DATE DUE

SEP 2 0 1988	
MAY - 3 1990	
JUN 0 8 1991	
MAR 1 8 1996	
JUN 0 5 1996	
JUL 08 1996	
JUL 2 9 1996	

Writing
for Television
and Radio

Wadsworth Series in Mass Communication

Rebecca Hayden, Senior Editor

GENERAL

The New Communications by Frederick Williams

Mediamerica: Form, Content, and Consequence of Mass Communication, 2d, by Edward Jay Whetmore

The Interplay of Influence: Mass Media & Their Publics in News, Advertising, Politics by Kathleen Hall Jamieson and Karlyn Kohrs Campbell

Mass Communication and Everyday Life: A Perspective on Theory and Effects by Dennis K. Davis and Stanley J. Baran

Mass Media Research: An Introduction by Roger D. Wimmer and Joseph R. Dominick

The Internship Experience by Lynne Schafer Gross

TELECOMMUNICATIONS

Stay Tuned: A Concise History of American Broadcasting by Christopher H. Sterling and John M. Kittross

Writing for Television and Radio, 4th, by Robert L. Hilliard

Broadcast Programming: Strategies for Winning Television and Radio Audiences by Susan Tyler Eastman, Sydney W. Head, and Lewis Klein

Advertising in the Broadcast and Cable Media, 2d, by Elizabeth J. Heighton and Don R. Cunningham

Strategies in Broadcast and Cable Promotion by Susan Tyler Eastman and Robert A. Klein

Modern Radio Station Practices, 2d, by Joseph S. Johnson and Kenneth K. Jones

The Magic Medium: An Introduction to Radio in America by Edward Jay Whetmore

Audio in Media by Stanley R. Alten

Television Production Handbook, 4th, by Herbert Zettl

Sight-Sound-Motion: Applied Media Aesthetics by Herbert Zettl

JOURNALISM

Reporting Processes and Practices: Newswriting for Today's Readers by Everette E. Dennis and Arnold H. Ismach

Excellence in College Journalism by Wayne Overbeck and Thomas M. Pasqua

When Words Collide: A Journalist's Guide to Grammar and Style by Lauren Kessler and Duncan McDonald

News Editing in the '80s: Text and Exercises by William L. Rivers

Reporting Public Affairs: Problems and Solutions by Ronald P. Lovell

Free-Lancer and Staff Writer: Newspaper Features and Magazine Articles, 3d, by William L. Rivers and Shelley Smolkin

Magazine Editing in the '80s: Text and Exercises by William L. Rivers

Newswriting for the Electronic Media: Principles, Examples, Applications by Daniel E. Garvey and William L. Rivers

This is PR: The Realities of Public Relations, 2d, by Doug Newsom and Alan Scott

Writing in Public Relations Practice: Form and Style by Doug Newsom and Tom Siegfried

Creative Strategy in Advertising by A. Jerome Jewler

Pictures on a Page: Photojournalism and Picture Editing by Harold Evans

Writing
for Television
and Radio

FOURTH EDITION

Robert L. Hilliard

Wadsworth Publishing Company
Belmont, California
A Division of Wadsworth, Inc.

Senior Editor: Rebecca Hayden
Production Editor: Deborah M. Oren
Managing Designer: Detta Penna
Designer: Louis Neiheisel
Copy Editor: Judith Hibbard
Cover Designer: Louis Neiheisel
Signing Representative: John Moroney

Printed in the United States of America

3 4 5 6 7 8 9 10—88 87 86

Library of Congress Cataloging in Publication Data

Hilliard, Robert L., date-
    Writing for television and radio.

    Includes index.
    1. Broadcasting—Authorship.   I. Title.
PN1991.7.H54   1984   808.2'2   83-6606
ISBN 0-534-02782-2

ISBN 0-534-02782-2

Preface

In recent years I have stressed two themes in speeches on communications: radio and television are the most powerful forces in the world today for affecting the minds and emotions of humankind; and whoever controls the media controls the political processes of a nation.

With the continued growth of media throughout the world and the development of new technologies, such as satellites, fiber optics, and lasers to facilitate the local, national, and international transmission of radio and television content even more effectively, the themes above have quickly moved from the category of concepts to inescapable truisms.

What do they mean to you, the radio and television writer?

In the world in which you live they suggest, most importantly, that with your choice of profession you have also chosen an awesome and inescapable responsibility. What you write directly affects the thoughts and feelings — and in many instances, the actions — of your listeners and viewers.

If we believe that freedom of communication is the keynote of a democratic society, then we also have to believe that all communications, including radio and television, must be open to the marketplace of ideas. All people should have the privilege and the opportunity to communicate any and all ideas to all other people. All people should have the right and the opportunity to hear those ideas or to turn them off. Only an informed, thinking society can remain free and be able to initiate and achieve individual and group self-realization. An uninformed public or one with access to only one side of a controversial issue is easy prey for the subverter of individual and group freedom.

A principal purpose of this book is to help you, as the writer of communications materials that influence people, to understand and implement the task of making available all forms of information and all shades of opinion. This is true whether you write drama, commercials, or news reports. Motivation to maintain and strengthen a free society through free media is not enough, however. One must know how to do it.

Since the first edition of this book appeared, it has been widely used for its bread-and-butter approach to writing. Departing from other books that concentrated on writing the television or radio play and put lower priorities on those areas of writing in which there were, in fact, higher realistic opportunities for jobs, this book concentrated on the practical areas of writing for professional careers in the field.

Its aim, however, has never been limited to a "how-to" approach. It attempts to demonstrate the practical potential of the media to affect people's thinking and actions humanistically and to serve the public interest by improved programming. It tries to establish sound aesthetic bases for all forms of television and radio writing. The chapter on drama, for example, is unique in its establishment of new principles of dramaturgy for television, based on an analysis of the potentials of the medium and on turning the restrictions of television and radio — analyzed in the chapters on the mass media and on production elements, as well as in the section on playwriting — to the advantage of the writer.

You will find several program-writing approaches in this book: those that have been tried frequently and successfully, including comments from practitioners in the field, especially those who would hire you to write similar scripts; those that have been tried only occasionally; and others that have not yet been tried, but which you may be motivated to use as practicality and conscience require.

This new edition, the fourth for *Writing for Television and Radio,* recognizes the changes that have taken place since the last edition and acknowledges the anticipated trends of the 1980s. In addition to updating and adding materials that reflect current practices (and of course, retaining materials that illustrate principles and techniques that have not changed), this edition notes those areas of writing in which opportunities have increased or decreased.

One such area, for example, is programming for specific audiences; the separate chapters in the previous edition on children's, women's, and minority and ethnic programs are more closely interrelated here in one long chapter. Another area that is offering more opportunities is industrial communications, and the material on instructional television use in business and organizations is expanded. Priorities in coverage of program types have been given to the areas of greatest potential employment for the broadcast writer, which currently are commercials, news and public affairs, and drama.

This edition also recognizes the effects of new technologies, although the means of distribution do not change the essential nature of the television or radio program or the techniques of writing them. The different kinds of opportunities available, for example, in the consistently advancing cable industry are noted. The National Association of Broadcasters Television and Radio Codes, included in previous editions, are omitted because they are no longer officially in use. However, this edition does add a glossary of terms, as suggested by a number of users of previous editions.

All types of broadcast writing—the play, the documentary, the commercial, the news program, the children's program, the feature, the woman's program, the talk program, the minority program, the music program, the special event, the education and information program, the variety show—are presented with the cautionary note that you can't learn through a book or in a classroom how to be a great writer. You can learn the potentials of a medium and the techniques, approaches, and forms of writing certain kinds of scripts. This may very well be sufficient to do a good job of writing the everyday programs that are considered commercially and professionally desirable. Becoming a great, or even a good, writer requires more: the psychological, sociological, political, environmental, educational, and aesthetic background and ability that we sometimes refer to as *talent*.

This book will introduce you to radio and television writing. If you learn and practice the techniques, you will be prepared to seek a job in the field. But this book will not automatically make you a good writer. If you have the talent and you learn the techniques and you write and write and write some more, then this book may be of some special value to you in achieving your goals. But if you don't have the ability and are not willing to work hard, then your time and efforts may be better invested in buying an easel or a plumber's wrench.

If you believe you have the talent, motivation, and dedication to study, learn, and practice hard, then I am pleased to have the opportunity to offer you a book that I think will help you go for it.

Contents

Writing
for Television
and Radio

1

The Mass Media

The television and radio writer aims at an audience that at one and the same time is very small and very large, that has much in common and almost nothing in common, that is a tightly knit group and a disunified mass.

Millions of people may be listening to or seeing the material developed by the writer. Yet any one group within this vast audience is apt to be a small one — usually a family group, at home, in everyday surroundings. The distractions of daily life are constantly at hand, continuously operative, and likely to pull the individual viewer or listener away from the program. Unlike theater and movie audiences, the television and radio audience is not captive. It has not paid a fee and if it doesn't like what it sees or hears it can turn the dial quickly to something else.

The play or film audience usually has read (or heard or seen) a review and knows something about what it is going to see. It chooses a specific show, and it rarely walks out. Not so the television or radio audience. Although most television viewers select specific programs and program formats (e.g., westerns, **sitcoms**), they can easily switch channels. Radio listeners may tune in a particular format, but if the talk-show subject or the type of music is not what they want at that moment they will search for something better. In addition, many viewers and listeners shop around the dial at random until they find something that grabs their attention.

The television or radio writer, therefore, must capture the imaginations of the audience as soon as possible. Each word, each picture must be purposeful, must gain attention and hold interest. Ideally, there should be no irrelevancies in the writing, no extraneous moments within the context of the particular program— although it must be granted that there are many programs that one sometimes thinks are entirely expendable.

With the growth of subscription (or pay) television (**STV**), audience motivation may change appreciably toward the end of the twentieth century. Although much of television and, especially, radio may remain advertiser-supported (or tax- and viewer-supported, as with public television and radio) and therefore free, the more popular programs will undoubtedly require fees, causing audiences to be much more selective.

Psychologists tell us that the smaller the group and the greater the physical distance between individual members of the audience, the better chance there is to appeal to the intellect. The physical groupings of the television and radio audience offer this opportunity to a greater extent than has been utilized thus far. On the other hand, because it is an audience that can remove itself quickly and easily with only the flick of a finger, emotional empathy also must be established. The use of universal emotional impressions is important because the audience is largely unknown to the writer and no immediate responses to determine the audience's reaction can be felt or measured.

Theater audiences and, to some degree, film audiences — or at least those within any given movie house — may have common interests or backgrounds: a common geographical location, the same relative economic or social status within the residential area of the city where the movie house is located, or similar educational backgrounds or cultural interests that prompted their attendance. The television and radio audience, as a whole, watching or listening to any one given performance is likely to have more diverse opinions, emotional prejudices, educational, social, and political backgrounds, and personal creeds than the theater or movie audience. The audience of the mass media is as varied as the population of the United States.

To make any single piece of material effective, the writer often tries to find a common denominator that will reach and hold as many as possible of the groups and individuals watching the more than 140 million television sets and listening to the more than 460 million radios in use in this country. Many critics have long suggested that financial rather than artistic or social considerations have controlled television and radio programming. The sponsor's primary aim frequently seems to be to present material that will not offend anyone. The sponsor and the producer thus far in the history of our mass media usually have searched for and often found the broadest common denominator, which frequently turns out to be the lowest. Rating organizations substantiate the advertising agency approach by measuring the percentages or numbers of people who allegedly watch any given program. Presuming that the ratings do have some validity — and many observers believe that the exceedingly small sample purportedly representing the entire American populace, as well as uncontrolled factors in interviewing techniques, nullify the claims of the rating systems — they do not usually measure accurately the audience's reaction, its potential buying power, or the effectiveness of either the program or the commercial message (although some of the rating systems attempt to do so).

Demographics have come to play a significant role in programming, particularly in radio. Stations analyze their markets and zero in on a target audience, orienting program materials to reach one or more specific age, sex, professional, economic, educational, or similar groups. Stations even determine which interest group might be listening in a particular place (home, work, car) at a particular time of day or night.

Reliance on quantitative measurement has prompted acceptance of the lowest common denominator. The cultural contributions of our mass media, with the exception of public broadcasting, have become, in large part, mediocre in quality and repetitive in nature. An outstanding casualty has been serious drama. In the 1960s, after a study of competition and responsibility in network television broadcasting, the **Federal Communications Commission (FCC)** stated: "By and large, episodes of television series are produced on the basis of 'formulas' — approved in advance by the network corporation and often its mass advertisers — which 'set' the characters, 'freeze' theme and action and limit subject matter to 'tested' commercial patterns." The pattern, with few exceptions, is still the same.

Spurred in part by audience interest in and the excellence of some British Broadcasting Corporation (BBC) and independent television series from the United Kingdom as well as by American-produced plays on public broadcasting channels, some specially made-for-television two- and three-hour presentations of good dramatic quality were produced in the 1970s and 1980s. The success of serial productions such as "Roots" resulted in a number of excellent multiepisode dramas. Opportunity does exist for the writer to develop scripts of high artistic value as well as scripts requiring a mastery of formula technique.

Radio and the Mass Audience

Radio is not limited by what can be presented visually. The writer can develop a mind picture that is bounded only by the extent of the audience's imagination. Sound effects, music, dialogue — even silence — are combined and integrated to provide the most effective presentation. However, the setting, physical characters, characterization, plot, and all of the other elements of the dramatic or nondramatic show must be conveyed through sound alone.

Radio permits the writer complete freedom of time and place. There is no limitation on the setting or on movement in time or space. The writer can create unlimited forms of physical action and can bypass in the twinkling of a musical bridge minutes or centuries of time. Orson Welles's radio adaptation of H. G. Wells's *War of the Worlds* is famous for its many provocative productions throughout the world. Television once attempted a smilar adaptation. It was unsuccessful. Limiting the action to what can be presented visually restricts the imaginative potentials of word and sound.

In listening to the sounds of any given radio program, the audience is not selective. It does not pick out what it wants, but hears only what the writer wants it to hear. In this way the writer controls the direction of the attention of the radio audience. Of course, different listeners may imagine the same sound stimulus in different ways because each person's psychological and experiential background is different. The radio audience "sees" a picture in its imagination. The radio writer can create this mind picture more effectively than can the writer in any other medium. The audience sees places, characters and events just as the writer wants and sometimes even experiences the emotions the writer wants. The subjectivity of the medium permits the writer to place the audience right alongside of or at any given distance from the character or performer. Voice distances and relationships to the microphone determine the view the audience has of the characters and of the setting. For example, if the audience is listening to two characters in conversation and the writer has the first character fade off from the microphone, the audience, in its imagination, stays with the second character and sees the first character moving away.

In radio a scene must be set in dialogue and sound rather than established through sight. This must not be done too obviously. Radio often uses a narrator or announcer to set the mood, establish character relationships, give information about the program participants, describe the scene, summarize previous action and even comment on the attitude the audience might be expected to have toward the program, the participants, or the characters in the play. This background material may be given through dialogue, music, sound, or, sometimes, even through silence.

Radio is, indeed, the art of the imagination. The radio writer is restricted only by the breadth and depth of the mind's eye of the audience. A vivid illustration of this and, appropriately, an example of good scriptwriting is Stan Freberg's award-winning spot "Stretching the Imagination."

MAN:	Radio? Why should I advertise on radio? There's nothing to look at ... no pictures.
GUY:	Listen, you can do things on radio you couldn't possibly do on TV.
MAN:	That'll be the day.
GUY:	Ah huh. All right, watch this. (AHEM) O.K. people, now I give you the cue, I want the 700-foot mountain of whipped cream to roll into Lake Michigan which has been drained and filled with hot chocolate. Then the royal Canadian Air Force will fly overhead towing the 10-ton maraschino cherry which will be dropped into the whipped cream, to the cheering of 25,000 extras. All right ... cue the mountain ...
SOUND:	GROANING AND CREAKING OF MOUNTAINS INTO BIG SPLASH!
GUY:	Cue the air force!
SOUND:	DRONE OF MANY PLANES.
GUY:	Cue the maraschino cherry ...
SOUND:	WHISTLE OF BOMB INTO BLOOP! OF CHERRY HITTING WHIPPED CREAM.
GUY:	Okay, twenty-five thousand cheering extras ...
SOUND:	ROAR OF MIGHTY CROWD. SOUND BUILDS UP AND CUTS OFF SHARP! Now ... you wanta try that on television?
MAN:	Well ...
GUY:	You see ... radio is a very special medium, because it stretches the imagination.
MAN:	Doesn't television stretch the imagination?
GUY:	Up to 21 inches, yes.

Courtesy of Freberg, Ltd.

The potentials of radio just described, however, are not necessarily reflected in radio as it currently exists. Except for commercials, which — aside from the ethics involved in purpose and content — can be highly artistic, the dramatic aspects of radio are virtually dormant. Some individual performers and producer/directors experiment with the potentials of radio, utilizing special effects and techniques in their programs (unlike the majority of disc jockeys, who primarily play records and tapes interspersed with commentary).

Bernard Mann, president of WGLD and other stations in North Carolina, has run the gamut from broadcast writing student to continuity writer to program director to station owner. He has stated:

> One of my great frustrations is that too little of the writing done for radio is imaginative. We have almost made it a part of the indoctrination program for copywriters at our radio station to listen to some of the old radio shows. During that time, listeners were challenged to use their imagination. Nothing has changed. The medium is still the same. The opportunity for the writer to challenge the listener is still there. It's just not being used very much. Of course, radio today has very little original drama, but every day thousands of pieces of copy are turned out with very little imagination. Often an advertiser will tell a salesperson, ''I can't use radio, I must have a picture,'' but I think that's radio's strength. The picture leaves nothing to the imagination, but a description will be colored by the listener to be more toward what he or she wants or likes.

Television and the Mass Audience

Television makes use of the same subjective potentials as radio, but is more specific in directing the attention and feeling of the audience. Television uses many of the techniques of theater and film, and the audience is directed through sight as well as through hearing. With its use of mechanical and electronic devices, television has more flexibility than theater, but because sight limits imagination it does not have as much flexibility as radio. Nevertheless, television can combine the sound and audience orientation of radio, the live continuous performance values of theater, the mechanical abilities of film, and its own electronic capacities. It is capable of fusing the best of all previous communications media.

Although it can break the dramaturgic unities of time and place, television is restricted by *physical* time and place. There are occasional multipart series and two- and three-hour drama specials, but most program lengths are one-half or one hour and the writer cannot develop a script as fully as might be desirable. Actual program lengths, after commercial and **intro** and **outro** credit time has been subtracted, run approximately twenty-one to twenty-four minutes for the half-hour program and forty-two to forty-nine minutes for the hour program.

The writer is hampered by the limitation of the camera view, by the limitation of settings for **live-type taped television** (live-type taped television refers to the taped program that uses the continuous action, nonedited procedure of the live show; it is done as if it were a live show) and by the comparatively small viewing area of the television receiver. The writer must orient the script more toward small groups on the screen at any one time and make more extended use of the close-up shot in studio-produced taped shows than in television filmed shows. These limitations prompted the intimate, subjective approach in dramatic writing and resulted, in television's so-called golden age, in the probing slice-of-life play. Most current television drama reflects these same limitations.

Even studio-bound taped television does have a reasonable freedom of movement, however. The camera serves, in a sense, as a moving proscenium arch. The writer may use **detail sets,** projections, electronic inserts, film clips, and multiple sets to achieve a broadening or a variety of place. The application and gradual domination of film technique in television production, and the concomitant movement of television's production centers from New York to Hollywood, changed some of the writing approaches; one result is that much of television consists of boxed-in versions of the motion picture.

Television combines both subjectivity and objectivity in relation to the audience, fusing two areas that are usually thought of as mutually exclusive. Through use of the camera and electronic devices, the writer and director frequently may give the audience's attentions and emotions a subjective orientation by directing them to specific stimuli. The close-up, the **split screen** and similar devices are especially useful. The television audience cannot choose, as does the theater audience, from the totality of presentation upon a stage. The television audience can be directed to a specific stimulus that most effectively achieves the purpose of the specific moment in the script. Attention can be directed to subtle reaction as well as to obvious action. At the same time, the television audience can be given an objective orientation in that the personality of the performer as a person can be brought more openly and directly to the viewer than can be done in the large auditorium of the theater or movie house. Although the purpose of most drama is to create illusion, the television narrator, master of ceremonies, announcer, actor, or other performer can achieve excellent nonillusionary relationships with the audience. The small screen and the intimacy of the living room create effects and require techniques different from those of a film shown in a movie theater.

Film critic Vincent Canby wrote in the *New York Times* that

> techniques and personalities of television are beginning to shape theatrical motion pictures — to make them smaller, busier and blander. . . . The first great wave of television directors who made their way to theatrical films — Arthur Penn, Sidney Lumet, George Roy Hill, Franklin Schaffner, John Frankenheimer — adapted themselves to the older medium. Even while they brought to Hollywood some of the frenetic tensions that were virtually a method of working in television when major shows were done live, these directors couldn't wait to exploit the cinema resources that then separated movies from television . . . imperial crane-shots and deep-focus vistas that . . . would have been out of the question in any live TV production . . . . Today the exact opposite is true — possibly because these TV people have grown up using film and tape. The television directors who are now switching to the big screen can't wait to reduce its dimensions, to make movies that look as much as possible like the sitcoms and so-called ''television movies.''

Do you, as a student and a viewer, see a symbiotic effect upon television as well?

The basic exposition of a television program should be presented through the action, logically and quickly. In radio it is more difficult to reach the audience through the action, and a narrator or announcer frequently is necessary. Remember that radio is aural and television essentially is visual; where a visual element in television can achieve the desired effect, it should take precedence over sound. In many instances dialogue may be superfluous. A story is told about a famous Broadway playwright, noted for his scintillating dialogue, who was hired to write a film script. He wrote a thirty-page first act treatment in which a husband and wife, on vacation, go up to their hotel room. Thirty minutes of witty and sparkling conversation reveal that the wife has become increasingly disturbed over her husband's attention to other women. An experienced movie director went over the script and thought it presented a good situation. He changed one thing. He substituted for the thirty pages of dialogue less than one page of visual directions in which the husband and wife enter the hotel, register, and walk to the elevator perfunctorily; the husband looks appraisingly at the female elevator operator, and a look of great displeasure comes over the wife's face as the elevator doors close. Sound should be considered secondary in television production; the essential ingredient is visual action. This principle applies to most nondramatic forms as well as to the play.

That many television writers have not yet learned the visual essence of their medium can be determined by a simple test. Turn on the audio but not the video of your television set. You will note that in almost every program, from drama to documentary, you will "see" just about as much as you would with the video on. Is television, as some critics say, still just radio with pictures?

Subject Matter

The writer not only faces a problem with the quality level of the material, but also faces concrete manifestations of this problem in the selection of specific subject matter. Television and radio writing are affected greatly by censorship. In commercial television and radio the control over the final script to be presented frequently rests in the hands of the advertising agencies representing the sponsor. In some cases, the person in charge of the television and/or radio division of the agency or of the individual account is an advertising executive, a businessperson with little or no knowledge of the artistic needs or potentials of the media. It has been alleged that three hostile postcards from a vacant lot will influence a sponsor or advertising agency to do almost anything. The sponsor, however, isn't the only potential censor. The originating network may reject material it deems unsuitable.

The growth of national spot advertising has gradually diminished agency control over individual television scripts, and network control has become predominant. Coincidentally, the gradual reduction of network radio programming has given control of content to local radio stations. The Television Bureau of Advertising's change of emphasis from selling national advertisers to selling local and regional sponsorship may ultimately move program control to the local television station as well. Local **cable** origination will enhance this move. The growth of direct broadcast satellite (**DBS**), which will bring programming direct to homes from distant sources, may obviate it.

A comparison of current programs with those as recent as the 1970s shows society's increased willingness, in all media, to discuss issues, use language, and reveal relationships that were previously taboo. Broadcasting, usually a follower rather than a leader of public taste and thought (except, perhaps, in the area of news information), is becoming more and more a reflection of real life.

Censorable Material

Censorship falls into two major categories: material that is *censorable* and material that is *controversial*.

Censorable material, as discussed here, is that which generally is considered not in good taste for the home television audience, although this same material might be perfectly acceptable in the legitimate theater or in films.

Controversial material, as discussed here, is material that is not necessarily in bad taste, but that conflicts with the beliefs, policies, or desires of the sponsor, the network, or the station — or of an outside group, to whose pressure the sponsor, station, and network usually succumb.

The FCC frequently acts as an arbiter of public taste. In addition to implementing the Communications Act of 1934, As Amended, which authorizes fines or license suspension for "communications containing profane or obscene words, language, or meaning," the FCC has by both suggestion and order acted, according to some people (particularly broadcasters), as a censoring body. Two prime examples: in 1971 the FCC issued an order requiring stations to review the lyrics of all records played to avoid any promotion, through those lyrics, of illegal drugs. In 1973 the FCC fined a station for its "topless" radio format — a phone-in format in which women, particularly, were encouraged to discuss their sex attitudes and practices. Through thinly veiled warnings to other stations the FCC successfully eliminated that short-lived but highly popular programming approach.

Yet times change. In the early 1980s a radio format became popular that is the same topless call-in program, but with a difference. The host is a therapist (usually a psychologist or psychiatric social worker) who, with the audience, listens to graphic details and purports to answer serious questions seriously.

The FCC constantly receives complaints concerning alleged obscenity. The most significant case of recent years, one that was like a ship without an anchor, was the "seven dirty words" case. The FCC found a George Carlin monologue on Pacifica-licensed radio station WBAI in New York "obscene," with "language that described sexual or excretory activities and organs patently offensive by contemporary community standards." Litigation in the 1970s finally resulted in a Supreme Court decision that narrowly upheld the FCC, stating that it was not unconstitutional to take action on "indecent" material that was in "nonconformance with accepted standards of morality." The Supreme Court decision, however, was interpreted to apply to this specific case only, and the FCC indicated that it would judge future similar cases on the merits of the particular complaint.

Broadcasting is coming closer to the realization that the facts of life cannot be made to disappear by banning them from public discussion or observation and pretending that they do not exist. Films are shown on television that only a few years ago would have been considered beyond the pale. Talk shows and documentaries deal with political and personal issues that would have been considered unthinkable in the 1970s. Sexual innuendos are common on television and explicit sexual references are not infrequent. Language reflecting the context of the characters and the situation is used more and more, although the most common four-letter words in real life have not yet — at this writing — made it to the living room screen.

But broadcasting remains very sensitive to public and political pressure and, even in a time of growth of freedom of expression on television, does not hesitate to pull back at even a hint of pressure, as is noted in the next section of this chapter.

Erik Barnouw, discussing censorship in the movies in his book *Mass Communication,* indicates an approach that just as readily may be applied to television and radio. Barnouw writes: "Banning evil example . . . does not ban it from life. It may not strengthen our power to cope with it. It may have the opposite effect. Code rules multiply, but they do not produce morality. They do not stop vulgarity. Trying to banish forbidden impulses, censors may only change the disguises in which they appear. They ban passionate love-making, and excessive violence takes its place."

Controversial Material

Censorship of controversial material is of concern to the writer. Controversial material refers to subject matter that in the broadest sense might disturb a viewer. Such material might relate to any area of public thinking, including certain aspects of political, social, economic, religious, and psychological problems. "When a story editor says, 'We can't use anything controversial,' and says it with a tone of conscious virtue, then there is danger," observes Barnouw.

There is a great danger to freedom of expression and the democratic exchange of ideas in U.S. television and radio because many media executives fear controversy. On the grounds of service to the sponsor and on the basis of high ratings for noncontroversial but mediocre entertainment, anything controversial has been avoided in too many cases. Many companies will refuse to sponsor a program with controversial material if they feel it will in any way alienate any potential customer anywhere. It can be said that if a sponsor permits a product to be identified with a controversial issue that may offend even small groups of citizens, there may be damage to the company's prestige. It can also be said, on the other hand, that anyone using the public airwaves has a responsibility not only to a private company, but to the public as a whole. Censorship of controversial material is particularly prevalent in dramatic programs. Reginald Rose, one of the great writers of television's golden age, who had some plays censored because they contained alleged controversial material, stated that such controversial productions help more than harm advertisers, and that people become more aware of the program and of the product, rather than barely noting the sponsorship of innocuous shows.

As far back as the early 1960s the FCC held hearings on television programming and, with few exceptions, heard almost all of the leading industries in this country state that the television programs they advertise on must be oriented toward their sales policies and must reflect their corporate images. Retired *New York Times* critic Jack Gould summed up in one of his columns the attitude of the television sponsor: "As a businessman governed by concern for his customers and stockholders, the advertiser wants to avoid displeasing any substantial segment of the public, wants to establish a pleasant environment for his product, wants to make sure the private life of a performer is not embarrassing to his company, and wants to skirt any possibility of being accused of taking one side in a situation where there are two sides."

Some sponsors do not succumb to pressure and they maintain the integrity of the programs they pay for. The Bell & Howell Corporation told the FCC that despite threats of boycott as a result of its sponsorship of controversial programs on the "Closeup" series, it would not abandon either the "conviction and faith that most Americans are fair-minded people who realize they must know more if our society is to survive" or "the principle that has served this country so well — the idea that the press should be free of advertising influence."

In the 1960s, often anything that was even vaguely controversial was censored: a talk by a clergyman on interdenominational friction was canceled by a network; a play about homesteading in the West was canceled because the sponsor didn't want anything presented that touched on the government giving economic help to farmers; the writer of a play about discrimination against a Black family, based on headline newspaper stories, was forced to change the protagonist to an ex-convict; one ironic example was the cancellation of a play about a network censoring a commentator, even after the script had been put into production and publicity about it had been released — the network that canceled the play had not long before censured one of its own top commentators.

Some censorship takes place not because of feared public reaction or even because of the sponsor's vested interest, but because of direct prejudice. One program, the true story of the owner of a large concern who was Jewish and who gave his entire fortune to fight cancer, was stopped by the sponsor because the play allegedly would give "Jewish department store owners" an unfair advantage over other department store owners.

Censorship that eliminates any material that might possibly put the sponsor's product in a poor light or that might suggest a competing product even obliquely, is responsible for a number of classic situations. Among them are the program dealing with the German atrocities of the 1930s and 1940s from which the sponsoring gas company eliminated all references to gas chambers, and the deletion of a reference to President Lincoln in another program because it was also the name of an automobile produced by a competitor of the sponsor.

In 1972 television writers representing the Writers Guild of America, West testified at hearings on press freedom held by the Senate Judiciary Committee's Constitutional Rights Subcommittee and chaired by Senator Sam Ervin. The writers said that scripts on controversial subjects are heavily censored by broadcast executives. David W. Rintels, head of the Guild's censorship committee, said that broadcast executives

> allow laughter but not tears, fantasy but not reality, escapism but not truth. . . . 75 million people are nightly being fed programs deliberately designed to have no resemblance at all to reality, nonsense whose only purpose is to sell snake oil and laxatives and underarm deodorants. . . . Writers by the dozens report that they have written characters who are black and have seen them changed to white. They have written Jews and seen them converted to gentiles. They have proposed shows about South African apartheid, Vietnam, old folks, mental disease, politics, business, labor, students and minorities; and they have been chased out of studios. . . . These instances are symptomatic of the rigorous and final institutionalization of censorship and thought control on television.

Rintels further stated that a poll of Guild members showed that 86 percent had experienced censorship of their work and that 81 percent believe that television is presenting a distorted picture of what is happening in America. He added that television drama fostered a "mythology which states that a punch in the mouth solves all problems and doesn't really hurt anyone."

At the same hearings Norman Lear, producer of a number of politically and socially aware — and sometimes controversial — sitcoms, praised the Columbia Broadcasting System (CBS) network for permitting his "All in the Family" to deal with subjects that were once forbidden on television, such as racial and religious bias and sexual impotence. But he made it clear that this was an exception and that "this country is ready for a lot more truth than it's getting." Lear has been foremost among television producers in breaking many of the censorship molds. It is not accidental that he has devoted his personal time and resources to fight those groups that would impose their concepts of morality on all the American people, including his development in 1981 of a national organization called People for the American Way.

Broadcasters rarely answer the charges of censorship of the kind brought by Rintels. The broadcast press, however, sometimes has something to say about the network and station prerogatives and responsibilities. An editorial by *Television/ Radio Age* publisher S. J. Paul put it this way:

In network entertainment programming, there is a behind-the-scenes battle that goes on — and has been going on for years — between writers and producers on one hand, and the establishment, i.e. the networks, on the other. The writers are seeking that so-called complete freedom to ply their craft. The networks, of necessity, must establish the guidelines within the canons of good taste. Establishing the criteria is a responsibility that the networks cannot duck. Anyone who has viewed the programs in this new season would have to conclude that all three networks have lowered their standards, particularly in the over-emphasis on violence and sex.

The arguments in favor of this kind of permissiveness have been recited many, many times — that we are now in a period of transition, that public tastes are changing along with moral standards, and that to muzzle creativity is to block progress and stifle the libido.

Actually, it requires more imagination to present entertainment in good taste than it does to present a dramatic series where this kind of sensationalism serves no end except questionable vicariousness, and, believe me, the writers know exactly what they are doing when they introduce these extraneous elements into a plot. . . .

There are certain types of entertainment fare that belong in the theater or motion pictures that are not applicable to television.

It has been said many times, television is the mass medium of family entertainment. It is an invited guest in the home. If it loses sight of this basic precept, it will further compound its many problems.

Many television and radio writers have found that censorship covers a far wider range than is specified in the **National Association of Broadcasters (NAB)** production codes and by individual stations and networks. Each sponsor has a special list of unacceptable subjects or ideas. For example, on one series sponsored by an automobile manufacturer no one ever had an auto accident, nor was one ever referred to by any character. One can find similar examples for almost every sponsored show on the air, and these are restrictions the writer who would write for that show must face. Although the most dramatic examples of censorship, as noted in this chapter, occur in plays, censorship applies as well to other forms of television and radio writing.

It does not have to be a question of either-or, however. In French television, for example, when material is presented that is generally deemed acceptable for a mature and intelligent audience but that may not be entirely acceptable to every family audience at home, an announcement before the program begins asks the viewers to watch the program with indulgence and to put the children to bed. On BBC programs there is virually no dialogue code. Although good taste is a general guide for writers, in a dramatic show, for example, a character can make any reference that is necessary to the play.

Censorship and politics   The history of censorship of controversial material in broadcasting is a long one and, unfortunately, one in which both broadcasters and the public never seem to learn the lesson of integrity and democracy. Certainly one of the United States' darkest and most shameful hours was the blacklist of the 1950s, when broadcasters cooperated with bigots to deny freedom of speech and the freedom to work to countless performers, directors, producers, and writers who were accused by self-proclaimed groups of superpatriots to be un-American. Broadcasters panicked, throwing courage to the winds and ethics out of the windows. Many careers and a number of lives were destroyed.

By the mid-1960s broadcasters were apologizing for broadcasting's past assault on democracy. They not only assured America that they would never again be intimidated into anti-American activity by self-serving groups, but also began to show their mettle by providing honest and stark coverage of the war in Vietnam (factual news coverage was considered controversial by some people). To be sure, the networks did not reveal the full extent of the overwhelming opposition of the American people to U.S. activities in Southeast Asia, particularly in the way they covered — and didn't cover — the many antiwar marches and rallies in Washington, D.C., and in other parts of the country. But news and documentary programs did delve into prison reform issues such as the Attica massacre; into citizen massacres such as those at Kent State and Jackson State Universities; into previously forbidden subjects such as homosexuality; into the women's liberation movement; into coverage that let the United States' dirty linen hang out, such as the Watergate hearings and the 1974 presidential impeachment proceedings; and into many social, political, environmental, educational, economic, and other problems that were critical and controversial. Not enough for some people; too much for others.

Yet in the early 1980s, as U.S. politics and attitudes began to grow conservative, broadcasting again began to display the behavior that only a few years before it had apologized for. Once again, self-proclaimed groups of patriots and moralists attempted to impose their beliefs on the rest of the United States. Two examples: A well-written, sensitive television series entitled ''Hello, Sidney'' portrayed the leading male character as a homosexual. The network quickly yielded to the censors and deleted from future scripts substantive clarifications of the character's sexual orientation and, of course, any plot lines that might have shown the character sympathetically in the context of his sexual preference. At about the same time, actor Ed Asner, the star of the "Lou Grant" series, made public statements about his beliefs concerning the war in El Salvador. Cries of "boycott" arose from those groups that decided that their beliefs should be the only permissible ones in our pluralistic society. Kimberly-Clark, the makers of Kleenex and other products, immediately withdrew its sponsorship. Shortly thereafter CBS cancelled the "Lou Grant" series, ostensibly on grounds of low ratings, although series with lower ratings remained on the air. The Americans for Democratic Action organization stated that cancellation of the series was "a veiled threat to freedom of broadcasting."

Without firm commitment to artistic (and political) freedom on the part of those who employ them, writers, too, live in a tenuous world.

Sydney W. Head, a leading teacher and writer in the communications field, has written that "television, as a medium, appears to be highly responsive to the conventional conservative values," and that a danger to society from television is that television will not likely lend its support to the unorthodox, but that "it will add tremendously to cultural inertia."

Censorship is the rule rather than the exception in American broadcasting. The great impact of the media and the ability of television and radio to affect the minds and emotions of people so strongly are clearly recognized by the media controllers, who represent the status quo of established business, industry, social, and political thought. The impact of the media is clearly reflected in the success and power of Madison Avenue. Commercials *do* sell products and services. This impact has enabled news and public affairs programs, even in their frequently limited and sometimes biased coverage of controversial issues, to become significant factors in changing many of our political and social policies and beliefs. Television is credited with bringing to much of the American population an understanding of the violence and prejudice practiced against Blacks through its coverage of the civil rights movement in the South. Watching hate in the street with the rest of the mob is one thing, watching it in your living room is another; television motivated many people to demand congressional action to guarantee all Americans civil rights. Although selective and limited in its coverage and hardly objective in its evaluation of the breadth and depth of the peace marches in Washington during the Vietnam war, the media nevertheless brought to people in their homes some of the horrors of Vietnam and some of the actions of millions of Americans who actively opposed the war. The result was nationwide citizen pressure that caused one president to end his political career and another president ultimately to wind down and end most of America's war activities in Southeast Asia. Live coverage of the Wategate hearings and the Nixon impeachment proceedings brought sharply to the American people information, ideas, and feelings, and in many cases, it motivated action that would not have otherwise come.

Frank Stanton, former president of CBS, has said:

The effect of broadcasting upon the democratic experience has gone far beyond elections. The monumental events of this century — depression, wars, uneasy peace, the birth of more new nations in two decades than had occurred before in two centuries, undreamed of scientific breakthroughs, profound social revolution — all these were made immediate, intimate realities to Americans through, first, the ears of radio and, later, the eyes of television. No longer were the decisions of the American people made in an information vacuum, as they witnessed the towering events of their time that were bound to have incisive political repercussions.

The writers who prepare continuity and background material for programs dealing with such issues and events can have the satisfaction of knowing that they are contributing to human progress and thought and are participating directly in changing society and solving problems of humanity. There are not too many professions in which one can accomplish this on such a broad and grand scale!

Theoretically, the writer can help to fulfill the responsibility of the mass media to serve the best interests of the public as a whole, can raise and energize the cultural and educational standards of the people, and thus can strengthen the country. Realistically, the best-intentioned writer is still under the control of the network and advertiser whose first loyalties seem to be directed toward their own interests and not necessarily toward those of the public. Occasionally, these interests coincide. The writer who wishes to keep a job in the mass media is pressured to serve the interests of the employer. It is hoped that conscience will enable the writer to serve the needs of the public as well.

2

Basic Elements of Production

Before the advent of videotape, television was a live medium. **Kinescope** recordings had very poor air quality. When the television industry began to move to the West Coast it adopted the so-called **Hollywood style** — the use of film and the style and technique of writing that go with it. Drama was no longer live, but prerecorded on film. News and public affairs, when done in the field, had of necessity always been on film. Although stations developed remote facilities for live coverage of on-the-spot happenings, stories were filmed and rushed to the studio for processing and airing on the regular news shows. Commercials were live in the early days — yes, Betty Furness did open that refrigerator door, live, on camera — but, it soon became easier and more efficient to prepare commercials as film inserts, even for otherwise live productions. Film soon became the production means for virtually all programs that by necessity or special design were not presented live.

When videotape came along in the 1950s many people looked for a revolution. **Magnetic tape** did replace film in many areas of television production, but film remained dominant in entertainment programs, particularly drama, and in news and commercials. With the refinement of videotape equipment and techniques, some inroads were made, but it wasn't until the early 1970s that something along the lines of a real revolution — or, perhaps, instant evolution — occurred.

By the 1980s videotape had surpassed the use of film for most television formats — news, documentaries, panels, game shows, soap operas. Film continued to be used for some documentaries, for dramatic programs, and for commercials and public service announcements (**PSAs**). With the introduction of electronic news gathering and electronic field production (**ENG** and **EFP**; the latter refers to use of **minicam** equipment to produce commercial and nonnews materials away from the studio), news became predominantly videotaped. Advantages of videotape over film include **instant replay,** reuse of videotape, sophisticated electronic editing facilities, and the lower cost of tape than of film.

In the early 1980s some film directors began to shoot their films on videotape. Film's superior resolution advantage began to decrease as videotape technology improved. In addition, film tends to lose some detail as it passes through the video system.

BM/E magazine has analyzed some of the advantages of tape:

Instant replay — it saves big hunks of time and money — if the first take is wrong, the director knows right away and can reshoot without leaving the set.

Totally quiet cameras that accommodate a wider range of light values and color temperatures than film cameras.

The current high-band VTRs [videotape recorders] — these lifted recording quality to the level the movie-makers wanted.

Ability of the current video cameras to use a range of lenses similar to that of film cameras.

The TV monitor as a large, well-lighted, easily multiplied viewfinder, which sees exactly what the camera sees.

Recent advances in editing technology which makes editing videotape easier and cheaper than the old standard film editing methods.

Recent developments in small van-mounted video production units, with two or three cameras feeding control equipment and recorders in the van. Set up time is usually much faster with this equipment than with portable movie units (for example, the camera can be warmed up on the way to the shooting site).

Capping it all is electronic processing of the program: color, aperture, gamma correction; picture enhancement of various kinds; dissolves, wipes, all the bag of special effects that the TV broadcaster today expects to come out of a smallish box when he punches the button.

The development of the ENG video equipment changed the nature of covering live news events in the 1970s. The lightweight portable television camera made it possible for the cameraperson to move into an event as quickly as the operator of the small 16-mm film camera, and permitted stations to get the story on the air immediately through instant playback from a videotape recorder (**VTR**) without waiting for the traditional processing of a film. The writer is affected because the time element for preparing intro, outro, and continuity materials for the finished studio report is considerably shortened where portable remote video equipment, rather than film equipment, is used.

Although television continues to change in many of its basic approaches as equipment becomes more sophisticated, radio — the older medium — has already largely explored its basic potentials. **Multiplexing**, **quadruplexing**, the **electronic synthesizer**, **automation,** and other technological changes present new opportunities for experimentation by the writer, producer, and director, but within relatively fixed formats.

Cable television is sometimes looked upon by the public as different from the broadcast television it has come to know. The difference is principally in the means of transmission as far as standard programming is concerned. The medium is still television, available to those who can afford to pay fees for the kinds of programs that otherwise would be on advertiser-supported "free" television. By the end of the twentieth century cable will probably be only a euphemism for subscription television — presuming **DBS**, **fiber optics**, or **lasers** do not replace cable as the technical conduit (as well as the accepted euphemism).

Cable and other new technologies do, however, provide some significant potentials and implications for the writer beyond the current practices of broadcasting. Cable permits and in many instances (as mandated by local franchising agreements) requires greater emphasis on local, sometimes live, programming than is found on most broadcast stations. The "pay" factor suggests the writing of material suitable for a more affluent and, therefore, a more culturally sophisticated audience than that of broadcast television. The requirement of local or live programming suggests more specific orientation of type and content of programs and awareness of limits dictated by live studio production, sometimes with limited equipment.

Most important, perhaps, is the development of cable's capabilities (and those of other new technologies) for service-oriented programming and two-way communication. With the introduction of computer-based instructional, economic (such as banking), marketing, and similar services, and the availability of response mechanisms in the receiving location, the writer's job may expand and in many instances change from the traditional creative pattern of broadcasting to that of computer program writer.

This chapter neither proposes nor pretends to present a comprehensive analysis of production techniques for either television or radio. It offers an overview of some of the basic and, in some cases, classic elements of production that directly affect writing technique. The writer must learn what the camera can and cannot do, what sound or visual effects are possible in the control room, what terminology is used in furnishing directions, descriptions, and transitions, and what other technical and production aspects of the media are essential for effective writing.

Radio

The primary technical and production potentials the radio writer should be aware of and should be able to indicate in the script, when necessary, pertain to microphone use, sound effects, and music. The writer should understand how the studio and control room can or cannot implement the purposes of the script.

The Microphone

The basic element of radio broadcasting is the microphone. The number of microphones used in a show usually is limited. For the standard program — a disc jockey or news program — only one is needed. Even in a dramatic show there may be only one or two for the announcer and the cast. Another may be used if there are any live sound effects. A musical group may require still another. A panel, discussion, or interview program may have a mike for each person or for every two people. Not all microphones are the same. The audio engineer selects certain types of microphones in terms of their sensitivity and uses for specific effects. The writer has only one important responsibility in this area: to indicate the relationship of the performer to the microphone. It is this physical relationship that determines the orientation of the listener. For example, the audience may be with a character riding in a car. The car approaches the edge of a cliff. The writer must decide whether to put the sound of the character's scream and the noise of the car as it hurtles down the side of the cliff on mike, thus keeping the audience with the car, or to fade these sounds into the distance, orienting the audience to a vantage point at the top of the cliff, watching the character and car going downward.

There are five basic microphone positions. The writer should indicate every position except **on mike**, which is taken for granted when no position is designated next to the line of dialogue. Where the performer has been in another position and suddenly speaks from an on mike position, then on mike should be written in.

On mike   The performer speaks from a position right at the microphone. The listener is oriented to the imaginary setting in the same physical spot as the performer.

Off mike   The performer is some distance away from the microphone. This conveys to the audience the impression that the sound or voice is at a proportionate distance away from the physical orientation point of the listener, which is usually at the center of the scene. The writer may vary this listener orientation; by removing the performer's voice but indicating through the dialogue that the performer has remained in the same physical place, the writer removes the listener and not the performer from the central point of action.

Fading on   The performer slowly moves toward the microphone. In the mind's eye of the listener, the performer is approaching the physical center of the action.

Fading off   The performer moves away from the microphone while speaking, thus moving away from the central orientation point.

Behind obstructions   The performer sounds as if there were a barrier between him or her and the focal point of the audience's orientation. The writer indicates that the performer is behind a door, outside a window, or perhaps under the bandstand.

The writer may indicate the need for special microphones. One is the filter mike, which creates the impression that the voice or sound is coming over a telephone. The voice at the focal point of the audience's orientation, even though speaking over the telephone, too, would be on mike. Another is the echo chamber, which creates various degrees of an echo sound, ranging from an indication that a person is locked in a closet to the impression of a voice in a boundless cavern.

Note the use of the five positions in the following sample material.

COMMENTARY	AUDIO
1. There is no mention of position. The character is assumed to be ON MIKE.	GEORGE: I'm bushed, Myra. Another day like the one today, and I'll just ... (THE DOORBELL RINGS) MYRA: Stay where you are, George. I'll answer the door. GEORGE: Thanks, hon. (DOORBELL RINGS AGAIN)
2. The orientation of the audience stays with George as Myra leaves the focal point of the action.	MYRA: (RECEDING FOOTSTEPS, FADING) I'm coming ... I'm coming. I wonder who it could be at this hour.
3. George must give the impression of projecting across the room to Myra who is now at the front door.	GEORGE: (CALLING) See who it is before you open the door.
4. Myra's physical position is now clear to the audience through the distance of her voice. Then as soon as we hear her ON MIKE, the audience's physical position arbitrarily is oriented to that of Myra at the door.	MYRA: (OFF) All right, George. (ON MIKE) Who is it?
5. This is an example of the behind-an-obstruction position.	MESSENGER: (BEHIND DOOR) Telegram for Mr. George Groo.
6. The physical orientation of the audience stays with Myra. George is now OFF MIKE.	MYRA: Just a minute. (CALLING) George, telegram for you. GEORGE: (OFF) Sign for me, will you Myra? MYRA: Yes. (SOUND OF DOOR OPENING) I'll sign for it. (SOUND OF PAPER BEING HANDED OVER AND THE SCRATCH OF PENCIL ON PAPER) MESSENGER: Thank you, ma'am. (SOUND OF DOOR BEING CLOSED) MYRA: (SOUND OF TELEGRAM BEING OPENED) I'll open it and ... (SILENCE FOR A MOMENT) GEORGE: (OFF) Well, Myra, what is it? (STILL SILENCE)
7. Note the complete shift of audience orientation. After Myra goes to the door the audience stays with her, hears George from the other end of the room, finally knows that George, who is coming on or fading on, is approaching the spot where the audience and Myra are. Finally, George is at that spot. Note the use of the term ON MIKE at the end, when the character comes to that position from another position.	GEORGE: (FADING ON) Myra, in heaven's name, what happened? What does the telegram say? (ON MIKE) Myra, let me see that telegram!

Although actual radio and television scripts are double-spaced throughout speeches, sound effects, music directions, and (for television) video directions, the scripts are single-spaced in this book to save space. You will also notice various script styles for the same kinds of programs. As far as possible, scripts have been presented exactly as they were written or produced, reflecting the real world of television and radio writing, where they do not necessarily conform in style and format from one station or production house to another.

The Studio

The physical limitations of a radio studio sometimes may affect the writer's purposes, so, if possible, the size of the studio should be checked to see if it is large enough. In addition, though most professional studios are satisfactorily equipped acoustically, some smaller stations are not, and the writer should attempt to determine whether it is possible to achieve the sensitivity of sound planned for the script.

The Control Room

The control room is the focal point of operation in which all of the sound, music, effects, and broadcast silence are coordinated — carefully mixed by the engineer at the control board and sent out to the listener. The control room usually contains the turntables on which transcriptions and recordings can be incorporated with the live action in the studio. The control room also contains recording and taping equipment that permit the capture of the program either for rebroadcast or for initial public broadcast at a later time.

The control board regulates the volume of output of all microphones, turntables, and tapes, and can fade or blend the sound of any one or combination of these elements.

Sound Effects

There are two major categories of sound effects: those that are recorded and those that are made manually or live. Virtually any sound effect desired may be found on records or tape. Examples range from various types of airplane motors to the crying of a baby. For split-second incorporation of sound into the live action of the program, however, manual or live effects are sometimes more effective. Manual effects include such sounds as the opening and closing of a door (coming from a miniature door located near the microphone of the sound effects operator) or the rattling of cellophane to simulate the sound of fire. Under this category fall natural effects — those emanating from their natural sources, such as the sound of walking feet in which the microphone might be held near the feet of a sound effects person marking time. In some instances entirely new combinations of sounds may be necessary, including an amalgamation of recorded, manual, and natural effects.

Inexperienced writers occasionally have a tendency to overdo the use of sound. Sound effects should be used only when necessary, and then only in relation to the psychological principles that determine the orientation of the listener. Reflect on your own orientation to sound when listening to the radio. For example, a high pitch, high volume, or rising pitch usually suggests a climax or some disturbing element, while a low pitch, or low volume, or descending pitch usually suggests something soothing and calm. However, combinations of these sounds and the relationship of specific sound to the specific situation can alter these generalizations. For instance, a low pitch in the proper place can indicate something foreboding rather than calm; the combination of a low pitch and a high volume, as in thunder and an explosion, can create anything but a soothing effect.

Sound can be used for many purposes and effects, as follows:

Establish locale or setting For example, the sound of marching feet, the clanging of metal doors, and the blowing of a whistle will suggest the locale or setting of a prison. The soft sounds of violin music, the occasional clatter of dishes and silverware, the clinking of glasses, and the whispered sounds of talking would suggest not only a restaurant, but perhaps an old-world Hungarian or Russian restaurant.

Direct audience attention and emotion Emphasis on a particular sound can specifically orient the audience. For example, the sudden banging of a gavel in a courtroom scene will immediately direct the mind's-eye view of the audience toward the judge's bench. In a sequence in which the audience is aware that a person alone at home is an intended murder victim, the sound of steps on a walk and the sound of knocking on a door, or the more subtle sound of the turning of a doorknob, will direct the audience attention toward the front door and orient the audience's emotions toward the suspenseful terror of inevitable and perhaps immediate violence.

Establish time The clock striking the hour or the crowing of the cock are obvious, oft-used, but nevertheless effective devices. The echo of footsteps along a pavement, with no other sounds heard, indicates a quiet street very late at night or very early in the morning. If an element referred to in the program, such as an airplane or the rumbling of a subway train, has been established as indicating a certain time, then the moment the sound effect signifying that element is used the audience will know the time.

Establish mood Anyone who has heard a dramatization of a Sherlock Holmes story is familiar with the mood created by the echo of a baying hound followed by the muffled strokes of a clock striking twelve. The creaking door of "Mystery Theater," one of the very few drama programs on radio in the 1980s, is a hallmark of mood setting, borrowed from the "Inner Sanctum" radio series of several decades earlier. The sounds of laughter, loud music, and much tinkling of glasses establish a much different mood for a party than would subdued whispers and the soft music of a string quartet. Sound may be used effectively as counterpoint in setting off an individual character's mood. The attitudes and emotions of someone who is worried, sullen, morose, and fretful may be heightened by placing the character in the midst of sounds indicating a wild, loud party.

Signify entrances and exits The sound of footsteps fading off and the opening and closing of a door, or the reverse — the opening and closing of a door and the sound of footsteps coming on — are unmistakable in indicating an exit or entrance. Transportation sounds and human and nonhuman sounds may be used to signify a character's coming to or leaving a place. The departure of a soldier from an enemy-held jungle island after a secret reconnaissance mission can be indicated by the sound of boat paddles, the whine of bullets, and the chatter of jungle birds and animals. If the bullet, bird, and animal sounds remain at a steady level and the paddling of the boat fades off, the audience remains on the island and sees the soldier leave. The audience leaves with the soldier if the paddling remains at an on-mike level and the island sounds fade off.

Serve as transition   For example, in a dramatic program, if the transition is to cover a change of place, the sound used may be the means of transportation. The young graduate is about to leave home to make it in the big city. Tender farewells are said. The farewells **cross-fade** into the sounds of a train, with appropriate whistles. The train sounds cross-fade into the sounds of the hustle and bustle of the big city. These sounds in turn cross-fade into a dialogue sequence in which the protagonist makes arrangements for renting a room. The change of place has been achieved with sound providing an effective transition.

If the transition is to cover a lapse of time, the sound may be that of a timing device, such as a clock striking three, the tick of the clock fading out and fading in again, and the clock then striking six.

The sound indicating the transition may not relate necessarily to the specific cause of the transition. It may be of a general nature, such as a montage of war sounds to cover a change of place or lapse of time when the action relates to a war. Sometimes a **montage**, or blending of a number of sounds, can be particularly effective when no single sound fits the specific situation.

In a nondramatic program, the transition may be between program segments, and sounds relating to the content of the next segment may be used for transition. In some situations the sounds may have a relationship to the program as a whole rather than to a specific circumstance, such as the use of a ticker or telegraph key sound as a transition device for a news program. On comedy shows sounds completely irrelevant to the material may be used for transitional purposes, serving at the same time, because of their irrelevance, as comedy material.

Create unrealistic effects   Note Norman Corwin's description in "The Plot to Overthrow Christmas" of the audience's journey to Hades, "to the regions where legions of the damnèd go."

(CLANG ON CHINESE GONG. TWO THUNDER PEALS. OSCILLATOR IN AT HIGH PITCH BEFORE THUNDER IS ENTIRELY OUT. BRING PITCH DOWN GRADUALLY AND FADE IN ECHO CHAMBER WHILE HEAVY STATIC FADES IN. THEN OUT TO LEAVE NOTHING BUT OSCILLATOR AT A LOW OMINOUS PITCH; THEN RAISE OSCILLATOR PITCH SLOWLY. HOLD FOR A FEW SECONDS)

Combinations of sound and music may be used to create almost any nonrealistic effect demanded, from the simplest to the most complicated.

Sound also may be used to achieve not only one, but a combination of the various purposes already noted. One of the classic sound effects sequences — to many people the best and most famous sequence of all — is the one that accompanied Jack Benny's periodic visits to his private vault. Younger people who have listened to the revivals of old-time radio programs have probably heard it too. The sounds used establish setting, orient the audience's emotions and direct its attention, establish mood, signify entrances and exits, serve as transitions between places and indicate lapses of time, and create nonrealistic effects.

SOUND: FOOTSTEPS ... DOOR OPENS ... FOOTSTEPS GOING DOWN ... TAKING ON
          HOLLOW SOUND ... HEAVY IRON DOOR HANDLE TURNING ... CHAINS
          CLANKING ... DOOR CREAKS OPEN ... SIX MORE HOLLOW FOOTSTEPS ...
          SECOND CLANKING OF CHAINS ... HANDLE TURNS ... HEAVY IRON DOOR
          OPENS CREAKING ... TWO MORE FOOTSTEPS (DIALOGUE BETWEEN THE GUARD
          AND JACK) ... LIGHT TURNING SOUND OF VAULT COMBINATION ... LIGHT
          TURNING SOUND ... LIGHT TURNING SOUND ... LIGHT TURNING SOUND ...
          HANDLE TURNS ... USUAL ALARMS WITH BELLS, AUTO HORNS, WHISTLES,
          THINGS FALLING ... ENDING WITH B.O. FOGHORN ...

Courtesy of J & M Productions, Inc.

The writer must keep in mind that many sounds, no matter how well or accurately done, sometimes are not immediately identifiable to the audience, and often may be confused with similar sounds. It may be necessary for the writer to identify the sound through the dialogue. For example, because the rattling of paper may sound like fire, and the opening and closing of a desk drawer may sound like the opening and closing of almost anything else, note the need for identifying dialogue in the following sequence and the attempt to make the designation of the sound logical and a natural part of the dialogue.

DICK: (RUFFLING THE PAGES OF A MANUSCRIPT) Just about the worst piece of junk
          I've ever done in my life.
ANNE: Well, even if you don't like it, I think it can become a best-seller.
DICK: (RUFFLING PAGES AGAIN) Three hundred and forty-two pages of pure un-
          adulterated mediocrity. Listen to them. They even sound off-key. (SOUND OF A
          DESK DRAWER OPENING) There. That's where it belongs. (SOUND OF MANU-
          SCRIPT BEING THROWN INTO THE DRAWER)
ANNE: Don't lock it up in your desk. I think it's good.
DICK: Nope! That drawer is the place where all bad, dead manuscripts belong. (SOUND
          OF DESK DRAWER CLOSING) Amen!

Music
Music is an important part of all radio programming. The writer should understand its several uses, including the following:

Content for musical program   Live music, in the form of an orchestra or a musical performer, has virtually disappeared from radio. Recorded or transcribed music is the primary content of radio today, as exemplified in the popular disc jockey type of program.

Theme for dramatic or nondramatic program   Those over fifty years old who heard the first few bars of "The Make Believe Ballroom" knew immediately that it was time for Martin Block, radio's first disc jockey. Those over forty remember that the first few bars of "Love in Bloom" meant that Jack Benny was about to make his entrance. Those over thirty know that "A Hard Day's Night" signaled the appearance of the Beatles. Although the theme identification with a person or group is not as strong as it was when radio required a sound theme to serve what today might be a visual cue on television, it still exists under certain circumstances. A twenty-year-old tuning in a radio music special would know that the initial playing of the song "Born to Run" signified that the special was about Bruce Springsteen.

Music may be used not only as a theme for a program as a whole, but also for a specific event or particular character. The action or character is immediately identifiable when the theme music is heard. This may be true in a dramatic program or with a personality on a nondramatic program. Theme music is used in dramatic shows, too — usually not during the action but principally for the opening, closing, and, sometimes, during the commercial breaks. Note the use of music as a theme in the following excerpts from the beginning and end of one program of a dramatic series entitled "The Delaware Story."

ANNOUNCER:	WDEL presents "The Delaware Story."
MUSIC:	THEME IN, UP, AND UNDER.
NARRATOR:	When we think of lawless robber barons and land pirates, our thoughts turn to the early wild and unsettled west. Yet, in the late seventeenth century ... if it had not been for the interference of the King of England, the State of Delaware, through the unscrupulous efforts of one man, might have become annexed to Maryland and never become a separate state at all.
MUSIC:	THEME UP AND OUT.
ANNOUNCER:	COMMERCIAL.
	And now, back to today's "Delaware Story." "The Man Who Almost Stole a State."
MUSIC:	THEME IN, UP, AND OUT.
NARRATOR:	In 1681 Charles II of England granted to William Penn a charter ...

[The narrator introduces the live dramatic action. Following the dramatic sequences, the narrator again resumes, completing the story.]

NARRATOR:	... but Talbot did not succeed in stealing a state, and he remains, fortunately, a not too successful chapter in "The Delaware Story."
MUSIC:	THEME IN, UP, AND OUT.

After the final commercial and program credits, the theme is again brought in, up, and out to close the show.

Bridge for program divisions or changing time or place   The musical **bridge** is the most commonly used device for transitions. Music lasting only a few notes or a few bars or, in some cases, of longer duration may be used to indicate the break between segments of the nondramatic presentation. For example, in the variety show the writer would indicate a music bridge following the completion of an act, before the master of ceremonies introduces the next act. Sometimes the bridge may also serve as a short musical introduction or finale. The musical bridge also may be used to distinguish the commercial insert from the rest of the program.

In the dramatic program the musical bridge frequently is used to indicate a change of place or a lapse of time. Care must be taken that the bridge is representative of the mood and content of the play at that particular moment. The musical bridge usually is only a few seconds long.

Note the use of the bridge separating dramatic sequences and narration in the following condensed excerpt, again from ''The Delaware Story'' series.

LORD BALTIMORE:	Go to Philadelphia and speak with William Penn. Ask him to withdraw. If he does not, then we can consider other methods.
MUSIC:	BRIDGE.
TALBOT:	(FADING IN) ... and if you choose to remain, we are left with only one recourse. I need not amplify, my dear Mr. Penn, need I?
PENN:	You have had my answer, Talbot. If you think you can frighten me from land legally deeded to me, then your presumptuousness is exceeded only by your stupidity.
MUSIC:	SNEAK IN SHORT BRIDGE.
NARRATOR:	Talbot returned to Maryland and immediately began his campaign to regain the land he believed rightfully belonged to Lord Baltimore ...
SOUND:	CROWD OF MEN'S VOICES, ANGRY, UNDER.
TALBOT:	We must fight for the right. I've called you together because we shall and must fight like vigilantes. Our first line of defense will be Beacon Hill. The firing of three shots means danger ... the blowing of horns will mean we assemble to ride. Are you with me?
ALL:	(SHOUTING) Aye! Aye!
MUSIC:	SNEAK IN SHORT BRIDGE.
NARRATOR:	And ride they did. Talbot now assumed dictatorial powers ...

Sound effect   For example, brass and percussion instruments often may be very effective in conveying the sound of a storm or in heightening the feeling of a storm presented through sound effects alone. Some effects cannot be presented potently except through music. How better could one convey on radio the sound of a person falling from the top of a tall building than through music moving in a spiral rhythm from a high to a low pitch and ending in a crash?

Background or mood   Music can heighten the content and mood of a sequence, especially in a dramatic presentation. Background music is an extremely important part of filmmaking, and is used effectively in nonmusical television plays. The music must serve as a subtle aid, however, and must not be obvious or, in some instances, even evident. The listener who is aware of a lovely piece of background music during a dramatic moment has been distracted from the primary purpose of the production. The music should have its effect without the audience consciously realizing it. Background and mood music should not be overdone or used excessively in the manner of the piano player accompanying a silent film. Well-known compositions should be avoided, to prevent the audience from being distracted from the dialogue by too great a familiarity with the music.

Sound and Music Techniques and Terms

Several important terms are used by the writer to designate the techniques used in manipulating sound and music. These techniques are applied at the **control board.**

Segue (*pronounced* seg-way)   The smooth movement from one sound into the next. This is particularly applicable to the transitions between musical numbers, in which one number is faded out and the next is faded in. Technically, it is used in the dramatic program as well as in the music show, but in the dramatic program the overlapping of sounds makes the technique a cross-fade rather than a **segue.**

An example in the music program:

ANNOUNCER: Our program continues with excerpts from famous musical compositions dealing with the Romeo and Juliet theme. First we hear from Tchaikovsky's *Romeo and Juliet* overture, followed by Prokofiev's *Romeo and Juliet* ballet, and finally Gounod's opera *Romeo et Juliette.*

MUSIC: TCHAIKOVSKY'S *ROMEO AND JULIET.*
SEGUE TO PROKOFIEV'S *ROMEO AND JULIET.*
SEGUE TO GOUNOD'S *ROMEO ET JULIETTE.*

ANNOUNCER: You have heard ...

An example in the dramatic program:

ANNOUNCER: And now, to today's mystery drama.
MUSIC: THEME IN AND UP, HOLD FOR FIVE SECONDS AND OUT, SEGUE INTO
SOUND: TINKLING OF GLASSES, VOICES IN BACKGROUND IN ANGRY CONVERSA-
TION, JUKEBOX PLAYING.

Cross-fade   The **dissolving** from one sound into another. The term **cross-fade** sometimes is used interchangeably with the term *segue*. The cross-fade is, however, the crossing of sounds as one fades in and the other fades out, and the segue is simply the immediate following of one sound by another. In the following example

MUSIC: THEME IN AND UP, HOLD FOR FIVE SECONDS, CROSS-FADE INTO THE
RINGING OF A TELEPHONE

the telephone ringing becomes blended for a second or two with the theme before the theme is entirely out, and then only the telephone ringing remains.

An example in a dramatic program:

CLARA: I don't know where Harry is, but if he's with some blonde in some bar ...
MUSIC: STAB IN BRIDGE, HOLD FOR THREE SECONDS, CROSS-FADE INTO SOUND
OF PIANO IN A BAR PLAYING SOFT ROCK.

Blending   Two or more different sounds combined and going out over the air at the same time. These may include combinations of dialogue and music, dialogue and sound effects, sound effects and music, or a combination of all three. The earlier example of the combination of tinkling glasses, angry voices in the background, and the playing of a jukebox is illustrative of blending dialogue, sound effects, and music. The blending of sounds may be used effectively to create nonrealistic effects.

Cutting or switching   The sudden **cutting** off of one sound and the immediate intrusion of another. It is a jarring break and sometimes is used for special effect purposes. It may simply designate the **switching** sharply from one microphone to another microphone or sound source. It also may be used for remotes:

ANNOUNCER: We now switch you to Times Square where Tom Rogers is ready with his
              "Probing Microphone."
CUT TO REMOTE, ROGERS AT TIMES SQUARE.
ROGERS: Good afternoon. For our first interview, we have over here ...

Fade in and fade out   Bringing up the volume or turning it down is a relatively simple operation. It frequently is used to fade the music under dialogue, as well as to bring it into the program and out of the program. The writer indicates that the music should be *faded in, up, under,* or *out*.

The following example illustrates the use of the fade-in and fade-out on the disc jockey show.

MUSIC: THEME, "You Rocked My Rocker with a Rock," IN, UP, AND UNDER.
ANNOUNCER: Good evening, cats, and welcome to the Rockin' Rollo Rock Repertory.
MUSIC: THEME UP, HOLD FOR FIVE SECONDS, THEN UNDER AND OUT.
ANNOUNCER: This is Rockin' Rollo ready to bring you the next full hour right from the top
              of the charts. And starting with number one on the rack, it's The Kitchen
              Sink and their new hit ...
MUSIC: SNEAK IN AND HOLD UNDER, "Clip Joint."
ANNOUNCER: That's right, you guessed it, The Kitchen Sink is smokin' away with "Clip
              Joint."
MUSIC: UP FAST, HOLD TO FINISH, AND OUT.

Television

Television drama production techniques continue to evolve. When drama production moved from New York to Hollywood, the live-type program multicamera shooting technique (called by some **New York style**) began to change into the single-camera technique of the film (called by some **Hollywood style**). The writer for television must therefore become familiar with both the traditional techniques of both television and film and with the combinations of these skills into the middle ground of videotape.

Although the television writer does not have to know the various coordinate elements of theatrical production as does the writer of the stage play, it is important to know how to use and integrate settings, lights, costumes, makeup, and the visual movement of performers into the dramatic or nondramatic script. The television writer, like the radio writer, can use all the elements of sound. In addition, the television writer must achieve at least a basic understanding of the special mechanical and electronic devices of the television medium. There are six major areas pertaining to television production that the writer should be aware of: the studio, the camera, the control room, special video effects, editing, and sound. A course in television production would be of value to the beginning writer.

The Television Studio

Studios vary greatly in size and equipment. Network studios, where drama series and specials are usually produced, have not only all the technical advantages of a television studio, but also the size and equipment of a movie sound stage. Some individual stations have excellent facilities, others are small and cramped. A large regional station may have one or two relatively small studios, limiting production to news and panel shows, while a nearby school system may have an instructional television studio that would be the envy of any commercial station. The writer should be aware of studio limitations before writing the script, especially where the show may be videotaped or produced live and it is necessary to avoid too many sets or large sets. Once extremely costly and difficult, exterior shooting is no longer a problem because of the availability of EFP video equipment.

The Camera

Whether the show is being recorded by a film camera or by a television camera on videotape, the basic movements of the camera are the same. Even the terminology is the same. The principal difference is the style: short, individual takes for the film approach, longer action sequences and continuous filming for the television approach. Because many television directors have moved to films and film directors to television, and with instant videotape editing, the two approaches have tended to move toward each other, combining elements of both.

In either case, the writer should consider the camera as a moving and adjustable proscenium through which the attention of the audience is directed just as the writer and director wish. There are three major areas of audience attention that may be changed via the camera: the distance between the audience and the subject, which includes the amount of the subject the audience sees; the position of the audience in relation to the subject; and the angle at which the viewer sees the subject. Various uses of the camera, including camera movement, lens openings, and types of shots, may be made to effect all of these approaches in varying degrees.

Camera movement may change the position, angle, distance, and amount of subject matter seen. There are six specific movements the writer must be aware of and be prepared to designate, when necessary, in the script.

Dolly-in and dolly-out The camera is on a **dolly** stand that permits smooth forward or backward movement. This movement to or away from the subject permits a change of orientation to the subject while keeping the camera on the air and retaining a continuity of action.

Zoom-in and zoom-out   Frequently used to accomplish the same purpose as the dolly, the **zoom** narrows the angle of view and compresses depth, making people or objects appear closer together. Some writers believe that psychologically the dolly is more effective, moving the audience closer to or further from the subject, whereas the zoom gives the feeling of moving the subject closer to or further from the audience.

Tilt up and tilt down   This consists of pointing the camera up or down, thus changing the view from the same position to a higher or lower part of the subject.

Pan right and pan left   The camera moves right or left on its axis. This movement may be used to follow a character or some particular action or to direct the audience attention to a particular subject.

Follow right and follow left   This is also called the **travel shot** or the *truck shot*. It is used when the camera is set at a right angle to the subject and either moves with it, following alongside it, or — as in the case of a stationary subject such as an advertising display — follows down the line of the display. The audience's eyes, through the camera lens pointed sharply to the right or left, pick up the subjects in the display. This shot is not used as frequently as are the previous ones.

Boom shot   Originally familiar equipment for Hollywood filmmaking, the camera boom became more and more part of standard television production practices. A crane, usually attached to a moving dolly, enables the camera to **boom** from its basic position up or down, at various angles — usually high up — to the subject. This is also known as a **crane shot**.

Note the use of the basic camera movements in the following scripts. In the first, using the standard television format, the writer would not ordinarily include so many camera directions, but would leave their determination to the director. They are included here to indicate to the beginning writer a variety of camera and shot possibilities. The left hand column, as shown here, would be written in on the mimeographed script almost entirely by the director.

VIDEO	AUDIO
ESTABLISHING SHOT.	DETECTIVE BYRON: (AT DESK, IN FRONT OF HIM, ON CHAIRS IN A ROW, ARE SEVERAL YOUNG MEN IN DUNGAREES, LEATHER JACKETS, AND MOTORCYCLE CAPS) All right. So a store was robbed. So all of you were seen in the store at the time of the robbery. So there was no one else in the store except the clerk. So none of you know anything about the robbery.
DOLLY IN FOR CLOSE-UP OF BYRON.	(GETTING ANGRY) You may be young punks but you're still punks, and you can stand trial whether you're seventeen or seventy. And if you're not going to cooperate now, I'll see that you get the stiffest sentence possible.

VIDEO	AUDIO
DOLLY OUT FOR LONG SHOT OF ENTIRE GROUP. CUT TO CLOSE-UP. PAN RIGHT ACROSS BOYS' FACES, FROM ONE TO THE OTHER, AS BYRON TALKS.	Now, I'm going to ask you again, each one of you. And this is your last chance. If you talk, only the guilty one will be charged with larceny. The others will have only a petty theft charge on them, and I'll see they get a suspended sentence. Otherwise I'll send you all up for five to ten.
FOLLOW SHOT ALONG LINE OF CHAIRS IN FRONT OF BOYS, GETTING FACIAL REACTIONS OF EACH ONE AS THEY RESPOND.	(OFF CAMERA) JOEY? JOEY: (STARES STRAIGHT AHEAD, NOT ANSWERING.) BYRON: (OFF CAMERA) Al? AL: I got nothin' to say. BYRON: (OFF CAMERA) Bill? BILL: Me, too. I don't know nothin'. BYRON: (OFF CAMERA) OK, Johnny. It's up to you.
TILT DOWN TO JOHNNY'S BOOT AS HE REACHES FOR HANDLE OF KNIFE. TILT UP WITH HAND AS IT MOVES AWAY FROM THE BOOT, INTO AN INSIDE POCKET OF HIS JACKET. CUT TO MEDIUM SHOT ON BOOM CAMERA OF JOHNNY WITHDRAWING HAND FROM POCKET. BOOM DOWN TO OBJECT IN JOHNNY'S HAND. (ORDINARILY, A BOOM SHOT WOULD NOT BE USED HERE. A ZOOM LENS WOULD BE EASIER TO USE AND AT LEAST AS EFFECTIVE.)	JOHNNY: (THERE IS NO ANSWER. THEN JOHNNY SLOWLY SHAKES HIS HEAD. IMPERCEPTIBLY, BYRON NOT NOTICING, HE REACHES DOWN TO HIS MOTORCYCLE BOOT FOR THE HANDLE OF A KNIFE. SUDDENLY THE HAND STOPS AND MOVES UP TO THE INSIDE POCKET OF HIS JACKET. JOHNNY TAKES AN OBJECT FROM HIS POCKET, SLOWLY OPENS HIS HAND.)

Although the format in the following, a film script, is different, note that the terminology and the visual results are virtually the same. The numbers in the left-hand column refer to each shot or sequence. Film scripts usually are shot out of sequence with all scenes in a particular setting done at one period of time. The numbers make it possible to designate easily which sequences will be filmed at a given time or on a given day, such as "Barn Set — sequences 42, 45, 46, 78, 79, 81."

FADE IN
1. EXT. BEACH — SUNRISE — EXTREME LONG SHOT.
2. PAN ALONG SHORE LINE AS WAVES BREAK ON SAND.
3. EXT. BEACH — LONG SHOT.
   Two figures are seen in the distance, alone with the vastness of sand and water surrounding them.
4. ZOOM SLOWLY IN UNTIL WE ESTABLISH THAT FIGURES ARE A MAN AND A WOMAN.
5. MEDIUM LONG SHOT.
   The man and woman are standing by the water's edge, holding hands, staring toward the sea. They are about sixty, but their brightness of look and posture make them seem much younger.

6. MEDIUM SHOT — ANOTHER ANGLE ON THEM.
   They slowly turn their faces toward each other and kiss.
7. CLOSE SHOT.
8. MEDIUM CLOSE SHOT.
   Their heads and faces are close, still almost touching.
       GLADYS: I did not feel so beautiful when I was twenty.
9. CLOSE SHOT — REGINALD
   as he grins
       REGINALD: Me neither. But we weren't in love like this when we
       were twenty. (CUT TO)
10. INT. BEACH HOUSE — ENTRANCE HALL — MORNING
    The door opens and Gladys and Reginald walk in, hand in hand, laughing.

As you study the scripts in the chapters dealing with specific program forms, you will note that the film script format usually is used only for the play. Virtually all other program types use the television script format.

Lenses

Although it is the director who must know what the camera lenses can do so that he or she may most effectively interpret the writer's intent, it would not hurt for the writer to obtain a working knowledge of what the camera can do focally. The following, from *BM/E* magazine, is a good introductory guide:

In the beginning, the user was confined to four lenses on a turret. This made framing a shot difficult as well as time consuming. With the old turreted camera there were only four focal lengths readily available, which necessitated a good deal of dollying with the resultant time loss and undesirable framing of a shot due to the limited number of focal lengths. Then along came the zoom lens with its great number of focal lengths immediately available. The director could now get the exact framing he wanted quickly. Now that it is here, can one zoom do everything? Of course not! The correct lens for your application may not be applicable to someone else's needs. A good studio lens is not a good remote lens although it may cover some remote applications. The remote lens works quite often at long focal lengths under low light levels requiring f stops of f/3 at 500mm or f/6 at 1000mm, or better. The average studio lens can attain 500mm with range extenders but it needs over 3 times more light at that focal length due to its limited aperture. . . . If your studio is small, you will need a lens with a wide angle so that it isn't necessary to dolly back to one side of the studio to get an overall shot of a set on the other side. Close focusing is necessary so that magnification is possible as well as interesting special effect shots. It should be noted here that two lenses with the *same* long focal length and different close focusing capability will magnify an object to a different degree, the greater magnification going with the closer focusing of the two. If commercial production is contemplated, then more capability will be demanded of the lens because agency people, as well as clients, want the dramatic eye-catching shot that will make the product memorable.

Taping time must be held to a minimum to earn more money for the station and less added cost to the advertiser. The lens can be of great help here. If a lense can, in fast sequence, go from an extreme close-up to a wide overall shot and back to a close-up then taping time will be lessened because there will be no need to stop the tape for different shot sequences.

However, if all that is done is news and weather, the simple good quality wide angle 10 to 1 lens may be all that is needed.

Add to this the ENG/EFP camera lenses that focus at a distance as close as three feet. Some lenses with macrocapability will focus even a few inches away from the subject.

Types of Shots

Among those directions most frequently written in by the writer are the shots designating how much of the subject is to be seen, as illustrated in the script examples a few pages back. Ordinarily, the determination is left up to the director, but in many instances the writer needs to capture a specific subject for the logical continuity of the script or for the proper psychological effect of that moment upon the audience. When the specific shot required might not be obvious to the director, the writer has the prerogative of inserting it into the script. Shot designations range from the close-up to the medium shot to the long shot. Within these categories there are gradations, such as the medium long shot and extreme close-up. The writer indicates the kind of shot and the specific subject to be encompassed by that shot. The use of the terms and their meanings apply to both the film and the television format. Here are the most commonly used shots:

Close-up　　This may be designated by the letters **CU**. The writer states in the script, ''CU Harry,'' or ''CU Harry's fingers as he twists the dials of the safe,'' or ''CU Harry's feet on the pedals of the piano.'' The **close-up** of the immediate person of a human subject will usually consist of just the face and may include some of the upper part of the body, with emphasis on the face, unless specifically designated otherwise. The letters **XCU** or **ECU** stand for *extreme close-up* and designate the face alone. The term *shoulder shot* indicates an area encompassing the shoulders to the top of the head. Other designations are *bust shot*, *waist shot*, *hip shot*, and *knee shot*.

Medium shot　　This may be designated by the letters **MS**. The camera picks up a good part of the individual or group subject, the subject usually filling the screen (but usually not in its entirety), and without too much of the physical environment shown.

Long shot　　The writer may state this as **LS**. The long shot is used primarily for establishing shots in which the entire setting, or as much of it as necessary to orient the audience properly, is shown. From the long shot, the camera may move to the medium shot and then to the close-up, creating a dramatic movement from an overall view to the impact of the essence or selective aspect of the situation. Conversely, the camera may move from the intriguing suspense of the extreme close-up to the clarifying broadness of the *extreme long shot* (**XLS**).

Full shot   This is stated as **FS**. The subject is put on the screen in its entirety. For example, "FS Harry" means that the audience sees Harry from head to toe. "FS family at dinner table" means that the family seated around the dinner table is seen completely. Some writers and directors use the designation **FF** for *full figure* shot.

Other   Variations of the above are given designations, sometimes on an ad hoc basis, that tell the director just what the writer has in mind. For example, if the writer wants two people in conversation to be the focal point of the shot, he or she might use the term *two-shot* or **2S**. If the two people are to fill the screen, *tight 2S* might be used, as in the next script example. Similarly, *medium two-shot* or M2S, *three-shot* or 3S, and other terms may be used as required.

The writer should be aware of any necessity to change lenses, focus the lenses, or dolly the camera for a new shot. Depending on the number of cameras used in the show — whether it is live or live-style videotaped — the writer should leave enough time between shots for the cameraperson to perform these functions properly.

Note the use of different types of shots in the following hypothetical script example. The video directions are necessary at the beginning of this script because the writer is dealing solely with pictures. Subsequent video directions may be left out by the writer, except, as at the end, where necessary to convey the meaning and action. You will note that in many of the actual scripts used in this book the writers provide very few video directions.

VIDEO	AUDIO
FADE IN ON LONG SHOT OF OUTSIDE OF BAR. ESTABLISH STREET FRONT AND OUT-SIDE OF BAR. DOLLY IN TO MEDIUM SHOT, THEN TO CLOSE-UP OF SIGN ON THE WINDOW: "HARRY SMITH, PROP." CUT TO INSIDE OF BAR, CLOSE-UP OF MAN'S HAND DRAWING A GLASS OF BEER FROM THE TAP. FOLLOW MAN'S HAND WITH GLASS TO TOP OF BAR WHERE HE PUTS DOWN GLASS. DOLLY OUT SLOWLY TO MEDIUM SHOT OF HARRY, SERVING THE BEER, AND MAC, SITTING AT BAR. ZOOM OUT TO WIDE SHOT, ESTABLISHING ENTIRE INSIDE OF BAR, SEVERAL PEOPLE ON STOOLS, AND SMALL TABLE AT RIGHT OF BAR WITH THREE MEN SEATED, PLAY-ING CARDS.	
	JOE: (AT TABLE) Harry. Bring us another deck. This one's getting too dirty for honest card players. HARRY: Okay. (HE REACHES UNDER THE BAR, GETS A DECK OF CARDS, GOES TO THE TABLE.)

VIDEO	AUDIO
TIGHT 2-S HARRY AND JOE	JOE: (TAKING THE CARDS, WHISPERS TO HARRY.) Who's the guy at the bar? He looks familiar.
	HARRY: Name of Mac. From Jersey some-place.
CUT TO CU JOE	JOE: Keep him there. Looks like somebody we got business with. (LOOKS AROUND TABLE)
CUT TO FS TABLE	Right, boys? (THE MEN AT THE TABLE NOD KNOWINGLY TO HARRY.)
	HARRY: Okay if I go back to the bar?
	JOE: Go ahead.
PAN WITH HARRY TO BAR. DOLLY IN TO BAR, MS HARRY AND MAC AS HARRY POURS HIM ANOTHER DRINK. MCU HARRY AS HE WRITES. CUT TO CU OF WORDS ON PIECE OF PAPER.	HARRY: (WALKS BACK TO BAR, POURS DRINK FOR MAC. SCRIBBLES SOMETHING ON PIECE OF PAPER, PUTS IT ON BAR IN FRONT OF MAC.)

Control Room Techniques and Editing

The technicians in the control room have various electronic devices for modifying the picture and moving from one picture to another — thus giving television its ability to direct the attention and control the view of the audience and to bypass the unities of time and place effectively. The technicians in the film editing room have the same capabilities except that the modifications are done during the editing process, whereas in live-type videotaped television the modifications may be done during the recording of the program. Further modifications can take place when editing the videotape. The writer should be familiar with the terminology and function of control room techniques and their similar function in film editing in order to know what the potentials of the medium are and to be able to indicate, if necessary, special picture modifications or special changes in time and/or place. The terms used have the same meaning in television and film.

The fade   The fade-in consists of bringing in the picture from a black (or blank) screen. (You've often heard the phrase *fade to black*.) The fade-out is the taking out of a picture until a black level is reached. The **fade** is used primarily to indicate a passage of time, and in this function serves much like the curtain or blackout on the legitimate stage. Depending on the sequence of action, a fast fade-in or fade-out or slow fade-out or fade-in may be indicated. The fade-in is used at the beginning of a sequence, the fade-out at the end. The fade sometimes also is used to indicate a change of place. The writer always indicates the fade-in or fade-out in the script.

The dissolve   The **dissolve** is similar to the cross-fade of radio. While one picture is being reduced in intensity the other picture is being raised, one picture smoothly dissolving into the next. The dissolve is used primarily to indicate a change of place, but is used sometimes to indicate a change of time. There are various modifications of the dissolve. An important one is the matched dissolve, in which two similar or identical subjects are placed one over the other; the fading out of one and the fading in of the other shows a metamorphosis taking place. The dissolving from a newly lit candle into a candle burned down would be a use of the matched dissolve. The dissolve may vary in time, and may be designated as a fast dissolve (almost a split-second movement) or as a slow dissolve (anywhere up to five seconds). At no point in the dissolve does either picture go to black. The writer always indicates the use of the dissolve in the script.

The cut   The **cut** is the technique most commonly used. It consists simply of switching instantaneously from one picture to another. Care must be taken to avoid too much cutting and to make certain that the cutting is consistent with the mood, rhythm, pace, and psychological approach of the program as a whole. The writer ordinarily is not concerned with the planning or designation of cuts in the television script, but leaves it up to the director. In the film script, particularly when the transition from one sequence to the next is a sharp, instantaneous effect rather than a dissolve or fade, the writer may indicate "cut to. . . ."

The superimposition   The **super**, as it is sometimes called, means the placing of one image over another, thus creating a fantasy kind of picture. This sometimes is used in the stream-of-consciousness technique when the thing being recalled to memory is pictured on the screen. To obtain necessary contrast in the superimposition, when the two pictures are placed on the screen together one picture must be of a higher light intensity than the other. The writer usually indicates the use of the superimposition.

The key or matte   A **key** is a two-source special effect where a foreground image is cut into a background image and filled back in with itself. A **matte** is a similar technique, but has the capability of adding color to the foreground image. Most television facilities have **character generators** (or **chirons** or **vidifonts**) that electronically cut letters into background pictures. Titles and commercial names of products are keyed or matted.

The wipe   This is accomplished by one picture wiping another picture off the screen in the manner of a window shade being pulled down over a window. The **wipe** may be from any direction — horizontal, vertical, or diagonal. The wipe may also blossom out a picture from the center of a black level or, in reverse, envelop the picture by encompassing it from all its sides. The wipe can be used to designate a change of place or time.

The split screen   In the split screen the picture on the air is actually divided, with the shots from two or more cameras occupying adjoining places on the screen. A common use is for phone conversations, showing the persons speaking on separate halves of the screen. The screen may be split in many parts and in many shapes, as is sometimes done when news correspondents report from different parts of the nation. One segment of the screen of virtually any size may be split off from the rest, as often is done in sports broadcasts; for example, one corner of the screen may show the runner taking a lead off first base while the rest of the screen encompasses the main action of the ball game.

Film and slides For live-type television production such as newscasts and in many college and university training studios, which may not have sophisticated film or videotape equipment, film clips (short lengths of 16-mm motion picture film) and slides are important. Slides provide visual information not available in the studio for news, sports, feature, and documentary programs. Film is sometimes used but has been largely replaced by videotape. Film clips are occasionally used in live-type videotaped drama to provide background exterior or stock shots.

Note the use of different control room techniques for modifying the picture and moving from one picture to another in the following hypothetical script example.

COMMENTARY	VIDEO	AUDIO
1. The fade-in is used for the beginning of the sequence.	FADE IN ON SHERIFF'S OFFICE. SHERIFF FEARLESS AND DEPUTY FEARFUL ARE SEATED AT THE DESK IN THE CENTER OF THE ROOM.	FEARLESS: I wonder what Bad Bart is up to. He's been in town since yesterday. I've got to figure out his plan if I'm to prevent bloodshed. FEARFUL: I've got faith in you, Fearless. I heard that he's been with Miss Susie in her room. FEARLESS: Good. We can trust her. She'll find out for us. FEARFUL: But I'm worried about her safety. FEARLESS: Yup. I wonder how she is making out. That Bad Bart is a mean one.
2. The dissolve is used here for a change of place without passage of time. This scene takes place simultaneously or immediately following the one in the sheriff's office.	DISSOLVE TO MISS SUSIE'S HOTEL ROOM. BART IS SEATED IN AN EASY CHAIR. SUSIE IS IN A STRAIGHT CHAIR AT THE OTHER END OF THE ROOM.	BART: I ain't really a killer, Miss Susie. It's only my reputation that's hurting me. Only because of one youthful indiscretion. SUSIE: What was that, Mr. Bart?
3. The superimposition is used here for a memory recall device.	SUPERIMPOSE, OVER CU BART, FACE OF MAN HE KILLED AS HE DESCRIBES SCENE.	BART: I can remember as well as yesterday. I was only a kid then. I thought he drew a gun on me. Maybe he did and maybe he didn't. But I shot him. And I'll remember his face as sure as I'll live — always. SUSIE: I guess you aren't really all bad, Mr. Bart.

COMMENTARY	VIDEO	AUDIO

AUDIO

BART: You've convinced me, Miss Susie. I've never had a fine woman speak to me so nice before. I'm going to turn over a new leaf. (WALKS INTO THE HALL. AN EARLY MODEL TELEPHONE IS ON THE WALL.) I'm going to call the sheriff. Operator, get me the sheriff's office.

4. The cut would be used without indication from the writer throughout this script.

VIDEO: PAN WITH BART TO THE HALL DOOR. CUT TO HALL AS HE ENTERS IT.

Here, the cut specifically indicates a different view of the character in the same continuous time sequence.

5. The wipe here moves from left to right or right to left. It designates a change of place. The use of the split screen indicates the putting of two different places before the audience at the same time.

VIDEO: HORIZONTAL WIPE INTO SPLIT SCREEN. BART IN ONE HALF, SHERIFF PICKING UP TELEPHONE IN OTHER HALF.

FEARLESS: Sheriff's office.
BART: Sheriff. This is Bad Bart. I'm going to give myself up and confess all my crimes. I've turned over a new leaf.
FEARLESS: You expect me to believe that, Bart?
BART: No, I don't. But all I'm asking is a chance to prove it.
FEARLESS: How do you propose to do that?
BART: I'm coming over to your office. And I'm not going to be wearing my guns.
SUSIE: That's all there was to it, Fearless. The more I talked to him, the more I could see that underneath it all he had a good heart.

VIDEO: WIPE OFF SHERIFF OFFICE SCENE. CU BART'S FACE AS HE MAKES HIS DECISION. FADE OUT. FADE IN ON MISS SUSIE SEATED ON HER BED.

6. The fade here indicates the passage of time. If this next scene were in the Sheriff's office, the fade would have indicated a passage of time and change of place.

7. The sustained opening on Susie is necessary, for live-type, continuous action television, to provide time for Bart to get off the set and for Fearless to get on. The fifteen or twenty seconds at the opening of this scene, in which we do not yet see Fearless, though Susie's dialogue indicates he is there, should be sufficient "cover" time.

(SHE WALKS TO THE SMALL TABLE AT THE FOOT OF THE BED, TAKES A GLASS AND BOTTLE, THEN WALKS OVER TO THE EASY CHAIR. WE SEE SHERIFF FEARLESS IN THE EASY CHAIR.)
Here, Fearless, have a sarsaparilla. You deserve one after what you've done today.
FEARLESS: No, Susie. It was you who really did the work. And you deserve the drink. (AFTER A MOMENT) You know, there's only one thing I'm sorry for.
SUSIE: What's that?

COMMENTARY	VIDEO	AUDIO
		FEARLESS: That Bart turned out to be good, deep down inside, and gave himself up. SUSIE: Why? FEARLESS: Well, there's this new gun I received this morning from the East that I haven't yet had a chance to use!
8. Fade is used to signify the end of a sequence, and — note the next scene — a passage of time and change of place.	THEME MUSIC IN AND UP STRONG. SLOW FADE OUT.	
9. Since this is a videotaped studio show, the film clip is stock footage of a well-known place, necessary for the exterior scene, not reproduceable in a studio. Such film clip inserts could be used at any time during the play itself.	FADE IN FILM CLIP OF SOUTH DAKOTA BADLANDS, THEN CUT TO TAPE OF FEARLESS AND SUSIE ON THEIR HORSES ON THE TRAIL WAVING GOODBYE TO BART, WHO RIDES OFF INTO THE DISTANCE.	
10. Key or matte, as noted earlier, permits the insertion of words onto the picture.	KEY CREDITS OVER THE SCENE AS FEARLESS AND SUSIE CONTINUE TO WAVE.	

Special Video Effects

Titles   The writer, though not responsible for the kinds of titling done, should be aware of the ability of the character generator, chiron, and vidifont machines to key words electronically with different colors into a picture and to roll them vertically or horizontally across the screen.

Nature effects   Though it is difficult to achieve realistic nature effects in some studios, it is possible to obtain some through special effects. These include snow, rain, smoke, and flame.

Miniatures   In lieu of film or live exteriors, a **miniature** of a setting that cannot be duplicated in full in the studio may serve very well for establishing shots. For example, a miniature of a castle may be used for an opening shot. The camera dollies toward the front gate of the miniature. Then a cut is made to the live set which may consist of the courtyard or an interior room. The use of stock film footage for such scenes is less costly and more authentic.

Detail sets   Detail sets serve to augment the close-ups of television. Where the camera might find it difficult to pick up the precise movements of the fingers turning the dial of a safe on a regular set, another camera may cut to a detail set of the safe and capture the performer's fingers in every precise action. Such shots are called *cut-ins* and usually are shot after the main action and edited into the finished tape.

Puppets, marionettes, and animation   These devices are particularly effective in commercial presentations and may be integrated easily into live action sequences. Animation is a staple and frequently the most creative approach in the production of commercials.

Chroma key   This electronic effect cuts a given color out of a picture and replaces it with another visual. Newscasts use this technique extensively where, for example, the blue background of the newscaster is replaced with a slide or a taped sequence.

Remotes   One or more cameras may be used at a place remote from the studio to send back material for incorporation into the program — live, as with a newscast, or taped, as with a play or documentary. An entire program may be done **remote**, such as a sports event.

Sound

Basically, sound is used in television in the same way as in radio, as analyzed earlier in this chapter. There are, however, some obvious modifications. The microphone in the television play usually is not stationary, but is on a boom and dolly to follow the moving performers. In the single-action shot of the film, it may be stationary if the actors do not move. Chest mikes, table mikes, and cordless mikes are also used, usually for the nondramatic studio program such as the interview and panel, but also occasionally for the drama in preset situations and positions. The dialogue and sound on the set emanate from and must be coordinated with the visual action. Off-screen sound effects may be used, but they clearly must appear to be coming from off-screen unless they represent an action taking place on camera. Sound may be prerecorded or, as in filmed productions, added after the action has been shot. Television may use narration, as radio does. In television the voice-over (**VO**) may be a narrator, an announcer, or the prerecorded thoughts of the character. Television uses music as program content, as background, and as theme. If a performer in television purportedly plays an instrument, the impression must be given that the person involved is really playing the instrument. Other uses of sound and music in radio may be adapted to television, as long as the writer remembers that in television the sound or music does not replace visual action but complements or heightens it.

_____ **For Application and Review**_____

Radio

1. Write a short sequence in which you use all five microphone positions.
2. Write one or more short sequences in which you use sound effects to establish locale or setting, direct the audience attention by emphasis on a particular sound, establish time, establish mood, signify entrances or exits, create transitions

between program segments, and create unrealistic effects. More than one of the above uses may be indicated in a single sequence.

3. Write one or more short sequences in which you use music as a bridge, as a sound effect, and to establish background or mood.

4. Write a short script in which you use the following techniques: segue, cross-fade, blending, cutting or switching, and fade-in or fade-out.

Television

1. Write a short sequence in the New York television-style script form in which you use the following camera movements: the dolly-in and dolly-out, the tilt, the pan, and the follow shot.

2. Write a short sequence in the Hollywood film-style script form in which you use the following camera movements: zoom, pan, boom, and change of camera angle.

3. Write a short sequence in television-style script form in which you, the writer, must indicate the following shots: CU, M2S, LS, FS, XLS, and XCU. Do the same thing using the film-style script.

4. Write a short sequence in television-style script form in which you, the writer, must designate the following effects: fade-in and fade-out, dissolve, superimposition, wipe, split screen, film insert, rear projection, and key.

5. Write a short sequence in film-style script form in which you, the writer, must designate the following effects: fade-in and fade-out, cut, and dissolve.

6. Watch several television programs and analyze the use of camera movements, types of shots, and switcher or editing effects. Can you determine the writer's contributions in relation to the use of these techniques as differentiated from the director's work?

3
Commercials and Announcements

harles "Chuck" Barclay, when he was director of Creative Services for the Radio Advertising Bureau, said: "Even the worst commercial, repeated often enough, sometimes produces results."

John Crosby, when he gave up writing television criticism for the *New York Herald-Tribune,* wrote in his final column: "I don't mind the commercials. It's just the programs I can't stand."

S. J. Paul, publisher of *Television/Radio Age,* wrote in one of his editorials: "The commercial-makers are themselves the stars of the radio-television structure. For in the short time frame of 20, 30, or 60 seconds a mood is created — a message is transmitted — and a sales point is made. This finished product is the result of many talents. In some cases, as it has often been remarked, the commercials are better than the programs."

Some commercials are awful because they insult our aesthetic sensibilities. Some are awful because they insult our logic and intelligence. Some are awful because they play on the emotions of those least able to cope with the incitements to buy, such as children.

Some commercials are good because they are, indeed, more aesthetically pleasing than the programs they surround. Some are good because they are educational and do provide the viewer with informational guidelines on goods and services.

All commercials are, however, designed to sell something — a product or service or idea. It is the existence of these commercials that provides the economic base for the United States broadcasting system as it is now constituted, and is likely to do so for the near future. Public television and radio, previously prohibited by FCC rules and regulations from carrying commercials, received authorization in 1982 to experiment with such advertising. Cable programming, thought by some subscribers to be an alternative to commercial-cluttered broadcasting, saw substantial gains in revenue from commercials in the 1980s. More and more cable systems and microwave operations are moving into subscription or pay television (STV), with the promise of commercial-free programming. Many critics, however, believe that as pay television gradually replaces free television, its operators will not be willing to forego the lucrative income from adding commercials to their programs.

Although cable advertising is still only a small percentage of that found on broadcast stations, copywriting approaches have already been pinpointed. These follow the general dictum that commercials on cable should not, as in broadcasting, try to be all things to all people, but should reflect the narrower demographic characteristics of the audience in the particular cable system.

In early radio and television there were few commercials, and many of these were provided gratis. In radio, for example, many of the first stations were operated by newspapers in order to promote the newspapers. Many others were operated principally to sell the receiving equipment manufactured by the stations' owners. It was not until late 1922, two years after regular broadcasting began, that station WEAF, New York City, carried the first sponsored program. When the sponsoring real estate firm's two advertised buildings were sold through the radio ads, commercial radio was born. In television the first stations, needing material, were happy to present films dealing with "electronics for progress" and showing "how rubber is made" — films that just happened to carry the clearly indicated brand names of the rubber company and the electronic appliance manufacturer and the other firms supplying the films.

Amost all of the writing of commercials is done in advertising agencies. In a few cases an advertiser, particularly on the local level, may prepare commercials in-house — sometimes not very well. Local radio commercials usually are prepared locally, frequently by someone connected with the station.

The commercial copywriter has a responsibility to the agency, advertiser, and station to create not only the most attractive message possible, but one that convinces and sells. At the same time, the power of the commercial (yes, many people believe that Madison Avenue can sell or convince anybody of anything!) charges the writer with the responsibility of being certain that the commercial has a positive and not a negative effect on public ethics and actions.

It is easier to do this with announcements, known more specifically as public service announcements or PSAs. These are similar to commercials in every way except they do not sell a product or service for money, and the station does not charge an advertising fee for them. PSAs are announcements on behalf of nonprofit organizations designed to raise funds or other forms of support for their activities.

Some Ethical Considerations

More and more the pressures of audiences, civic and citizen organizations, some professions, and the federal government are changing the approaches to commercial writing and presentation. At one time some commercials were blatantly racist. Since the civil rights movement of the 1960s, racism in the media, including commercials, gradually lessened. But even as anti-Black stereotypes waned, organizations were formed to combat media racism against other groups, as well as to keep a watchful eye on portrayals of Blacks. Writers should check even a seemingly innocuous reference to or portrayal of a Black, Asian-American, Hispanic, Native American or other minority with a qualified spokesperson from that group for unintentional and inadvertent stereotyping.

Most advertisers and agencies have recognized the need not only to avoid stereotyped portrayals of minorities, but also to include them — particularly Blacks — as nonstereotyped characters in programs and commercials. Some of the cynical among us might suggest that economics plays at least as large a part in this action as does ethics. Over 500 stations have some sort of programming for Blacks and about 125 radio stations program totally for Blacks, reflecting the increasing buying power of this group. It is hoped that it won't be necessary for writers, producers, agencies, and networks to look at the buying power of other minorities before making an ethical decision to include representatives of these other groups regularly and positively in programs and commercials.

Prejudicial portrayals have not been limited to race. Negative ethnic references, particularly those related to national origin, have also needed pointing out and correction. One of the most flagrant areas of stereotyping still existing is that of women. If Blacks, for example, were portrayed in commercials the way women are, there would be a national scandal. The women's movement, particularly through the efforts of the National Organization for Women (NOW), has instituted forceful action against insulting media stereotypes, including the stereotyping of women in subservient roles in society. One study of commercials by NOW showed that in 42.6 percent of the commercials women were doing household work, in 37.5 percent their role was to provide help or service to men, and in 16.7 percent their main purpose was for male sex needs. In only 0.3 percent of the commercials were women shown as independent individuals. Women have been presented, by and large, as vacuous, usable *things*. It is not surprising that a *Good Housekeeping* survey found that one-third of women have at one time or another turned off commercials because they found them offensive.

The public image created of a person or a race or an ethnic group or of women affects the acceptance of that individual or group into the mainstream of economic endeavor — specifically the job market and other opportunities that relate to the job market. Given the current situation where male-dominated business and industry generally keep women's pay lower and deny women equal opportunity to compete with men for top-paying jobs, some people believe that there is a "hidden agenda" behind the commercials and other representations of women in the media. That is not to say that the commercial writers, producers, and ad agency representatives consciously and with overt deliberation are conspiring to keep women in a certain economic — and hence social–political–sexual — place; but the role of their subconscious or unconscious might be examined in light of the product they turn out.

Ethical considerations relate not only to portrayals of people, but to representations of products. For years, the National Association of Broadcasters (NAB) Codes constituted a degree of self-regulation by the industry of a number of areas of content and practice, including length and frequency of commercials, permissible products and services to be advertised, and ethical guidelines for the representation of products and for comparing products of competitors. For example, in the 1970s, responding to pressures from the FCC and citizen groups, the NAB Code reduced the number of minutes of commercials in children's programs and introduced content restrictions. These included a ban on nonprescription medications, conformity to safety rules and regulations for products advertised to children, separation between program content and advertising messages by an "appropriate device," and disclosure of additional costs for toys, such as the need to purchase batteries. In March 1982, the NAB suspended its Television and Radio Codes following a U.S. District Court finding that part of the Television Code was illegal. With the suspension of the Code, even the minimal protection for children began to disappear. Even earlier, the **Federal Trade Commission (FTC)** was forced to abandon its proposals to ban advertising products that may be considered harmful to children — such as cereals and other food containing principally sugars — and the promotion of premiums for children. In January 1983, the Code was officially dropped.

When pushed hard enough the broadcasting industry does take action. Perhaps the greatest pusher of drugs has been broadcasting, which daily and nightly exhorts millions to buy this or that patent medicine to cure almost anything and everything. Congress began to fear that broadcast advertising was contributing to the growing drug culture, and in response to indications that governmental action might soon be necessary, the members of the industry who subscribed to the NAB Code adopted guidelines, some of which are still adhered to on a voluntary basis by many stations.

Some writers may find guidelines restrictive; others may find that they stimulate more responsible writing. All writers will find they require awareness of what may and what may not specifically go into a commercial, in form, purpose, and content. All, it is hoped, will also identify with the statement in *Television/Radio Age* by a creator of commercials who believes that "accounting to a set of practical, working rules allows a good balance of involvement with the industry and accountability to the consumer public. It's hard to try and dupe, or con the viewer when you feel 'we are they' . . . and realize that you are only cheating yourself."

Lengths of Announcements and Commercials

Announcements and commercials differ mainly in that most of the former are PSAs and promote not-for-profit ideas, products, and services — which may include ideological participation through personal time, energy, or money contributions — while the latter sell products and services for profit. Some announcements are clearly commercial in nature, though not directly paid for by some advertiser or agency, such as a **cross plug** by the station for one of its upcoming programs. Another difference is in the length; commercials are usually twenty, thirty, or sixty seconds (sometimes ten) and announcements frequently are ten seconds in length and sometimes less than that, filling a ten-second station break with the station identification (**ID**). The techniques of persuasion used in announcements, including the public service kind, and commercials are identical. On occasion the forms differ and, of course, content is different.

Many copywriters, in writing announcements and commercials for radio, use a word count scale to determine the number of words that will go into a given time segment of a radio announcement or commercial; at best, such word counts are approximate. The length of individual words, the complexity of the ideas, the need for emphasis through pause and variation in rate, and the personality of the performer delivering the announcement are some of the factors affecting the number of words that may be spoken effectively in a given length of time. Some generalizations may be made, however. The 10-second ID contains about 25 words; the 20-second announcement, about 45 words; the 30-second announcement, about 65 words; the 45-second announcement about 100 words; the one-minute announcement, about 125 words; the minute-and-one-half announcement, about 190 words; and the two-minute announcement, about 250 words. These word counts cannot be applied to television, except in the instance of a continuous spoken announcement, because the visual action in television may be expected to take up a portion of the time without dialogue or verbal narration.

Spot announcements may be commercial or noncommercial. The noncommercial kind are PSAs. Commercial spots may be inserted either within the course of a program or during the station break. You may find some form of industry or FCC guidelines on total number of and time allowed for commercials in specified program lengths when you enter the professional field.

Spots may be of varying lengths. Most commercials are thirty seconds long, although when the economy is up, there is a marked increase in sixty-second spots. Some advertisers have occasionally attempted the *split thirty* commercial — that is, combining two fifteen-second commercials for two of its products into one thirty-second spot. Agencies generally have opposed this, however, believing that most products or services need more than fifteen seconds to be presented and sold effectively. Spots are frequently twenty, forty, and fifty seconds long, particularly in radio.

Announcements may be of varying forms and kinds. The station-break announcement will include a station identification, and accompanying or following it may be a PSA, a news flash, a **service announcement**, a cross plug for one of the station's other programs or, of course, a commercial message. Sometimes commercial messages are tied to service announcements, such as a brief "weather report brought to you by . . ." or the latest "news flash brought to you by. . . ." Spot announcements of the same type are sometimes bunched together into a particular break in a given program (if not enough commercial time has been sold, they may all be public service announcements).

The ID

The purpose of the station break is for the station identification, or **ID**. The ID is usually ten seconds long. If accompanied by a commercial announcement, it may be two seconds long, followed by an eight-second commercial. The ID consists of the call letters of the station, the city in which the station is located and, sometimes, the operating frequency of the station. Occasionally, the station will attempt to find an identifying phrase to go with the ID.

A simple, direct ID would be: "You are listening to NBC, 660, WNBC, New York."

A special identification for radio would be: "America's number one fine music station, WQXR and WQXR-FM, New York."

CBS-TV has used the following audio-video slogan as a special identification:

VIDEO	AUDIO
SLIDE: Channel 2's "Eye"	Keep your eye on Channel 2. CBS, New York

Some radio stations use singing commercials for IDs as promotion material. A frequently used break was the video picture of the identifying seal of the NAB, with the voice-over (VO) announcing that "This seal of good practice identifies this station as a subscriber to the code of the National Association of Broadcasters," followed by the name of the station, its channel and city.

In writing an ID, the writer must remember that an ID is a public relations trademark for the station and must be identifying and distinctive at the same time.

The following IDs illustrate how a station has established an identification between its format, beautiful music, and its key promotional word, gold. The first ID reminds new or infrequent listeners of the format; the second ID doesn't have to.

With beautiful music ... this is gold at FM-100 ... WGLD, High Point

At FM-100, this is gold ... WGLD-FM, High Point

IDs are of special interest to advertisers insofar as research has indicated that ten-second commercials hold the attention of 40 percent more viewers throughout the time period than do the more standard thirty-second commercials. Announcements promoting the station or any of its particular programs are called **promos**.

Public Service Announcements (PSAs)

Announcements in the public service frequently are given as part of the ID, and may be of any length. The local station usually receives such announcements in a form already prepared by the writer for the distributing organization. The following is an example of the station ID and the PSA presented together:

This is _____, your election station. If you've been listening to the important campaign issues on _____, you'll want to vote on Election Day. Register today so you can.

Many organizations issue radio and television kits containing various forms and lengths of announcements. One of the ten-second PSAs of the American Foundation for the Blind, designed for broadcast during a station break, reads:

There is a book without pages. For the latest information about the Talking Book for the blind contact the Library of Congress or the American Foundation for the Blind, 15 West 16th Street, New York City.

Here's the same idea expanded into forty seconds:

ANNOUNCER: Besides being visually or physically handicapped so that they can't read ordinary books, Talking Book readers come in: black, yellow, white, Spanish, French, German, mystery addicts, sports nuts, philosophers, psychologists, child, adult, and teenage. . . .

And so do Talking Books.

No matter what your age, race, or interest, if physical limitations prevent you from reading ordinary books, your Library will mail you as many records as you can read.

You can register with the Talking Book Division of the

_____, _____
　　　　　(library or agency)　　　　　　　　　　　　　(street address)
_____, and start reading some
　　　　　　　　　(city, state, zip)
good records.

Reprinted with the permission of the American Foundation for the Blind, Inc.

The American Heritage Foundation's nonpartisan ''Register, Inform Yourself, and Vote'' program issued PSAs ten, twenty, thirty, and sixty seconds long. The following examples illustrate the form the PSA may take.

———————————————————————————O———————————————————————————

● *Analyze each of the following announcements. Determine the kind of writing approach in each and the kind of material added with each subsequent time extension.*

———————————————————————————O———————————————————————————

10-SECOND ANNOUNCEMENT
ANNOUNCER: You can't vote if you're not registered. Protect your right to vote. Register now at _____, _____, _____.
　　　　　　　　　　(place)　　　　　　　　(dates)　　　　　　　(hours)

20-SECOND ANNOUNCEMENT
ANNOUNCER: The right to vote is a great right. It helps you run your government. But you can't vote unless you're registered. Register now so you can vote on Election Day. Register now at

_____, _____, _____
　　　　(place)　　　　　　　(dates)　　　　　　　(hours)
Register now.

30-SECOND ANNOUNCEMENT
ANNOUNCER: It's not much bigger than a phone booth. But it's the place where your town gets its schools built and its streets paved. What is it? It's your precinct voting

booth. And you'll be locked out of this year's important election on _____
(date)
— if your name's not in the book … the voter's registration book. So get your
name in the book.
Go to _____, _____, _____
(place)   (dates)   (hours)
Register before the deadline _____. Register now.
(date)

60-SECOND ANNOUNCEMENT

ANNOUNCER: It's not much bigger than a telephone booth. And it's open only a couple of
days a year. But it's the place where your schools are built, roads are paved,
streets are lighted. What is it? It's the voting booth in your precinct. And you'll
want to be there on Election Day, along with your friends and neighbors, helping
to make the decisions that make your town a better place to live in. But — is your
name in the book? Because if it isn't — if you haven't registered — you'll never
see the inside of that voting booth. So be sure you aren't left out. Registration
closes _____. Go now to _____ and get your name in the book. And then,
            (date)   (place)
on Election Day, we'll see you at the polls.

Courtesy of American Heritage Foundation

PSA Types

Service groups, government agencies, and other organizations devoted to activity
related to the public welfare, such as public health departments, educational associations, societies aiding the handicapped, and ecology groups, among others, have
devoted more and more time in recent years to special television and radio work-
shops for their regular personnel and volunteer assistants. The PSAs on voting just
given, presented by such an organization, are general spots and illustrate form only.
PSAs are written specifically, too, for special program types and in terms of special
occasions. They are written to fit into disc jockey, news, women's, sports, and
other programs. They may be prepared for delivery with a weather bulletin or with a
time signal. They can relate to a given national or local holiday. The following
examples illustrate how the ''organization'' writer may go beyond the general spot
announcement.

WASHINGTON'S BIRTHDAY SPOT
(20 Seconds, Radio)

This is station _____ reminding you that a holiday like Washington's Birthday brings a
sort of break into the routine of daily living. This applies also to America's estimated 400,000
legally blind people — or had you thought of them as a group apart? They certainly aren't.
For information about blindness contact your nearest agency for the blind or the American
Foundation for the Blind, 15 West 16th Street, New York City.

TIME SIGNAL
(20 Seconds, Radio)

ANNOUNCER: It's _____ ... and right now an emotionally disturbed child in
              (time)
              _____ needs your help and understanding. This is National Child
    (town or area)
    Guidance Week. Observe it ... and attend the special program on emotionally
    disturbed children in _____ presented by the _____
              (town or area)
    PTA, on _____ at _____.
         (date)   (place)

DISC JOCKEY PROGRAM
(30 Seconds, Radio)
(after million-record seller)

DISC JOCKEY: _____ ... a record that sold a million copies. Easy listening,
    (title and artist)
    too. But here's a figure that's not easy to listen to: Over 1,000,000 American
    children are seriously emotionally ill. During National Child Guidance Week,
    the _____ PTA, in cooperation with the American Child
    Guidance Foundation, is holding a special meeting to acquaint you with the
    problems faced by children in _____. It's
                          (town or area)
    to your benefit to attend. Be there ... _____
                        (date and address)
    ... learn what you can do to help.

LOCAL WEATHER FORECAST
(20 Seconds, Radio)

ANNOUNCER: That's the weather forecast for _____, but the outlook for children
                       (town or area)
    with emotional illness is always gloomy. This is National Child Guidance
    Week, and you can help by learning the facts about the problem in
    _____. Attend the _____ PTA meeting
    (town or area)
    on _____ at _____.
        (date)   (place)

- *The preceding announcements on child guidance specify the time, date, place, and sponsor of a meeting. What if there is no meeting scheduled? Reread the previous announcement written for the disc jockey show and then read the following announcement, written for the same show, but without the information on a specific meeting. Note how the specifics are transferred smoothly into generalities — and vice versa.*

DISC JOCKEY PROGRAM
(30 Seconds, Radio)
(after million-record seller)

DISC JOCKEY: _____ ... a record that sold a million copies.
(Title and Artist)

Easy listening, too. But here's a figure that's not easy to listen to: Over 1,000,000 American children are seriously emotionally ill. During National Child Guidance Week, many PTA groups, in cooperation with the American Child Guidance Foundation, are holding special meetings concerning these problems faced by children. Find out when your meeting will be ... and attend.... Learn what you can do to help.

Prepared for American Child Guidance Foundation, Inc.
by its agents, Batten, Barton, Durstine & Osborn, Inc.

The good PSA is like the good commercial: it puts the product or service in the setting, using the strongest attention-getting and persuasive elements, including personalities, drama, and other special needs. Before you get to the analyses of good announcement writing in the remaining part of this chapter, what persuasive devices do you find in the following American Foundation for the Blind PSAs, in addition to their illustration of these elements?

CLORIS LEACHMAN
(60 Seconds, Radio)

I'm Cloris Leachman. Sometime actress ... ah ... speaking about blindness ... thinking about blindness. I'm suddenly blind for these few moments ... I've closed my eyes. I've shut out any light with my hands and I'm struggling to contend with it. Am I suddenly gifted with musical genius ... because I'm blind ... ? No. Am I hard of hearing? Hardly. I'm thinking about these things because I've had occasion. Sometimes as an actress, to ah ... think about it and ... and now, this day for the American Foundation for the Blind. But it's something for us all to think about — if you want to find out more about it you can write to FACTS, F-A-C-T-S FACTS, Box One-eleven, New York one-double-oh-eleven.

(30 Second Spot, TV)

VIDEO (PICTURE)	AUDIO (SOUND)
LONG SHOT OF MAN AND DAUGHTER. HE IS ABOUT TO SHAVE. FILLS HAND WITH LATHER, AND PROCEEDS TO SHAVE. DAUGHTER READS FROM BOOKLET.	When a man becomes blind he must learn to do everyday things — like shaving — all over again. His daughter is helping him to learn with the aid of a brand-new teaching guide available right now in both braille and printed editions.
LOGO: Teaching Guide, American Foundtion for the Blind, Box 111, New York 10011	For information write: Teaching Guide, The American Foundation for the Blind, Box one eleven, New York one double oh eleven.

30 SECONDS, RADIO

If you're physically or visually handicapped, you still have the right to vote. It's protected by law. Here, in California, the law is the Election Code, Section 14423. It says, in general, that if you're physically or visually handicapped, you may be helped at the polls by no more than two persons you designate. So, don't let a visual or physical handicap keep you from the polls this election year. This message was brought to you as a public service by the American Foundation for the Blind and this station.

(A similar spot to the one above, incidentally, is prepared for every state in the Union.)

Good PSAs, like good commercials, vary in type and format and utilize the approach that most effectively reaches the target audience. For example, as noted in the upcoming section Commercial Formats, the testimonial is a successful and widely used technique. The following PSA on behalf of abused children uses this approach, with the voice of the parent relating his or her own experience.

Being a parent is the toughest job in the world. Parents Anonymous understands that. No matter how much you want to be a good parent, sometimes the little things a child does make you lose control. I could never handle my daughter crying. When she cried, I hit her. Parents Anonymous helped me stop. If you want help, call Parents Anonymous at 1-800-882-1250.

Written and produced for Parents Anonymous by
K. Ladd Ward and Co.

Commercials

Writing the commercial is not just technique, talent, and an inspiration at 3 A.M. that turns out to be the Clio Award storyboard. (The Clio Awards, represented by a statuette similar to the Oscar of the movies, are jury-selected and presented annually at the American TV and Radio Commercials Festival.) It is attitude, basic preparation, tested procedure, and, in some instances, guts and/or a hard head. Two consistent award winners, Roy Grace and John Noble — creators of the Volkswagen ads — stated in the *DDB* (Doyle Dane Bernbach) *News* that the best ad may end up in a back drawer unless the creators believe in it strongly enough to sell it to the account executive. Grace said that "50% is doing the work, and 50% is fighting for it. . . . Too many young people are willing to do the work, but at the first No they surrender. You can be the greatest talent in the world, the greatest team doing the greatest work, but if you're not willing to defend it, it'll never see the light of day." Noble warned that "there are account men who can talk young creative people out of a concept very easily. But if it's been approved by the Creative Department, that means it ain't a bad ad when it goes up there. There may be certain problems, but for creative people to come back immediately after seeing an account man and say 'We can't do this because so-and-so says we can't do this' is wrong. There should be a battle."

Clearly, the commercials field is not for the writer who wishes to hide behind the typewriter in a secluded place and not be bothered with the outside world except to pass along the sheets of genius to the outstretched hands of a benevolent and understanding producer.

Robert Levenson, as creative director of the Doyle Dane Bernbach advertising agency, suggested in the *DDB News* some guidelines for judging what is a good commercial. He starts out with two basic assumptions:

(1) We are looking at a storyboard of a commercial or at a comp. of an ad. The advertising hasn't run yet, so we have zero hindsight. (2) We have agreement on a strategy or a position or a copy platform or something, so when we decide whether the advertising is good or not, it's the advertising that we're talking about and nothing else. O.K. What do we look for? . . . There is only one first right answer in my opinion: The commercial should be on the product. . . . If the commercial is on the product, the only right second question is: is it clear? I think if we stopped right there, we might upgrade half the commercials on the air because half the commercials I see leave me not knowing what product they're talking about or what they're saying about whatever they're talking about. So, if the commercial we're looking at is clearly on the product, we're halfway home.

In other words, the discipline of keeping your eye on what you're selling and how clearly you're selling it is half the battle. . . . What I left out is that, even though a commercial is on the product and is clear, it's not necessarily good. What I left out, of course, are all the skills, the talents, the instincts, the hard work that the best creative people bring to their jobs. The best creative people understand discipline and they understand direction and they understand soundness. They also understand that those things aren't enough. But they also understand that you can't make good advertising without them.

The discipline comes first. Then we get to . . . attention-getting, warm, human, life-like, funny and all the rest. . . . Sometimes, with some products, you don't have to go too far past the discipline. That was true years ago with Polaroid. All we did was have Garry Moore and Steve Allen stand up there — live — and take a Polaroid picture. A minute of copy later, there it was. The audience applauded like crazy, people went out and bought Polaroid cameras by the tens of millions. . . . And what did we do? We let the product be the star of the commercials.

Here's the test: If you look at a commercial and fall in love with the brilliance of it, try taking the product out of it. If you still love the commercial, it's no good. . . . Don't make your commercials interesting; make your products interesting.

Barbara Allen, copywriter and teacher of television and radio writing, set forth five preliminary steps in putting commercials together: (1) know the product or service, (2) pick the central selling idea, (3) choose the basic appeal, (4) select the format, and (5) start writing.

Techniques of Writing Commercials

Emotional appeals   The appeal of the commercial is an emotional one. By emotional we do not mean the evoking of laughter or tears. Emotional appeal means, here, the appeal to the nonintellectual, nonlogical aspects of the prospective customer's personality. It is an appeal to the audience's basic needs or wants. For example, one of the basic wants in our society is prestige. Look at the next commercial you see for an automobile. Does it appeal to logical, to intellectual needs? Does it recommend that you buy the car because it is shorter than the other makes, thus enabling the driver to find a parking space more easily? Does it emphasize lower horsepower as one of the car's major advantages, enabling the owner to save on gasoline and at the same time still achieve the maximum permissible miles-per-hour on our highways without risking a speeding ticket or, more importantly, one's life? Sometimes, in a buyer's market, yes. Sometimes, in a real or manufactured gas shortage, yes. But most of the time the appeal is to prestige or to our emotional needs, not to logic.

The development of commercials for the compact car is a good case in point. "Big car room" became an important ingredient in selling small cars. The compact must be bigger than the competing compact. One couldn't own a small car; one had to own a king-sized small car! And how many automobile commercials show the driver climbing into the car to be seated next to a woman looking as much as possible like Farrah Fawcett. The emotional implication is, of course, that men who drive this make of automobile have sitting with them women who look like movie stars. This is the prestige factor again. Or, so goes the implication, if the prospective customer does not have such women immediately available, the very presence of the automobile in his driveway will attract them. This would be an appeal to power, in this instance the power to draw women — a strong emotional appeal to sexist attitudes.

There are a number of basic emotional appeals that have been particularly successful and on which the writer of commercials may draw as the motivating factor within any individual commercial. The appeal to self-preservation is perhaps the strongest of all. Drug commercials, among others, make good use of this appeal. Another strong appeal is love of family. Note the next commercial you see presented by an insurance company. Other widely used emotional appeals include patriotism, good taste, reputation, religion, loyalty to a group, and conformity to public opinion.

The following commercial illustrates, primarily, the effective use of the appeal to prestige. The implications are that if one does not serve Libby's foods, one does not have *good taste,* is not a *smart shopper,* and, by further implication, would not have the prestige of sophistication and intelligence of those who do serve Libby's. The use of emotional appeals does not mean, of course, that the implications may not be valid.

● *As you read the commercial see if you can find an additional emotional appeal and a sample of logical appeal.*

VIDEO	AUDIO
1. MCU ANNOUNCER BESIDE LIBBY'S DISPLAY.	ANNOUNCER: LIBBY'S presents a word quiz. What is the meaning of the word "epicure?" Well, according to our dictionary the word means a person who shows good taste in selection of food. And that's a perfect description of the homemaker who makes a habit of serving ...

VIDEO	AUDIO
2. INDICATES DISPLAY.	LIBBY'S famous foods. Yes, everyone in every family goes for
3. INDICATES EACH PRODUCT IN SYNC (IF POSSIBLE CUT TO CU LIBBY'S PEACHES ... THEN PAN IN SYNC).	LIBBY'S Peaches ... Fruit Cocktail ... LIBBY'S Pineapple–Chunks, Crushed or Sliced ... Pineapple Juice ... LIBBY'S Peas ... Beets ... Corn–Whole Kernel or Cream Styled ... LIBBY'S Tomato Juice ... Corned Beef Hash ... and LIBBY'S Beef Stew. AND right now, smart shoppers are stocking up
4. HOLDS UP LIBBY'S COUPONS (IF POSSIBLE CUT TO CU LIBBY'S COUPONS).	on LIBBY'S famous foods ... because there's still time to cash in those LIBBY'S dollar-saving coupons you received. You can save a whole
5. MOVE IN FOR CU LIBBY'S DISPLAY.	dollar on this week's food bill. So stock up now on LIBBY'S famous foods ... and cash in your LIBBY'S coupons and save! Always make LIBBY'S a "regular" on your shopping list!

Courtesy of Libby's Famous Foods

You may have noted the appeal to love of family in the statement that ''everyone in every family goes for. . . .'' The logical appeal was the emphasis, at the end of the commercial, on the saving of money through the use of Libby coupons. (Should this commercial have stressed ''nutritious'' food as another logical appeal?) Logical appeals are those that strike the intellect, the logical, analytical thinking processes. An example of a logical appeal would be that which, with accurate information, emphasizes that the electronic structure of the television set being advertised has certain elements that make it longer lasting or that provide a clearer picture than other makes. This kind of logical appeal may be contrasted with the emotional appeal that ignores the organic functioning of the television set but emphasizes the shape, color, or styling of the cabinet, items having nothing to do with the logical purpose of a television set.

Commercials often only *seem* to use logical appeals; closer examination of many commercials reveals that the appeals are really emotional in content. Emotional appeals are far more effective in commercial advertising than are logical appeals.

Audience analysis Before choosing and applying the specific emotional or logical appeals, the writer must know, as fully as possible, the nature of the audience to whom the message is directed. In the mass media it is often impossible to determine many specifics about a given audience at a given air time. The audience is a disunified mass of many attitudes and interests, economic, social, political, and religious levels, spread out over a broad geographical area — particularly in television. When advertisers sponsored entire programs and were, indeed, identified with particular programs and personalities, the writer could make some judgment on the kinds of people who watched that particular show. Since the spot ad began to replace the full-sponsor program, it has been harder for the writer to make such an analysis.

Demographics — the science of analyzing the audience makeup as a base for specific commercial content and technique and, in radio, for a particular station format and sound — is essential to successful promotion and advertising. There are some basic elements of audience analysis that the writer may apply in both television and radio. These are: age, sex, size, economic level, political orientation, primary interests, occupation, fixed attitudes or beliefs, educational level, ethnic background, geographical concentration, and knowledge of the product. The writer should try to include appeals to all the major groups expected to watch the given program and commercial. Be careful, however, not to spread the message too thin. Here are several award-winning commercials that appeal to a large audience segment, but at the same time contain some specific appeals that relate to a few particular characteristics of the audience. As you analyze each of these commercials for the specific audience appeals, determine toward what kind of audience each might be particularly aimed.

VIDEO	AUDIO
1. MAN AND WOMAN AT DINING ROOM TABLE, EATING DINNER. WOMAN LOOKS DEPRESSED.	1. WOMAN: Joey called this morning. MAN: So, how's Joey ... Joey?!?
2. CLOSEUP OF MAN.	2. MAN: What's wrong?
3. CLOSEUP OF WOMAN.	3. WOMAN: Nothing. MAN: Nothing?
4. CLOSEUP OF MAN.	4. MAN: Our Joey called 2000 miles ... the kids alright?
5. CU OF WOMAN.	5. WOMAN: Fine. MAN: Sally? WOMAN: Fine.
6. CU OF MAN.	6. MAN: The kids are fine, Sally's fine ... So why did he call? WOMAN: I asked him that, too.
7. CU OF WOMAN CRYING.	7. MAN: And why are you crying? WOMAN: Cause Joey said, "I called, just cause I love you, Mom."
8. MAN PUTS ARM AROUND WOMAN, AND KISSES HER.	8. SINGERS: Reach out, reach out and ...
SUPER: REACH OUT AND TOUCH SOME-ONE. BELL SYSTEM LOGO.	

Courtesy of American Telephone and Telegraph Company, Long Lines Department

Today will stay with you for the rest of your life.

Today you're bringing home your new baby and your wife.

And all around are people who mean the world to you,

sharing your jubilation,

part of the Pepsi Generation.

C'mon, c'mon, c'mon, c'mon and have a Pepsi Day.

C'mon, c'mon, c'mon and taste the Pepsi way.

Your baby's home, your family's here,

to celebrate and hold her near.

C'mon, c'mon and Have a Pepsi Day.

You're the Pepsi Generation.

Have a Pepsi Day!

VIDEO	AUDIO
CUT TO BICYCLIST RIDING DOWN STREET.	May a little bitey bite of sunshine come your way come your way
AERIAL VIEW OF BICYCLIST RIDING DOWN STREET.	
SIDE VIEW OF BICYCLIST RIDING PAST WATER FOUNTAIN.	(MU)
CUT TO BICYCLIST RIDING ON HIGHWAY.	a little bite of love and happiness
CUT TO SIDE VIEW OF BICYCLIST ON HIGH BRIDGE SURROUNDED BY TREES.	everyday, everyday I wish you
CUT TO SIDE VIEW OF BICYCLIST ON HIGHWAY.	no good-byes
CUT TO PAN ACROSS OF CU OF BICYCLISTS.	but a new friend every morning
CUT TO BICYCLIST RIDING IN COUNTRY NEAR FIELDS.	clear blue skies are the simple things in
CUT TO BICYCLIST RIDING ON HIGHWAY IN COUNTRY IN THE RAIN.	life that are good and true that's the world I wish for you
CUT TO CU OF COCA-COLA CAP ON BOTTLE BEING OPENED.	It's the real thing
CUT TO SIDE VIEW OF BICYCLIST DRINK-ING COKE.	may you always have someone
CUT TO BICYCLISTS FIXING THEIR BIKES AND DRINKING COKE.	to share all your happy moments through
CUT TO PAN UP OF COKE BEING POURED INTO GLASS.	somebody who will sit
CUT TO CU OF BICYCLIST DRINKING COKE.	and laugh and share some Coke
CUT TO GIRL AND BOY ON BLANKET IN GRASS DRINKING COKE.	with you
CUT TO BICYCLIST RIDING IN TUNNEL.	because they're the real things
CUT TO BICYCLIST RIDING IN SMALL COUNTRY TOWN.	and I'd like to fill your life with
CUT TO CYCLIST RIDING PAST HOUSES WITH TWO ELDERLY LADIES STANDING IN FRONT.	the real thing

Courtesy of The Coca-Cola Company, McCann-Erickson, Inc.

VIDEO	AUDIO
FADE IN:	NARRATOR: Next time she wants a ciga-rette give her a kiss instead.
SC 1 MCU Black Couple side by side. Woman puts cigarette in mouth. Man takes cigarette away and gives her a kiss.	
DISSOLVE TO:	
SC 2 TITLE "For tips on quitting call us American Cancer Society" (sword) FADE OUT	For tips on quitting call the American Cancer Society.

The research done by the creative agency team goes beyond preliminary audience analysis. Even after the commercial is created, it is not finalized until it is tested, evaluated, rewritten, and reproduced in terms of audience-reaction research. The concept of advertising agency research has grown over the past three decades. Indeed, when intensive television advertising began in the early 1950s, "creative" research hardly existed at all. David Ogilvy, chairman of Ogilvy & Mather International advertising agency, stated in *Television/Radio Age* that "research has helped us create more effective advertising. But all this research is creating a serious problem. Instead of creating *one* campaign for each product, we are now called upon to create half a dozen, for testing. Nobody can do that for very long without running out of ideas."

Familiarization with product   Earlier in this chapter we noted Robert Levenson's stress on the product itself as the key to a good commercial. Before the writer can apply audience analysis or choose emotional appeals, it is essential that he or she become thoroughly familiar with the product. This does not mean that the male writer needs to use a particular girdle before preparing an ad for it or that the female writer must test a particular shaving cream before writing the commercial for it — and this is not meant facetiously because in both cases testing the product on a personal basis is possible. In addition to personal observation or use of the product, the writer should get as much information as possible about it from those closely connected with it. A good source of information is the research department of the company. From the information obtained about the product and from the personal feeling developed about it (woe to the writer who develops an antipathy toward the product!), the writer can then coordinate the audience analysis with emotional and logical appeals and develop a unique or novel way of presenting the product most effectively to the audience.

The writer should either have or develop flexible and receptive tastes when it comes to particular products. The ad agency may be fortunate enough to land an account for a product with built-in excitement: a revolutionary camera like the Polaroid or a low-cost, high-gas-mileage, long-lasting-engine small car with large seating capacity and storage space like the Volkswagen — successful commercials for both of which are included in this chapter, and whose success subsequently prompted many similar products and advertising campaigns. On the other hand, the writer may have to deal with a seemingly prosaic product like a pill for indigestion or a long-standing and accepted product like telephone service and still have to be able to open up his or her imagination to creating an ad that will have the entire country saying "try it, you'll like it" and "reach out and touch someone."

What kind of product will you be writing about if you become a successful commercials copywriter? Over the years the leading advertising categories on television have changed little, with the four largest advertising groups remaining rather static: (1) food and food products, (2) toiletries and toilet goods, (3) automotive, and (4) proprietary medicines. Other leading advertisers are confectionary and soft drinks, soaps, cleansers and polishers, and household equipment and supplies.

Organization of the commercial   Because the commercial's primary purpose is to persuade, the writer should be aware of the five basic steps in persuasive technique. First, the commercial should get the attention of the audience. This may be accomplished by many means, including humor, a startling statement or picture, a rhetorical question, vivid description, a novel situation or suspenseful conflict. Sound, specifically the use of pings, chords, and other effects, effectively attracts attention, too.

Second, after attention is obtained, the audience's interest must be held. Following up the initial element with effective examples, testimonials, anecdotes, statistics, and other devices, visual or aural, should retain the audience's interest.

Third, the commercial should create an impression that a problem of some sort exists, related vaguely to the function of the product advertised. After such an impression has been made, then, fourth, the commercial should plant the idea in the audience's mind that the problem can be solved by use of the particular product. At this point the product itself might even first be introduced. Finally, the commercial must finish with a strong emotional and/or logical appeal, one that achieves the fifth step in persuasion — getting action. This final step prompts the audience to go out and buy the product.

All of the award-winning commercials given here as examples illustrate the five steps of persuasion, some of them in clear sequence, others not so obviously, but nevertheless effectively.

The Xerox "Hannigan" commercial is an example of expert compacting of all of the five steps of persuasion in a tight sequence of a relatively few seconds. The first frame of the storyboard has the attention factor. The second frame holds the attention with a reinforcement of the initial example. The third frame indicates that a problem exists. The fourth frame shows how the problem can be solved. The subsequent frames — most of the commercial — solidify frame four and stimulate the desired action. Following the storyboard is the script, providing an example of how the video is written by the copywriter before it is turned into visual representations by the art department.

SECRETARY: (SAYS NAMES THROUGHOUT) Hannigan . . . Flannigan . . . Mulligan . . . Finnigan . . .

ANNCR: (VO) The firm of Hannigan, Flannigan, Mulligan, Finnigan, Gilligan and Logan had a big name . . .

but a small office. Too small for a copier with an automatic sorter.

Until Xerox created the 3400 small copier.

With its automatic sorter . . .

It made up to 15 sets of documents in a small amount of time

and a small amount of space. Which made . . .

Hannigan, Flannigan, Mulligan, Finnigan, Gilligan, Logan . . .

. . . and O'Rourke, very happy. (SUPER: XEROX)

Courtesy of Xerox Corporation
(Needham, Harper & Steers, Inc.)

VIDEO	AUDIO
EXHAUSTED SECRETARY SORTING COPIES INTO SETS.	SECRETARY: (Says names throughout) Hannigan ... Flannigan ... Mulligan ... Finnigan ... V.O.: The firm of Hannigan, Flannigan, Mulligan, Finnigan, Gilligan, and Logan had a big name ... but a small office ... too small for a copier with an automatic sorter.
DISSOLVE TO ... SAME SECRETARY AS SHE WALKS TO 3400 IN THE OFFICE. HAND COMES IN AND STARTS MACHINE. WE SEE SORTING OPERATION.	Until Xerox created the 3400 small copier. With its automatic sorter ... it made up to 15 sets of documents in a small amount of time and a small amount of space.
CUT TO TAKING OUT COMPLETED SETS.	Which made ...

VIDEO	AUDIO
SECRETARY O'ROURKE HANDS OUT COMPLETED SETS TO PARTNERS. SECRETARY O'ROURKE GIVES A RELIEVED SMILE. SUPER: XEROX	V.O.: Hannigan, Flannigan, Mulligan, Finnigan, Gilligan, Logan ... ... and O'Rourke, very happy.

Courtesy of Xerox Corporation
(Needham, Harper & Steers)

● *See if you can find the steps of persuasion in the following announcements, two of them award-winning commercials and one a PSA. The Alka-Seltzer spot is now a classic and a direct, clear statement on a product solving a problem. How do these commercials differ from the previous one not only in the use of the five steps of persuasion, but in the approaches used within each step? You should conclude that the five steps of persuasion are a guide, not a mandate, in the structure of a commercial.*

60-SECOND TV SPOT

VIDEO	AUDIO
OPEN ON RUGGED-LOOKING MAN AT COCKTAIL PARTY SMOKING CIGARETTE AND TALKING.	RUGGED MAN: (OC) (Speaking sympathetically) Hey, Harry, you look like you haven't seen the sun for a month. You ought to get out more.
CUT TO REVEAL AN ANEMIC-LOOKING MAN. CUT TO RUGGED-LOOKING MAN.	HARRY: (OC) I go out. What do you mean go out? RUGGED-LOOKING MAN: You'd feel better if you got out in the great outdoors ...
RUGGED-LOOKING MAN STRETCHES EXPANSIVELY, ATTEMPTING TO CONVEY THE JOY OF THE OUTDOORS. CUT TO HARRY, THE ANEMIC-LOOKING MAN. HE REACTS AGGRESSIVELY, AS THOUGH HE HAS BEEN PERSONALLY ATTACKED BY THE RUGGED-LOOKING OUTDOORSMAN.	... stretched your muscles ... got your lungs full of fresh air. HARRY: (Angrily ... feeling he has been personally attacked.) What fresh air? You call the air around here fresh air?
CONTINUE WITH HARRY'S DIATRIBE. HE PUFFS ON A CIGARETTE. CONTINUE WITH HARRY, SMOKING AS HE TALKS.	HARRY: It's like living in a coal mine, it's so polluted around here. HARRY: You know what you see on your windowsill in the morning? Soot! This thick. (He gestures with fingers.)
OTHERS GATHER AROUND HARRY, ALL OF THEM SMOKING.	HARRY'S VOICE CONTINUES: And in traffic — in your car — carbon monoxide.

PAN ACROSS CIGARETTES OF ONLOOKERS.

ECU CIGARETTES.

ECU CIGARETTES.

PAN UPWARD FROM ONLOOKERS TO
SMOKE RISING TO CEILING.
SCREEN FULL OF SMOKE.

FREEZE FRAME ON HARRY'S FACE, SEEN
DIMLY THROUGH SMOKE.

HARRY'S VOICE CONTINUES: Every day it's
killing you.
HARRY CONTINUES: You want me to get
more fresh air ...
HARRY: ... then start doing something
about the air pollution in this town.
HARRY: Tear down the smoke stacks ...

HARRY: Get rid of that big incinerator out
on the flats ...
ANNOUNCER: (VO) If you'd like to do something about air pollution, we suggest you
start with your own lungs.

Courtesy of American Cancer Society

60-SECONDS

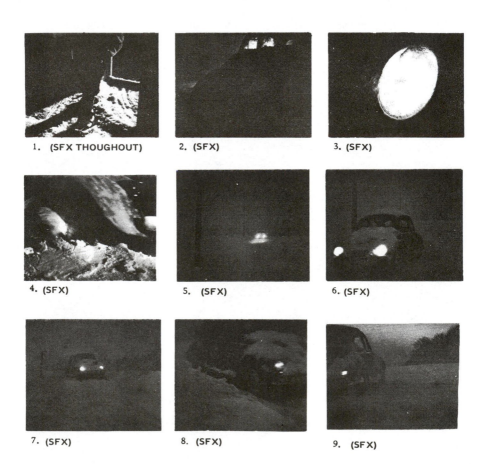

1. (SFX THOUGHOUT)   2. (SFX)   3. (SFX)

4. (SFX)   5. (SFX)   6. (SFX)

7. (SFX)   8. (SFX)   9. (SFX)

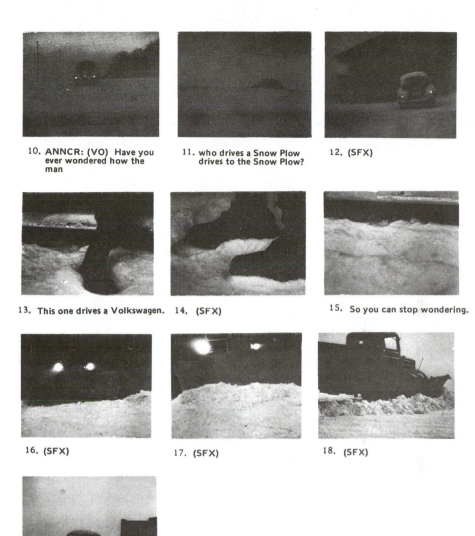

10. **ANNCR: (VO)** Have you ever wondered how the man

11. who drives a Snow Plow drives to the Snow Plow?

12. **(SFX)**

13. **This one drives a Volkswagen.**

14. **(SFX)**

15. So you can stop wondering.

16. **(SFX)**

17. **(SFX)**

18. **(SFX)**

19. **(SFX)**

Doyle Dane Bernbach Inc.
for Volkswagen of America

30 SECONDS

VIDEO	AUDIO
OPEN MCU MAN SEATED AT TABLE IN RESTAURANT. BEHIND HIM YOU SEE OTHER CUSTOMERS AND WAITER WHO IMITATES THE MAN'S GESTURES.	SFX: Restaurant noises. Low murmur, clatter of dishes, knives and forks. MAN: Came to this little place. Waiter says, "Try this, you'll like it." "What's this?" "Try it, you'll like it." "But what is . . . ?" "Try it, you'll like it." So I tried it. Thought I was going to die. Took two Alka-Seltzer.
CUT TO TWO ALKA-SELTZER DROPPING IN GLASS OF WATER. PAN ACROSS ASPIRIN BOTTLE AND TWO ASPIRINS. CONTINUE PAN ACROSS ROLL OF ANTACIDS AND TWO ANTACIDS. CONTINUE PAN TO FOIL PACK OF ALKA-SELTZER.	ANNCR VO: For headache and upset stomach, no aspirin or antacid alone relieves you in as many ways as Alka-Seltzer. For headache and upset stomach.
CUT BACK TO CU MAN IN RESTAURANT.	MAN: Alka-Selzer works. Try it, you'll like it!

Courtesy of Miles Laboratories and Wells, Rich, Greene, Inc.

Writing styles   The writer constantly must be aware of the necessity for keeping the commercial in good taste. Although there have been commercials that were repugnant to individuals or groups, the sponsor tries not to alienate a single potential customer. The style should be direct and simple. If the commercial is to seem sincere, the performer presenting it must have material of a conversational, informal nature that permits him or her to present it so that the audience really believes what it hears or sees. This does not mean that the writer uses ultracolloquial or slang words. The vocabulary should be dignified, though not obtuse; it must be attention-getting, but not trite. Usually, the writer will avoid slang and colloquialisms entirely unless these forms have a specific purpose in the commercial.

The writer should be certain that the writing is grammatically correct. Action verbs are extremely effective, as are concrete, specific words and ideas. If an important point is to be emphasized, the writer must be certain to repeat that point in the commercial, although in different words or in different forms. One exception is the presentation of a slogan or trademark the sponsor wants the audience to remember; in this case word-for-word repetition is important. Keep in mind that for television the visual rather than the aural picture frequently is the key. Some commercials on television can be virtually all visual, as with the Volkswagen ''Snow Plow'' spot.

The writer should avoid, if possible, the use of superlatives, false claims, phony testimonials, and other elements of obvious exaggeration. Even setting aside ethical considerations, a commercial with such elements might be a mistake; it might antagonize a large part of the audience, even if it is particularly effective in deceiving another part. Network commercials are sometimes more honest than those on independent stations. Frequently, the commercial on the small station is not only presented but also written by the disc jockey or announcer who may have sold the show or the air time in the first place. Extravagant claims sometimes are made in order to keep the account.

The Television Storyboard

Commercial continuity is basically the same for both radio and television. However, it must be remembered that although the radio commercial must convey everything through sound, the television commercial is essentially visual. The television announcement should be able to hold the viewer with the picture. Some producers seem to lack confidence in the visual effectiveness of their own spots. Listen to the sound on your television set the next time there is a commercial break in the program. Chances are you will be to able to hear it all the way to the refrigerator, or even, depending on your acuity and tastes, all the way to the wine cellar. The visual continuity in the commercial should be such that the technician does not have to turn up the sound for every advertising message. Well-written commercials should not rely on a high volume of sound, nor should the video be treated merely as an adjunct to the audio. In fact, commercial producers (and account executives and sponsors) like to see, as fully as possible, the visual contents for a prospective commercial in its early stages. For this purpose a **storyboard** is used. The storyboard usually is a series of rough drawings showing the sequence of picture action, optical effects, settings, and camera angles, and it contains captions indicating the dialogue, sound, and music to be heard. A good example is the award-winning Eastern Airlines ''River Raft'' storyboard.

60 SECONDS

1. (MUSIC)

2. (MUSIC)

3. (MUSIC)

4. (MUSIC)

5. WELLES: Away from it all in the Caribbean, . . .

6. there's more for father and son to share than just scenery. (PAUSE)

7. (MUSIC)

8. (MUSIC)

9. (MUSIC)

10. (MUSIC)

11. There's a true family vacation of learning and sharing memories together.

12. Of living the kinds of experiences you don't find at home. (PAUSE)

13. (MUSIC)

14. (MUSIC)

15. (MUSIC)

16. Come with us on Eastern Airlines, . .

17. for a summer to remember at a price your family can afford.

18. Call your travel agent.

19. Or Eastern. The Wings of Man.

Created by Young & Rubicam
International for Eastern Airlines

There are frequently many refinements from the storyboard that sells the commercial to the advertiser to the finished film or tape that sells the product to the viewer. Some producers work from storyboards alone. Others want scripts, either in the Hollywood or New York style, containing the visual and audio directions and dialogue. The following noncommercial commercial, a highway safety PSA from the U.S. Department of Transportation, provides a comparison between the storyboard and the script.

60 SECONDS

C-1 I want to watch the sun come up another fifty years.

C-2 I want to write a novel that will bring the world to tears.

C-3 And I want to see Venice.

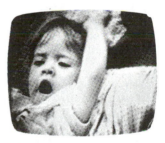

C-4 I want to see my kids have kids. I want to see them free.

C-5 I want to live my only life. I want the most of me.

C-6 I want to dance. I want to love. I want to breathe.

C-7 Janie died. On an endless road in America.

C-8 Because a lonely man was driving drunk out of his mind.

C-9 Problem drinkers who drive are responsible for more than 40 deaths every day. Get the problem drinker off the road.

C-10 I want to know what's out there beyond the furthest star.

C-11 I even want to go there if we ever get that far. And I want to see Venice.

C-12 Help. Do something about the problem drinker. For his sake. And yours.

60 SECONDS

VIDEO	AUDIO
FADE UP ON MLS OF WIFE, HUSBAND AND CHILD IN LARGE HAMMOCK. MOVE IN TO MCU OF MOTHER AND CHILD.	JANIE SONG: I want to watch the sun come up another fifty years
DISSOLVE TO LEFT SIDE MCU SHOT OF ALL THREE.	I want to write a novel that will bring the world to tears
DISSOLVE TO MCU OF FRONT SHOT OF MOTHER AND CHILD.	And I want to see Venice
DISSOLVE TO CU OF CHILD.	I want to see my kids have kids
DISSOLVE TO CU LEFT SIDE SHOT OF MOTHER AND CHILD.	I want to see them free
DISSOLVE TO MLS OF ALL THREE — MOVE IN TO MS.	I want to live my only life I want the most of me
DISSOLVE TO LEFT SIDE MS OF MOTHER AND CHILD.	I want to dance
DISSOLVE TO MS OF RIGHT SIDE OF MOTHER AND CHILD.	I want to love
DISSOLVE TO CU LEFT SIDE OF MOTHER AND CHILD.	I want to breathe
FREEZE FRAME AND DISSOLVE TO B & W.	ANNCR VO: Janie died On an endless road in America
PULL BACK FROM B & W PHOTO IN A PICTURE FRAME AND DOLLY PAST EMPTY BED	Because a lonely man was driving drunk out of his mind
	Problem drinkers who drive are responsible for more than 40 deaths every day Get the problem drinker off the road. JANIE SONG: I want to know what's out there beyond the furtherest star I even want to go there if we ever get that far
TITLE: "GET THE PROBLEM DRINKER OFF THE ROAD." FADE TO BLACK.	And I want to see Venice.

- *Go back over the two storyboards and analyze them in terms of product or service emphasis (does the product stand alone?) and organization (the five steps of persuasion).*

Placement of Commercials

As noted earlier, commercials are of various length; the length frequently depends on placement. Knowing if the spot is to be a station break, a hitchhiker, a participating announcement on radio, or a program announcement on television can help the writer analyze the audience, particularly as to its psychological attitude or physical behavior at the time it hears or sees the spot. Here are the major areas of placement.

IDs and service announcements   The station identification, as already stated, usually is a ten-second break. Attached to the ID may be an eight-second commercial for television or a longer one (for a longer break) for radio. A service announcement accompanying an ID may be from five to ten seconds long, consisting of a commercial message accompanying public service information, such as a time signal or weather report. For example:

It's _____ P.M., Soporific Watch Time. See the Soporific Wrist Alarm — date and calendar — twenty-one jewels.

Chain breaks   The chain is another name for the network. The time available between the network station identification and the local station identification is sold to advertisers either on a network or local basis. This is an especially good source of revenue for local stations. Television advertisers on the chain break usually fill the time with twenty-second commercial films. Radio advertisers use an announcement of about fifty to sixty words in length.

Thirty- and sixty-second announcements   As noted at the beginning of this chapter, programs do not end at the thirty- or sixty-minute mark. Time is allowed for the ID and one or more commercials. In some instances, a sponsored program following another sponsored program will start late to permit more time for the ID and announcements. Sometimes the network affiliate will fade out a program early or fade in a program late to permit more time for commercials in the time break. Twenty-second, thirty-second and full-minute commercials are most often used for both television and radio.

Participating announcements   When a show is unable or unwilling to get just one sponsor, it may get a number of participating advertisers. The various advertisers jointly share the cost of the entire program, and the length and frequency of their commercials vary in proportion to the share of the program cost they have contributed. Disc jockey shows on radio, with their frequent commercial announcements, and films on television, with their sometimes constant interruptions for commercials, are examples of the **participating announcement** program.

Program announcements   When a single sponsor has purchased the entire show, either as a one-shot arrangement or a series, all the commercials on that program will come from that sponsor. The commercials are called program announcements. The sponsor may space the commercials into short announcements or lump the commercial time for one long announcement.

The program announcements for the longer programs — half-hour, hour, or ninety-minute shows — follow a fairly standard transitional form. Each one builds on the previous one, but nevertheless contains enough variety so that the audience is not bored by repetition. The average show usually has three program announcements: at the beginning, in the middle, and at the end. Occasionally there are four commercials, divided into short opening and closing "billboards," and two insertions within the program itself.

Co-op announcements   These are the commercials of several sponsors who have purchased a particular network show. They differ from participating announcements in that the co-op sponsors are in different cities; the announcements are given simultaneously rather than consecutively on the same show. The network leaves fixed commercial time in the program for the local station to fill in with the message from the co-op sponsor in that locality.

Commercial Formats

There are five major format types for commercials: the straight sell, the testimonial, humor, music, and dramatization. Any single commercial may combine two or more of these techniques.

The straight sell   This should be a clear, simple statement about the product. Be careful about involving the announcer or station too closely with the product. Do not say "our product" or "my store" unless a personality is presenting the commercial, when the combination of testimonial and straight sell techniques may permit such personal involvement.

The straight sell may hit hard, but not over the head and not so hard that it may antagonize the potential customer. The straight sell is straightforward and the statement about the product is basically simple and clear. The writing technique sometimes stresses a gimmick, usually emphasizing something special about the product, real or implied, that makes it different or extra or better than the competing product. Sometimes the straight sell is built around a slogan characterizing the special attribute, which accompanies the product in every commercial. The following fifty-second award-winning radio commercial is an example of the straight sell with a gimmick that features both a personality and a slogan.

SFX:	CLOCK GONGING. HORSE AND CARRIAGE.
ORSON WELLES:	It's 3 A.M. in the French Quarter of New Orleans. How'd you like the best cup of coffee in town? And a beignet. That's a square donut without a hole.
SFX:	PEOPLE TALKING, DOORS OPENING AND CLOSING, PLATES RATTLING.
ORSON WELLES:	This is the place. Morning Call. Find a stool at one of the elbow-worn marble counters and while you're waiting for your order, take a look around.
MUSIC:	EASTERN THEME FADE UP AND THROUGHOUT.
ORSON WELLES:	The place hasn't changed much in the past 100 years. Same counters, same foot rail. Same mirrors where you can watch and be watched sipping coffee and sprinkling powdered sugar on hot beignets that still cost a nickel. Only in New Orleans ... one of the places that make Eastern what it is ... the second largest passenger carrier of all the airlines in the free world ... the Wings of Man.

Created by Young and Rubicam International for Eastern Airlines

Sometimes the straight sell is essentially a simple presentation enhanced and made exotic with an attention-getting visual or sound device, such as the theme song in the thirty-second spot entitled "Afloat."

AFLOAT

SINGER: There's a fragrance

that's here today . . .

and they call it

Charlie.

A different fragrance

that thinks your way.

Yeah, they call it Charlie.

Kinda young. Kinda now.
Charlie.

Kinda free. Kinda wow.
Charlie.

Kinda fragrance that's
gonna stay. And it's here
now.

Charlie.

ANNCR: (VO) Now the world
belongs to Charlie, by
Revlon.

Courtesy of Revlon, Inc.
(Grey Advertising, Inc.)

The testimonial   The testimonial commercial is very effective when properly used. When the testimonial is given by a celebrity — whose status is likely to be quite a bit higher than that of the average viewer — the emotional appeals of prestige, power, and good taste are primary. What simpler way to reach the status of the celebrity, if only in one respect, than by using the same product he or she uses? The writer must make certain that the script fits the personality of the person giving the endorsement.

A winner of many awards and a coup in celebrity advertising featuring one of the most prestigious artists of the century is the following commercial for Polaroid with Sir Laurence Olivier.

60 SECONDS

VIDEO	AUDIO
LS OLIVIER, CAMERA IN HAND, AP-PROACHING VASE OF FLOWERS FROM OUT OF DARK BACKGROUND.	FOOTSTEPS
MLS OLIVIER, HOLDING UP AND POINTING TO CAMERA, FLOWERS IN FOREGROUND.	OLIVIER: Polaroid's new SX-70.
MS OLIVIER PREPARING CAMERA TO TAKE PICTURE.	
MS OLIVIER POINTING TO BUTTON ON CAMERA.	OLIVIER: Just touch the button …
MCU OLIVIER TAKING PICTURE OF FLOWERS.	
CU OLIVIER TAKING PICTURE OF FLOWERS, ONE PICTURE OUT OF CAMERA.	OLIVIER: Now, these pictures,
CU OLIVIER TAKING PICTURE OF FLOWERS, TWO PICTURES OUT OF CAMERA.	OLIVIER: developing themselves, outside the camera,
CU OLIVIER TAKING PICTURE OF FLOWERS, THREE PICTURES OUT OF CAMERA.	OLIVIER: are hard and dry.
MCU THREE PICTURES STILL ALMOST BLANK.	MUSIC.
CU THREE PICTURES, FLOWERS BARELY BEGINNING TO SHOW.	OLIVIER: There's nothing to peel,
CU THREE PICTURES, FLOWERS SHOWING A LITTLE MORE.	OLIVIER: nothing even to throw away,
CU THREE PICTURES, FLOWERS EMERG-ING MORE.	OLIVIER: nothing to time.
CU THREE PICTURES, FLOWERS CONTINUE TO EMERGE.	MUSIC
CU THREE PICTURES, FLOWERS BECOM-ING CLEARER.	MUSIC
CU THREE PICTURES, FLOWERS MORE CLEAR.	OLIVIER: In minutes, you will have a finished photograph of such dazzling beauty

VIDEO	AUDIO
CU THREE PICTURES, FULLY PRINTED.	OLIVIER: that you will feel you are looking at the world for the first time.
XC FINISHED SINGLE PICTURE.	MUSIC
MCU OLIVIER HOLDING CAMERA OPENED.	OLIVIER: The new SX-70 Land Camera.
MCU OLIVIER HOLDING UP CAMERA CLOSED.	OLIVIER: From Polaroid.

Doyle Dane Bernbach Inc. for Polaroid Corporation

An alternative to the traditional celebrity testimonial is the testimonial from the average man or woman — the worker, the homemaker, the person in the street with whom the viewer at home can more easily identify. Through such identification the viewer may more easily accept the existence of a common problem in a commonly experienced physical, economic, or vocational setting and, concomitantly, may more readily accept the solution adopted by the person in the commercial — using

1. (MUSIC THROUGHOUT) ANNCR: (VO) Robert Ammon...

2. Michigan.

3. Mrs. James Simonds... New Hampshire.

4. Mrs. Frank O'Brien...

5. Alabama.

6. Mrs. Travis Wiginton... California.

7. Robert Geroy...

8. North Carolina.

9. James Edelstein... Wisconsin.

10. **Mrs. D. M. Olson...**
    Minnesota.

11. **Ask them whether an**
    American Tourister
    is a great suitcase to have...

12. **when you hit the road.**

Doyle Dane Bernbach Inc. for American Tourister

the sponsor's product. You see this form frequently with laundry products and cosmetic comparisons. The following is an example which has an interesting variation: not using the actual person referred to.

Sometimes, when emotional appeals are dominant, an "everyman" or "every-woman" approach is used, as in the following:

60 SECONDS, RADIO

Hello, I'd like to tell you something about myself. I used to be a drunk, and a chronic drunk driver. In the ten years between my first arrest and having my license revoked I racked up 19 major traffic violations, I caused 6 serious accidents, injured 3 people besides myself and had my license suspended twice. I was still driving and drinking. Then one night I was driving home after work and I had a few and I hit this kid on a bicycle. He died before they could get him any help. He was just 11 and a little younger than my oldest boy. I'm living with that now. I was too drunk to see him then, but I can see him now ... and I remember.

ANNCR: This message was brought to you by The General Motors Corporation.

General Motors Corporation "Safer Driver Radio" series
Created by Robert Dunning, N. W. Ayer & Son, Inc., New York

This announcement does not promote a product, but, instead, a public service idea. It is, therefore, educational in nature and is what is termed an *institutional* commercial — one that does not sell a product but is designed to create good will for the sponsor.

The writer should be careful in the use of testimonials in programs aimed at children. Children are particularly susceptible to exhortations of hero and heroine figures, including both live and animated performers, who may appear on a given program. Strong pressures by citizen groups and other public interest sources have prompted many broadcasters to remove such testimonials from the commercial content on children's shows. An FCC Policy Statement on Children's Television has suggested the avoidance of "host selling and other sales techniques that blur the distinctions between programming and advertising."

Humor Just as public attitudes toward humor change over the years, so do the humorous approaches in commercials. Always an effective attention-getter, humor in commercials, to be successful, must reflect the humorous trends of the times. At one time the gag or one-liner was the staple of commercial humor, but has largely been replaced by more gentle humor, by parody, by satire. In a sense, this approach is a return to the past when Bob and Ray as Harry and Bert Piel, the beer brewers, provided some of the finest humor in broadcasting, on commercials and programs both. Henry Morgan did it on radio even before there was television, with parody so sharp that he lost sponsors — even while the satirization of the sponsors was selling their products and making them money. Stan Freberg has been one of the more prolific practitioners of the parody. The following ad featuring Dick and Bert — among the more recent of successful exponents of humorous commercials — contains outrageous moments, yet maintains enough reality of the characters and the situation it satirizes to make them and the product believable. In addition, it uses the techniques of persuasion to show how the product being advertised solves a general as well as a specific problem.

TICK TOCK CITY

DICK:	Welcome to Cal's Tick Tock City.
BERT:	Thanks …
DICK:	Where the big hand is on dependability and …
SFX:	SMALL METAL OBJECT FALLING
DICK:	The little hand …
BERT:	Is on the floor.
DICK:	Snaps right back on.
BERT:	I want to buy some digital watches for gifts. Do you have National Semi Conductor?
DICK:	(LAUGH) No. We make our own somewhere.
BERT:	Well, I wanted to get the National Semi Conductor Chronograph. It's a watch and a stopwatch. It's the thinnest on the market.
DICK:	This is the thinnest watch we make. This watch tells time and weighs fish.
BERT:	I don't think …
DICK:	You just slip the mackerel in this harness …
BERT:	No-no … the National Semi Conductor Chronograph has an exclusive tritium night-light that lets you read it day or night without pushing buttons. And the battery has a 3 year warranty.
SFX:	DRAWER OPEN
DICK:	No chronograph. I got this phonograph watch.
BERT:	What?
DICK:	Put one of these teenie weenie records on …
SFX:	HISS OF A RECORD
VOICE:	The time is 5:68 (SKIP) :68 (SKIP) :68 …
SFX:	RECORD SCRATCH AS NEEDLE IS MOVED OVER IT.
DICK:	Just needs a new needle …
BERT:	Well, how about alarm watches?
DICK:	We got coo-coos, gongs, and buzzers.
BERT:	Well, National Semi Conductor has the only tritium alarm on the market. It actually chirps and you can read it at night.
DICK:	Here's one you don't have to read. It squirts your arm every hour …
BERT:	What???
DICK:	Actually, It just wets on your wrist.
BERT:	Are those little diapers?

DICK: Prevents wrist rash.
ANNCR: For great chronographs and alarm watches, look for National Semi Conductor, the
          longest name in digital watches.
DICK: If you don't like the gasoline model, I've got diesel ...
SFX: STARTING ENGINE
BERT: It's a little bulky.
DICK: But it gets 12 hours to the gallon.

Courtesy of Dick Orkin Creative Services, Inc.

Sometimes humor tends toward the bizarre. A problem of this kind of commercial is that the humor is overwhelmed and the audience is turned from the product to the technique by the gimmick. One award-winning commercial that found a proper balance of all elements and was extremely popular is the following ''P-A-R-K-A-Y'' spot.

30 SECONDS

VIDEO	AUDIO
1. OPEN ON LITTLE GIRL SITTING ON FRONT PORCH AT WICKER TABLE. BEGIN SLOW MOVE IN ON HER AS SHE SINGS.	KID: P-A-R-K-A-Y, P-A-R-K-A-Y.
2. CUP SPEAKS WITH LID.	CUP: Butter.
3. LITTLE GIRL PAUSES, THEN BEGINS SINGING AGAIN.	KID: (SIGH) P-A-R-K-A-Y, P-A-R ...
4. CUP SPEAKS WITH LID.	CUP: Butter.
5. LITTLE GIRL PAUSES AGAIN, SIGHS, THEN LIFTS LID OF CUP & TASTES. SHE CONSIDERS THEN CHANGES HER LITTLE SONG.	KID: (SIGH) (TASTES) B-U-T-T-E-R, B-U-T-T-E-R.
6. CUP SPEAKS ONCE MORE WITH LID.	CUP: Parkay!
7. LITTLE GIRL PAUSES, CONSIDERS, THEN CHANGES SONG ONE LAST TIME.	KID: (SHRUGS) P-A-R-K-A-Y, P-A-R-K-A-Y.
8. CUT TO LIMBO SHOT OF SOFT PARKAY PACKAGES & SUPER: *PARKAY MARGARINE FROM KRAFT. THE FLAVOR SAYS BUTTER.*	ANNCR: Parkay Margarine from Kraft. The flavor says butter.

Permission for use of this material has been granted by Kraft, Inc.
(Needham, Harper & Steers, Inc.)

Some humorous commercials use what seems to be a juxtaposition of seemingly incongruous elements — but the topicality makes the point clear, as in the following example.

10 SECONDS

1. **(SILENT)**

2. **ANNCR: (VO) If gas pains persist ...**

3. **(SFX)**

4. **Try Volkswagen.**

Doyle Dane Bernbach Inc. for Volkswagen of America

Some advertisers and agency people believe that one of the problems with the really top-notch humorous commercials was that the audience got so involved with the humor that it didn't pay enough attention to the product. Many producers believe that parodies have been overdone, that any satire in commercials has to be fresh, innovative, and unique. The parody should be so good that the public will want to hear it over and over again. The most effective parodies have been those with a story line, even a limited one, in which the situation is dominant. Within the situation are the references to the product. The following example is a classic of this type.

30 SECONDS

VIDEO	AUDIO
OPEN ON HUSBAND SITS UP IN BED IN SLIGHT TRANCE, OBVIOUSLY UNABLE TO SLEEP. WIFE IS IN BED BESIDE HIM.	HUSBAND: I can't believe I ate that whole thing.
	WIFE: You ate it Ralph.
	HUSBAND: I can't believe I ate that whole thing.
	WIFE: No Ralph, I ate it!
	HUSBAND: I can't believe I ate that whole thing.
	WIFE: Take two Alka-Seltzer.
CUT TO TWO ALKA-SELTZER DROPPING IN GLASS OF WATER. PAN ACROSS ASPIRIN BOTTLE AND TWO ASPIRINS. CONTINUE PAN ACROSS ROLL OF ANTACIDS AND TWO ANTACIDS. CONTINUE PAN TO FOIL PACK OF ALKA-SELTZER.	ANNCR. V.O.: For headache and upset stomach, no aspirin or antacid alone relieves you in as many ways as Alka-Seltzer. For headache and upset stomach.

VIDEO	AUDIO
CUT TO CLOSE UP OF HUSBAND.	WIFE: Did you drink your Alka-Seltzer?
	HUSBAND: The whole thing.

Courtesy of Miles Laboratories and Wells, Rich, Greene, Inc.

Music   The musical commercial has always been one of the most effective for having an audience remember the product. How many times have you listened to a song on radio or television, been caught up in its cadence, and then suddenly realized it was a commercial and not the latest hit tune?

Producer Susan Hamilton stated in *Broadcasting* magazine that "music is still basically an emotional thing. And the reason we are producing commercials that sound like records is to try and grab the listeners. We're always told that when a commercial comes on the radio kids immediately turn the dial. But when you make your spots sound like songs, there's a chance you may be able to reach those kids before they reach those dials." In fact, some commercials such as Pepsi-Cola's "The Girl Watcher's Theme," Alka-Seltzer's "No Matter What Shape," and Coca-Cola's "I'd Like to Teach the World to Sing," did become hit songs. Because it has to be singable the musical commercial usually follows the contemporary trend — the hit pattern of the particular year.

Music has been so effective in writing commercials that many of us have come to identify and remember Coca-Cola, McDonald's, and United Air Lines, among others, first with their theme music and only secondarily with a particular sales message. One of the most effective examples, now a classic, is the following:

60 SECONDS

VIDEO	AUDIO
	SONG:
CUT TO CU OF GIRL'S FACE AND SINGING.	I'd like to buy the world a home and furnish it with love. Grow apple trees and snow white turtles doves
PB TO REVEAL GIRL SINGING WITH BOY AND GIRL WITH COKE BOTTLE ALSO SINGING.	
DISS TO PAN ACROSS OF BOYS AND GIRLS IN NATIVE DRESS WITH COKE BOTTLES IN HAND AND SINGING.	I'd like to teach the world to sing (sing with me) in perfect harmony (perfect harmony) and I'd like to buy the world a coke and keep it company.
	It's the real thing.
DISS TO SIDE VIEW OF ROWS OF BOYS AND GIRLS IN NATIVE DRESS AND SINGING.	I'd like to teach the world to sing (what the world wants today)
DISS TO PAN ACROSS OF ROWS OF BOYS AND GIRLS IN NATIVE DRESS SINGING.	In perfect harmony (perfectly) I'd like to buy the world a Coke.
DISS TO PAN ACROSS OF COKE BOTTLES IN HANDS OF BOYS AND GIRLS.	and keep it company
DISS TO CU OF GIRL'S FACE AND SINGING.	It's the real thing (Coke is)

VIDEO	AUDIO
DOUBLE EXPOSE CU GIRL'S FACE SINGING OVER CROWD SHOT TO PB TO REVEAL CROWDS OF BOYS AND GIRLS OF ALL NATIONS ON HILL WITH CRAWLING TITLE AND MATTE: SUPER: ON A HILLTOP IN ITALY WE ASSEMBLED YOUNG PEOPLE FROM ALL OVER THE WORLD TO BRING YOU THIS MESSAGE FROM COCA-COLA BOTTLERS ALL OVER THE WORLD. IT'S THE REAL THING. COKE.	What the world wants today Coca-Cola. It's the real thing. What the world wants today Coke is. Coca-Cola.

> Courtesy of The Coca-Cola Company. Words and music by Roger Cook, Roger Greenaway, William Becker and Billy Davis. McCann-Erickson, Inc.

Dramatization A dramatization is, in effect, a short play — a happening that creates suspense and reaches a climax. The climax is, of course, the revelation of the attributes of the product. In the classic structure of the play form, the resolution is the members of the audience all rushing out of their homes to buy the particular product. Dramatizations frequently combine elements of the other major commercial forms, particularly music, testimonials, and humor. Here are several award-winning commercials in the dramatization form.

• *As you study them, (1) determine which forms, in addition to drama, they contain, and (2) analyze their use of the five steps of persuasion, including their use of emotional appeals.*

---

60 SECONDS

VISUAL	AUDIO
1. COUNSELOR WALKING DOWN STEPS OF ROW HOUSE.	SONG: "Hey, look at you lookin' at the sunrise …
2. CU OF COUNSELOR TALKING TO BOY.	"There's such a brighter …
3. BOY BEING PULLED UP.	"look in your …
4. COUNSELOR AND BOY WALKING DOWN SIDEWALK, TALKING.	"eyes.
5. COUNSELOR AND BOY CROSSING STREET.	"Now that I know you've felt the wind …
6. COUNSELOR AND THREE KIDS WALKING DOWN SIDEWALK.	"that's blowing, reaching out …
7. PAN OF COUNSELOR AND KIDS.	"and wanting life's good things.
8. LONG SHOT OF PLAYGROUND GATE OPENING AND KIDS WAITING.	"Now that you're seein' …

VISUAL	AUDIO
9. OPEN GATE AND KIDS RUSHING IN.	"All things grow.
10. CU OF COUNSELOR TURNING AROUND.	(MUSIC UP)
11. COUNSELOR PASSING BALL TO BOY.	
12. COUNSELOR JOGGING TO BOY BEHIND FENCE.	"There is more love in …
13. CU OF JOSÉ.	"you than anyone …
14. COUNSELOR ASKING BOY TO FOLLOW.	"I know.
15. COUNSELOR WITH ARM AROUND JOSÉ, INTRODUCING HIM TO KIDS.	"You take time for friends …
16. COUNSELOR PLAYING CHECKERS WITH KIDS, GIRL DRINKING COKE.	"and simple talking …
17. CU OF COUNSELOR DRINKING COKE.	"Sippin' Coke …
⅛—. LS OF COUNSELOR SWINGING BOY AROUND.	"enjoyin' life's …
19. PAN OF KIDS DRINKING COKE AGAINST FENCE.	"good things. It's the Real Thing.
20. CU OF PRODUCT AGAINST FENCE.	"Oh … Coca-Cola.
21. PAN OF KIDS AGAINST FENCE.	"It's the Real Thing.
22. PRODUCT AGAINST FENCE.	"Oh … Coca-Cola.
23. COUNSELOR GIVING JOSÉ A COKE.	"It's the Real Thing.
24. PRODUCT AGAINST FENCE WITH SUPER: "It's the real thing, Coke."	"Oh … Coca-Cola.
25. COUNSELOR WITH JOSÉ ARM IN ARM. SUPER: "It's the real thing. Coke."	"It's the Real Thing."

Courtesy of The Coca-Cola Company. McCann-Erickson, Inc.

The next commercial is a combination of the dramatization and documentary forms.

60 SECONDS

ANNCR. (VOICE OVER):
With divers working a quarter mile down these days, how do you . . .

keep track of them without big, unmanageable cables.

In Britain, the Royal Navy is developing a monitoring system that uses optical fibers made by the people of ITT.

OFFICER: Give me a readout on No. 1 diver.
TECHNICIAN: Respiration and heart rate normal.

OFFICER: Ready No. 2 diver. Test for leaks and send him down.

ANNCR.: The ITT optical fibers are threads of glass that can be built . . .

right into the air hose — and over them, a laser beam can flash medical reports . . .

sixteen conditions that signal an emergency.

TECHNICIAN: Diver in distress.
OFFICER: What's the problem, Bob?
TECHNICIAN: EKG is unstable.

OFFICER (V.O.): Operate emergency procedure.
ANNCR.: Who knows how many lives this ITT cable will save—

once it's out of the laboratory.
OFFICER (V.O.): Not bad, chaps.

Courtesy of International Telephone and Telegraph Corporation.
(Needham, Harper & Steers, Inc.)

60 SECOND SPOT
Poker Game

VIDEO	AUDIO
LS A FRIDAY NIGHT POKER GAME	HOWARD COSELL: The Friday night game at Carl's and someone's playing with marked cards.
CU OF DEALER.	DEALER: Five card draw, gentlemen, jacks or better to open.
CU 1ST PLAYER.	1ST PLAYER: I open for two.
CU 2ND PLAYER.	2ND PLAYER: I'll see you.
CU 3RD PLAYER:	3RD PLAYER: I never win at this game. By me.

VIDEO	AUDIO
LS OF GAME.	HOWARD COSELL: All these men know who's playing with the marked cards but they don't mind.
	DEALER: Cards.
	1ST PLAYER: I'll take two.
	2ND PLAYER: Let me have three.
CU OF 2ND PLAYER.	HOWARD COSELL: He's the one, he's blind and the cards are marked in braille. They're made available by the American
SUPER ADDRESS.	Foundation for the Blind. Brailled cards are just one of the hundreds of aids and appliances made and adapted for blind people. If you want a catalog, write BLIND AIDS, Box 111, New York 10011.
	1ST PLAYER: I've got three Queens.

Courtesy of the American Foundation for the Blind

An interesting combination of dramatization and humorous satire is the following noncommercial commercial. If the copywriter finds it difficult to "sell" a product in a commercial, will she or he find it more difficult to "unsell" a product?

————————————————————◯————————————————————

• *What writing techniques (i.e., steps of persuasion, emotional appeals) does the following use to unsell a product? Do its writing techniques differ from those of the "commercial" commercial?*

————————————————————◯————————————————————

JOHN AND EVIE
(60 Seconds)

MUSIC:	SMOKE GETS IN YOUR EYES
GIRL:	(NORMAL) John ...
BOY:	(NORMAL) Evie ...
GIRL:	(BIT ROMANTIC) John ...
BOY:	(BIT ROMANTIC) Evie ...
GIRL:	(GIGGLY) John ...
BOY:	(GIGGLY) Evie ...
GIRL:	(MORE ROMANTIC) John ...
BOY:	(MORE ROMANTIC) Evie ...
SOUND:	Lighting cigarette ... and Puffing
GIRL:	John ...
BOY:	Evie ...
GIRL:	(UPSET) John!
BOY:	(PERSISTING) Evie!
SOUND:	KISS
GIRL:	(BLOWING AWAY ANNOYING SMOKE) John ...

BOY:	(BLOWING AWAY SMOKE) Evie …
GIRL:	(SLIGHT COUGH) John …
BOY:	(SLIGHT COUGH) Evie …
GIRL:	(LOOKING FOR JOHN) John???
BOY:	(LOOKING FOR EVIE) Evie???
GIRL:	(INCREASED COUGHING) John …
BOY:	(INCREASED COUGHING) Evie …
GIRL:	(FRANTIC COUGHING AND CALL FOR HELP) Johnnnnn!!!
BOY:	(FRANTIC COUGHING AND CALL FOR HELP) Evieeeee!!!
MUSIC:	COUGHING AND MUSIC FADE OUT
ANNCR:	The American Cancer Society reminds you that smoking cigarettes is a drag and you'd better believe it.

Other commercial forms Two of the most effective appeals involve family and children. The viewer identifies strongly and is left with a good feeling toward the product, service, or idea. Here are two award-winning examples:

60 SECONDS

VIDEO	AUDIO
LONG SHOT OF CAB ON COUNTRY ROAD.	"I was raised on country sunshine
CU OF GIRL IN CAB.	
LS OF KIDS ON SWING.	Green grass beneath my feet
LS OF CAB.	
KIDS ON HORSE.	Runnin' thru fields of daisies
KIDS ON TREE FISHING.	Wadin' thru the creek
LS OF FATHER ON TRACTOR.	
PAN OF CAR WITH GIRL.	You love me and it's invitin'
SHOT OF HAY LOFT.	To go where life is
MOTHER ON PORCH.	More excitin'
LONG SHOT OF CAB.	But I was raised
CU OF FATHER REACTING TO CAB.	On country sunshine
CU OF CAB.	
CU OF GIRL ON SWING REACTING TO CAB.	I was raised
CU OF BOY IN HAY LOFT.	On country
BOY JUMPS OUT OF HAY LOFT.	sunshine. I'm a happy
MOTHER ON PORCH REACTING TO GIRL.	With the simple
LONG SHOT OF CAB ARRIVING AT HOUSE.	Things — a Saturday night dance
PRODUCT SHOT.	A bottle of Coke
GIRL GREETS FAMILY.	The joy that the Bluebird brings
	I love you please believe me
CU OF GREETING.	And don't you ever leave me
CU OF FAMILY ON PORCH.	Cause I was raised on country sunshine
CU OF KIDS DRINKING COKE.	It's the real thing
PRODUCT SHOT.	Like Coke is

VIDEO	AUDIO
GUY GETTING OUT OF TRUCK.	That you're hoping to find
GIRL AND GUY EMBRACE.	Like country sunshine, it's the real thing
COUPLE ON SWING.	Coca-Cola."
SUPER: "It's the Real Thing."	

Courtesy of The Coca-Cola Company. McCann-Erickson, Inc.

60 SECONDS

MONTAGE OF CHILDREN:

I love you, Daddy.
He brung me to the circus once.
I love my daddy more than everything.
My daddy is sweet.
My daddy is regular.
My daddy is skinny.
Sometimes when I'm riding in the car with him
   he goes so fast I'm sort a scared.
Slow down daddy.
He might skid and drive the car off the road.
When Daddy drives I worry because
   he has lots a crashes.
A policeman can come right around the
   corner and my Dad might get arrested.
I wish he would come back.
He didn't come home yet.
I want him to come back.
I'm scared.
I would feel worried about him.
I get scared because he goes so fast.

ANNCR:

If you don't care about your own safety, remember that those who love you do. Please slow down. This message was brought to you by the General Motors Corporation.

General Motors Corporation "Safer Driver Radio" series
Created by Robert Dunning, N. W. Ayer & Son, Inc., New York

Combining the visual and aural content of the commercial with the product is an example of good creative art as well as successful selling. The following thirty-second spot for Revlon entitled "Mountain" is an example. Another approach is a narrated dramatization, sometimes combining additional elements such as a theme song or theme music with variations on lyrics for different spots, as in the McDonald's "Hot Stuff" commercial which also follows. Additionally, it has a point of view and a societal learning situation with which a large segment of its viewers can identify.

(HUNTING HORN) (MUSIC) ANNCR: (VO) Come to find the beautiful fragrance of Jontue.

Sensual . . . but not too far from innocence. Jontue.

(MUSIC) (HUNTING HORN) The beautiful fragrance . . . (MUSIC) Sensual . . .

but not too far from innocence. Jontue from Revlon. Wear it and be wonderful.

Courtesy of Revlon, Inc.
(Grey Advertising, Inc.)

VIDEO	AUDIO
BOY ATTEMPTS TO STUFF BASKETBALL	SONG: You, you're the one
HE MISSES	You're tryin' for perfection
GIRL ATTEMPTS MOVE ON BALANCE BEAM	You, you're the one
SHE MISSES	Standin' up to close inspection

VIDEO	AUDIO
BOY TRIES AGAIN	Workin' harder everyday
MISSES AGAIN	To get it right this time
GIRL TRIES AGAIN	Giving up is not your way
MISSES AGAIN	You really want to shine
CU BOY'S FACE. LOOKS DETERMINED	You
PULL BACK AS HE STUFFS IN BALL	You're the one
HE STUFFS BALL IN ACTUAL GAME	SFX: KA-CHUNK-BOOM/STUFF EFFECT
CU OF EXALTED LOOK ON HIS FACE	SONG: The feelings great now
CU GIRL'S FACE, LOOKS DETERMINED	You
PULL BACK	You're the one
SHE EXECUTES MOVES PERFECTLY	SFX: JOYOUS APPLAUSE/CROWD NOISE
THEY GO TO MCDONALD'S	It's time to celebrate now
HAMBURGERS ON GRILL	That's why we're cookin' just for you
EATING	Cause you demand a lot
BOY SMILES/EATS	Right now nothing else will do
GIRL SMILES/EATS	So we serve you fast and hot
THEY LOOK AT EACH OTHER	At McDonald's
MORTISE	We do it all for you.

Copyright, McDonald's Corp. 1979
(Needham, Harper & Steers, Inc.)

When you consider the combinations possible among the five major types of commercials, you have, as a writer, a seemingly infinite number of formats to work with. Sometimes you can start with the type. For example, a renowned performer singing your commercial: a classic combination of testimonial and music. You can sometimes tailor your ad and even your entire campaign around this personality. Conversely, you can develop the theme of your campaign, such as AT&T's highly successful ''Reach Out and Touch Someone,'' and hope to attract a well-known singer to participate in it. The following musical testimonial with Lena Horne is an excellent example.

MUSIC UNDER
ANNCR: *The Bell System presents Lena Horne for Long Distance.*
MUSIC UP
LENA SINGS: Reach out, reach out and touch someone.
                Reach out, call up and just say "hi."
                Reach out, reach out and touch someone.
                Wherever you are,
                You're never too far,
                They're waiting to share your day ...
MUSIC UNDER
LENA SPEAKS: You far away from folks you love? Pick up the phone and have a nice long visit. That's what I do to chase the blues. And it works!

MUSIC UP

LENA SINGS: People from coast to coast
Calling up friends to keep them close.
Families who care so much
Keeping in touch ...
Reach out, reach out and touch someone (To End)

Courtesy of American Telephone and Telegraph Company, Long Lines Department
(Music by Davis Lucas, Lyrics by Don Wood)

In the 1980s, creative writers and producers began to combine elements of existing commercial types with the increasing entertainment emphasis on science fiction (i.e., *Star Wars, Star Trek, E.T.,* and other film and television features) into ''new wave'' commercials. *Broadcasting* magazine described these as ''surrealistic and sex-oriented and distinguished by quick cuts, bands of light, bright colors, loud rock music, optical illusion and a minimal amount of dialogue.'' Although this commercial type seemed to build up a sponsor's general image, there is still some question as to whether it has been effective in actually selling specific products or services.

One of the classic statements on radio commercials was made in 1949 by Maurice B. Mitchell, director of broadcast advertising for the NAB. The continuing validity of the five points presented by Mr. Mitchell was emphasized by *Broadcasting* magazine on September 10, 1973, when it reprinted Mr. Mitchell's 1949 statement under the headline: ''Second time around: words about radio still ring true.'' Reprinted in part here, we might say ''third time around, still true.'' Although Mr. Mitchell's comments related to radio advertising in general, they are in some instances specifically and in other instances by implication oriented toward the job of the commercial continuity writer. Mr. Mitchell stated:

How can you use radio more effectively? What are the things you can do to get greater results from radio? I would tell you five simple things — the five points into which all our study and all our research can be boiled down.

No. 1. Before you can use radio for maximum effectiveness, you have got to understand your objectives. Before an advertiser, before a retailer sets up his radio advertising budget or buys any time, he should know what he expects to advertise and to whom he expects to address his advertising message. What do you want from radio and whom do you want to talk to? It's just that simple. . . .

No. 2. The retailer should take advantage of a technique we have found to be overwhelmingly successful — the beamed program technique. If you know what you want to say and you know whom you want to say it to, you can buy a vehicle that will, without waste, talk directly to the people you want to address. It's a rifle shot at a target, not a buck-shot at a barn door. . . .

No. 3. We think the retailer who wants maximum success from advertising should advertise his strong departments and his strong lines, advertise his in-demand merchandise and advertise it on the radio regularly. . . .

No. 4. You've got to have the kind of copy that will do the selling job right. Not just ''copy'' — not just the stuff you poke out with one finger on the typewriter for your newspaper *and* your radio advertising . . .

sometimes. One of the things we've never been able to understand is why an advertiser will put phrases in his advertising copy that people would never say aloud. Did you ever hear of a woman who called her husband on the phone and said to him, "Would you mind stopping in at Jones's Department Store today and buying me a pair of slippers because, there, quality and variety go hand in hand?" A lot of advertisers are saying that sort of thing every single day of the week. Don't you think perhaps she might actually say, "I wish you'd buy me a pair of slippers at Jones's because their sale ends today, and I can't get downtown"? She is telling her husband specifically what she wants, specifically why she wants it, and she makes a decision to buy for a specific reason.

One of the best examples I've seen is the copy of an advertiser who used the radio recently to advertise purses. In his early advertising, he was using this kind of copy: "Stop in here for a purse because we have purses that will help complete a smart costume ensemble at budget prices." Now, nobody buys "a smart costume ensemble at budget prices." But when he later began to say, "Here's where the working girl will always find a purse at $8.98," or "Here's where you'll find plastic bags that wash as easily as your face," or "Here's where you'll find plastic bags and purses in bright colors that will go with your dark suit," he was talking to people in the terms in which they thought of his merchandise. He was talking specifically to the listeners about the specific things his merchandise could do for them, and he wasn't being vague and saying, "This merchandise which we have to sell has this attribute." He was saying, "*You* ought to buy this because this will do this for *you*."

We also think the kind of copy that produces the maximum results for a retailer is truthful, believable copy. If you will sit down and take the trouble to find out those things that you can say about your goods that are truthful and that are believable, then you have taken a step towards greater success in radio. That kind of copy sticks in a person's mind for a long time. It doesn't always produce results *today,* but continual repetition will cause people to remember the store that uses that kind of advertising. Joske's (of San Antonio) continual repetition of "the largest store in the largest state," and similar slogans used by other great stores, stay in the minds of many people who aren't planning a purchase the first time they hear it. The fact that when they do get around to buying they'll remember that here's where they've wanted to stop — that's the real effect of that kind of copy. Truthful copy, like truthful clerks, is a lot more convincing. Very few retailers would instruct their clerks to deliberately lie to a potential buyer. Yet many retailers don't deliberately lie but — let me say — deviate somewhat from the bare facts in their advertising.

Most important of all, invite your customer to take direct action. Don't say: "You should buy a pair of slippers because they're wonderful," but say: "Come on down to our store tomorrow morning at 10 o'clock and go into the entrance just off Main Street. You don't even have to go upstairs — the slippers are right near the door. You can buy them and be out in five minutes." You've given a direct invitation to take direct action.

I've heard some taxi-cab advertising recently that impressed me. Typical was a line of taxi cabs that said, "Here's where you can have dependable, clean, efficient taxi service." Now I don't particularly care if the taxi-cab company is run efficiently. If it isn't, I assume they'll go bankrupt and somebody else will come around when I call. Dependability is certainly not the key customer advantage for a taxi-cab company to promote as a basic reason for calling a cab. On the other hand, I have heard another taxi company say, "It's raining out today! Don't get wet! Call a taxi. Call this number. Be sure you call this number if you need a taxi. And if you need a taxi, call this number." They're talking to me about a service I'm liable to need right then in terms of why I might need it and they make sure I can find it if I do.

One of the things I get a big kick out of, and I'm sure many other advertising men do, is the Christmas approach — "Be sure you bring something home to your wife that will put the lovelight in her eyes." I can put the lovelight in my wife's eyes without the help of any advertising. But there are some other reasons why I might buy her a Christmas present. Some pretty good, sound selling reasons. "Put the old lovelight in your wife's eyes" looks wonderful on a typewriter, but it sounds silly in advertising and doesn't persuade anybody. The direct-action copy approach, talking to people in terms that they understand, in the terms in which they think of the use of the merchandise themselves, will sell.

No. 5. Coordinate your advertising. . . . How do you coordinate your advertising? It's very simple. You display radio-advertised merchandise at the place where you said it could be bought. . . . Make sure you promote your radio programs in all of your other advertising media. . . . Conversely, use radio to make your other media work better. . . . Let radio give emphasis and increased publicity to all of your other advertising purchases.

For Application and Review

1. For both television and radio, choose a product, a program, and a station. Develop a commercial for each, using the following considerations: audience analysis; logical and emotional appeals; familiarization with the product and its basic place in the commercial; and the five steps of persuasion: attention, interest, impression of a problem, solving of a problem, getting action.
2. Using the same considerations, write a PSA for television and a PSA for radio.
3. Write a television and radio ID for your local stations.
4. Watch and listen to several commercials and analyze the specific emotional appeals used. Write television and radio commercials in terms of the analysis of the audience in your locality, using one or more of the following emotional appeals in each commercial: prestige, power, good taste, self-preservation.

5. Watch and listen to television and radio commercials until you are certain you can identify each of the following formats: the straight sell, the testimonial, humor, music, dramatization. Write short television and radio commercials that illustrate each of these forms.

4

News
and Sports

News

Any real happening that may have an interest for or effect upon people is news. The television or radio reporter has a limitless field. Anything from a cat up a tree to the outbreak of a war may be worthy of a transmission to the mass media audience. The gathering of news, however, is not our primary concern here. The writing of news broadcasts is.

Sources of News

Two major agencies, the **Associated Press (AP)** and **United Press International (UPI)**, which serve as news sources for the newspapers, also service television and radio stations. The same information given to newspapers is made available for broadcasting. For broadcast purposes, however, the news writing style should be changed so that the stories become shorter and more pointed, oriented toward the needs of television and radio transmission. In television, in addition, the news stories are not used alone, but are coordinated with visual elements such as films, tapes, photographs, and **wirephotos**. A number of organizations provide special news material, particularly pictorial matter, for television. Special newsreel and photo companies operate in almost every city containing a major television station. The large networks have their own news gathering and reporting organizations.

All television and radio stations of any consequence, even small local stations, subscribe to at least one wire service. The small station also may use more immediate sources for local news, such as telephoned reports from city agencies or even private citizens, special information from the local newspapers, word-of-mouth communications, and sometimes special reporters of their own. The local news story must be written from scratch and, for television, written to fit in with the available visual material.

In the large station, the news is usually prepared by writers in a special news department. Most small stations do not have separate news departments, so news broadcasts are prepared by available personnel. The continuity department, if there is one, prepares the special local reports. Generally, the job will fall to the program director or to the individual announcer. The news received through teletype, as well as from local sources, is edited in the large station by the producer or director of the news program or by the individual commentator. The commentator on the small station does this job. The announcer has to make certain that the news reports he or she reads on the air fit his or her personality, vocabulary, and, often, station policy. More important, the amount of news prepared must fit the time limit of the show and the organization of the news must adhere to the format of the program. A writer preparing news for a particular program and for a particular announcer will edit it so that it conforms to the above requirements as the specific case demands. For example, the *Washington Post* has described how Steve Steinberg, chief writer for ABC news reporter and commentator Howard K. Smith, matched "his style to the speaking habits and story preferences of Smith. For example, you will not hear Smith say the word 'particularly' on the air. Steinberg doesn't use it because Smith can't pronounce it. And Smith likes to set up stories with historical backgrounds. . . . If it was up to Howard, everything in the show would begin: 'On July 4, 1776. . . .' "

Special Considerations

Local news   One of the spurs to radio and television news was the FCC's **prime-time rule**, requiring return to local stations by the networks of one-half hour of time during the prime viewing hours for local originations. The most common pattern for use of the additional local programming time was to increase the half-hour news show to one hour. This included not only straight news and commentary, but public affairs programming of a feature and **minidocumentary type**. In major markets local news programs began to become viable competition with network news broadcasts, in many instances even strong competition for even the most popular entertainment programs. One of the reasons for the surge of local news was the development of the minicamera, or ENG, which permits immediacy in local news gathering. This, in turn, affected the form of local news; it became more people-oriented, more informal in nature. Stations developed local "magazine" approaches, including not only the traditional feature material, but adding new concepts such as consumer advocate reports, investigative reporting and special reports on vital and frequently controversial issues such as educational practices, racial discrimination, child abuse, and feminist concerns.

The FCC requirement for ascertainment of community needs played a significant role in the reorientation of local news content. More and more local stations dealt more and more with the gut concerns in the communities. Instead of simply reporting on what happened, stations became oriented toward the problems of their towns and cities, as specified in the FCC **Ascertainment Primer**, and sought solutions to these problems. The approach is basically the same, whether the local station is in a large city or a small one. In *Radio/Television Age,* Robert E. Shay, as director of broadcasting at WCBS-TV in New York City, stated: "The entire station is geared to people. We basically want to show them how to cope. If we discuss housing, we talk to the people with the problems and not so much with the experts." Dick Dudley, as president of the Forward Communications Group, discussed in *Radio/Television Age* the news approach of WSAU-TV, Wasau, Wisconsin: "In a small market such as ours, the interest of the audience is quite often vastly different from that of a major metropolitan market. Thus we have to develop a more acute news sense of our community and area. The network news covers most major stories with a broad brush. We have to utilize a finer news approach to fulfill our commitments to our community."

An AP study showed that over 80 percent of all radio listeners, regardless of age, economic status, or format of the stations they listen to, want full news programs. They prefer local news, but also want national and international coverage. They want the news to be serious, informative, and to relate to their personal needs and interests. These findings are of particular interest to the news producer and writer for the regional or local station. Many broadcasters believe that local news has become so ingrained that even the abolition of ascertainment requirements does not substantially affect it.

Special status of television news   The attitude of the people of the United States toward television news places the writer (and producer) in a position of great influence and ethical responsibility. Surveys continue to show that television is considered by most Americans to be the most believable of all mass media and the major source of their news information. One of the questions asked in the yearly surveys is which of the media should be given more credibility in instances where news reports conflict; about half the public chooses television, about a quarter picks newspapers, and the remainder is divided between magazines and radio. About twice as many people say they get more of their news from television than from newspapers. In light of the power they have to affect the minds and emotions of people, what personal restraints and commitments are there or should there be on televisions newswriters and producers? What, if any, outside guidance or controls — such as regulation by the federal government — should there be?

Fairness and Equal Time   Broadcast news also has a special status in that it is affected more than any other type of programming by the FCC's two most controversial regulations: the **Fairness Doctrine** and the **Equal Time rule**. Any presentation of an issue of controversy in a given community must contain all the major sides of that controversy. As with editorializing, if a station is proven to the satisfaction of the FCC not to have presented the controversial issues "fairly," it may be required to provide comparable broadcast time for those sides considered to have been omitted. The Equal Time rule applies to political affairs only and requires a station to provide equal time on the air to all bona fide candidates for a given office, preventing the station, in effect, from providing one candidate with an advantage in reaching the public. Although it is generally accepted that broadcasters are against the Fairness Doctrine and that citizen groups are for it, a survey of stations by *Television/Radio Age* found a substantial minority of program directors and station managers in favor of it. William Sheehan, when president of ABC

News, stated: "I don't think the Fairness Doctrine is a problem. It doesn't inhibit enterprising broadcast journalism at all. During all this time we've been operating under it, ABC has continued to present news and documentary programming in a frank and hard-hitting manner and no subject has been taboo." On the other hand, Thomas Frawley, as president of the Radio and Television News Director's Association, advocated abolishment of the Fairness Doctrine: "What it all boils down to is that the Fairness Doctrine is as strong or as weak as the sitting Commission decides it will be. Which strongly suggests that there's nothing really consistent about it. . . . The Commission has been saying all along that it isn't judging news content, just balance. But the mere fact that the Doctrine is there at all, whether it is administered strictly or not, inhibits broadcasters from doing a lot of the courageous things in news that they want to do." Many broadcasters believe that the Fairness Doctrine is in violation of the First Amendment by restricting freedom of speech; some broadcasters and virtually all public-interest groups representing the viewing public believe that the Fairness Doctrine prevents those in control of the broadcast media from unduly influencing public thought and belief by slanting the news, and that it extends freedom of speech by making it more easily available to all points of view.

Those who oppose equal time — including almost all broadcast executives — believe that it limits the amount of political coverage stations provide because it requires equal time for minority as well as majority candidates. Those who favor Equal Time believe that it prevents the broadcast media, particularly in small markets with a limited number of stations, from eliminating minority or dissenting political opinions or giving unfair advantage to one major party candidate over another.

As long as the Fairness Doctrine and Equal Time rule are in operation, however, the newswriter constantly must be alert to their provisions and should be certain that any given script — even a segment of a news broadcast or news feature — is not a violation of federal regulations. One way in which writers can do this is to do thorough research on a given subject and to obtain as many varying opinions as possible on a controversial issue before preparing it for broadcast. Although this means more work, it also should guarantee a much more valid and in-depth news story.

Format

In some instances the writer may do little more than prepare the transitional continuity for a particular program, leaving out the news content itself. It is then up to the individual commentator to edit the news to fit his or her own announcing abilities, personality, and the program approach. In many cases the writer prepares only the opening and closing for a program, the broadcaster or a special writer filling in the news portions with wire service reports and other materials. The basic radio news format has changed little over the years, except that the fifteen-minute news program has on many radio stations become five minutes. A still valid format, retained here from an earlier edition of this book for nostalgia as well as illustrative purposes, and out of respect for one of the country's greatest journalists, is the following prepared format for an Edward R. Murrow fifteen-minute news broadcast.

EDWARD R. MURROW — FORMAT

BRYAN: The FORD ROAD SHOW presents EDWARD R. MURROW with the news ... This is
            George Bryan speaking for Ford, whose new Interceptor V-8 engine brings you
            gas-saving Precision Fuel Induction.
            (One minute commercial) — Now, Edward R. Murrow.

MURROW: (11 minutes of news) ..... I'll be back in a moment with the word for today. Now, a
            word from George Bryan.

BRYAN: (1-minute 30-second commercial) Now here is Mr. Murrow with his word for the day.

MURROW: Word for the day.

BRYAN: The FORD ROAD SHOW has presented Edward R. Murrow with the news. This is
            George Bryan speaking for Ford, whose new Interceptor V-8 engine brings you
            gas-saving Precision Fuel Induction. Listen through the week for the other FORD
            ROAD SHOWS with Bing Crosby, Rosemary Clooney, Arthur Godfrey, and the
            morning World News Roundup.

CBS Radio Broadcast

   **The Murrow format is for a network program. The following format is for a local
station news broadcast.**

WBSM NEWS FORMAT

:30 BEFORE THE HOUR:
     ANN: (READ THREE SHORT HEADLINES) THESE STORIES AND MORE AFTER ABC
            REPORTS ON WORLD AND NATIONAL EVENTS. SET YOUR WATCH TO WBSM. THE
            TIME AT THE TONE IS _____ O'CLOCK.

:00 ABC NEWS (NETWORK)

:05 LOCAL NEWS (PLAY NEWS SOUNDER CART)
     ANN: IT'S _____ DEGREES AT _(TIME)_. I'M _____,
            WBSM TOTAL INFORMATION NEWS, BROUGHT TO YOU BY
            (READ SPONSOR TAG).
     (READ THREE STORIES, USE ONE ACTUALITY)

:07 ANN: WBSM NEWS TIME _____.
     (PLAY COMMERCIAL :60)

:08 ANN: (COMPLETE THE NEWS)

:10 ANN: THE NEWS IS BROUGHT TO YOU BY _____(SPONSOR TAG)_____.
            WBSM NEWS TIME _____. NORM MCDONALD'S WEATHER FORECAST IS NEXT.
     (PLAY :30 WEATHERCAST)
     ANN: IT'S _____ DEGREES IN DOWNTOWN NEW BEDFORD. I'M _____,
            WBSM TOTAL INFORMATION NEWS. OUR NEXT NEWS AT _____ O'CLOCK.

NOTE: WHEN GIVING TIME, USE "DIGITAL" TIME.
        EXAMPLE: FIVE MINUTES PAST FIVE IS "FIVE-OH-FIVE."

Courtesy of WBSM, New Beford, Massachusetts

   Some local, independent stations use the wire services almost exclusively for
their news programs. Even when that is done, a format must be prepared containing
an opening, a closing, and transitional lead-ins for the specific organizational parts
of the newscast, including the commercials. Here is such a format:

FIVE MINUTE NEWS FORMAT — SUSTAINING

OPEN: Good (morning) (afternoon) (evening).
             The time is _____.
             In the news _____.
             (Note: use 4 stories ... mixing national, world and local by order of importance).*
ANNCR: More news in just a moment.
TAPE: COMMERCIAL (if logged)
ANNCR: In other news _____.
             (NOTE: use 2 stories ... national, world and/or local).
ANNCR: WGAY weather for the Washington area _____.
             (NOTE: use complete forecast, including temperature, humidity and winds).
CLOSE: That's news and weather ... I'm   (anncr. name)

*Total local news content: 3 stories in entire newscast.

Courtesy of WGAY, FM & AM, Washington and Silver Spring

Styles of Writing

The writer of the news broadcast is, first of all, a reporter whose primary duty is to convey the news. The traditional five Ws of news reporting must apply. In the condensed space of a few sentences, comparable to the lead paragraph of the newspaper story, the television or radio report must contain information as to What, Where, When, Who, and, if possible, Why. In addition, the television and radio newswriter must include as many of the details as possible within the limited time devoted to the story. The key word is *condensation*.

The writer must be aware of the organization of the broadcast in order to provide the proper transitions, which should be clear and smooth between each story. The writer should indicate to the audience the different divisions of the broadcast. For example, note the introduction: ''Now here is Mr. Murrow with his word for the day,'' in the earlier Edward R. Murrow format. Similar divisions might be: ''And now the local news,'' or ''Now, the feature story for the day,'' or ''Now, the editor's notebook.''

The writer must be aware of the content approach, whether it is straight news, analysis, or personal opinion, so as not to confuse editorializing with news. It is wise not to try to fool the audience, at least not too often, although some news commentators have been doing so for years. Distortion of stories or the presentation of only one side of the picture can change a news story into an opinion comment. Incomplete statements and the excessive use of color words can do the same thing. Avoid unnecessary sensationalism. Remember that the newscaster is coming into the home as a guest, and is generally accepted as a personal visitor. The approach should be informal, friendly, and — ideally — honest.

Inasmuch as the announcer tries to establish an informal and friendly relationship with the audience, avoid unnecessarily antagonizing or shocking stories, particularly at the very beginning of the broadcast. Consider the time of the day the broadcast is being presented — whether the audience is at the dinner table, seated comfortably in the living room, or rushing madly to get to work on time. The writer should think of the news as dramatic action. The story with an obvious conflict (the war, the political campaign, the divorce case, the baseball pennant race) attracts immediate attention. Because action is important, write the stories with verbs. The immediacy of television and radio, as opposed to the relatively greater time lapse between the occurrence and reporting of the incident in print journalism, permits the use of the present tense in stories about events that happened within a few hours preceding the newscast. The television and radio writer should be cautious in the use of questions as opposed to direct statements as the opening element of a story. Although the rhetorical question is an excellent attention-getting device in speech making, the nature of objective broadcasting makes its use in radio and television dubious. Rather than beginning with a question such as: "What will happen to nuclear disarmament negotiations . . . ?," it is more dramatic to say: "The question in all the capitals of the world tonight is: What will happen to nuclear disarmament negotiations?" Uninformed approaches to the news should be avoided. It is better to give whatever details are available without comment than to say: "This is an incomplete story, but. . . ."

The writer should begin the news story with precise, clear information. The opening sentence should be, if possible, a summary of the story as a whole. Be wary of including too many details. Remember that the audience hears the news only once and, unlike the newspaper reader, cannot go back to clarify particular points in the story. The audience must grasp the entire story the first time it hears it. The writing, therefore, must be simple and understandable and, without talking down to the audience, colloquial in form. This does not imply the use of slang or illiterate expressions, but suggests informality and understandability. Repetition must be avoided, and abstract expressions and words with double meanings should not be used. The information should be accurate and there should be no possibility of a misunderstanding of any news item. Make certain that the terminology used is correct. For example, don't refer to a figure in a story as a "car thief" if the person has not been convicted and is, in actuality, an "alleged car thief."

Keep in mind the essential differences between radio and television newswriting. Although both stem from the tradition of print journalism, each has modified the newspaper approach according to individual characteristics.

Radio newswriting is closer to newspaper reporting than is television newswriting. Where the television report can show the event happening, sometimes even with an on-the-spot reporter narrating the happening and including eyewitness accounts, the radio report may have to include more extensive written details, particularly verbal descriptions of scenes, people, and actions. Neither, however, unless providing coverage in depth in a fifteen- or thirty-minute broadcast, is as detailed or as lengthy as the newspaper report. The latter provides more space for analysis and for repetition of major points. Television and radio do not have such space or, more accurately, time. Probably the most difficult job for the writer of television or radio news is to select out of the sometimes myriad details of information the most salient points and present them in twenty or thirty seconds. Selection for television, as noted in the sports news script later in this chapter, frequently depends on the availability of visuals. Choose words as carefully as if you were conveying critical information in the limited space of a telegram or on a billboard.

Keep in mind your audience, your news announcer, and your station format. Is the station oriented toward straight news, seriously presented? Is it competing with another station for audience through emphasis on personalities rather than on format and content? Is the announcer for the particular time slot someone who is known for and who has been successful with a special style? Is the audience at that particular time in a hurry, or leisurely sitting in living room easy chairs? Combining all the variables will dictate your writing style. Generally, the newswriting style should be conversational. Sometimes you want to enable the announcer to talk to the audience as though he or she were sitting in their living room with them. Sometimes you want to present a father or mother figure who conveys an image of being totally trustworthy and unimpeachably authoritative. Many critics attribute Walter Cronkite's success to such an image.

Remember that good writing is good writing, whether in print or on the air. Words must flow and convey clear meaning. Don't be ambiguous. Be dramatic, but not melodramatic. For example, if a forest fire has destroyed one hundred acres of timber, don't say that "One million square feet of wood went up in smoke"; say that "Enough timber went up in smoke to build forty eight-room houses." Even if you don't have a visual, make it visual in the audience's imagination.

Keep in mind the AP study cited earlier; how does the reporting of each event affect the lives of your listeners and viewers? For example, without making political judgments, how would you report, in a way meaningful to the people in your community, the gathering of almost one million people in New York City on June 12, 1982, to call for a halt to nuclear development.

The writer must help the announcer to convey numbers accurately and to pronounce words correctly. The writer should not put long numbers in figures, but should write them out in words. It is sometimes helpful to place the numerical figures in parentheses. The writer should avoid using long, difficult words or tongue-twisters. After foreign words and difficult names the writer should place in parentheses a simplified sound spelling of the word. Both the AP and UPI wire services provide such guides. For example, note the following UPI guide to names in wire service stories during one day of the 1982 Israel-PLO conflict in Lebanon.

TODAY'S PRONUNCIATION GUIDE

-14-

ARAFAT, YASSER (YAH'-SEHR AHR-AH-FAHT'), P-L-O LEADER

BEGIN, MENACHEM (MEH-NAHK'-UHM BEH'-GIHN), ISRAELI PRIME MINISTER

BEKAA (BEH-KAH'), VALLEY IN CENTRAL LEBANON

CHAMOUN, CAMILLE (KAH-MEEL' SHAH-MOHN'), LEBANESE CHRISTIAN LEADER

EITAN, RAFAEL (RAH-FAH-EHL AH-TANN), LIEUTENANT GENERAL, ISRAELI ARMY CHIEF OF STAFF

GEMAYEL, BESHIR (BEH-SHEER' GEH-MAH-YEHL'), LEBANESE PHALANGIST OFFICER

HABIB (HAH-BEEB'), PHILIP, SPECIAL U-S MIDEAST ENVOY

SARKIS, ELIAS (EHL'-EE-AHS SAHR-KEES'), PRESIDENT OF LEBANON

SHAMIR, YITZHAK (YIHTS-HAHK SHAH-MEER), ISRAELI FOREIGN MINISTER

UPI 07-14-82 04:30 AED

United Press Broadcast Wire

Approach

Putting a news broadcast together involves many people. The writer is only one — but in a way the central — figure, tying together into a script everything that is to go over the air. The writer may be many people — producer, reporter, cameraperson, announcer, editor — contributing to a script. Or the writer may be one person doing one job or many different jobs — including writing the script.

"Manufacturing the News at Channel 6," a *Philadelphia Magazine* article by William K. Mandel, provides an insight into many factors that affect and result in a script for "Action News," the 6 P.M. news program of television station WPVI, Philadelphia.

Life at Action News starts early in the morning. By 8:30 A.M. film crews have come to the brightly lighted, compact newsroom on the fourth floor of the WPVI Building to pick up their morning's assignments. A photographer who shoots only silent film is already in the suburbs, getting film to use in that evening's "wrap," a segment of five-to-ten second news stories about events in outlying areas that would normally never make it to the air. . . .

[The news director, assignments editor, and executive producer] gather around a blackboard and chalk in the day's stories. Then they decide which reporters and camera crews will cover them. There's never a shortage of stories — most of them are either gleaned from the hundreds of press releases that flood the newsroom each day or are submitted by the staff of TV reporters. A few of them are assigned to beats (e.g. City Hall, police headquarters, education). By knowing what's scheduled in their area of expertise, they can advise where it might be advantageous to send a camera. . . .

. . . the biggest cross TV news has to bear is the charge of superficiality. With 31 stories in 16 minutes, how can anything be in depth? "TV news *is* strictly surface," admits news director Mel Kampmann. "We're the headline, the first paragraph. If you took all the words we used in a 30-minute show, you wouldn't fill more than half the front page of the *Bulletin*. But that copy is all of the topgoing news you'd need that day. Anyone who wants to know total background involvement of a news story should go to a newspaper or news magazine and get it. TV news does not have time to dwell." Anchorman Larry Kane knows the limitations of his medium. "It's just a basic summary. Our achievement is getting a fast-paced, well-mixed diet of the day's events into a fresh, interesting format." "You can't equate an in-depth story with time on the air," says executive producer Howard Glassroth in defense of TV. Visual impact is worth a lot of words. A 30-second film of a fistfight is just as good as a three-page description of it. Better. And a 90-second clip plus narration is often the distillation of several hours of reporting. Each reporter has to know how to use the tools of TV journalism — the camera and microphone — to slice a story crosswise properly and get a true segment of what's going on. . . .

. . . By 4 P.M. the early edition Action News starts taking shape. . . . By now, every reporter is back and filmed reports have been edited or are in the process of being edited. . . . "We have some very definite guidelines on what we put on the air, and how we do it," says Kampmann. "We always want to be able to *show* the viewer instead of *tell* him. If there's a story about the new airport tax, we'll show planes taking off at the airport rather than some guy talking at City Council. If the milk board has changed some prices, we'll show an interior shot of a supermarket. People can hear with their ears. They don't have to watch someone reading them the news. They should be able to see something while they're listening. If we don't have film, our artist works up an illustration to superimpose. . . ."

"In addition to straight news, a TV news program must also include sports and weather," Kampmann explains. . . . "people don't want to hear about cold fronts and occluded fronts. Nobody knows what they are, anyway. . . . Weather reporter Jim O'Brien will be telling people how to dress their kids for school tomorrow, whether to carry an umbrella, and what to wear if they are going out at night. It will be a service told in a way that people use the weather."

[Anchorman Kane, following the show,] likes to be back at his desk by 7:30, to start updating and rewriting the 6 P.M. show for the 11 o'clock offering. The shows usually have a different lead story and sound.

Although specific orientations and logistic approaches differ, the basic cohesion of many elements from many sources into a final script is the same at all stations. The person responsible for the script, whether designated a writer at a network or performing the duties of an announcer and/or producer and/or editor and/or writer at a medium-sized or small station, must consider all of the policy, personality, and procedural aspects, as in the process followed for "Action News."

Types of Broadcasts
The most common type of television and radio news broadcast is the straight news presentation, on radio usually in five- or fifteen-minute segments and on television usually in fifteen-minute and half-hour periods. There are also commentator personalities who present news analysis and/or personal opinions on the news. Sometimes these are included in the straight news show. In recent years news analysis in depth, stressing feature stories and dramatic aspects of the news, has become more common. Networks and stations frequently have specials that probe the news. Many of these programs utilize serious research and present their findings in documentary or semidocumentary form. Although usually under the direction of the news department, the documentary and feature are covered here in a separate chapter. Other news-show types, such as the panel discussion and the interview, are also covered in a separate chapter on talk programs.

In addition to the general news program, there may be straight news shows devoted to specific topics, such as the international scene, financial reports, garden news, consumer affairs, educational or campus news, and so forth. The approaches within these categories may vary, of course, such as stressing the public service aspect or the human interest elements.

Most news programs are a combination of the live announcer or announcers, film and tape for television and audiotape for radio of the recorded events, other visuals for television, and in some cases where a story is breaking at that moment, live remotes. There can be, as well, multiple pickups from various studios, involving reporters closer to the scenes of the events. Networks frequently present news roundups from various parts of the country and, on radio and through satellite on television, from various parts of the world. There are also frequent — though, perhaps, not frequent enough — on-the-spot news broadcasts that show or narrate the event actually taking place. The live remote is one of the most important contributions television can make and deserves fuller utilization.

Organization of the News Program

There are specific kinds of news programs, as previously indicated, including those emphasizing a special topic or a special approach. In the straight news program the writer should look for a clear and logical organization, no matter what the topic or approach. One such organization is for the placement of stories to follow a topical order, that is, the grouping of similar stories into sections, although the order of the sections themselves may be an arbitrary one. A geographical grouping and order is another organizational form. For example, the news coverage may move from North America to Europe to Asia to South America to Africa to the rest of the world. Another frequently used grouping organizes the material into international, national, and local news categories. The order of presentation often moves, within these categories, from the largest (international) to the smallest (local). Probably the most common approach is to place the most important story first in order to get and hold the audience's attention, much as does the lead story in the newspaper.

The organization is determined, in part, by the audience being reached. The early morning newscast on television is for people getting ready for work and on radio is for **drive-time** commuters. In the midmorning newscast stories frequently are chosen and placed to appeal primarily to women, the bulk of the listening group at that time. In the early evening the organization usually is one that will reach most effectively the listener or viewer who has just returned from work. The news broadcast just before prime time on television frequently seeks to reach a family group watching together. The time of day is also important in relation to what the audience already knows of the news. In the early morning newscast it is desirable to review the previous day's important late stories. In the late evening broadcasts the current day's news should be reviewed and the audience should be prepared for the next day's possible happenings.

The physical format of the news show may vary. It may begin with an announcer giving the headlines, then a commercial, and then the commentator coming in with the details. It may start with the commentator beginning directly with the news. It may be a roundup of different reporters in different geographical areas.

───────────────────○───────────────────

● *In the following pages, purposely presented in haphazard order, is a UPI news report.*
(1) How would you rearrange this material to develop a news broadcast oriented around a clear, effective organization? Organize the newscast along geographical lines; organize it according to international, national, and local news; organize it along topical lines, grouping similar types of stories; organize it according to the importance of the stories.
(2) After you have practiced organizing the material, analyze the writing itself to determine whether: the five Ws are clearly included; the principle

of conflict is utilized; clarity, simplicity, and the direct statement are evident; informality is present.
(3) What kind of news broadcast is this? Straight news? Commentary? Documentary? Rewrite this news broadcast into at least one form other than its present orientation.

———————————————————————————○———————————————————————————

THE PRESIDENT WAS HANDED A SETBACK ON THE HILL TODAY WHEN THE HOUSE VOTED 324-86 TO OVERRIDE HIS VETO OF A COPYRIGHT BILL. IT WAS THE FIRST SUCCESSFUL OVERRIDE VOTE IN EITHER THE HOUSE OR SENATE OF ANY OF REAGAN'S SEVEN VETOES.

ADMINISTRATION OFFICIALS FEAR THAT IRAN MAY BE PREPARING TO TAKE THE 22-MONTH PERSIAN GULF WAR TO IRAQI TERRITORY WITH AN INVASION BID TO TOPPLE THE REGIME OF PRESIDENT SADDAM HUSSEIN (SAH-DAHM HOO-SAYN').

THE U-S EMBASSY IN SAN SALVADOR SAYS A BADLY DECOMPOSED BODY FOUND NEAR THE CITY COULD BE THE CORPSE OF MISSING AMERICAN JOURNALIST JOHN SULLIVAN. OFFICIALS SAY THE BODY MAY BE HARD TO IDENTIFY POSITIVELY.

A MICHIGAN MAN ALREADY IN CUSTODY FOR SHOOTING HIS MOTHER WILL FACE ADDITIONAL CHARGES FOR THE SLAYINGS OF FIVE MEMBERS OF AN ALLENDALE FAMILY. THE FAMILY WAS FOUND SHOT TO DEATH IN THEIR RURAL HOME FOUR MONTHS AGO.

(MILWAUKEE)--A MILWAUKEE ATTORNEY SAYS HE WILL ISSUE AN ATTEMPTED MURDER WARRANT TODAY FOR FUGITIVE PATRICK JOHN O'SHEA IN THE WOUNDING OF A WISCONSIN POLICE OFFICER. O'SHEA ... ALREADY CONVICTED IN THE DEATH OF A MASSACHUSETTS POLICE SERGEANT ... WAS BEING SOUGHT IN THE SHOOTING OF SERGEANT LEWIS TYLER OF SUBURBAN BROOKFIELD WHO WAS IN CRITICAL CONDITION WITH A HEAD WOUND. HE WAS WOUNDED DURING A HIGH SPEED CHASE FRIDAY NIGHT.

THE STATE DEPARTMENT CREDITS SYRIAN SECURITY FORCES FOR TURNING BACK A CROWD OF ANTI-AMERICAN PROTESTORS WHO STORMED THE U-S EMBASSY IN DAMASCUS TODAY ... CALLING FOR AN ARAB BOYCOTT OF AMERICAN GOODS.

THE SYRIAN CROWD ALSO CALLED FOR THE OUSTER OF U-S ENVOY PHILIP HABIB FROM THE LEBANON PEACE TALKS. HE PARTICIPATED IN ANOTHER ROUND OF TALKS TODAY IN BEIRUT. THE LATEST CEASE-FIRE APPEARED TO BE HOLDING IN BEIRUT FOR A THIRD NIGHT.

WESTERN NEGOTIATORS SAY AN AGREEMENT HAS BEEN REACHED ON A SET OF GOVERNING PRINCIPLES FOR NAMIBIA. THE PRINCIPLES INCLUDE GUIDELINES FOR FREE ELECTIONS IN THE TERRITORY NOW RULED BY SOUTH AFRICA.

THE HOUSE ENERGY AND COMMERCE COMMITTEE HAS OVERWHELMINGLY
APPROVED AN ADMINISTRATION PLAN TO COUNTER CUBAN PROPAGANDA BROADCASTS.
UNDER THE PLAN, A SPANISH-LANGUAGE RADIO STATION WOULD BE SET UP IN FLORIDA.

(BOSTON)--GOVERNOR EDWARD KING HAS SIGNED INTO LAW A BILL ESTABLISHING
THE MASSACHUSETTS TECHNOLOGY PARK CORPORATION. THE STATUTE MANDATES THE
CREATION OF A 19-MEMBER CORPORATION TO SELECT A SITE FOR THE MASSACHUSETTS
MICROELECTRONICS CENTER AS ITS FIRST PROJECT. UP TO 20-MILLION-DOLLARS WILL BE
PROVIDED BY STATE FUNDS THROUGH A BOND ISSUE FOR THE CONSTRUCTION OF THE
FACILITY. EIGHTEEN SEMICONDUCTOR COMPANIES AND EIGHT ENGINEERING SCHOOLS
WILL BE UTILIZING THE CENTER.

THE COMMERCE DEPARTMENT SAYS RETAIL SALES FELL ONE-AND-ONE-HALF PERCENT
IN JUNE ... AFTER TWO MONTHS OF INCREASES. AN ALMOST SEVEN PERCENT DROP
IN AUTOMOBILE SALES IS BEING BLAMED AS A MAJOR FACTOR IN THE DECLINE.

LABOR DEPARTMENT FIGURES SHOW FLINT, MICHIGAN, MAINTAINED ITS STANDING AS
HAVING THE HIGHEST UNEMPLOYMENT RATE OF THE NATION'S METROPOLITAN AREAS.
STAMFORD, CONNECTICUT, HAD THE LOWEST UNEMPLOYMENT RATE.

PRESIDENT REAGAN TOLD A NATIONAL CONVENTION OF COUNTY WORKERS IN BALTI-
MORE TODAY THAT HIS NEW FEDERALISM PROGRAM TO BREAK UP THE WASHINGTON
BUREAUCRACY WILL BE SENT TO CAPITOL HILL BY THE END OF THIS MONTH.

NEW MEXICO HEALTH OFFICIALS SAY THE PLAGUE THAT KILLED AN 11-YEAR-OLD BOY
WAS NOT CONTAGIOUS. OFFICIALS SAY THE PLAGUE WAS THE BUBONIC FORM ... NOT THE
PNEUMONIC FORM THAT CAN BE TRANSMITTED FROM PERSON TO PERSON.

UPI 07-13-82 09:55 PED

Another organizational approach frequently used is to concentrate on one major
news story, with the orientation of all other news around that story. As an illustration, here is one of the most significant news stories of recent decades.

Here is today's news:
President Ford said at a news conference today that he pardoned former President Nixon
because of his concern for Mr. Nixon's health and because he felt that attention to Watergate
was distracting the country from more important needs.

[The announcer then went on to give the background of the news conference and the
major emphasis of the questions.]

President Ford stated that there was absolutely no deal made between him and Mr. Nixon
for a pardon as a part of Mr. Nixon's decision to resign.
The first question put to Mr. Ford was:

[The taped excerpt, audio for radio, video for television, was inserted here, with similar introductory material and appropriate tape inserts following.]

Following the report on the news conference, which dealt almost entirely with President Ford's pardon of former President Nixon, the program reported on congressional attitudes and action concerning the appropriation of funds for a staff and other transitional services for Mr. Nixon, dealt with some congressional charges concerning White House briefings being flown to Mr. Nixon in California, the latest developments in the Watergate trials, and news and commentary on the relationship of President Ford's pardon for Mr. Nixon to pardon or amnesty for those who refused to fight in Vietnam.

On this particular news day, the most important continuing stories happened to be interrelated and happened to deal with national affairs. Following this coverage, the news broadcast went into the other news of the day, including international events.

Rewriting

One of the newswriter's duties, particularly on the local level, is *re*writing. A smaller station without a news-gathering staff is sometimes almost totally dependent on the newswire. The announcer, given sufficient time and energy, edits those stories that can appropriately be adapted to include a local angle, evaluating their impact on the community. In effect, the announcer *re*writes the news. As noted earlier, news broadcasts are organized into homogenous groupings. Finding a unifying thread that means something special to the listener in that community frequently requires rewriting. For example, segments in a topical grouping of stories dealing with the economy might be rewritten to reflect their relationship to the local unemployment figures.

Perhaps the most common form of rewriting is updating. An important story doesn't disappear after it is used once. Yet, to use exactly the same story in subsequent newscasts throughout the day is likely to turn away those listeners who hear it more than once and conclude that the station is carrying stale news. Updating is an important function of the network newswriter. There are several major areas to look for in updating news stories. First, the writer determines if there is any further hard news, factual information to add to the story. Second, if the story is important enough it is likely that investigative reporting will have dug up some additional background information not available when the story was first broadcast. Third, depending on the happening's impact on society, it will have been commented upon after its initial release by any number of people from VIPs to ordinary citizens. In addition, a story may by its very nature relate to other events of the day.

Note the final paragraph in the material earlier in this chapter on WPVI's "Action News." Television stations with their own news staffs try to rewrite the news from one newscast to the next, not only updating it, but also reorienting it toward a different audience. How many times have you been disappointed or even angry when the 11 P.M. news coverage was virtually the same as the 6 P.M. newscast, especially when there was an important happening about which you were eagerly awaiting further information?

Remotes

One of the most exciting aspects of media news writing and reporting — and viewing and listening — is the remote. On both radio and television the remote brings the audience directly to the scene of the event, as it is happening, live. Some remotes are reports following the event, equivalent to the reporter phoning in the story to the newspaper the moment after it has happened. The remote usually is handled by someone who is a combination writer-reporter, because the material must be gathered, written, and reported on by the same person. Louis Alexander of Houston, Texas, is a writer who is a reporter, handling remotes for networks and stations throughout the country. He is also a professor of journalism who teaches that news reporting is a partnership between reporter and editor, one knowing best what has happened and the other knowing best how and what to fit into the overall picture. Alexander describes the duties and procedures of handling the remote broadcast from his vantage point as a writer as well as a reporter. Although his description specifically relates to a radio remote, the basic concepts as they apply to the writer are equally true for television.

Remote feeds enable the radio reporter to beat the other media with the news. The sound of the voice coming over the phone, broadcast by the station, adds to the listeners' excitement by reminding them that they are hearing it from the very scene of the action — political convention, freeway accident, sports arena or close by the launching pad. Some experienced reporters arrange a continuous feed, live, during the event. Most remote feeds, however, must fit into scheduled newscasts. Most stations can connect a studio recorder to the incoming telephone line and record it directly; and some stations have special high-fidelity telephone lines that preserve most of the voice quality.

A remote feed from the scene of action — live — is a continuous report of what is going on. You need a good knowledge of events and the people involved in them, and quick articulation and recognition of what's going on. For a pre-planned event, several days in advance, or longer, order a telephone line from the phone company in that local area. For an extra charge you may have them install a line with higher voice quality. Make arrangements in advance with local authorities or their public relations representative for a spot with good visibility and good access to whatever information services will be provided locally.

First the reporter gathers information and records statements by the participants or observers, then reads the notes and decides what is most important to pass on to the . . . audience. This enables the reporter, while listening to the actualities, to decide which statements are the most significant as well as good technical quality. . . . For the preplanned event, do your homework: gather background information, write a few short pieces to fill in during quiet, inactive moments, and learn to identify as many as possible of the main personages by their faces and their voices. Arrange with your news director the schedule of times to be on the air and the cues that switch the broadcast between studio and remote site. Come on the air before the main action starts and set the stage for the listener: provide the background needed to understand and appreciate what is about to happen. Then provide continuing word pictures of events, conditions, attitudes. Be sure to switch to the studio, or to a colleague, on cue; also switch whenever you are on the verge of running out of worthwhile things to report. Before you sign off from the remote site, be sure to acknowledge local assistants and summarize what has happened, unless the studio newscaster plans to do that.

The process for the remote feed which is not live is slightly different. The reporter writes the story, holding it to whatever length is desirable or required — 40 seconds, one minute, two minutes or more. If the story includes an actuality, the reporter writes an intro, times the actuality to fit into the overall time allotted for the story, and inserts a transition phrase after the outcue, to pick up the thread of the text. The reporter then cues the tape to the beginning of the actuality.

Feeding the story over the telephone is technically easy. It is simplest when the reporter is feeding without an actuality: telephone the station's news room, advise you are ready to feed, wait for the studio personnel to connect a recorder onto the receiving line, count "3-2-1" to allow time for the recording to roll, read the story to the end, with a sign-off that indicates you are on the scene: "This is John Smith, at the Johnson Space Center in Houston." The ordinary telephone transmits most levels of the human voice with good quality, and many stations have at least one telephone line which the phone company has upgraded to high-fidelity reproduction. The recorded story comes onto the tape in the studio with good sound quality — with just enough of a "remote tone" to remind the listener that the voice is coming from the scene of the action.

When the reporter is feeding an actuality the process has additional technical requirements: a tape recorder which has the appropriate circuitry — a few of the better quality models have it; and a line that plugs into the recorder's output and has two alligator clips on the other end. The reporter unscrews the telephone mouthpiece and removes it (although some telephone company regulations forbid this, the practice is nevertheless generally accepted) and connects the alligator clips to the two terminals within the telephone mouthpiece. The reporter connects the microphone to the tape recorder, providing a circuit that can feed into the telephone, alternately, the recording or the reporter's voice. The reporter speaks through the microphone and listens through the telephone receiver. With the actuality cued on the tape recorder, the reporter feeds the story through the microphone, switches on the actuality at the proper point, and switches back to the microphone for the ending.

Some reporters like to record the entire story, even when there is no actuality included. Then they feed it from the recorded version to the radio station. This has the advantage of enabling the reporter to send the best version the first time, eliminating fluffs and repeats, and may also hold down the telephone charge for long distance time.

The following is a script prepared and used by Alexander for the kind of remote described above, covering a sports event that, as later years proved, changed the entire structure of professional tennis and, for women, affected other sports as well.

National Public Radio
Friday, Sept. 21 (1973)
TENNIS

The largest crowd ever to watch a tennis match saw Billie Jean King upset Bobby Riggs last night in three straight sets.

The exhibition was a $100,000 — winner take all — answer to the question, "Can a good woman player beat a good man player?"

King, at 29, is the world's number one woman player. Riggs at 55 has won 40 national and world championships.

King won by outplaying Riggs — catching him out of position with passing shots and cross-court shots — never letting Riggs set up the lobs and trick shots for which he is famous. The scores were 6-4, 6-3, 6-3.

Riggs said afterwards that King played well within her game, but he couldn't get his own game started. "She made better shots off my best shots," Riggs said.

In the Astrodome the crowd of 30,000 mostly expected Riggs to win — yet they cheered more loudly for King. An estimated 40 million people watched over television throughout the United States and 35 other countries.

Today King is back in the Viriginia Slims women's tournament in Houston. She has a third round match to play, and she said she has to fight against a letdown after last night.

For National Public Radio, this is Louis Alexander in Houston.

Some Television Considerations

The types, styles, organization, and approaches are essentially the same for the television and the radio news broadcast. The combinations of studio, recorded, and live remote materials apply to both media. The most important difference is the obvious one: television is visual. The reporter, feeding a remote or in the studio, must have a visual personality. In the past several decades the television news personalities — such as Murrow, Huntley and Brinkley, Cronkite, Walters, Rather — have become the stars of television. (This was true of radio as well, when it was *the* medium for broadcast news, with its Gabriel Heatter, Lowell Thomas, Fulton Lewis, Jr., Elmer Davis, and H. V. Kaltenborn.) The physical setting should be interesting and attractive, consistent with the concept of informational and exciting news. Even the presentation of content that in itself may be undramatic should be visually stimulating. For example, watch the techniques and gimmicks introduced by weather reporters in the nightly weather segment of the news program. Television news should stress the visual and may use videotape, film, tape, slides, photographs, inanimate objects, and, where necessary for emphasis or exploration in depth, even guests in the studio. Except for relatively extensive use of an anchorperson to keep together the physical continuity of the program or, through that person's special personality, to instill confidence or, as a star, to motivate viewing by the audience, the television news program should *show* the news, not *tell* about it. We have all seen television news programs where a reporter merely read the news to us and we felt that we might as well have heard it on radio and not taken time to sit down in a living room to watch. Even when insufficient time or great distance or geography makes it impossible to show a film or tape of the event or carry it as a live remote, a blow-up photo or a slide of the scene or of the persons involved may be used as a background to the reporter's narration.

Writing the script that appears over the air is only the final stage of a long, arduous, and frequently complicated process. Planning and development begin early in the day, even for a program such as ''CBS Evening News with Dan Rather,'' which may not go on until the evening. Many preliminary materials precede the finalization of an actual script: (1) CBS Program Log is distributed on the morning of the show, showing all the film pieces used on the morning news, midday news, evening news, and even on the other network news programs from the previous day. (2) Written about 6 or 7 A.M. and distributed around 8:30 A.M. is a "CBS News Insights" sheet, with logs, which shows who is assigned to what coverage, what the planned assignments are for the day, and with a domestic and foreign "Who's Where" so that any member of the staff is reachable at all times. (3) About 11 A.M. a "Who Does What" rundown is distributed, showing which associate producers and which reporters are doing what and where. (4) About 11:15 A.M. a "Morning Line" is issued, with more information on the big stories and who is assigned to them. (5) About 12:30 or 1 P.M. a "Prelineup" is completed, providing a list of the stories expected to be used on the program. (6) About 3:30 P.M. or shortly thereafter the technical "Lineup" comes out, listing the stories that will be on, their sequence and times. (7) About 5 P.M. there is an "Editorial Lineup" with more exact information on where each story is. (8) Up until show time there are "Lineup Revisions," incorporating any changes warranted following the time the first lineup was prepared. (9) The rundown sheet and the final script itself are prepared.

The following are selected examples of this material, to give you an indication of some of the preparation that goes into the final product. Here, all pertaining to the same broadcast, are the (1) prelineup, (2) technical lineup, (3) rundown, and (4) first part of the final script. These are facsimiles of the sheets actually used for the program, including the pencil and ink changes made by the producer, director, and talent. Note the changes in the position of stories from the prelineup to lineup to rundown to script.

PRELINEUP — THE CBS EVENING NEWS WITH DAN RATHER — MONDAY, JULY 19, 1982

1. IRAQ/LARRY PINTAK	BAGHDAD-LONDON
2. CLUSTER BOMBS/BILL PLANTE	WASHINGTON, SHREVEPORT & MEMPHIS
3. BALANCED BUDGET/LESLEY STAHL	WASHINGTON
4. HEAT WAVE/BERNARD GOLDBERG	NEW YORK, BOSTON & PHILADELPHIA
5. MIDWEST WEATHER/DERRICK BLAKLEY	DES MOINES, OMAHA & CHICAGO
6. COMA/STEVE YOUNG	NEW YORK

POSSIBLES:

1. FUNDING/FRANK CURRIER	CHICAGO
2. PRISONER RELEASE/BOB FAW	TEL AVIV
3. DEER HUNT/CHARLES KRAUSE	MIAMI
4. CHILDREN OF WAR/RICHARD ROTH	DAMASCUS
5. FOREIGN MINISTERS/BOB SIMON	WASHINGTON
6. WEST BEIRUT/ALLEN PIZZEY	DAMASCUS
7. WHALING/MARTHA TEICHNER	LONDON
8. NIMMO/ERIC ENGBERG	WASHINGTON
9. CHINA CRIMINALS/BRUCE DUNNING	NEW YORK
10. LAW/FRED GRAHAM	WASHINGTON

TELOPS:

1.	VIKING SHIP	LONDON
2.	PALACE SECURITY	LONDON
3.	IRAN FIGHTING	NEW YORK
4.	CRASH FUNERAL	CHARLOTTE
5.	ASBESTOS LEAK	RICHMOND

LINEUP — THE CBS EVENING NEWS WITH DAN RATHER — MONDAY, JULY 19, 1982

1. OPEN   LIVE

2. Rather   Live

3. CLUSTER BOMBS/BILL PLANTE   WASH 2:00

4. Rather   Live
   LTP: Iran Fighting   VTR/   NY

5. IRAQ/LARRY PINTAK   VTR/   1:30   Baghdad

6. Rather   Live
   BUMPER: Goldberg–Blakley   VTR/
7. 1stCMCL (Shell/Termnex)   VTR/20 1:10

8. Rather   Live

9. HEAT/BERNARD GOLDBERG   VTR/   1:45   NY

10. Rather   Live

11. WATER/DERRICK BLAKLEY   VTR/   :55   Chi
    Deer Hunt/KRAUSE   1:10   Miami
12. Rather   Live
    BUMPER: Stox   VTR/

13. 2ndCMCL (Budwsr/A-1Sauce)   VTR/20 1:10

14. Rather   Live

15. BALANCED BUDGET/LESLEY STAHL   WASH 1:45

16. Rather   Live

17. FUNDING/FRANK CURRIER   VTR/   1:45   Chi

18. Rather   Live
    BUMPER: Young   VTR/

19. 3rd CMCL <u>(Conoco/AllSt)</u>   VTR/**20**1:10

20. Rather   Live
     LTP: Funeral   VTR/   Charlotte

21. COMA/STEVE YOUNG   VTR/   3:00   NY

22. Rather   Live
     BUMPER: Roth   VTR/
23. 4thCMCL (FreeNSoft/Midas/FlaOJ) VTR/**20**1:30

24. Rather   Live

~~25. El SALVADOR/BILL MOYERS~~   ~~LIVE 1:45~~   ~~NY~~

26. Rather   Live
     LTP: Palace Security   VTR/   Lon
27. (CHILDREN OF WAR/RICHARD ROTH) VTR/ 1:45   Damascus

28. Rather Goodnight   Live

29. 5thCMCL (Pepsodent/Fle&TckCllr) VTR/**20**1:05

30. CTN: Universe   VT/

<u>RUNDOWN</u>

CBS TELEVISION NETWORK

CBS EVENING NEWS WITH DAN RATHER

Monday, July 19, 1982
6:30-7:00 PM, EDT
7:00-7:30 PM, EDT (Update)   Pages

			Pages
Beirut Kidnap	1 Rather	–Pres of American U in Beirut kidnapped	1
Iran-Iraq War	2 Rather/ PINTAK	–War now swinging in Iraq's favor, but it needs help from other Arab countries	2
Scolding Israel	3 Rather/ PLANTE	–U.S. holds up arms shipment because of Israel's use of cluster bombs in Beirut; <u>Sec of State Schultz</u> meets with <u>Saudi and Syrian foreign ministers</u>	3
Promo	(Graphic)	–Next: Hostile Elements	3

———————————— ANNOUNCEMENTS ————————————

Hostile Weather	4 Rather/ GOLDBERG/	–Northeast heat makes life unbearable for man and beast; 4 <u>Men;</u>	4

	BLAKLEY	–But Midwest rains make life all wet for man and crops: millions in crop damage	5
FL Deer Kill	4Rather/ KRAUSE	–Deer kill is now useless because of delays caused by conservationists; Lt. James Farrier (FL Fish and Game Comm); Cleveland Armory (Fund for Animals)	6
Insanity Defense	4Rather	–Atty Gen endorses insanity defense crackdown	7
Stock Market	(Graphic)	–DJI down 2.57 to 826.10	7

──────── ANNOUNCEMENTS ────────

Emergency Bill	5Rather	–Reagan signs emergency bailout for fed agencies	8
Budget Rally	4Rather/ STAHL	–Cabinet & 130 congressmen turn at rally for balanced budget amendment as do non-supporters; Pres Reagan; Rep Jim Wright (Maj Ldr); Sen Alan Cranston (D-CA); Rep Claude Pepper (D-FL); VP Bush	8-9
Hi Poverty Level	Rather	–31.8-mil people living below the poverty level	10
Unemploy Problms	4Rather/ CURRIER	–States having difficulties paying federal loans to pay unemployment benefits; Man; Woman; Agaliece Miller (Illinois Dept of Labor)	10-11
House Buys Down	Rather	–Housing starts down Americans cannot afford	12
2 Rates Dropped	Rather	–Fed reducing discount rate charges member bks for loans, prime lending down ½%	12
Chrysler Quarter Promo	Rather/ (Graphic)	–Chrysler has successful second quarter ; –Next: Back from the Brink	12 12

──────── ANNOUNCEMENTS ────────

State Appointee	Rather	–Kenneth Dam, Dep Sec of St; D Fischer to leave	12
Crash Victim ..Funeral	Rather/LTP	–Funeral for Jacobs' attended by daughter, Sonya once the only woman on death row	12
Coma Survival	Rather/ YOUNG	–Emergency medicine now able to save 50% more coma victims; Richard Friswell (Head Injury Fndtn) Edward & Marge Garvey; Maurice Chappy Garvey	13-14

| Promo | (Graphic) | —Next: Children of War | 14 |

⸺ ANNOUNCEMENTS ⸺

Buckingham .."Scandal"	Rather/LTP	—<u>Michael Trestrial</u> protector of Roy Fam resigns; Intruder appears in ct today; <u>Queen E II, Prince Phil</u>	15
Palestinian ... Children	Rather/ ROTH	—Israel releases 200 Palestinian chil- dren today many living in refugee camps	16
Sign Off	Rather	—Good night	16

⸺ ANNOUNCEMENTS ⸺

1 Repositioned to follow PLANTE in 7:00 East/ 2 Repositioned to follow Beirut kidnap tell in 7:00 East/ 3 Repositioned to top and updated in 7:00 East/ 4 Updated in 7:00 East/ 5 Added in 7:00 East

1 RATHER	Good evening: This is the CBS Evening News, Dan Rather reporting.
2 RATHER	President Reagan signalled Israel loud and clear today ... that the American public is displeased with Israel's use of certain U.S.-supplied weapons of war. Bill Plante reports:
3 PLANTE	(TRACK UP)
PLANTE/OC	President Reagan decided this morning to hold up a shipment of artillery shells much like the controversial cluster bombs ... while the administration reviews the Israeli explanation.
VO/TEXAS PIX GRAPHIC BEGINS	4,000 of the 155 MM shells, which are assembled at this Texas munitions plant were scheduled to be shipped to Israel today or tomorrow. They function in much the same fashion as the air dropped cluster bomb which the U.S. no longer produces but which the Israelis have stockpiled and is the type they are believed to have used in Beirut.
VO:	The cluster bomb opens in mid air to release some 650 miniature bombs about the size of golf balls, which rotate to earth and explode on impact. The weapon is intended for use against such vehicles as trucks and radar vans. Israel has admitted using the cluster bombs, according to White House sources, but claimed that in so doing they abided by the secret conditions in their agreement with the U.S.--and that in any case, they use them only against military targets. The Israeli letter conceded that many of its military targets were in the midst of populated areas, but argued that civilian casualties were not intentional. White House sources said the administration was not satisfied with the Israeli explanation, which it received only after repeated requests. That is why Mr. Reagan and his senior staff ordered the review and the hold on the new shipment. Officials here agree privately that whether this temporary sanction amounts to anything more than a slap on the wrist for Israel now depends entirely on the outcome of the peace negotiations. The Syrian and the Saudi foreign ministers, who met today with Secretary of State George Schultz, will confer tomorrow with President Reagan about how to achieve peace in Lebanon. But the Syrian made it plain again today that his nation is unwilling to even talk about taking in the remnants of the PLO. Bill Plante, CBS News

<u>3</u> RATHER	In Lebanon, the Beirut ceasefire is into its second week. All sides seemed to be practicing restraint . . . on the eve of tomorrow's White House talks.
	Within the general calm, there was at least one notable act of violence.
	The acting president of the American University of Beirut . . . David Dodge . . . was kidnaped by gunmen on the West Beirut campus.
	The gunmen have not been identified, and have not been heard from.
<u>4</u> RATHER	The war between Iraq and Iran seems to be going Iraq's way . . . at least for now. Iraqi jets hit two cities inside Iran . . . <u>Khorrambad</u> and <u>Ilam</u> . . . and Iran reports many civilian casualties.
	But some experts expect an Iranian counter-attack.
	Westerners are being advised to leave the Iraqi port city of <u>Basra</u> . . . an Iranian objective.

——— o ———

	In Baghdad, Larry Pintak has more on the war . . . from Iraq's point of view:
<u>5</u> PINTAK	(TRACK UP)
PINTAK:	We hold our gun with one hand . . . the Iraqis are fond of saying . . . with the other we build. Building their army for war and building their country into a modern state. The people say they remain ready to fight, but lately the talk has been of the desire for peace. News from the front still dominates the media, with the government claiming new Iraqi gains almost every day.
	Countless numbers have perished in the past six days as Iraq's army has fought to defend its soil against the Iranians. The battlefields are littered with corpses . . . Baghdad says the Iranian death toll has reached ten thousand. But it claims its own losses have been light. Scores more have been maimed.
	Iraq repulsed Iran's initial drive but the fighting continues. Desperate scrambles for water by the Iranian POWs tells the story . . . temperatures reaching 150 degrees and searing winds. To silence the guns Baghdad wants the help of its fellow Arabs.
PINTAK O/C:	This could lead to a dramatic realignment in the Middle East balance of power. Diplomatic sources say Iraq has called for a gathering of Arab moderates to discuss a way to end the war. A summit in Baghdad where Egypt would be welcomed after four years as an outcast, and radical Syria, Libya and South Yemen would be barred.
	Larry Pintak, CBS News, Baghdad
<u>8</u> RATHER	Somewhere in the United States, this was a pleasant day. But not in the Midwest, where hurricane-force winds and buckets of rain ruined millions of dollars in crops. And not in the northeast, where temperatures rose even faster than tempers. How hot was it? Bernard Goldberg tells you:
<u>9</u> GOLDBERG	TRACK
	It's hot, it's muggy, it's hazy . . . and it's turned the Big Apple into a baked apple.
NY TOURIST	The kids are used to the heat and so am I.
BG	Where are you from?
TOURIST	Arizona.
BG	Today was another scorcher — the fourth day in a row that temperatures hovered around 100 degrees.
SOT NYER	It's tough, cause a guy like me, walking around, it sure gets ya.
BG	And it was tough for the horses that pull carriages and tourists around the city. Two of them dropped dead yesterday, victims of heat exhaustion. A third keeled over — too hot, too tired to get up. So today, the city pulled all the horse-drawn carriages off the street and said they'd stay off until the temperature dropped to below 90.

And the rest of the northeast was sweltering too. In Boston — 98 degrees, a record — it dawned on a lot of people today. Literally. It was so hot, they slept on the beach. In Portland, Maine — 94 degrees, another record — the water slide ride at the Aqua-Bagen Park was the hottest ticket in town. And they haven't sweated this much on Capitol Hill since the last election.

In Jersey City, New Jersey — 98 degrees — where they've had no drinking water since a main broke last Thursday ... they were doling fresh water out from tanks in front of City Hall.

(SOT GUY WITHOUT SHIRT:	Without water, it's pretty rough, man)
BG	Today, the water was running again, but still had to be boiled before drinking.
SOT GUY WITHOUT SHIRT TAKES WATER AND POURS IT ON HIS HEAD AND SAYS:	Good, feels good.
VO: PEOPLE AT FOUNTAIN, BABY ASLEEP	For some people the best way to beat the heat was to be out ... out cold.
	BG CBS News NY

Courtesy of CBS News

News Special Events

The dramatic nature of media-covered special events in the United States in the past twenty years, such as moon landings, Vietnam protest marches, Watergate hearings and impeachment proceedings, Abscam hearings, and antinuclear rallies, stimulated interest in this aspect of broadcasting as never before, and enhanced the image and role of broadcasting as a whole.

The special event is usually under the direction of the news department and is essentially something that is taking place live and is of interest — critical or passing — to the community. It is usually a remote, on-the-spot broadcast. Special events usually originate independently and include such happenings as parades, dedications, banquets, awards, and the openings of new films and supermarkets. Political conventions and astronaut launchings are, perhaps, more significant kinds of special events. Some special events allow no time for preparation; others are planned sufficiently in advance to permit preparation in depth by the writer and producer.

Sometimes special events are merely introduced, presented without comment, and — occasionally — summarized or critiqued when over. Sometimes they are narrated on radio and are accompanied by commentary on television. The opening and closing material and, frequently, transition and filler material are provided by the writer. The latter two are sometimes handled directly by the broadcaster who is assigned to the event and who presumably is an expert on the subject being covered.

Most special events are more effective on television than on radio. If the event is for presentation within a regular news program, it is frequently prerecorded (see the section on remotes earlier in this chapter). The picture captures the action and the commentary provides background and clarifying information. Films or tapes of special events usually are edited and sometimes carefully prepared beforehand in terms of format, transitions, introductions, and additional material to be recorded. Sometimes they are so fully prepared that they take on the characteristics of the special feature rather than the special event. There is often only a fine line between the special event and the feature and any given program might be either one or a combination of the two. The feature and its ultimate refinement, the documentary, are discussed in the next chapter. Suffice to note now, in terms of difference between the two forms, that the special event is a broadcast covering an actual happening that is part of the current mainstream of life, whereas the feature may or may not be part of current events and is usually devised, developed, and executed by the broadcaster or other producing organization.

Techniques   For events other than those which require only a short intro and outro, the writer should collect as much material as possible. News stories, maps, press releases, historical documents, books, photographs, and similar sources can be pertinent and helpful in preparing continuity. Copy should be prepared for all emergencies as well as for opening, closing, transition, and filler uses. Material should include information on the personalities involved, the background of the event, and even on probable or possible happenings during the event.

Coverage in depth of a special event requires considerable preliminary work. Russ Tornabene, when vice president and general manager of the NBC Radio Network, stated the following regarding special events: "Extensive research goes into the preparation of material to be used as background for broadcasting special events. For example, a research document prepared for the Olympics runs to about 500 pages. For the primaries and political conventions there are several books prepared, each with several hundred pages. They are even tabbed for quick reference, with color-coded sections, for various categories such as candidates, issues, etc. The job of the writer, therefore, in preparing background material for special events is an important one. In addition, the correspondents doing the broadcasts add to the basic book with research, interviews and materials of their own."

Because the form of the special event is extemporaneous, the material, though prepared as fully as possible, should be simple, straightforward, and informal, and should sound as though it were ad-libbed.

Types   As previously noted, some special events are simply coverage of the event taking place. They do not require commentary and the writer needs to prepare only an appropriate opening and closing. The following illustrates continuity that may be used for a continuing special event that is broadcast more than once:

PRGM: FCC HEARINGS

DATE:
TIME:
ANN: Good morning.
          Good afternoon.
          In just a few moments, your city station will bring you the _____ day of the Federal Communications Commission hearings on network television policies and practicies.

             The hearings are taking place in Washington, D.C., before the entire Federal Communications Commission.

          We take you now to Washington, D.C.

* * *

That concludes this (morning's) (afternoon's) session of the FCC hearings on network television policies and practices. Your city station is bringing you these important broadcasts direct from Washington, D.C., in their entirety, through the week of February 5th. We are interested in your reaction to these broadcasts. Write, FCC Hearings, WNYC, New York 7. And join us again (at 1:45) (tomorrow morning at 10) for the next session.

Courtesy of the Municipal Broadcasting System—
Stations WNYC, WNYC-FM, WNYC-TV — New York City

Other types of special events permit and require the development of transition and background material during the event. The best example of this kind of special event is the broadcast of the live sports event, which is discussed later in this chapter under ''Sports.''

One type of special event virtually indistinguishable from a feature is that which has been carefully preplanned and developed and is a special event only because it is being presented in front of an audience. Productions of the arts fall into this category — though who could say that such an event is not a feature or vice versa. When the station participates in the preparation for the event, the writer can provide special input as to its actual development and perhaps its outcome. When the station does not participate in the actual action of the event — such as a concert or recital — the writer's job is somewhat different. There may be a need to prepare only the opening and closing, as in the following example. (Note the detailed video directions; SC refers to *studio card* or card bearing the indicated information.)

VIDEO	AUDIO
OPENING:	
Cover shot of Choral Group	Channel Five presents ...
Super Slide: L-20	the INTERCOLLEGIATE CHORAL FESTIVAL ...
	The festival, which was held last evening at William Neal Reynolds Coliseum, included choral groups from ten colleges throughout North Carolina ... and a massed chorus of over 450 voices.
Super SC: Dr. Knud Anderson	The director is Dr. Knud Anderson of the New Orleans Opera House.
Super SC: Willa Fay Batts	Piano Soloist is Willa Fay Batts;
Super SC: Beatrice Donley	Alto Soloist, Beatrice Donley; and
Super SC: Mary Ida Hodge	Accompanist, Mary Ida Hodge. And now ... The Premiere INTERCOLLEGIAGE CHORAL FESTIVAL OF NORTH CAROLINA:
CLOSING	Channel Five has presented The Premiere
Super Slide: L-20	of THE INTERCOLLEGIATE CHORAL FESTIVAL OF NORTH CAROLINA, directed
Super SC: Dr. Knud Anderson	by Dr. Knud Anderson.

Courtesy of WRAL-TV, Raleigh, N.C.

Sports

At one time the sports department of a station or network was an offshoot of the news department. But the phenomenal growth of live sports event coverage gave sports new status in broadcasting and more and more sports divisions are separate, independent functions. The smaller the station, of course, the greater the likelihood that sports will be a function of the news department, rather than a separate entity. The writing of sports is similar to the writing of news. If anything, the style for sports broadcasts must be even more precise and more direct than for news broadcasts. The language is more colloquial and though technical terms are to be avoided so as not to confuse the general audience, the writer of sports may use many more expressions relating to a specialized area than can the writer of news.

Types of Sports Programs

The straight sportscast concentrates on recapitulation of the results of sports events and on news relating to sports in general. Some sportscasts are oriented solely to summaries of results. These summaries may come from wire service reports or from other sources of the station. Material that is rewritten from newspaper accounts or that is taken from the wires should be adapted to fit the purpose of the particular program and the personality of the broadcaster.

The sports feature program may include live or recorded interviews with sports personalities, anecdotes or dramatizations of events in sports, human interest or background stories on personalities or events, or remotes relating to sports but not in themselves an actual athletic event.

A sports show may amalgamate several approaches or, as in the case of the after-event critique or summary, may concentrate on one type alone. Many sports news shows are combinations of the straight report and the feature.

The most popular sports broadcast is, of course, the live athletic contest while it is taking place. In some instances economic or legal factors prevent the direct broadcast of the event, and it is recorded and broadcast at a scheduled time after the event has taken place.

Organization of Sports News

Formats for the sports news broadcast parallel those of the regular news broadcast. The most common approach is to take the top sport of the particular season, give all the results and news of that sport, and work toward the least important sport. In such an organization the most important story of the most important sport is given first unless a special item from another sport overrides it. Within each sport the general pattern in this organization includes the results first, the general news (such as trades, injuries, and so forth) next and future events last. If the trade or injury is of a star player or the future event is more than routine, such as the signing for a heavyweight championship fight, then it will become a lead story. The local sports scene is usually coordinated with the national sports news, fitting into the national reporting breakdowns. The local result or story, however, will usually be the lead within the given sports category and sometimes the local sports scene will precede all other sports news. Formats vary, of course.

The sports segment of the regular thirty-minute evening news program of a large regional station, WCVB-TV, Boston, follows the results format, except when a significant happening in the world of sports clearly demands the lead position, as in the following on-air script.

VIDEO	AUDIO
Hall of Fame Slide	Almost all of your favorite baseball cards came to life today in Cooperstown, New York, to bestow the game's highest honor on four of its members . . .
VC/VO	Former Commissioner Happy Chandler, along with former New York Giant short stop Travis Jackson were among the foursome inducted today. . . . Joining them was the only man to win the MVP award in each league, Frank Robinson . . . who won the award in 1961 with Cincinnati and again in 1966 with the Baltimore Orioles. . . . And, of course, baseball's all time home run king Hank Aaron who surpassed the Babe in 1974 while with Atlanta and wound up with 755 homers and a lifetime batting average of .305. . . . As for greatness, there was none more satisfying for Aaron than today. . . .
SOT at :31 Hall of Fame Slide	We'll hear some more from the new inductees tonite at 11. . . . If these are what the dog days of August are all about, Red Sox fans could be in for a long month. . . . The Sox dropped their third straight to the White Sox today in Chicago, 4-3 the final. . . .
VC/VO	Chicago scored first in the third after Bruce Hurst retired the first eight batters. . . . Aurelio Rodriguez walked and scored all the way from first on rejuvenated Ron LeFlore's double. . . . Two innings later Harold Baines made it three-zip
SOT at :14 VO at :21	It's gone. . . . The Red Sox got on the scoreboard when Gary Allenson gets the go ahead on three and oh and Ron LeFlore probably wished he never swang. . . . A four-base error as Allenson comes all the way around to cut the lead to 3-1. . . . Singles by Dwight Evans, Jim Rice and Carney Lansford cut it to three to two but that's as close as it got. . . . Which wasn't the case for Third Base Umpire Tim McLellond and Ralph Houk . . .

VIDEO	AUDIO
	McLellond can obviously read lips, even from over 100 feet away. . . . He gives Houk the gate and the Major gives McLellond his nickel's worth before heading for his first early shower of the season. . . . Dennis
SOT at :55	Lamp came on for Jerry Koosman to nail it down. . . .
	The Sox head for Baltimore now, looking at four games with the Orioles. . . .

VO			
Cleveland	4	0	
Milwaukee	1	0	3rd
Baltimore	2		
Kansas City	4		
Detroit	8		
Toronto	5		
Seattle	0		
California	9		6th
Minnesota	3		
Oakland	1		6th
Yankees			
Texas		Tonight	

VC/VO   In the National League almost 58,000 showed up at Vet Stadium in Philadelphia today but Leon Durham of the Cubs sent them home disappointed. . . . This first inning shot to center of Dick Ruthven put the Cubs up 2-0. . . . 7-2 the final, the Cubs snap a four game losing streak.

VO		
St. Louis	5	
Montreal	4	
Pirates	4	
Mets	3	
Dodgers	9	
Braves	4	8th
San Diego	8	
Cincinnati	6	
San Francisco		
Houston	Tonight	

Bruce Litzke is back in the winner's circle for the first time in 15 months. . . . Despite a two over par round of 73 today, Litzke took the Canadian Open. . . .

VC/VO   Litzke wasn't the only player with a case of the bogies today. . . . Tommy Valentine, who started the day just two shots back, misses this putt on 15 to give Litzke a three shot lead. . . . Onto 16 Hal Sutton nailed his approach shot stiff but Litzke does him one better as he tucks a wedge shot inside Sutton for a very makable bird. . . .

VIDEO	AUDIO
	Despite not having won all year until today, Litzke has pocketed over $206,000. . . .
VC/VO	Over at the Back Bay Racquet Club today it was the finals of the Pepsi Challenge Open Racquetball Tournament. . . . This is the women's final. . . . Nan Higgins in the yellow shirt from Haverhill goes three sets with Judy Bryant in blue. . . . Higgins takes the open title for the second year in a row. . . . More than 180 players from around New England began the tournament on Friday. . . . After Higgins was crowned, George Viera of Brockton took the men's open title from Dennis Acedo in two sets. . . . The winners each receive a weekend for two in New York City. . . .
Strike Slide	The NFL opens its exhibition season next week in Canton, Ohio, with the Hall of Fame game. . . . The Preseason slate seems to be immune from a pending player strike but not so for the regular season. . . . One of the principals in the ongoing dispute, Players Association Executive Director Ed Garvey, was a guest today on *ABC's This Week with David Brinkley* and
VC SOT	spelled out the what, where's and when of the strike. . . .
Hickman Slide	More sad news today in the world of motor sports. . . . 39 year old Jim Hickman died today from injuries he suffered in an accident yesterday in Milwaukee. Hickman is the third to die this weekend while racing a high speed vehicle. . . .
Waltrip Slide	Yet still the races go on. . . . Today Darrel Waltrip held off a late charge to win the Talladega 500 Stock Car race. . . .

Courtesy of WCVB-TV, Boston

● *One of the most difficult aspects of writing the sports news script is the writer's dependency on the availability of visual material for not only the content but also the form and sometimes even the organization of the script. Given the available visuals above, could you have written any of the segments differently?*

Sports Special Events

The live on-the-spot coverage of an athletic contest is the most exciting and most popular sports program. The newspaper and magazine cartoons showing a viewer glued to a television set for seven nights of baseball in the summer or seven nights of football, basketball, and hockey in the fall and winter are no longer exaggerations.

The sports special event can be other than a contest, however. Coverage of an awards ceremony, of an old-timer's day, of a Cooperstown Hall of Fame induction, of a retirement ceremony are all special events that are not live contests on the playing field or court.

The contest Although the jobs of television and radio broadcasters differ, those of the continuity writers are essentially the same. In television the broadcasters are announcers, and not narrators as they are in radio. Even if they wanted to, the television broadcasters would find it difficult to keep up with the action as seen by the audience, except in slow games such as baseball. Since sports are visual to begin with, the less description by the television broadcaster the better. The television announcer is primarily an encyclopedia of background information. The radio announcer needs background information, too, but sometimes is too busy with narration to use very much of it.

The sports broadcaster must have filler material; that is, information relating to pre-event action and color, statistics, form charts, information on the site of the event, on the history of the event, about the participants, human interest stories, and similar materials that either heighten the audience's interest or help clarify the action to the audience. This material must be written up and must be available to the broadcaster to be used when needed, specifically during lulls in the action, and in pregame and postgame opening and closing segments. At one time staff writers prepared this material. More recently, sports broadcasters have been expected to be experts in their field and to know and to provide their own filler material. Former sports stars have been hired to do "color" at live events, providing first-hand technical and human interest information not usually known to the nonplayer. Because of indications that too many sportscasters were not objective, but were "homers" who might falsify, distort, or suppress facts to aid the attendance and public relations of the home team, the FCC required that the sports broadcast must disclose "clearly, publicly, and prominently" during each athletic event whether the announcers are being paid, chosen, or otherwise controlled by anyone other than the station.

The primary function of the writer for the live contest is that of a researcher and outliner. The script may be little more than an outline and/or a series of statistics, individual unrelated sentences, or short paragraphs with the required background and transition continuity. The following outline is more complete than most. Note that the material contains not only the opening and closing format, but also includes the commercial format so that the announcer knows when to break, and has the lead-in script material for the commercial. Each page of the opening and closing formats are set up so that after the first page the announcements of network sponsors or local sponsors may be inserted without disrupting the continuity.

PROFESSIONAL HOCKEY — OPENING BILLBOARD

VIDEO	AUDIO
Up from black	Sneak theme
FILM	
PROFESSIONAL HOCKEY	ANNCR: Coming your way now is PROFES-
(Super)	SIONAL HOCKEY, the fastest game in the world ...
	and BIG match it is —
SUPER (NAME OF TEAMS)	the _____ against
	the _____.
	(Theme up and under)

VIDEO	AUDIO
CBS SPORTS (Super)	ANNCR: This is the _____ in a series of exciting matches that will be brought to you every Saturday afternoon during the season ...
BEST IN SPORTS (Super)	As part of the continuing effort of CBS SPORTS to present the BEST IN SPORTS all the year around. (Theme up and under)
NATIONAL LEAGUE HOCKEY (Super)	ANNCR: This is an important regular season contest in the National Hockey League ... hockey's MAJOR league ...
NAME OF STADIUM (Super)	being brought to you direct from famed _____ in _____. (Theme up and under)
NAME OF TEAM	ANNCR: So now get ready to watch the match between the _____ and the _____ ...
NAMES OF SPORTSCASTERS (Super)	with description by _____ and _____. Now let's go to (Name of Stadium) _____ (Theme up and hold)

CLOSING BILLBOARD

VIDEO	AUDIO
PROFESSIONAL HOCKEY	You have just seen a presentation of fast-moving PROFESSIONAL HOCKEY ...
NATIONAL LEAGUE HOCKEY	one of the big regular season matches of the NATIONAL HOCKEY LEAGUE ... the MAJOR league of hockey. (Theme up and under)
NAME OF TEAMS	Today's exciting contest was between the _____ and the _____.
NAME OF STADIUM	Played on the _____ home ice, the famed _____ in _____. (Theme up and under)
NEXT SATURDAY	We invite you to join us again NEXT Saturday afternoon for another big Professional Hockey Match ...
NAME OF TEAMS	Next week's televised contest will bring together the (Name of Team) _____ and the (Name of Team) _____ at the (Name of Stadium) _____. (Theme up and under)
NAMES OF SPORTSCASTERS	The description of today's match has been provided by _____ and _____.

VIDEO	AUDIO
PROFESSIONAL HOCKEY is a CBS TELEVISION NETWORK Presentation PRODUCED BY CBS SPORTS	This presentation of PROFESSIONAL HOCKEY has been produced by CBS SPORTS. (Theme up and hold)

HOCKEY COMMERCIAL FORMAT

Before Opening Face-Off — "Very shortly play will be starting here at (Name of Arena) and we will have action for you."
(1 minute commercial)

First Period — During 1st period of play three 20 second commercials are to be inserted at the discretion of each co-op station. Audio Cue: "There's a whistle on the ice and the score is _____ & _____."

1st pause during play-by-play.	.20 seconds
2nd pause during play-by-play.	.20 seconds
3rd pause during play-by-play.	.20 seconds

End of First Period — "That is the end of the first period and the score is _____ & _____."

Middle First Intermission — "In just a moment, we are going to have more entertainment for you during this intermission."

Before Second Period Face-Off — "Very shortly, play will be starting in the second period at (name of arena) and we will have more action for you."
(1 minute commercial)

Second Period — During 2nd period of play three 20 second commercials are to be inserted at the discretion of each co-op station. Audio Cue: "There's a whistle on the ice and the score is _____ & _____."

1st pause during play-by-play.	.20 seconds
2nd pause during play-by-play.	.20 seconds
3rd pause during play-by-play.	.20 seconds

End of Second Period — "That's the end of the second period and the score is _____ & _____."
(1 minute commercial)

Middle Second Intermission — "In just a moment we are going to have more entertainment for you during this intermission."

Before Third Period Face-Off — "Very shortly play will be starting in the third period here at (Name of Arena) and we will have more action for you."
(1 minute commercial)

Third Period — During third period of play three 20 second commercials are to be inserted at the discretion of each co-op station. Audio Cue: "There's a whistle on the ice and the score is ‗‗‗‗‗‗‗ & ‗‗‗‗‗‗‗."

1st pause during play-by-play.	.20 seconds
2nd pause during play-by-play.	.20 seconds
3rd pause during play-by-play.	.20 seconds

End of Third Period — "That is the end of the game and the score is ‗‗‗‗‗‗‗ & ‗‗‗‗‗‗‗."
(1 minute commercial)

Statistical Wrap-up

Before Closing Billboard — "This wraps up another National Hockey League telecast. Final score ‗‗‗‗‗‗‗ & ‗‗‗‗‗‗‗."

By permission of CBS Television Sports

In the preceding format the writer prepared a fair amount of actual script continuity. In the following football format there is less dialogue prepared but considerably more directions provided for the actual telecasting process. The planning is more precise, with time segments and total elapsed time after each segment.

NFL TODAY, PART 1 — PRE GAME

00:00	Open and Tease the Day	2:30
02:30	Commercial 1	1:02
03:32	Football Segment 1	7:30
	(includes 2-minute field report supplied by NFL Films)	
11:02	Commercial 2	1:32
12:34	Sports News Segment	5:00
	(probably include 1½ to 2-minute non-football feature supplied by NFL Films)	
17:34	Commercial 3	1:32
19:06	Football Segment 2	7:25
	(includes 2-minute feature supplied by NFL Films)	
26:31	Commercial 4	1:02
27:33	Close	1:02
28:35	Game Opening Billboard	1:00
29:35	System	

CUE: WE'LL BE READY FOR THE START OF TODAY'S NATIONAL
   FOOTBALL LEAGUE GAME AFTER THIS WORD FROM YOUR
   LOCAL STATION. (Pause) THIS IS CBS.
Note: 72-Second Station Break

NFL TODAY, PART II — GAME

01:00   Announcers set scene 1:10

LEAD TO COMMERCIAL 1

CUE: WE'LL BE READY FOR THE START OF TODAY'S GAME
        IN JUST A MOMENT.
02:10   Commercial 1 .... 1:32
        (On doubleheaders this will be a 2-minute position)
03:42   Announcers set starting lineups, cover coin toss ceremony if
        going on at time 1:18
05:00   Kickoff — First Quarter
        Commercials 2, 3 and 4
        CUE: During Action — WITH (time) REMAINING IN THE (_____)
                QUARTER, THERE'S A TIME OUT WITH THE SCORE
                (team & score) AND (team & score).
        Note: If there's a problem with the clock, we'll use: IN THE
                (_____) QUARTER, THERE'S A TIME OUT WITH THE SCORE
                (team & score) AND (team & score).
        Unless there are regional commercial positions, we will not employ these
        cues except at the end of the quarters; countdown cues will be used.
        End of First Quarter
        Commercial 5 and NFL PSA 1:45
        CUE: THAT'S THE END OF THE FIRST QUARTER WITH THE
                SCORE _____
        Second Quarter
        Commercials 6, 7, 8 & 9
        Note: Network promos will be in fixed positions following commercials
                7 & 16. In the vast majority of cases we hope that these will be
                12-second videotape announcements that can be included in the
                commercial reel. If, for any reason, they are straight copy, the
                announcements should still be held to 12 seconds.
        CUES WILL BE THE SAME AS THOSE LISTED FOR FIRST QUARTER.
        End of First Half

NFL TODAY, PART II — HALFTIME

00:00   CUE: THAT'S THE END OF THE FIRST HALF WITH THE
                SCORE _____ .... :10
00:10   Commercial 10 (90 secs.) Note: On the second games of doubleheaders
        this will be a 60-second position. If there are first game sponsors involved
        in the second game, one 30-sec. commercial will shift to position 1 .... 1:32
        STATION BREAK CUE: WE'LL JOIN JACK WHITAKER IN CBS
        CONTROL AFTER THIS WORD FROM YOUR LOCAL STATION.
01:42   System (from Coord) .... :10
01:52   Station Break (62 seconds) 1:05

02:57   (a) Sports News Segment 5:20
             (includes 1-minute commercial as part of total time) Note: This
             segment will include 2:30 feature supplied by NFL Films.

08:17   (b) Football Scores & Hilites 5:00

13:17   CUE TO BILLBOARD: WE'RE ALMOST READY TO BEGIN THE
             SECOND HALF WITH (team) KICKING TO (team) .... :10

13:27   Middle Billboard .... :31
             Title Slide — National Football League — :05
             Copy: "Today's National Football League game is being sponsored
                 by _____."
             Sponsor A — :05
             Sponsor B — :05
             Sponsor C — :05
             Sponsor D — :05
             Copy: "Today's game will continue in just a minute."

13:58   Commercial 11 .... 1:02

15:00   Second Half Kickoff — Third Quarter
             Commercials 12, 13 & 14
             CUES WILL BE THE SAME AS THOSE LISTED FOR FIRST QUARTER.
             End of Third Quarter
             CUE: THAT'S THE END OF THE THIRD QUARTER WITH THE
                 SCORE _____. WE NOW PAUSE FOR A WORD
                 FROM YOUR LOCAL STATION. (SYSTEM)
             Note: If the station break does not fall at the end of the third quarter
                 (see Station Break Summary), the cue will be as follows: WE'LL
                 RETURN TO (stadium) AFTER THIS WORD FROM YOUR
                 LOCAL STATION. (SYSTEM)
             Station Break (62 seconds) and NFL PSA 1:45
             Fourth Quarter
             Commercials 15, 16 & 17 (see note following commercials 6, 7, 8 & 9)
             CUES WILL BE THE SAME AS THOSE LISTED FOR THE
             FIRST QUARTER.
             End of Game
             Commercial 18 .... 1:02
             Note: In all games this commercial will be scheduled in fourth quarter
                 action should sufficient commercial opportunities occur.
             CUE: THAT'S THE END OF THE GAME AND THE FINAL SCORE
                 IS _____. WE'LL BE BACK AT (_____)
                 STADIUM IN JUST A MOMENT.
             Play-by-play announcers will fill as required (Note: Should be maximum
             of 4 minutes) and then cue to Pro Football Report.
             CUE: NOW WE TAKE YOU TO (Announcer) IN CBS CONTROL FOR
             PRO FOOTBALL REPORT.
             Note: On doubleheader dates we will cue directly to station identification.
             CUE: STAY TUNED FOR (team vs. team) GAME IMMEDIATELY
                 FOLLOWING THIS WORD FROM YOUR LOCAL STATION.
                 (Pause) ... THIS IS CBS.

Blackout markets carrying a first game will have to cover the second game with a STAY TUNED FOR PRO FOOTBALL REPORT.

NFL TODAY, PART III — POST GAME

00:00	Program Segment 1	4:00
	(Scores of 4 games, VTR hilites on 2 of 4)	
04:00	Commercial 1	1:02
05:02	Program Segment 2	4:00
	(Scores of 4 games, VTR hilites on 2 of 4)	
09:02	Commercial 2	1:02
10:04	Program Segment 3	4:00
	(Scores of 4 games, VTR hilites on 2 of 4)	
14:06	Commercial 3	1:02
15:08	"Goodbye" and Closing Billboard	1:00

Note: This will have to be pre-taped and racked on separate machine so that it can follow any commercial position. ... System should be included on tape.

Station Note: There will be no fill procedures. The Post Game Show on first games will run 16:08 regardless of the end time of the game. See Doubleheader Procedures for instructions on second game sign-offs.

The _____ Show was produced by CBS Television Sports

————————————————————O————————————————————

● *What significant differences, if any, are there in the preparation of the rundown sheet for a network sports event and for the following local sports event?*

————————————————————O————————————————————

VIDEO	AUDIO
OPENING: LONG SHOT OF SPORTLAND:	(BOOTH ANNCR.) Now live from beautiful Sportland on U.S. 1 north of Raleigh — WRAL-TV presents ...
CUE THE MUSIC — SUPER L-317-s	Bowling from Sportland ... the exciting new bowling show where each week you'll
PAN SLOW RIGHT	see the top bowlers in this area compete for prizes and the title of King of the Hill —
CUT TO CU OF BOWLER	plus a chance to win $10,000 should they bowl a perfect 300 game. Now here's your
ZOOM BACK SLOWLY	bowling host, Jim Heavner.
DROP SUPER AND ZOOM IN ON JIM HEAVNER, FADING OUT THE MUSIC	(JIM) Hello, ladies and gentlemen, I'm Jim Heavner and I'll be your host ... (DOES WARM-UP) (INTRODUCES BOWLERS) (DOES THE INTERVIEW) (THEN RIGHT BEFORE THE START OF THE FIRST GAME) We'll start our first game right after this important message.

VIDEO	AUDIO
CUT TO STUDIO FOR BREAK ONE:	(SIXTY SECONDS)
BACK LIVE:	(STARTS FIRST GAME) (AFTER FIRST GAME, WE WILL HAVE INTERVIEWS ONLY IF WE ARE INSIDE OF 0:15) (CUT TO SECOND BREAK WITH CUE — WE'LL START OUR SECQND GAME RIGHT AFTER THIS IMPORTANT MESSAGE)
CUT TO STUDIO FOR BREAK TWO:	(SIXTY SECONDS)
BACK LIVE:	(START SECOND GAME) (WE SHOULD HAVE FINISHED SECOND GAME PRIOR TO 0:38) (IF WE'RE RUNNING NEAR OR OVER THIS KILL BREAK THREE) (TIME PERMITTING CUT TO THIRD BREAK WITH CUE — WE'LL START OUR THIRD GAME RIGHT AFTER THIS IMPORTANT MESSAGE)
CUT TO STUDIO FOR BREAK THREE:	(SIXTY SECONDS)
BACK LIVE:	(STARTS THIRD GAME) (AFTER GAME, TIME PERMITTING, HE INTERVIEWS WINNER AND LOSER HANDING THEM THEIR ENVELOPES) (IF WE NEED A PAD, HEAVNER BRINGS OUT CHARLIE BOSWELL FOR THE BOWLING TIP OF THE WEEK) (IF FURTHER PAD IS NEEDED USE FOURTH PROMO CUTAWAY) (CLOSE IS REVERSE OF THE OPENING —
PAN LEFT	HEAVNER BOWS OUT)
CUT TO LONG SHOT OF SPORTLAND WITH MUSIC	(BOOTH ANNCR.) Live from beautiful Sportland on U.S. 1 north of Raleigh WRAL-TV has presented bowling from Sportland ... be with
SUPER SLIDE: L-317-s AND CUE MUSIC	us again next week when top bowlers in this area again compete for prizes and the title of King of the Hill — plus a chance to win $10,000 on Bowling from Sportland — Bowling from Sportland was directed by Ross Shaheen.
SUPER SLIDE: L-207-s	
SUPER SLIDE: L-307-s	
SUPER SLIDE: L-317-s: MUSIC UP AND OUT:	
BLACK:	

By permission of Sportland, Inc.

The noncontest   The principal difference between this special event and the live contest is that this one can be more completely prepared for and, in some instances, even can be outlined in terms of anticipated sequences. Although it should come over as extemporaneous, the writer can, through **preinterviewing** and working with the producer and director in setting up certain actions, write an outline that contains specific happenings rather than noncontent transition phrases. The following detailed rundown was adapted from a network presentation.

RUNDOWN SHEET ON STADIUM REMOTE
Football Coach Tribute

Approx. 2:15 P.M.:	Panoramic view of Stadium. Key in: "Football Coach's Last Game." Announcer voice-over.
Approx. 2:55 P.M.:	Panoramic view of half-time ceremonies at Stadium. Key in: "Football Coach's Last Game." Announcer voice-over.
Approx. 4:50 P.M.:	Announcer introduction to closing minutes of football game. Feature scoreboard clock running out. Key in: "Football Coach's Last Game" over action on field as gun sounds ending game. Interviewer describes closing moments of game.

1. Interviewer stations Football Coach on the field facing the field camera. Bands of the competing universities line up behind Football Coach and Interviewer.
2. Band music concludes and Interviewer thanks the bands on behalf of Football Coach. (Interviewer's mike should be fed into stadium public address system for any narration while on field.)
3. Football Coach and Interviewer walk up ramp to field house followed by special guests. At entrance to field house they are picked up by camera on dolly and led down the hall of the University dressing room. The University squad and the opposing team's captain follow closely.
4. Interviewer introduces some friends and former players of Football Coach, with brief comments from the guests and from Football Coach. It is hoped that the Presidents of both Universities can be present, and that the President of Football Coach's University can quote from letters written to Football Coach by prominent persons in government and in other fields. At some point during the proceedings an outstanding national football coach will talk to Football Coach from station studio via split screen.
5. At conclusion of program Interviewer presents Football Coach with award from Network.
6. Brief comment from Football Coach to his University alumni throughout the country.

For Application and Review

1. Clip out the front page stories from your daily newspaper and organize them for a radio news broadcast according to each of the following approaches: topical; geographical; international, national, local; from most to least important, regardless of category. Write the script for a fifteen-minute straight news broadcast for radio, using one of the organizations developed above.
2. Rewrite the radio broadcast you have developed in the exercise above for a television news program, utilizing photos, film, tape, and other visuals.
3. Prepare the opening and closing continuity and the filler material for a live local broadcast — for television and radio both — of the next athletic event in your community. Rewrite your material as though the same event were to be broadcast over a national network.
4. Find out what special event worthy of news coverage, other than an athletic contest, will take place in your community in the near future. Prepare the opening and closing, transition, and filler material for radio. Include, if possible, an interview with one or more personalities taking part in the event. Revise for television the material you prepared for radio.

5

Features and Documentaries

eatures and documentaries are usually under the direction of the news department of the television or radio station or network. They deal with news and information and, frequently, opinion; they are sometimes pertinent to current events, sometimes of a historical nature, and sometimes academic, cultural, or abstract without necessarily relating to an immediate or major issue of the day.

The Feature

The feature or, as it is sometimes called, the special feature, falls somewhere between the special event and the documentary. The special event is coverage of an immediate newsworthy happening, sometimes unanticipated, and the special feature is preplanned and carefully prepared. There are special events, of course, such as sports events, that are preplanned. The difference is that in the special event the producer is covering a happening as it unveils and does not know what the outcome is going to be. In the feature the outcome is known and, indeed, the program may have been well-rehearsed as well as prerecorded. The broadcaster usually has more control over the sequence of events in the feature than in the special event. The special event usually is live, while the feature usually is filmed, taped or, if live, produced from a script or at least a routine sheet or detailed rundown sheet. Special events usually are public presentations that television and radio arrange to cover. Features usually are prepared specifically for television or radio presentation and generally are not presented before an in-person audience. The special event is part of the stream of life, but the feature is designed by a producing organization.

Features usually are short, two to five or fifteen to thirty minutes in length — the former for fillers and the latter for full programs of a public service nature. The subject matter for the feature varies. Some sample types: the presentation of the work of a special service group in the community, a story on the operation of the local fire department, an examination of the problems of the school board, a how-to-do-it broadcast, a behind-the-scenes story on any subject, from raising chickens to electing public officials. The feature offers the writer the opportunity to create a program of high artistic quality closely approaching the documentary.

Writing Approach

Because it does come so close to the documentary, the feature requires careful research, analysis, and evaluation of material, and writing based on detail and depth. That does not mean that it requires a full and complete script. Because the feature is composed, frequently, of a number of diverse program types — such as the documentary, the interview, the panel discussion and the speech — it may be written in **routine sheet** or **rundown form**. Some features have combinations of script, rundown sheet, and routine sheet.

Because the feature is usually a public service presentation it often contains informational and educational content. But it doesn't have to be purely factual or academic in nature. It can even take the form of a variety show or a drama — or certainly have elements of these forms within the program as a whole. The feature is an eclectic form and can be oriented around a person, an organization, a thing, a situation, a problem, or an idea. The following example is principally oriented toward an organization (the Red Cross) but also includes a problem (disaster work) and a situation (a specific disaster in the Harrisburg area and a specific technique, artificial respiration). Note that this feature was produced by a local commercial station as part of a regular public service series and is a live-type program with film inserts.

HOW RED CROSS DOES IT

VIDEO	AUDIO
SLIDE #1 TRI-STATE STORY	MUSIC: RECORD "RED CROSS SONG" IN AND OUT BEHIND STATION ANNOUNCER: As a public service, WEHT presents TRI-STATE STORY — a half hour
SLIDE #2 RED CROSS EMBLEM	prepared through the cooperation of the Springfield Chapter of the American Red Cross. Here to introduce our guests for this evening is Mr. John Smith, Director of Pub- lic Relations for the Springfield Red Cross. Mr. Smith:
CAMERA ON SMITH	(MR. SMITH THANKS ANNOUNCER AND INTRODUCES TWO GUESTS, MR. HARVEY AND MR. JONES. THEN ASKS MR. HARVEY TO SPEAK.)
CAMERA ON HARVEY CLOSEUP OF PHOTOS ON EASEL	(MR. HARVEY TELLS OF RECENT DISASTER WORK IN HARRISBURG AREA, SHOWING PHOTOGRAPHS OF SERVICE WORKERS. HE WILL RISE AND WALK TO THE EASEL.)

VIDEO	AUDIO
CAMERA ON SMITH AND JONES	(MR. SMITH INTRODUCES MR. JONES. THEY DISCUSS SUMMER SAFETY SCHOOL FOR SWIMMERS. JONES LEADS INTO FILM WITH FOLLOWING CUE): "Now I'd like our viewers to see a film that was made at Lake Roundwood during last year's Summer Safety School."
SPECIAL FILM	(8:35) (SILENT — JONES LIVE VOICE-OVER)
CAMERA ON JONES	(JONES INTRODUCES ARTIFICIAL RESPIRA-TION DEMONSTRATION.)
CAMERA ON TWO BOYS	(JONES DESCRIBES METHODS OFF CAMERA.)
CAMERA ON SMITH	(SMITH THANKS JONES AND HARVEY AND GIVES CONCLUDING REMARKS.)
SLIDE #3 TRI-STATE STORY	MUSIC: THEME IN AND UNDER STATION ANNOUNCER: Tri-State Story, a WEHT Public Service Presen-tation, is on the air each week at this time. Today's program was prepared through the cooperation of the Springfield Chapter of the American Red Cross.

By permission of American National Red Cross

"Day By Day" was an award-winning feature series on a public television station. As with the Red Cross feature, note how the basic introduction of the main idea (in "Day By Day," the world of the deaf) leads into the building of an understanding of the subject through background, discussion, and demonstration. It is, in dramatic terms, a rising action, moving the audience along to greater interest and empathy. This is a desired technique in writing the feature. Without expensive technical requirements such as location filming, and using only one set and a demonstration area, the writer-researcher of "Day By Day" was able to obtain variety and excitement.

———————————————————————————◯———————————————————————————

- *What are the different program forms and techniques used in this run-down sheet? Without increasing the budget, is there any additional or different material or approaches you, as writer, would have used?*

———————————————————————————◯———————————————————————————

DAY BY DAY

WUCM-TV
Delta College
University Center, Michigan

3:00 P.M. (Live) & 7:30 P.M. (Repeat)

Partial Script

Host/Prod. — A. Rapp   Direct. — M. Baldwin
Anncr. — L. Scott   Vid. Eng. — H. Conley
Vol. Prog. Coord. — J. Arvoy   Writer/Resch. — K. Semion
                                        Series Sec. — B. Meyers

Guests — 8
Segments — 2 (Same Topic)

VIDEO	AUDIO
BLACK	
VT OPEN (SLIDE MONTAGE)	TAPE THEME ("DAY BY DAY")
	ANNCR. (STAND OPEN)
	THE FOLLOWING PROGRAM IS PRODUCED
	IN THE STUDIOS OF WUCM-TV FROM
	DELTA COLLEGE AT UNIVERSITY CENTER,
	MICHIGAN. THIS IS DAY BY DAY.
	(PAUSE)
	LIVE AT 3 REPEATED ON VIDEO TAPE AT
	7:30 P.M.
	YOUR HOST IS ANDY RAPP AND I'M
	LAMARR SCOTT.
MS OF ANNCR.	ANNCR. (SPEC. OPEN): IMAGINE, IF YOU
	CAN, A WORLD OF UTTER SILENCE.
	(PAUSE)
	IMAGINE THAT YOU COULD CLOSE YOUR
	EARS AS YOU CAN CLOSE YOUR EYES,
	AND THERE WOULD BE NO FOOTSTEPS,
	NO WHISTLING WIND. IMAGINE THE
	WORLD OF THE DEAF. TODAY, WEDNES-
	DAY, DECEMBER 12, WE'LL EXPLORE THE
	WORLD THAT HAS INCLUDED SUCH
	GREAT PERSONS AS THOMAS EDISON
	AND JOHANN SEBASTIAN BACH.
	AND NOW, HERE'S ANDY.
	APPROX. 1 MIN.

VIDEO	AUDIO
WS OF SET	HOST & ANNCR. (AD LIB CHAT): — NATIONAL "DING-A-LING" DAY
SHOW PHONE NOS.	— ASK FOR TELEPHONE CALLS APPROX. 2 MIN.
SEGMENT #1 4 GUESTS WALK ON SET AND SIT	SEGMENT #1 ANNCR. (GUEST INTRO.): IT'S EASY TO THINK NEGATIVELY WHEN YOU THINK OF DEAFNESS, AND THAT'S WHY TEACHING DEAF PERSONS TO DEVELOP POSITIVE SELF-IMAGES IS AN IMPORTANT GOAL OF OUR GUESTS. BERT POOS (PAHZ) IS SUPER-INTENDENT AND DEAN OF STUDENTS FOR THE DEAF IN FLINT. HIS WIFE, EDIE POOS (PAHZ), IS COORDINATOR OF THE HEARING IMPAIRED PROGRAM AT MOTT COMMUNITY COLLEGE IN FLINT. EARL JONES IS AN IN-STRUCTOR AT THE MICHIGAN SCHOOL FOR THE DEAF AND DIRECTOR OF THE MOTT ADULT EDUCATION PROGRAM FOR THE DEAF. AND MARIE ERICKSON IS AN INTERPRETER FOR THE MOTT COLLEGE PROGRAM.
(DISCUSSION AREA) VID. SPOT EFFECT SIGN READER	HOST (INTERVIEW) #1: FOUR GUESTS. TOPIC: "THE PROBLEMS OF BEING DEAF OR HARD OF HEARING." APPROX. 10 MIN.
SEGMENT #2 (DEMONSTRATION AREA) DEAF STUDENTS PERFORM PANTOMIME SKIT	SEGMENT #2 HOST (INTERVIEW) #2: FOUR GUESTS DEMO. NARRATED BY GUEST ON DISCUSSION SET. GUEST INTROS STUDENTS. APPROX. 10 MIN. ANNCR. (SPEC. CLOSE): THIS POEM, CALLED THE WORLD OF SILENCE, WAS WRITTEN BY A DEAF PERSON: "THE RING OF BELLS — WHAT IS IT? THE RUSTLE OF LEAVES, CAN YOU HEAR IT? CAN YOU HEAR THE CLOCK TICK TOCK. A BABBLING BROOK, A FRIEND'S HELLO, THE BARK OF A DOG, THE TELEPHONE'S RING? TO ME, THESE SHOULD NOT MEAN A THING. BUT I CARE — I CARE. I FEEL THE SOUNDS I CANNOT HEAR." FOR ANDY RAPP, THIS IS LAMARR SCOTT,

VIDEO	AUDIO
	WISHING YOU A GOOD EVENING.
RANDOM SHOTS OF GUESTS	TAPE THEME ("DAY BY DAY")
BLACK	

Courtesy of WUCM-TV, Delta College
University Center, Michigan; Andersen Rapp, Executive Producer

The following is from an NBC radio feature series entitled "Emphasis."

---○---

● *As you analyze it, note (1) in what ways, if any, as a network program, it differs from the previous two non-network feature examples; (2) what special writing approaches and techniques mark it as a radio, rather than a television, presentation. Rewrite it as a network television feature.*

---○---

Even if you go to Washington with a closed mind, keep your eyes open. Bill Cullen, At Ease. More after this for Best Western Motels.

Just about everybody who gets to Washington sees the Lincoln Memorial ... most get to the Smithsonian Institution ... and some even manage to find Ford's Theater ... where Lincoln was shot.

But there are hundreds of monuments in the nation's capital that hardly any visitor notices ... and that most Washingtonians themselves know little about. For instance, there are thirty statues of men on horseback ... which may be one or two too many. Some of the riders ... like Ulysses S. Grant ... you may have heard of ... but there are a lot of other generals there that no one now remembers. In the middle of DuPont Circle there is an elegant marble fountain held up by some partly draped ladies. The fountain honors a Union admiral in the Civil War named DuPont. The man who designed the fountain was Daniel Chester French ... one of this country's great sculptors. French also did a lovely statue of a deaf girl learning sign language. It's at Florida Avenue and Seventh Street.

If your taste runs more to nostalgia, there are relief sculptures of 1926 automobiles on the Capitol Garage ... and, for modernists, a lot of strictly abstract sculpture will go on display at the Hirshhorn Museum next year.

When somebody wants to put in a piece of decoration or sculpture, Washington is where they want to do it ... and you can spend weeks there just looking around.

Bill Cullen, Emphasis, At Ease.

Now a word for Best Western.

Courtesy of NBC News

Procedure

If we consider the feature a minidocumentary — and in many instances it is exactly that — the procedure for its preparation is similar to that of the documentary. After a topic is chosen, a preliminary outline is developed and research is done. As with the "Day By Day" series, the writer and researcher are frequently the same person. Following completion of the research a rundown sheet or, as it is sometimes called, a working script, is prepared. Usually much more material is obtained than necessary, and the working script provides a base for editing, organization, content, and time. Ideally, the final working script and the transcript of the program as aired would be identical, except that the transcript would contain the complete program material, including actualities or interviews and other nonannouncer material. Some producers prepare their scripts in rundown or working script form, without the actualities. Others include the complete actualities.

The following are the working script and excerpts from the transcript with the actualities for the same program from CBS Radio's "The American Challenge" series. They illustrate the form the writer uses after he or she has completed the research and, in this instance, after the producer has put together the necessary material. A preliminary working script would not usually contain the timing and the precise quotes of the interviewee, but would indicate the name of the person to be interviewed and the gist of the material sought. A final working script, however, for final editing, would contain the fuller information. Although this series is no longer on the air, the host, Walter Cronkite, continues to do similar programs on radio.

THE AMERICAN CHALLENGE

pgm 10   ward   to live free

MUSIC THEME   up 3 seconds then under for
    CRONKITE: The American Challenge. Thirty Special Reports this weekend brought to you by

---

THEME UP TO END AT :13
    CRONKITE: This is Walter Cronkite, CBS News, reporting on the CBS Radio Network. In a time when the relationship between Great Britain and the colonists in America was steadily growing worse, Thomas Jefferson wrote: "The God who gave us life gave us liberty at the same time; the hand of force may destroy, but cannot disjoin them."
    That's not true anymore. Drugs, electrical stimulation of the brain, the techniques of behavioral psychology can leave life, while taking liberty. An American Challenge, after this.
(COMMERCIAL INSERT)
    Defining freedom is probably a job better left to philosophy students and the people who put dictionaries together. Historian Blanche Cook, a teacher at New York's John Jay College of Criminal Justice believes it is easier to say what freedom is not.
        In: You start looking at what . . .
    Runs: :30
        Out: . . . and stops this man.
    Behavioral psychologist B. F. Skinner believes that a concern for freedom has outlived its time.
        In: I think you can show . . .
    Runs: :36
        Out: . . . then the behavior will change.
    Our very survival, says Dr. Skinner, depends upon controlling people. And the techniques for maintaining that control are available.
        In: I think we have that . . .
    Runs: :16
        Out: . . . to use it.

For historian Cook, the problem is quite different.

        In: We're using this really splendid ...

     Runs: :25

       Out: ... which could free us, really.

To find freedom and the limits of freedom. A matter for debate and an American Challenge; to make liberty more than a word stamped on our coins.

This is Walter Cronkite, CBS News.

#10 — TO LIVE FREE
(MUSIC)

WALTER CRONKITE: THE AMERICAN CHALLENGE. Thirty special broadcasts this weekend. This is Walter Cronkite reporting on the CBS Radio Network.

In a time when the relationship between Great Britain and the colonists was steadily growing worse, Thomas Jefferson wrote, "The God who gave us life, gave us liberty at the same time. The hand of force may destroy, but cannot disjoin them."

That's not true anymore. Drugs, electrical stimulation of the brain, the techniques of behavioral psychology can leave life, while taking liberty. An American challenge, after this.

* * *

CRONKITE: Defining freedom is probably a job better left to philosophy students and the people who put dictionaries together. Historian Blanche Cook, a teacher at New York's John Jay College of Criminal Justice, believes it is easier to say what freedom is not.

BLANCHE COOK: You start looking at what the various police departments, for instance, have done with the technology that came out of Vietnam. The most bizarre thing of all is a fancy program: plant an electrode into somebody's brain who steals a lot, let's say, and gets arrested all the time. And he's going downtown to the supermarket, let's say, and all of a sudden the computer picks up that his adrenalin is going fast, and his heartbeat is going fast, and they figure out, well, he's going to steal something. The computer programs a shock, and stops this man.

CRONKITE: Behavioral psychologist B. F. Skinner believes that a concern for freedom has outlived its time.

B. F. SKINNER: I think you can show that we are misguided in our insistence on the right of the individual, for example, to breed as he wants, or to consume more than a reasonable share of the resources of the world, to pollute the environment. There are not real freedoms, they are the products of our present culture. And if we can change that culture, then the behavior will change.

CRONKITE: Our very survival, says Doctor Skinner, depends upon controlling people, and the techniques for maintaining that control are available.

SKINNER: I think we have that. We have the rudiments of it. And we have to change our culture in such a way that we will be permitted to use it.

CRONKITE: For historian Cook, the problem is quite different.

COOK: We're using this really splendid technology, which could be used to feed people, you know, to really make our lives very comfortable, we're using it to control people. I think that's the really big challenge: how do we use the technology that we have, which could free us, really.

CRONKITE: To find freedom, and the limits of freedom, a matter for debate, and an American challenge, to make liberty more than a word stamped on our coins.

This is Walter Cronkite, CBS News.

As noted above, the feature and the minidocumentary are sometimes one and the same. The growth of the minidocumentary in the 1980s suggests the need for a special section on this program form, and it is found after the following section on the documentary.

The Documentary

It is sometimes said that next to the drama the documentary is the highest form of television and radio art. Many broadcast news personnel say that the documentary, combining as it does news, special events, features, music, and drama, *is* the highest form. At its best the documentary not only synthesizes the creative arts of the broadcast media, but it also makes a signal contribution to public understanding by interpreting the past, analyzing the present or anticipating the future. Sometimes it does all these in a single program, in highly dramatic form, combining intellectual and emotional meaning.

Types

Robert Flaherty is considered a seminal figure in the development of the modern documentary. His "Nanook of the North," completed in 1922, set a pattern for a special type of documentary film. This type went beneath the exterior of life and carefully selected those elements that dramatized people's relationships to the outer and inner facets of their world. Flaherty started with an attitude toward people: he eulogized their strength and nobility in a hostile or, at the very least, difficult environment.

Pare Lorentz, noted for his productions of "The Plow That Broke the Plains" and "The River" under Franklin D. Roosevelt's administration in the 1930s, forwarded another type of documentary: the presentation of a problem affecting a large number of people and the ways in which that problem could be solved. Lorentz's type of documentary called for positive action on the part of the viewer to remedy an unfortunate or ugly situation. A third type of documentary is exemplified by the British film "Night Mail," produced by innovator John Grierson. The details of ordinary, everyday existence — in this instance the delivery in Britain of the night mail — are presented in a dramatic but nonsensational manner. In this type we see people and/or things as they really are; we receive factual information without a special attitude or point of view expressed or stimulated.

These types (the student of documentary writing is urged to view these films) provide the bases for writing the television and radio documentary. The documentary for the mass media may use one of the three approaches or — and this frequently is the case — combine two or more of the types in varying degrees.

Form

Although the documentary is dramatic, it is not a drama in the sense of the fictional play. It is more or less a faithful representation of a true story. This is not to say, however, that all documentaries are unimpeachably true. Editing and narration can make any series of sequences seem other than what they really are. The documentary form is flexible. The semidocumentary or fictional documentary has achieved a certain degree of popularity. Based on reality, it is not necessarily factual. It may take authentic characters but fictionalize the events of their lives; it may present the events accurately but fictionalize the characters; it may take real people and/or real events and speculate, as authentically as possible, in order to fill in documentary gaps; it may take several situations and characters from life and create a semitrue composite picture. Some of Norman Corwin's semidocumentaries raised radio to its highest creative levels.

Although the documentary deals with issues, people, and events of the news, it is not a news story. It is an exploration behind and beneath the obvious. It goes much more in depth than does a news story, exploring not only what happened but, as far as possible, the reasons for what happened, the attitudes and feelings of the people involved, the interpretations of experts, the reactions of other citizens who might be affected, and the implications and significance of the subject not only for some individuals, but also for the whole of society.

The difference between the news story and the documentary may sometimes not relate so much to content as it does to approach. Where the news report is oriented toward objectivity, the documentary is oriented toward interpretation and often presents a distinct point of view. For example, a news program on a murder in New York City may present fully all the known factual material. A documentary on the same subject — such as the classic "Who Killed Michael Farmer?" (part of which is given later in this chapter) — covers considerably more in background and character exploration and provides an understanding and an impact that otherwise would be missing.

The documentary is filmed or taped in the field. The fact that a program may be done outside the studio, however, does not guarantee that it will be a good one or a better one than that done only in the studio. Sometimes small stations can't send out crews for the time it takes to prepare the program effectively, and a documentary may be done in the studio with already existing materials and good transitional narration. However, actualities — the people and events live on tape — always make for a better documentary, all other factors being equal.

Procedure

Essentially, the documentary contains the real words of real persons (or their writings, published and unpublished, including letters if they are not living or cannot possibly be reached and there is no record of their voices), the moving pictures of their actions (or photos and drawings if film or tape is unavailable or they lived before motion pictures) and, concomitantly, the sounds and visuals of real events. These materials, sometimes seemingly unrelated, must be put together into a dramatic, cohesive whole and edited according to an outline and then a script. A good documentary script cannot be created in the isolation of one's bedroom, no matter how much inspiration one may find there.

First, the writer must have an idea. What subject of public interest is worthy of documentary treatment? The idea for the program frequently comes not from the writer, but from the producer. Increasing hunger and starvation in the world? Murder and violence by a given government to supress political enemies? Political and economic discrimination against minorities? Corruption in a country's leadership? Economic crises and unemployment? Threat of nuclear holocaust? What about something on the scenic pleasures of southern California? Or the experience of riding a train across Siberia? Or the life and times of Leonardo Da Vinci?

A documentary does not have to be controversial, but can be more a feature of the how-it-works or how-it-was or how-to type. The very use of live people and live events, however, does make most documentaries pertinent to ongoing life and therefore, to a greater or lesser degree, controversial.

The investigative documentary came into focus through coverage of events such as Watergate, the Nixon impeachment proceedings, the Pentagon Papers, and similar national and international happenings, and became popularized — and institutionalized — through the CBS weekly program "60 Minutes."

All documentaries should have a point of view. What is the *purpose* of the particular documentary you are preparing? To present an objective many-sided view of a community's traditions and problems? By lack of criticism, to justify violence as a means for international political gain? To show the courage of a minority group in a hostile social environment? To show the effects of pollution on a friendly natural environment? To show that the only way to find true rejuvenation of body and spirit is to spend all of one's vacation time in encounter groups (or health clubs or dude ranches or hot tubs) in southern California? To what degree will the writer's personal beliefs (or those of the producer, network executives, agency representatives, or sponsor) determine program content and orientation?

When the subject and the point of view are determined, the real work starts: from thorough research in libraries, to personal visits to people and places, to investigations of what video and audio materials on the subject are already available. When the research is completed, the writer can prepare a more definitive outline.

Until the material is accumulated and editing begins, and work on a final script is started, the writer's work may seem temporarily in abeyance. Not so! As a writer, you may be involved intricately in the production process. You may suggest the specific materials to be obtained, sometimes recommend the orientation these materials should take, and even help gather them. In terms of getting actualities on tape, you may write transition material, including lead-ins and lead-outs and, in some cases, the questions and even some of the answers for interviews. You may prepare preliminary narration to tie the materials together as a final script begins to take shape in your mind. As the materials come in you will constantly revise your outline, make it more and more complete, and begin to juxtapose narration with the filmed or taped material.

After all the materials have been gathered and have been seen and/or heard many times by the writer the development of a final script can begin in earnest. The final script is used for the selection and organization of the specific materials to be used in the final editing and taping of the program. It is not surprising, in terms of the high degree of coordination and cooperation needed to complete a good documentary, that in many instances the writer also serves as the producer and/or the director or editor.

Sometimes an entire documentary may come from just a few minutes of tape that carries material available to no other reporter or station. The writer may decide that this material would make a good beginning or a good ending, and plan the rest of the program around it. For example, a network may have an exclusive film of a minute's duration of a secret meeting between the heads of two major world powers. From this, with the aid of stock footage, interviews, commentary, and further taping or filming not even necessarily related directly to the event, a documentary program can be created.

Technique

Human interest is the key to good documentary writing. Even if you want to present only facts, and even if the facts seem stilted and dry, make them dramatic. Develop them in terms of the people they represent. Even if the subject is inanimate — such as a new invention — endow it with live attributes; indeed, we have all known machines that seem more alive than some people we have known! The documentary script should be developed in dramatic terms: the exploration of character, the introduction of a conflict (the problem that creates the happening requiring documentary treatment), and the development of this conflict through the revelation of the complications involved until a crisis is reached. Although the big things create the action, the little things, the human elements, are important in creating and holding interest.

The documentary utilizes many elements of the drama, including background music, special settings for television, exotic nonrealistic and visually unproducible settings in radio, narration, special effects, and, in the semi- or fictionalized documentary, actors portraying real persons, living or dead. A narrator is almost always used in the documentary. Use the narrator judiciously. Too much narration distracts. Don't let the program sound or look like a series of educational interviews or lectures. Make the points clear and concise. Sometimes relatively important material must be deleted, for legal or time reasons, from the presentations of actual persons. A narrator frequently can summarize on-the-spot materials that cannot be presented as actualities.

Application: Radio

Process   A radio documentary may be produced with virtually no budget and little equipment save two or three tape recorders and some tapes. One such documentary, produced as a college course project at the University of North Carolina and the recipient of a national award for public service reporting, illustrates how simple and direct the documentary-making process can be.

● *If you are studying this chapter as a member of a class or other writing group, plan to write and produce, with your colleagues, a similar documentary based on a problem in your community.*

First, the class decided on a subject: the problems of the small farmer in the Piedmont region of North Carolina (where the university is located) and the possible relationships of these problems to politics.

The three major documentary types were combined in the purpose of the documentary: to present information in a straightforward, unbiased manner; to show by implication that there was a problem that had to be solved and to indicate several possible solutions; and to present the farmer as a persevering person in a difficult economic environment. It was decided that not only farmers, but also experts from the university should be interviewed and their tapes edited in a sort of counterpoint fashion.

Research was the next step, with as much material as could be found on the

problem gathered from an examination of all available literature and from preliminary talks with farmers and persons familiar with the farm problem. The subject and
purpose were clarified further and, on the basis of the projected findings of the
documentary, specific interviewees were chosen — farmers in terms of size, location, and crop of the farm, and experts in terms of their academic department and
special area of study.

A careful distillation of material already gathered led to the formation of a series
of pertinent and interrelated questions to be asked of the farmers and the experts.
After the interviews were completed, a script containing the narration and a description of the taped material to be inserted was developed from all the material
available, including tapes, library research, and personal interviews. An analysis of
the script indicated places that were weak, some because of the lack of material and
others because of the superfluity of material. Further field work and the addition and
pruning of material resulted in a final script, ready for the editing process.

The following are excerpts from a composite of the script and a verbatim transcription of the program. The final script is shown in capitals; the material in
parentheses is that actually recorded and incorporated into the program with the
narration. Note here the use of numbers indicating the tape and **cut** to be used, with
notations of the first and last words of each cut to help the editor.

————————————————————O————————————————————

- *One criticism of this script may be that it tries to cover too many sub-*
jects. Another may be that it is not sufficiently dramatic. If you find any
validity to these criticisms, take the material contained in the script and
other material that you can get through your personal research, and re-
write this documentary in outline form, improving on it as you think
necessary.

————————————————————O————————————————————

THE PIEDMONT, NORTH CAROLINA FARMER AND POLITICS

OPEN COLD:	TAPE #1, CUT 1, DUPREE SMITH: "I WOULD LIKE VERY MUCH … BEST PLACE TO WORK."
	(I would like very much to spend my entire life here on the farm because I feel like being near the land and being near the soil and seeing the operation of God on this earth is the best place to live and the best place to work.)
MUSIC:	IN, UP, AND UNDER
NARRATOR:	THIS IS THE SMALL FARMER IN THE PIEDMONT OF NORTH CAROLINA.
MUSIC:	UP AND OUT
NARRATOR:	YOU ARE LISTENING TO "THE PIEDMONT, NORTH CAROLINA FARMER AND POLITICS." THE VOICE YOU JUST HEARD WAS THAT OF DUPREE SMITH, A FARMER IN PIEDMONT, NORTH CAROLINA. IN RURAL AMERICA A CENTURY AGO THE FARM PROBLEM WAS AN INDIVIDUAL ONE OF DIGGING A LIVING OUT OF THE LAND. EACH FARMER SOLVED HIS OWN INDIVIDUAL PROBLEMS WITHOUT

GOVERNMENT AID. NEARLY EVERYONE FARMED. TODAY, BECAUSE OF INCREASING COST OF MAINTAINING CROPS, LARGER SURPLUSES, HEAVIER STORAGE COSTS AND LOWER FARM INCOME, THE SMALL FARMER IN NORTH CAROLINA, AS WELL AS ACROSS THE NATION, HAS BEEN UNABLE TO DEPEND ON HIS LAND FOR A LIVING. PRODUCTION CONTINUED TO GROW, SURPLUSES MOUNTED. FARM INCOMES FELL AND THE GOVERNMENT SUBSIDIES NECESSARILY GREW.

PROFESSOR KOVENOCK: TAPE #2, CUT 1: "THE COMMON PROBLEMS ... ARE THESE."
(The common problems shared by almost all national farmers today and, at the same time, most North Carolina farmers, are these.)

NARRATOR: YOU ARE LISTENING TO PROFESSOR DAVID KOVENOCK OF THE POLITICAL SCIENCE DEPARTMENT OF THE UNIVERSITY OF NORTH CAROLINA.

KOVENOCK: TAPE #2, CUT 2: "FIRST OF ALL ... SHELTER FOR HIS FAMILY."
(First of all, a decline in the income going to the farmer — a problem of — this is particularly for, let us say, the marginal farmer, the farmer with a small operation in North Carolina and the rest of the country — the problem of obtaining employment off the farm, that is, some relatively attractive alternative to continuing an operation on the farm that is becoming insufficient for feeding, clothing, and buying shelter for his family.)

NARRATOR: THIS IS DUPREE SMITH'S PROBLEM.

SMITH: TAPE #1, CUT 2: "YES, THAT WAS MY DESIRE ... PART TIME AND WORKING."
(Yes, that was my desire after returning from service, was to go back to nature and live and raise a family where I felt that I would enjoy living to the fullest. For several years, on this same amount of land, I was able to support my family and myself adequately. For the last year or two, this has been on the decrease. The decline has been to such extent, that I've had to go into other fields — my wife helping part time and working.)

NARRATOR: WHAT SPECIFICALLY ARE DUPREE SMITH'S PROBLEMS?

KOVENOCK: TAPE #2, CUT 3: "THE COMMON PROBLEM ... OCCUPATIONAL PURSUIT?"
(The common problem shared by the North Carolina farmer and by the national farmer would be, first of all, the condition of agriculture, the relationship of the supply of agricultural commodities to the demand and, of course, consequently, the price that the farmer receives which, of course, now is somewhat depressed. The second major problem is the condition of the rest of the economy as a whole — that is, is it sufficiently good so that the farmer has some alternatives to continuing his, currently, rather unsatisfactory occupational pursuit?)

NARRATOR: FARMERS ARE MARKETING MORE, BUT ARE RECEIVING LOWER PRICES FOR THEIR CROPS AND PRODUCE. DR. PHILIPS RUSSELL, A FORMER COLLEGE PROFESSOR AND RETIRED FARMER, HAS THIS TO SAY:

PHILLIPS RUSSELL: TAPE #3, CUT 1: "THE FARMER HAS BEEN LOSING ... IN AN UNPROTECTED MARKET."

(The farmer has been losing out everywhere, because he has to buy the things that he needs in a protected market and he has to sell in an unprotected market.)

NARRATOR: WHAT IS THE FARMER'S ANSWER TO THIS PROBLEM? FARMING HAS BECOME A BUSINESS INSTEAD OF A WAY OF LIFE. THE FARMER IS FORCED TO CURTAIL HIS ACTIVITIES ON THE FARM IN ORDER TO SUPPORT HIS FAMILY. DR. RUSSELL SAYS:

RUSSELL: TAPE #3, CUT 2: "THAT'S THE ONLY WAY ... 24-HOUR FARMER."
(That's the only way that a man can continue in farming — is to make some extra money in town to spend it out in the country because he's losing everywhere as a 24-hour farmer.)

NARRATOR: FARMER HARRY WOODS COMMENTS:
HARRY WOODS: TAPE #4, CUT 1: "I WOULD HATE ... AT THIS TIME."
(I would hate to have to try — let's put it that way — right at this time.)

INTERVIEWER: TAPE #1, CUT 1 (CONT.): "WOULD YOU LIKE ... IT FULL TIME?"
(Would you like to be able to work it full time?)

WOODS: TAPE #4, CUT 1 (CONT.): "WELL, I ENJOY ... IT'S PRETTY ROUGH."
(Well, I enjoy farming. I enjoy it, but as far as actually making a living out of it, I would hate to think that I had to do it, because it's pretty rough.)

NARRATOR: MANY BELIEVE THAT THE BASIS FOR SOLVING THE PROBLEM LIES AT THE FEDERAL GOVERNMENT LEVEL. HARDEST HIT IS THE FARMER WHO CAN LEAST AFFORD IT, THE SMALL COMMERCIAL FARMERS WORKING INFERIOR LAND. THEY LACK ADEQUATE CAPITAL TO IMPROVE THEIR HOMES. MUCH OF THEIR EFFORT GOES INTO PRODUCING THEIR OWN FOOD. OFTEN THEY DON'T HAVE THE MECHANICAL AIDS TO MAKE THEM MORE EFFICIENT. THEY ALSO GET LITTLE BENEFIT FROM THE SUBSIDIES AND HIGH SUPPORTS BECAUSE THEIR YIELD IS LOW AND THEY CAN'T AFFORD TO STORE UNTIL THE GOVERNMENT MAKES PAYMENT.

RUSSELL: TAPE #3, CUT 3: "IF FARMING ... THAT'D BE FATAL."
(If farming is to be continued, and the country still has to rely on the farms for three very important things: food, feed, and fiber, and if the farming system collapses, we won't have enough fiber, and in case of war, that'd be fatal.)

*   *   *

NARRATOR: BESIDES PRICE SUPPORTS, STORAGE AND SOIL BANKS, THE GOVERNMENT SPENDS SOME TWO AND A HALF BILLION DOLLARS TO OPERATE ITS OTHER FUNCTIONS FOR THE IMPROVEMENT OF FARMING. THERE IS LITTLE AGREEMENT AS TO JUST WHAT ROLE GOVERNMENT SHOULD PLAY IN ASSISTING THE FARMER. FARMER HARRY WOODS HAD THIS TO SAY:

WOODS: TAPE #4, CUT 2: "THE FARM PROBLEM ... TO HAVE THEM."
(The farm problem has been with us ever since I've known anything about the farm, and there have been both sides in, and it's never been solved yet. Until they really get down to business and want to solve it, why, it never will be. Now, you said something about politics, why, you know, and I think that everybody else realizes that there is politics in the farm program as they are administered. By the time that they go into the Congress and come out, you know what happens, and, it's difficult to ever

	work out something that, well, that is workable. But, as far as Republicans or Democrats, why, we've had farm problems under both parties, and I think we'll continue to have them.)
KOVENOCK:	TAPE #2, CUT 4: "THERE'S COMMON AGREEMENT ... THIRTY-EIGHT CENTS." (There's common agreement, common ground for agreement, that during the last seven or eight years that farm income has gone down roughly twenty-five per cent. The farm purchasing power is at the lowest point since sometime during the 1930's. Further, we have relatively great social dislocations among farmers and non-farmers in rural America due to the relative decline of the position of the farmer in the economic sphere. We now have more employees in the Department of Agriculture than we've ever had before, and, of course, they are serving fewer farmers. The size of the surplus is, of course, grounds for common agreement. It's multiplied six or seven times; it's now worth, roughly, seven billion dollars. And, of course, the farmer's share of the dollars that we spend in the grocery store has declined now to a low point of thirty-eight cents.)

*   *   *

MUSIC	IN AND UNDER
NARRATOR:	THESE ARE THE PROBLEMS.
MUSIC:	FADE OUT
NARRATOR:	THE ANSWERS ARE NOT APPARENT. THE FARM INCOME DILEMMA SPELLS TROUBLE, NOT ONLY FOR THE FARMERS, BUT FOR THE PEOPLE WHO DO BUSINESS WITH THEM, POLITICIANS, GOVERNMENT OFFICIALS AND TAX PAYERS ALIKE. WHAT DOES THE FARMER, AS A MEMBER OF THE AMERICAN SOCIETY, DESERVE? PROFESSOR S. H. HOBBS OF THE SOCIOLOGY DEPARTMENT OF THE UNIVERSITY OF NORTH CAROLINA HAD THIS TO SAY:
HOBBS:	TAPE #5, CUT 1: "ONE IS THE PROBLEM ... ECONOMIC SYSTEM." (One is the problem of maintaining income adequate to maintain a level of living comparable with other groups. This does not mean that farmers deserve an income equal to that of any other group, but he does deserve to have an income that enables him to live comfortably in the American economic system.)
NARRATOR:	IN A REGULATED, PROTECTED, AND PARTIALLY SUBSIDIZED ECONOMY SUCH AS OURS, THE FARMER REQUIRES CONSIDERABLE PROTECTION. THE TASK IS TO DEVISE NEW METHODS WHICH WILL PROVIDE HIM WITH AN ADEQUATE INCOME FOR THE VITAL FOOD WHICH HE PRODUCES.
SMITH:	TAPE #1, CUT 1: "I WOULD LIKE ... PLACE TO WORK." (I would like very much to spend my entire life here on the farm because I feel like being near the land and being near the soil and seeing the operation of God on this earth is the best place to live and the best place to work.)
MUSIC:	IN, UP, HOLD, UNDER.
NARRATOR:	YOU HAVE BEEN LISTENING TO "THE PIEDMONT, NORTH CAROLINA, FARMER AND POLITICS." THIS PROGRAM WAS A STUDENT PRODUCTION OF THE RADIO PRODUCTION CLASS IN THE DEPARTMENT OF RADIO,

	TELEVISION AND MOTION PICTURES OF THE UNIVERSITY OF NORTH CAROLINA. ASSOCIATED WITH THE PRODUCTION WERE: BUD CARTER, YOSHI CHINEN, JIM CLARK, WILLIAM GAY, ROGER KOONCE, JOHN MOORE, ANITA ROSEFIELD, ALEX WARREN, ANNE WILLIAMS, STEVE SILVERSTEIN AS ENGINEER, AND WAYNE UPCHURCH, YOUR ANNOUNCER.
MUSIC:	UP AND OUT.

Structure   One of the broadcasting's finest documentaries was CBS's "Who Killed Michael Farmer?" an exploration in depth of a murder, the murderers, and their environment. It is not only a classic, but remains an excellent example today of how to write documentaries. Part of the documentary is presented here, with bracketed comments analyzing the structure of the script and some of the writing techniques used.

WHO KILLED MICHAEL FARMER?

OPENS COLD:

MURROW:	This is Ed Murrow. Here is how a mother and a father remember their son — Michael Farmer.
ET:	MR. AND MRS. FARMER: MRS. FARMER: Michael was tall and very good looking. He had blond hair and blue eyes. Maybe I'm prejudiced as a mother, but I thought he had a saintly face. MR. FARMER: He was always laughing and joking. He was a very courageous and spirited boy. He was athletic, even though he walked with a limp from an attack of polio when he was ten years old. He was an excellent student who had great plans for his future. It's a hard thing to realize that there is no future any longer.
MURROW:	Michael Farmer died on the night of July 30, 1957. He was fifteen years old. He was stabbed and beaten to death in a New York City park. Boys in a teen-age street gang were arrested for this crime. Ten gang members — under fifteen years of age — were convicted of juvenile delinquency and committed to state training schools. Seven other boys — fifteen to eighteen — stood trial for first degree murder ... were defended by twenty-seven court-appointed lawyers. Their trial lasted ninety-three days; ended last Tuesday. This was the verdict of an all male, blue ribbon jury.
ET:	JUROR: We found Louis Alvarez and Charles Horton guilty of murder in the second degree, and we also found Lencio de Leon and Leroy Birch guilty of manslaughter in the second degree. We found Richard Hills and George Melendez not guilty because we believe these boys were forced to go along with the gang the night of the murder. We also found John McCarthy not guilty because we were convinced, beyond a reasonable doubt, that this boy was mentally sick and didn't know what was going on at any time.
MURROW:	It would seem that this case now is closed. All that remains is for a judge to pass sentence. Under the law, the gang alone is guilty of the murder of Michael Farmer. But there is more to be said. More is involved here than one act of violence committed on one summer night. The roots of this crime

go back a long ways. In the next hour — you will hear the voices of boys and adults involved in the case. This is *not* a dramatization. The tragedy first became news on the night of July 30, 1957. At 6:30 on this steaming summer evening in New York City, the Egyptian Kings and Dragons gang began to assemble. They met outside a neighborhood hangout — a candy story at 152nd Street and Broadway, in Manhattan's upper West Side. They came from a twenty-block area … from teeming tenements, rooming houses and housing projects. One of their leaders remembers the number of boys present this night.

[A standard method of effectively opening a radio documentary is to select carefully out of the mass of taped material several short statements by persons involved and present them immediately in order to get the audience attention and interest as well as to tell, sharply and concretely, what the program is about. This is especially effective here in the opening statements of Mr. and Mrs. Farmer. The stark nature of the beginning of the program — it opens cold, no introduction, no music — lends force to the opening. Short opening quotes are not usually sufficient, however, to provide enough background information. The narrator condenses and states in terse terms the necessary additional material. The type of documentary is suggested close to the beginning. The statement: "But there is more to be said. More is involved here … the roots of crime go back a long ways" indicates the line of development: not only will the event and the people involved be explored in depth, but a problem will be presented and solutions will be sought.]

ET: GANG MEMBER:
We had a lot o' little kids, big kids, we had at least seventy-five — then a lot of 'em had to go home before nine o'clock; we was supposed to leave at nine o'clock but then we changed our plans to ten o'clock, you know. So I told a lot o' little kids I don't wanna see them get into trouble, you know, nice guys, so I told them they could go home. So they went home. They left us with around twenty-one kids.

MORROW: People sitting on the stoops and garbage cans along this street watched them … grouped together, talking excitedly. They called each other by their nicknames: Magician, Big Man, Little King, Boppo. No one bothered to ask what they were talking about. This boy remembers.

ET: GANG MEMBER:
They were talking about what they were going to do and everything. They were going to fight and everything. But they'd never planned nothing. They just said we were gonna go to the fight and we were just gonna get some guys for revenge. They said we ain't gonna let these Jesters beat up any of our guys no more.

MURROW: The Jesters are a street gang in an adjoining neighborhood — Washington Heights, where Michael Farmer lived. The two gangs were feuding. Boys on both sides had been beaten and stabbed. There is evidence that this night the gang planned to surprise and attack any Jesters they could find. They came prepared for a fight.

ET: GANG MEMBER:
Some picked a stick and some had got some knives and chains out of their houses and everything. One had a bayonet. No, a machete.

MURROW: Holding these weapons they lingered on the corner of a brightly lit street in the heart of a great city. A police station was one block away. One gang leader went to a candy story ... telephoned the President of a brother gang ... requested guns and cars for the night's activity ... was told: "We can't join you. We have troubles of our own tonight." Shortly after nine PM, the gang walked to a near-by park ... was followed there by some girl friends. A gang member, 14 years old, continues the story.

ET: GANG MEMBER:
We went down to the park and sat around for a while. Then we started drinking and we drank whiskey and wine and we was drunk. Then we started talkin' about girls. We started sayin' to the girls that if they get us to bring us some roses an' all that — that if we get caught to write to us and all this.

MURROW: In one hour, Michael Farmer would be dead. The gang prepared to move out. Some had doubts.

[Suspense is an important ingredient of the documentary. But it is not the suspense of finding out what is going to happen. The documentary is based on fact: we already know. The suspense is in learning the motivations, the inner feelings, the attitudes of the persons involved even as the actual event is retold. This is implied in the narrator's previous speech.]

ET: GANG MEMBER:
I didn't wanna go at first, but they said come on. So then all the big guys forced me to go. I was scared. I was worried. I realized like what I was doing I'd prob-ably get in trouble.

MURROW: They left the park and headed for trouble at about ten PM. They walked uptown toward the neighborhood of the rival gang — the Jesters. They walked in two's and three's to avoid attention. Along the way, they met, by chance, this boy.

ET: GANG MEMBER:
I was walkin' uptown with a couple of friends and we ran into Magician and them there. They asked us if we wanted to go to a fight, and we said yes. When they asked me if I wanted to go to a fight, I couldn't say no. I mean I could say no, but for old-times sake, I said yes.

MURROW: He was a former member of the gang — just went along this night, "For Old-times Sake." Next stop: Highbridge Park ... within the territory of the Jesters. Michael Farmer lived one block from the park. In the summer, the Egyptian Kings and Dragons fought the Jesters at the park swimming pool. This pool is closed at ten PM but not drained. Boys in the neighborhood frequently slip through a breach in the gate to swim here late at night. The Egyptian Kings and Dragons regrouped near the pool. Two gang members continue the story.

ET: GANG MEMBERS:
FIRST BOY: We were waiting over there, in the grass. Then two guys went down to see if there were a lot of the Jesters down there. To check. I was kind of nervous; felt kind of cold inside.
SECOND BOY: They sent three guys around the block. We walked around the block to see how strong the club was we was gonna fight. To see if they had lots of guys and what-not. What we saw, they had lots of big guys. I'd say about nineteen, twenty or eighteen, like that. And we figured it out so we kept on walking around the block.

MURROW: While their scouts prowled the neighborhood, Michael Farmer and his friend, sixteen-year-old Roger McShane, were in Mike Farmer's apartment ... listening to rock 'n' roll records. This is Mrs. Farmer.

[We can see the use here of D. W. Griffith's technique of dynamic cutting: switching back and forth between two or more settings and two or more persons or groups of people who are following a parallel course in time and in action. The actions of the gang have been presented in chronological order. Now time is moved back, and the actions of Michael Farmer and Roger McShane will catch up in time and place.]

ET: MRS. FARMER:
They stayed in his room playin' these new records that they had bought and Michael came out to the kitchen, just as I asked my husband what time it was, to set the clock. It was then five after ten. He asked for a glass of milk and as he walked from the kitchen, he asked, "I'm going to walk Roger home." And that was the last time I saw him.

MURROW: Both boys had been warned by their parents to stay out of Highbridge Park at night. But, as they walked along the street on this steaming July evening, they decided to sneak a swim in the park pool. At this pool, the Egyptian Kings and Dragons were waiting for their scouts to return. Here is what happened next; first in the words of Roger McShane; then in words of the gang members.

ET: McSHANE AND EGYPTIAN KINGS:
McSHANE: It was ten-thirty when we entered the park; we saw couples on the benches, in the back of the pool, and they all stared at us, and I guess they must 'ave saw the gang there — I don't think they were fifty or sixty feet away. When we reached the front of the stairs, we looked up and there was two of their gang members on top of the stairs. They were two smaller ones, and they had garrison belts wrapped around their hands. They didn't say nothin' to us, they looked kind of scared.
FIRST BOY: I was scared. I knew they were gonna jump them, an' everythin' and I was scared. When they were comin' up, they all were separatin' and everything like that.
McSHANE: I saw the main body of the gang slowly walk out of the bushes, on my right. I turned around fast, to see what Michael was going to do, and this kid came runnin' at me with the belts. Then I ran, myself, and told Michael to run.
SECOND BOY: He couldn't run anyway, 'cause we were all around him. So then I said, "You're a Jester," and he said "Yeah," and I punched him in the face. And then somebody hit him with a bat over the head. And then I kept punchin' him. Some of them were too scared to do anything. They were just standin' there, lookin'.
THIRD BOY: I was watchin' him. I didn't wanna hit him at first. Then I kicked him twice. He was layin' on the ground, lookin' up at us. I kicked him on the jaw, or some place; then I kicked him in the stomach. That was the least I could do, was kick 'im.
FOURTH BOY: I was aimin' to hit him, but I didn't get a chance to hit him. There was so many guys on him — I got scared when I saw the knife go into the guy, and I ran right there. After everybody ran, this guy stayed, and started hittin' him with a machete.

MURROW: The rest of the gang pursued Roger McShane.

ET: <u>McSHANE:</u>

I ran down the hill and there was three more of the gang members down at the bottom of the hill, in the baseball field; and the kids chased me down hill, yelling to them to get me.

MURROW: Members of the gang remember.

ET: <u>EGYPTIAN KINGS AND McSHANE:</u>

FIRST BOY: Somebody yelled out, "Grab him. He's a Jester." So then they grabbed him. Mission grabbed him, he turned around and stabbed him in the back. I was ... I was stunned. I couldn't do nuthin'. And then Mission — he went like that and he pulled ... he had a switch blade and he said, "you're gonna hit him with the bat or I'll stab you." So I just hit him lightly with the bat. SECOND BOY: Mission stabbed him and the guy he ... like hunched over. He's standin' up and I knock him down. Then he was down on the ground, everybody was kickin' him, stompin' him, punchin' him, stabbin' him so he tried to get back up and I knock him down again. Then the guy stabbed him in the back with a bread knife.

THIRD BOY: I just went like that, and I stabbed him with the bread knife. You know, I was drunk so I just stabbed him. (LAUGHS) He was screamin' like a dog. He was screamin' there. And then I took the knife out and I told the other guys to run. So I ran and then the rest of the guys ran with me. They wanted to stay there and keep on doin' it, so I said, "No, come on. Don't kill the guy." And we ran.

ET: FOURTH BOY: The guy that stabbed him in the back with the bread knife, he told me that when he took the knife out o' his back, he said, "Thank you." McSHANE: They got up fast right after they stabbed me. And I just lay there on my stomach and there was five of them as they walked away. And as they walked away the ... this other big kid came down with a machete or some large knife of some sort, and he wanted to stab me too with it. And they told him, "No, come on. We got him. We messed him up already. Come on." And they took off up the hill and they all walked up the hill and right after that they all of 'em turned their heads and looked back at me. I got up and staggered into the street to get a cab. And I got in a taxi and I asked him to take me to the Medical Center and get my friend and I blacked out.

MURROW: The gang scattered and fled from the park. This boy believes he is the last gang member who saw Michael Farmer this night.

ET: <u>GANG MEMBER:</u>

While I was runnin' up the footpath, I saw somebody staggering in the bushes and I just looked and turned around, looked up and kept on runnin'. I think that was the Farmer boy, he was staggerin' in the bushes.

[The suspense has been built and a climax reached. The selection and editing of taped materials to tell the story of the assault and murder are done magnificently. Excerpts from the taped interviews were selected to follow a chronological pattern   present the actions, to feelings, and attitudes of the gang members in terms of increasing tempo and violence. Various physical and emotional viewpoints are presented, all relating to one another and building the suspense into an ultimate explosion. The documentary should be dramatic. Is there any doubt about the existence of drama in the preceding sequence? The audience is put into the center of the action, feeling it perhaps even more strongly than if the incident were fictionalized and presented, as such incidents frequently are, on a police series. Could any line of a play be more dramatic than, in context, "That was the least I could do, was kick 'im," or "(LAUGHS) He was screamin' like a dog," or "The guy that stabbed him in the back with the bread knife, he told me that when he took the knife out o' his back, he said 'Thank you'"?]

MURROW:	He left behind a boy nearly dead ... continued home ... had a glass of milk ... went to bed. But then.
ET:	GANG MEMBER:
	I couldn't sleep that night or nuthin' 'cause I used to fall asleep for about half an hour. Wake up again during the middle of the night. My mother said, "What was the matter with you? Looks like something is wrong." I said, "Nothin'."
MURROW:	That boy used a baseball bat in the attack. This boy used a bread knife.
ET:	GANG MEMBER:
	First I went to the river to throw my knife away and then I went home. An' then I couldn't sleep. I was in bed. My mother kept on askin' me where was I and I ... I told her, you know, that I was in the movies. I was worried about them two boys. If they would die ... I knew I was gonna get caught.
MURROW:	At Presbyterian Medical Center, Roger McShane was on the critical list. Before undergoing major surgery that saved his life, he told about the attack in Highbridge Park. The official police record reveals what happened next. The speaker: New York City's Deputy Police Commissioner, Walter Arm.
ET:	COMMISSIONER ARM:
	A member of the hospital staff notified the police, and patrolmen of the 34th precinct arrived at the hospital a few minutes afterwards and learned from the McShane boy that his friend Michael Farmer was still in the park, under attack. The patrolmen rushed to the park, where they found the Farmer boy just before 11:00 PM. He was lying on the ground off the footpath and moaning in pain. The policemen were soon joined by detectives and young Farmer told them, "The Egyptian Kings got me." The Farmer boy made this comment as he was being rushed to the hospital at 11:05 PM. The parents of the boy were notified.
MURROW:	Mr. and Mrs. Farmer continue the story.
ET:	MR. AND MRS. FARMER:
	MR. FARMER: The Sergeant from the 34th Precinct called us, and asked who I was, and was I the father of Michael Farmer. I said I was, and he said, "Well, your boy is in Mother Cabrini Hospital, in serious condition." I identified myself further, as a fireman in this area, and he said, "Oh, I'll come right down and give you a lift down to the hospital." So this sergeant drove us down to the hospital; as we walked in, the officer who was on duty there called the sergeant, and he said the boy had died fifteen minutes earlier.
	MRS. FARMER: And the sister there in the hospital took us downstairs to identify the body. He had an expression as though he was just calling for help.
	MR. FARMER: Well, it was real bad ... he was my number one boy.
MURROW:	This boy had never been in trouble with the police. Several Egyptian Kings and Dragons claim they often saw him with the Jesters; assumed he was a member.

The Jesters say neither Farmer nor McShane belonged to their gang ... and according to police, there is no evidence to the contrary. From the Jesters, police learned which boys might have been involved in the assault at Highbridge Park. At 6:30 AM, this gang member heard somebody knocking at the door of his apartment in a housing project.

ET: GANG MEMBER:

I hear this knockin' on the door. I didn't think it was the police, you know. 'Cause, you know, I thought I wasn't gonna get caught, so I was layin' in bed and told my mother, "Mommie, I think that's the milkman knockin' on the door or somebody." She said, "Why don't you answer it," and I said, "No, I'm in my underwear." So she says, "OK, I'll go." She opened the door and my mother comes over, "You get in any trouble last night?" And I says, "No, Mommie, I didn't get in no trouble last night." And then she says, "Well, there's a police-man over here, wants to see you." And I says, "What for," and he says, "Some-thin' that happened last night," and I says, "OK," then, I started thinkin' of trying, you know, runnin' away from the house, so I put on my clothes and acted innocent, you know. He said to me, "You know what happened last night?" I say, "No, No. I don't know a thing that happened last night. I was in the car from ten on." He says, "Oh, if that's the truth, you have nothin' to worry about. You like to come down to the police station with us?" And I said, "OK."

MURROW: Another gang member spent the morning in Children's Court, pleading inno-cent to a robbery committed two weeks earlier. He was released, pending a hearing. When he returned home, police were waiting to question him about the murder of Michael Farmer. This is the boy who used a bread knife in the assault at Highbridge Park.

ET: GANG MEMBER:

Well, when we was goin' to the ... to the paddy wagon, the detective, he kept wipin' his feet on my suit. So I told him to cut it out, and he still won't cut it out. So then, then the Sergeant says, "Cut it out," so then he said, "Why don't you mind your business," and he kept on doin' it. He kept on wipin' his feet on my suit, and I just got the suit out of the cleaners, that's all. I told him, "I just got the suit out of the cleaners," and he says to me, "That's just too bad. That suit belongs in the garbage can." So he kept on wipin' his feet on my suit, and he kept on sayin', "You murderer" and all this. They kept on sayin', "You're gonna get the electric chair, you're gonna get the electric chair." He kept on sayin' that to me; he made me mad. If I had a gun, I would have shot them all.

MURROW: He told us, "I hate cops." The police say his story of what happened in that paddy wagon is fantasy. They also deny threatening another gang member who explains why he wanted to be caught.

ET: GANG MEMBER:

I was crackin' up 'cause I wanted them to hurry up and come and get me and get it over with, so when I got picked up, I felt safe then. We went in the car and then they threatened me. I mean, not exactly a threat, but they told me what was goin' to happen: I'd get beat up if I didn't talk. So I told them, "Tell me, who was the guy that squealed?" They told me, "Who do you think you are, Dillinger or somebody — ya gonna get even with the guy?" I said, "No, I just wanted to know." They said, "No." So they took me to the Precinct; it made me laugh to see all the guys sitting there in the ... in the ... when I walked in, everybody said, "Ha ha," and started laughin' so I felt all right with the fellas then. My girl was sitting there anyway, and she ... she had the knives.

MURROW: Police found two hunting knives in the bureau drawer of a fifteen-year-old girlfriend of the gang. Two gang members admitted that they gave these knives to the girl after the assault at Highbridge Park. The police record continues.

ET: COMMISSIONER ARM:
The search of the gang during their interrogation yielded five knives, several garrison belts and a heavy length of chain. All of the young men arrested made full admissions to police officers and to representatives from the staff of District Attorney Hogan. At 8:00 PM the following day, seven of the boys were charged with homicide, two others were charged with attempted homicide, and ten others were charged with juvenile delinquency.

MURROW: Police said, "This is the largest group of boys ever arrested for a New York City killing." Statistically, they were among 58 youths in the city arrested in 1957 for murder and non-negligent manslaughter ... among more than three thousand youths under twenty-one arrested in the nation last year for crimes of major violence ... and among an estimated one million youths arrested for crimes of all kinds. The father of Michael Farmer attended the preliminary court hearing of the gang members later indicted for the murder of his son. As he watched them arraigned before a judge, he made a judgment of his own.

ET: MR. FARMER:
They are monsters — in my mind I classify them as savage animals. That's all. I don't think that they have any civilization in them. I think they're just two-legged animals. They haven't any concept of living with other people, outside of to show that they can do something worse than the other or to claim any sort of notoriety. These boys didn't even hang their heads, most of them, when they came to court. They stood erect and looked around the court for their relatives. And so forth. One of them had a small smirk when they looked in our direction. They should be put away, and kept away. Or if the penalty is death, to be executed. Certainly they set themselves up in the form of a judge, jury and execution squad in the case of my son. All in the matter of minutes. This is pure jungle activity.

[Thus far the script has told what happened. In the material dealing with actions and attitudes after the crime was committed, the script begins to imply that there is more to the story than what happened, that the persons involved are not the two-dimensional characters of the television fiction series. Yet, the act was so grievous and wanton that it is not too difficult to come to the same conclusion as Mr. Farmer. This speech indicates a division in the script. Can we simply leave the story there — this is a jungle and the only solution is to destroy the animals therein? The script begins to explore motivation, begins to get behind the problem.]

MURROW: Two detectives told the judge at the gang's arraignment, "These boys showed no remorse and gave us little cooperation." At their murder trial, some of the boys testified that police beat and frightened them into making confessions. The police officers accused denied this under oath. First reports on this crime suggested that at least one gang member had stabbed for thrills. Police said the fourteen-year-old boy who used a bread knife in the attack told them, "I always wanted to know what it would feel like to stick a knife through human bone." This same boy denied to us that he said that; gave us three other reasons for his crime. First.

ET: GANG MEMBER:
I told you I didn't know what I was doing. I was drunk. I went out, you know, I . . . you know, I was drunk, I just went like that, and I stabbed him.

MURROW: We asked him, "Did you know the boy you stabbed?" Answer: "No, but I thought he was a Jester." Question: "Had the Jesters ever done anything to you?" Answer:

ET: GANG MEMBER:
They kept on callin' me a Spick. They kept on saying, "You dirty Spick, get out of this block." Every time I go in the pool, they said to me the same thing. I don't bother them, 'cause, you know, I don't want to get into no trouble with them, but one day they beat me up. You know, there was about five of them, and they wouldn't leave me alone. They beat me up, and I had to take a chance to get the boys so we could beat them up.

MURROW: He said his third reason for stabbing a boy he did not know involved his fear of gang discipline.

ET: GANG MEMBER:
See, because we say before, if anybody don't beat up somebody, when we get back, he's gonna get beat up. So I say, "OK." They got special guys, you know, to keep their eyes on the boys. Anyone who don't swing out is gonna get it when we come back. They got to pass through a line; they got about fifteen boys over here, and fifteen boys over there, and you know, in a straight line, like that. They got to pass through there and they all got belts in their hands.

MURROW: So far, we have heard that a boy was killed because other boys — most of them under fifteen — got drunk, wanted revenge, feared gang discipline. Only one boy charged with murder pleaded not guilty on grounds of insanity. He was declared legally sane. But a psychiatrist testified in court that this boy was epileptic and "incapable of premeditating and deliberating." Court-appointed defense council did not request psychiatric examination of the other six boys on trial for their lives. The jury that convicted some of them heard very little about their mental and emotional make-up. Our reporter tried to get psychiatric reports on the other gang members too young to be tried for murder. He questioned Marion Cohen, head of the treatment service, New York City Youth House. She told him.

ET: MISS COHEN AND REPORTER:
COHEN: We see our function as holding boys remanded temporarily by Children's Court until disposition of their case is made by a judge. While the boy is here, we try to study and diagnose his problem.
REPORTER: Well, now, the younger members of the gang that killed Michael Farmer were brought here. Did you study the individual boys; make reports on them for the judge who was going to try them?
COHEN: No, we did not.
REPORTER: Why not?
COHEN: Because the judge did not request it.
REPORTER: Is this usual practice?
COHEN: No, in most cases, judges are interested in finding out as much as they can about the individual boy's problems, in order to differentiate his needs.

REPORTER: But in this case, nothing was found out about the mental make-up or the individual needs of these boys. Is that right?

COHEN: Yes.

REPORTER: Do you usually wait for the court to request such studies?

COHEN: No, when we are fully staffed, we do a study on every boy who is here for more than a week.

REPORTER: Why didn't you study these boys then?

COHEN: Because we are two-thirds under-staffed. We have only four case-workers for three-hundred boys.

MURROW: The New York City Youth House is a brand-new five-million-dollar building. It has a swimming pool, self-service elevators — the most modern equipment. But there are only four case-workers for three hundred boys. Reason: low pay and a shortage of trained personnel. Our reporter continues his conversation with Marion Cohen.

ET: MISS COHEN AND REPORTER:

REPORTER: Can you make any generalizations about the gang members you have studied?

COHEN: Yes, these are kids who essentially feel in themselves weak and in-adequate ... and have to present a tough facade to others. Of course, most adolescents feel insecure. But these boys have a distorted idea of what real adequacy is. They become easy prey for leaders whose sole drive is aggressive. They are egged on by their peers to establish a tough reputation ... each kid daring the other to go one step farther. They have to compete on a level of violence.

MURROW: It would seem that members of the Egyptian Kings and Dragons gang fit the pattern. Consider the statement of this fourteen-year-old gang member who participated in the assault at Highbridge Park.

[The interviews with the experts may be considered transition material. It is established that there is a problem. Some of the reasons for the problem are tentatively suggested. The audience now is ready for exploration of the problem and a clarification of the reasons.]

ET: GANG MEMBER:

I didn't want to be like ... you know, different from the other guys. Like they hit him, I hit him. In other words, I didn't want to show myself as a punk. You know, ya always talkin', "Oh man, when I catch a guy, I'll beat him up," and all of that, you know. So after you go out and you catch a guy, and you don't do nothin', they say, "Oh man, he can't belong to no gang, because he ain't gonna do nothin'."

MURROW: Are we to believe that a boy is dead — murdered — because those who killed him fear being called "punks"? Another gang member says he acted to pro-tect his reputation. He calls it "rep."

ET: GANG MEMBER:

Momentarily, I started to thinking about it inside: did I have my mind made up I'm not going to be in no gang. Then I go on inside. Something comes up den here come all my friends coming to me. Like I said before, I'm intelli-gent and so forth. They be coming to me — then they talk to me about what they gonna do. Like, "Man, we'll go out here and kill this guy." I say, "Yeah." They kept on talkin' and talkin'. I said, "Man, I just gotta go with you." Myself, I don't want to go, but when they start talkin' about what they gonna do, I say, "So, he isn't gonna take over my rep. I ain't gonna let him be known more than me." And I go ahead just for selfishness. I go ahead, and get caught or something; sometimes I get caught, sometimes I don't. I'm in some trouble there.

MURROW: That boy admits that he kicked and punched Roger McShane during the attack at Highbridge Park ... didn't stab him because he didn't have a knife. We asked, "Suppose you had a knife; would you have used it? Answer:

ET: GANG MEMBER:
If I would of got the knife, I would have stabbed him. That would have gave me more of a build-up. People would have respected me for what I've done and things like that. They would say, "There goes a cold killer."

MURROW: He wants people to say, "There goes a cold killer." He is only fourteen years old — the same age as the boy who used a bread knife in the Highbridge Park attack ... and who told us why he too wants to be known as a "cold killer."

ET: GANG MEMBER:
It makes you feel like a big shot. You know some guys think they're big shots and all that. They think, you know, they got the power to do everything they feel like doing. They say, like "I wanna stab a guy," and then the other guy say, "Oh, I wouldn't dare to do that." You know, he thinks I'm acting like a big shot. That's the way he feels. He probably thinks in his mind, "Oh, he probably won't do that." Then, when we go to a fight, you know, he finds out what I do.

MURROW: Some gang members told police that they bragged to each other about beating and stabbing Farmer and McShane ... wanted to make certain they would be known as "tough guys." According to the official police record, this was the reaction of their parents.

ET: COMMISSIONER ARM:
During the hours that the boys were rounded up and brought to the police station, many of their parents came to the scene. They expressed shock and bewilderment and disbelief over the fact that their boys were being questioned by police and might have had a part in this hideous crime. When they finally realized that this was true, they still couldn't believe it.

MURROW: One mother told our reporter.

ET: MOTHER OF GANG MEMBER AND REPORTER:
MOTHER: I had absolutely no problems with him. Everyone in the neighborhood can vouch for that. When I walked out there this morning, all my storekeepers and everythin' just can't believe that my son is mixed up in anything like this. (SIGH) I have no idea what I can do for him right now. I doubt if there is anything we can do for him right now.
REPORTER: Do you plan to go over to see him?
MOTHER: Of course I have to go to see my child. (SOBBING) I can't let him down now. Even though he was wrong, I still can't just turn my back on him. (SOBBING)

MURROW: Parents went to see their sons in jail; and how did they react when they saw them? One boy said:

ET: **GANG MEMBER:**
My mother said she was ashamed of me, and everything, and I told her that it wasn't my fault and I couldn't help it. My father wanted to kill me at first, and after I explained to him what happened he was still ... he was still like ... felt bad about it, ashamed to walk the streets after somethin' like that, but then you know, he wouldn't touch me then, after I told him what happened.

MURROW: The statement of another gang member.

ET: **GANG MEMBER:**
My father understood. He didn't actually understand, but you know, he didn't take it as hard as my mother. My mother ... it came out in the newspapers, she had a heart attack. It's a lucky thing she's alive today.

MURROW: One mother talked to her son in the presence of the other boys arrested. Here is what she said, according to this gang member present.

ET: **GANG MEMBER:**
When she sees him she says to him, "How did it feel when you did that to Farmer? It was good, eh?" You know, jokin' around with the kid. So we told her, "You know what your son did?" I says, "He stabbed him in the back." She says, she just went like that, shrugged her, you know, shoulders. Then we didn't pay any attention to her, because ya know, you don't like to see a mother actin' like that with a kid ya know.

MURROW: What is known about the mental and emotional make-up of parents whose children commit crimes? Dr. Marjorie Rittwagen, staff psychiatrist for New York Children's Courts, gave us some statistics.

ET: **DR. RITTWAGEN:**
We find that some seventy-five to eighty percent of parents of children who are brought into this court are emotionally ill or have severe personality or character disorders. They include sociopathic personality disorders, alcoholics and the like. And about ten percent of this seventy-five to eighty percent are commitably psychotic — in fact, some parents go completely berserk in Court, threaten judges and are sent to psychiatric wards for observation. Most of these parents are so overwhelmed with their own problems that they ignore their children. Kids feel not so much rejected as nonentities. Usually, in these homes, there are no fathers.

MURROW: There are no fathers in the homes of five of the seven gang members tried for the murder of Michael Farmer. Four of these boys live with their mothers; one with his grandparents. His mother told our reporter why she left her son.

ET: **MOTHER OF GANG MEMBER AND REPORTER:**
MOTHER: He has lived with my mother all his life from birth. (SOBS) I lived there up to two, three years ago. It seems like since I left my child everything has happened. (SOBS) Not that I just walked out on him, but when I planned to get married I spoke to him. He said, "Well, go ahead, you have to have some happiness; you can't just stay with me all the time." So I said, "Will you be willing to come with me?" He said, "No, I don't want to leave my grandparents." (SOB) REPORTER: Do you think that it would have been important if he had stayed with you?
MOTHER: I think it would have been important had I stayed with him and not leave him at the age of fifteen. I wouldn't advise that to anyone who has a boy, or any other child. (SOBS)

MURROW: Eleven of the eighteen boys arrested in the Farmer case come from homes broken by desertion, divorce or death. Children's Court psychiatrist Marjorie Rittwagen says this is the pattern.

ET: <u>DR. RITTWAGEN:</u>
Some seventy to eighty percent of our children come from homes broken by desertion or divorce. Most of the children stay with their mothers. At critical times in their lives they are left in a fatherless home. They're almost afraid to relate too closely to their mothers, and are often driven into the streets to seek companionship with a gang. They find the superficial group relationship more comfortable than individual ones. In fact, difficulty in relating to people is one of their big handicaps. They don't talk out their problems, they act them out.

MURROW: Example: this thirteen-year-old boy. He lives with a mother married and divorced three times. She works to support him ... cannot spend much time with him. Her son has plenty of problems, but she doesn't know about them.

ET: <u>GANG MEMBER:</u>
I never tell her about my problems. One reason is that if I tell her my problems, like some guys were beating me up, she would keep me in the house ... and wouldn't let me go out. Or if I tell her I'm doing badly in school, she'll probably hit me. Or if I tell her I had an argument with a teacher, or something like that, she'd probably hit me. She don't give me a chance to explain, you know. She just comes out, and pow, she hits me. I don't tell her anything.

MURROW: He doesn't talk out his problems; he acts them out — sometimes by firing a beebee gun at adults.

ET: <u>GANG MEMBER:</u>
Tell you the truth, I used to shoot people myself. Sometimes I would shoot the people I don't like too much, you know. (LAUGHS) I would be up on the roof and they would be walkin' by with packages or something — and pow, I would shoot them.

MURROW: Violence is all around him, he says.

ET: <u>GANG MEMBER:</u>
Usually I go for horror pictures like "Frankenstein and the Mummy" or things like that. I like it when he goes and kills the guy or rips a guy in half or something like that. (LAUGHS) Or when he throws somebody off a cliff. You know, all them exciting things.

MURROW: Next: the gang member who used a bread knife in the Highbridge Park attack. He lived with his mother and step-father; told us he often quarreled with his mother; wanted his step-father to spend more time with him.

ET: <u>GANG MEMBER:</u>
I'll ask him to take me boat-riding, fishing, or some place like that, ball game. He'll say, "No." He don't go no place. The only place where he goes, he goes to the bar. And from the bar, he goes home. Sleep, that's about all he do. I don't talk to my parents a lot of times. I don't hardly talk to them — there's nothing to talk about. There's nothing to discuss about. They can't help me.

MURROW: They can't help me! What he wants, he says, is to be like his favorite comic book hero.

ET: <u>GANG MEMBER:</u>
Mighty Mouse — he's a mouse — he's dressed up like Superman. He's got little

pants — they're red. The shirt is yellow. You know, and then he helps out the mouse. Everytime the cats try to get the mouse, Mighty Mouse comes and helps the mouse, just like Superman. He's stronger than the cats. Nothing can hurt him.

MURROW: Another boy told us: "My father doesn't want to hear my troubles. They make him mad." Reason:

ET: <u>GANG MEMBER:</u>
He wants me to be better than my other brother. That's why every time he comes to me and say, "You see, you gonna be like your brother. The one that's in the Tombs. If you keep on doing wrong, you gonna be like him." He kept on telling me that, so I said, "Well if he wants me to be like him, I'm gonna be like him." So I started doing wrong things. And then he says to me, "I don't wanna catch you in trouble." Well, in one way he should have got me in trouble before, because he found a gun that I had ... you know, I had a home-made. And he found it, and he didn't say nothin', he just broke it up and threw it away and kept me in the house for one day. He should have took it to the police or somethin', and told them that I had it. Maybe I would have been sent to the Youth House or someplace, before, and I wouldn't have gotten into so much trouble, and I would have learned my lesson.

MURROW: This was his first arrest. But ten of the eighteen boys involved in the Farmer case had previous records as juvenile offenders; some for such minor offenses as trespassing or chalking names on buildings; others for serious crimes, including assault, burglary and attempted grand larceny. Three gang members were under the supervision of probation officers. But how much supervision does a boy on probation get, in New York City? Clarence Leeds is Chief Probation Officer at Children's Court.

[The script is now fully into the problem as it concerns the characters of the story. The transitions, through selecting and editing, are excellent, moving logically, yet not obviously, from the boys to the parents. The statements of the boys and the parents all follow a pattern, validating the diagnosis of the sociologist and the psychiatrist. Now the documentary can attempt an investigation of the solutions to the problem, those attempted and those still to come.]

ET: <u>CLARENCE LEEDS:</u>
Our probation officers have minimum case loads of between sixty and seventy delinquent boys apiece. This means that at best they can talk to each boy perhaps once a month. And you can't give a child the guidance and help he needs by seeing him that infrequently. We are doing just about double the number of case loads and investigations that we're equipped to handle and possibly as a consequence of this, about thirty per cent of the boys on probation commit new offenses which will bring them to the attention of the court once again.

MURROW: Three Egyptian Dragons on probation participated in the murder of Michael Farmer. Another member of this gang had served one year in a state training school for juvenile delinquents ... was diagnosed as a "dangerous psychopath" ... but received no psychotherapy. Reason: there are 500 boys in this institution; only one psychiatrist and one pscyhologist to treat them. Five months after this "dangerous psychopath" was released from the institution, he

stabbed Roger McShane at Highbridge Park. Who is to blame? John Warren
Hill, Chief Justice of New York's Children's Court, told us why many very disturbed children are released quickly by state institutions.

ET: JUDGE HILL:
It is a shocking fact that children committed to state institutions by this court
often are discharged from these institutions within four to six months without
having received any real treatment or help. Why? Because our state facilities
for the long term care of delinquent children are so shockingly inadequate
that our state institutions must make these discharges quickly in order to
make room for new court commitments. For while the rate of delinquency has
increased in New York City ... there's not a single additional bed provided in
our state institutions for delinquent children, aside from some few which the
city made available for use by the state. But that was a bare nothing compared
to the great need which has developed increasingly in this area.

MURROW: Children released from New York institutions are put on parole. The Egyptian
Dragon diagnosed as a "dangerous psychopath" was assigned to a youth
parole worker ... was under the supervision of this worker at the time of the
Farmer murder. But how closely was he watched? Joseph Linda is in charge of
youth parole workers, New York City area.

ET: JOSEPH LINDA:
Each of our youth parole workers supervises about 80 boys, and in some cases,
about 100 boys, because of staff shortage. This means that they may see these
boys as infrequently as once every two months.

MURROW: Youth parole and probation agencies are non-existent in half the counties of
this nation. In most of the other counties, they are understaffed, according to
a survey by the National Probation and Parole Association. Some responsibility
for supervising problem children often is shifted to the schools by the courts.
This happened in the case of several Egyptian Kings and Dragons brought to
court prior to the murder of Michael Farmer. The speaker, Murray Sachs,
court liaison officer, Board of Education, New York City.

ET: MURRAY SACHS:
The courts had made a number of requests in the helping of these youngsters.
The unfortunate thing about these children was this: they would refuse to
come to school. Not coming to school, they wouldn't be doing the things that
we think are constructive and helpful. Those, we know, have such deep-rooted
behavior problems and must be dealt with on that basis by specialists who are
equipped to handle it, and, for heaven's sake, our community, our citizens
should not expect the school to do that. It seems that the only one that might
help them would be the institution where they might be placed, and given
individualized and controlled assistance, of one kind or another. Again we're
faced with the serious problem of there's just no place for them.

MURROW: In the richest state of the nation, long-term institutional care is not available
for eighty per cent of delinquent children under twelve years of age. No state
institution for these children exists. The few private institutions are jammed.
One gang member involved in the Farmer case committed five offenses before
he was twelve years old. Within a week or two after each arrest, he was set

free in the community. At twelve, children are eligible for state training schools. But even then it is difficult to place them because of overcrowding. John Warren Hill, Chief Justice of New York's Court, sums up the result.

ET: <u>JUDGE HILL:</u>
In a great number of cases of very disturbed children, children who should be removed from the community, this court has been unable to find any placement for the child and our only alternative has been to place these children on probation, which, of course, means their return to the community.

MURROW: They are sent back to the streets — unhelped, unsupervised. Set free in the community, what do they do with their time? Listen to one boy describe a typical summer day in his neighborhood of brick tenements in Manhattan's upper west side.

ET: <u>GANG MEMBER:</u>
I usually get up at ·11 or 12 o'clock, you know. I sleep late. And then I will go out and see the guys, sitting on the stoop, you know, doing nothin'. I would sit there with them, and sometimes they will say, "Let's split and go to a movie," so I would go to the movie with them. Or sometimes we would try and get a game of stickball or somethin' like that. Our block is crowded, we didn't hardly have a chance to play because the busses kept going back and forth, back and forth. We couldn't do nothin'. So that we just sit, then when it got to night-time, well, you know, we would go around and say, "Come on, man, let's go break windows for some excitement" or "Come on man, let's go boppin'." Then we would go and look for guys, to beat 'em up. Then we would come back. And then, (LAUGHS) we would sit on the stoop, man, and we'd hear a cop car outside and we would all fly up to the roof, or somethin' like that. Then, we just come down and start talkin' and talkin'.

MURROW: Consider the day of another boy, sixteen years old. He makes the rounds of schools, pool halls, and candy store hangouts. He works for a syndicate ... sells marijuana cigarettes to other children and smokes them himself.

ET: <u>GANG MEMBER:</u>
I'd get the dough by sellin' it. I'd take about four or five a day. It keeps me goin'. All depends ... when I get up in the morning I take one or two; three hours later take another one. If I ain't got nothin' to do, I just feel like goofin', crackin' up and everythin'. I just take another one. Go to a dance, take two or three. If you don't get it easy, you try all kinds of — not violence, but you see an easy dollar to rob, you rob it. You see somethin' to pawn, you pawn it.

MURROW: Boys troubled and adrift in the community formed the gang that killed Michael Farmer. Sociologists call gangs of this breed "anti-social groups" or "fighting gangs." They exist in most of our large cities. According to police estimates there are 134 of these gangs in Los Angeles County; 24 in Miami; 110 in New York, including the Egyptian Kings and Dragons.

[You have read about two-thirds of the documentary script. The voices and sounds of realism have been presented. The thoughts and feelings of as many different and varied persons as might be found in a Shakespearean tragedy have been explored. "What" happened moved into "why" it happened into the evolution of a problem that demands a solution. Much as do the films of Pare Lorentz, "Who Killed Michael Farmer?" then examines the possible solutions to the problem. The final few pages of the documentary script sum up:]

ET: GREENHILL REPORT:
            Residents trace the origin of juvenile crime to parents' inability to control their
            children, racial issues, newcomers in the area, lack of police protection, intimi-
            dation of teachers and policemen by youth gangs, and a lack of restrictive
            measures in Highbridge Park. Persons interviewed reported 16 major incidents
            leading to death or hospitalization in the last three years. Ten of them in the
            last two weeks. Most of the incidents had not been reported to police for fear of
            gang retaliation. Among the population in general, there were attitudes of hope-
            lessness and fear. A large number of people expect gang retaliation after the
            present crisis has quieted down. They are cynical and see no way of preventing
            retaliation for it always occurred in the past. About 40 percent of children be-
            tween the ages of 3 and 16 reacted immediately with a variety of physical and
            emotional symptoms. For the first time, some children began to carry knives for
            their own protection.

MURROW: One boy in the neighborhood who fears for his life is Michael Farmer's friend,
            Roger McShane — a State's witness at the murder trial of the Egyptian Kings
            and Dragons. During the trial, McShane received two death threats in the mail.
            One letter said: "You are alive. But if them guys get the chair, we will kill you."
            That threat possibly came from a crank. But no one can be sure — least of all
            Roger McShane.

ET: McSHANE:
            There's nothing you can do except protect yourself. It's just gonna get wilder
            and wilder. I mean, it's just gonna get worse. You can't have a policeman walk-
            ing around with every boy or girl that leaves his house at night. And follow him
            to the store if he has to go to the store or follow him up to the show or you can't
            have a policeman follow each individual all around the neighborhood just so
            they can be protected.

MURROW: The parents of Michael Farmer.

ET: MR. AND MRS. FARMER:
            MR. FARMER: I'm very much afraid for my son Rayme. Rayme's 14. Who knows
            the rest of these Egyptian Kings won't come up looking for him, or trying to
            extend their activities; make themselves a little bit more infamous. You can't
            reason with the type of minds that they have. You don't know what they'll come
            up with next.
            MRS. FARMER: I'm worried about all of us. There was a time when I'd run down at
            night for milk, or to mail a letter, now I wouldn't go down the street after nine
            o'clock. I just have that terrible feeling that something is lurking there in the dark.

MURROW: Fear remains in this community. A new summer approaches ... and according
            to one volunteer youth worker in the area already there are danger signals.

ET: YOUTH WORKER:
            The situation is beginning to look critical once again. We find that one of the
            Egyptian Kings apparently not involved in the Michael Farmer killing is now
            trying to reorganize a gang and is recruiting in the area. Unless something is
            done very quickly with this particular gang, we are definitely going to run into
            the same situation in a very short time. You can't say whether that will be six
            months or a year from now, but if this gang is allowed to reorganize again,
            there may be more killings and something had better be done, fast, if we are
            interested in saving other children from the fate of Michael Farmer.

MURROW: What has been solved by the verdict of a jury and the commitment of 15 boys to institutions which are ill-equipped to rehabilitate them; and because of overcrowding, may soon return them to the community? The problem of juvenile crime continues. The experts may list all sorts of causes. But they agree on one answer to why these conditions continue to exist: We permit them to. This is Ed Murrow. Good Night.

"Who Killed Michael Farmer?"
© Columbia Broadcasting System, Inc. Written and produced by Jay L. McMullen.

Application: Television

The basic approaches and techniques are essentially the same for the television and radio documentary. The most important difference, obviously, is the use of visuals in television. Where the radio documentary gathers words and sounds, the television documentary adds film, tape, photos, and graphics. Where the radio program must use dialogue and/or narration to describe something, the television program needs only the picture itself. Television has the advantage of the motion picture's "visual writing," the ability to tell a story more concisely and sometimes more meaningfully through showing instead of telling.

The picture may be the primary element in any given sequence in the television documentary, with the narration and taped dialogue secondary. The people and their actions may be actually seen and thus understood, rather than being imagined through verbal descriptions of what they did and saw. On the other hand, the words of the people and the narrator may be the prime movers, with the pictures merely filling in visually what is being described in words.

The series thus far in television history that have best exemplified the human interest and dramatic as well as the investigative fact-digging aspects of the documentary have been "See It Now" and "60 Minutes." Robert Chandler, as vice-president for administration of CBS News, explained that on "60 Minutes" there are no script materials as such prepared before the program sequence goes on site for interviewing and taping. He stated:

> Once we have an idea for a program, which can come from a newspaper article, a letter, an observation by one of our staff or from any other source, we investigate the possibility through research of the subject and, sometimes, through a site visit by the producer or researcher. After the site visit a research report is prepared and we decide whether to go with that story. If we do, then phone calls are made to line up the interview. A crew goes out and gets everything set up some four or five days before the correspondent gets there. Except for the research report, nothing in the nature of script materials has yet been prepared. The closest to prepared materials of a written nature are some areas for questioning that the producer gives to the correspondent prior to the interviewing. When the filming is completed — and that may be as much as five hours for a 15-minute sequence — the producer and correspondent look at the material and decide how to structure it — what to use and what to discard. At this stage, fairly late in the game, formal writing takes place. It consists principally of the narration and necessary bridges to pull the materials into a coherent whole. Later on a formal opening for the program is written. The writer for "60 Minutes" writes to the existing film. A single excep-

tion sometimes occurs on site, when the correspondent may do a "stand-up" sequence on camera on location. This is usually a brief sequence which is written on location and spoken to the camera.

—————————————————O—————————————————

• *As you read the following "60 Minutes" script, make notes on your analysis of the program structure and the writing techniques used. Follow the general style of the commentary that accompanies the "Michael Farmer" documentary.*

—————————————————O—————————————————

WARNING: LIVING HERE MAY BE HAZARDOUS TO YOUR HEALTH!
Esther Kartiganer, Producer

HARRY REASONER: Just like the warning on a package of cigarettes or a bottle of iodine, the signs were there for everyone to see for many months, but it was a situation where not much seemed to happen until this week. We're talking about the Love Canal.

The Love Canal is an area of Niagara Falls, New York, with a romantic name and an increasingly depressing history. There was a man named Love who wanted to build the canal. He went broke. Then the city and the Hooker Chemical Company used his empty ditch to bury used and dangerous chemicals. When it was full it was covered up. The city built a school on the site, and a middle-class community grew up around the school.

A couple of years ago, they found the chemicals were seeping out into the air and dirt and affecting people's health. In the past nine days, the canal has been very much back in the news: new studies showing chromosome damage in people living in areas not previously proven dangerous; a decision to evacuate about 700 families temporarily at federal expense. But there's still no agreement on how serious is the problem. As one federal official put it, the only sure thing is that something up there has made some people sick. The thing is, you have to go there to get the feel of it. We went back to the site of the first problems.

The silence here is very loud. Although you get the occasional sound of a plane overhead and kids playing and dogs barking in the street a couple of hundred feet away, what you hear inside the chain-link fence is the silence. It is like Flanders Field, but there are no flowers here, just the wistful evidence that someone tried to grow some once to make a pretty place. You hear the silence and you feel endangered, because this enemy is so pervasive and impersonal. Grown men and women, here only briefly, feel endangered. I don't know who left this ball here, but I know you stop and think a couple of times before you pick it up.

The school is probably the saddest. They say it smells bad inside, and it sits right on top of the dead and choked canal where the danger is buried. It is like those scenes in a horror movie where the suspense of ordinary things builds towards something nameless. The school is probably the saddest, because it reminds you that only a couple of years ago there were unremarkable people here, people who saw only the normal shadows in the dark, people who saw no irony in a routine sign.

What we are looking at tonight is a basic question. There were all kinds of warning signs after the state moved in 1978. In the beginning, there didn't seem to be any doubts.

It was a horror story, and the State of New York treated it like one. They declared a health emergency. At a cost of $10 million, the state bought 239 homes and permanently moved the people out of the first two rings around the vicious ditch. Then they put up a chain-link fence around the area which was to define the limits of the danger. They even printed this fancy brochure — "Love Canal: A Public Health Time Bomb" — explaining proudly how they had handled the health emergency. That was 1978. This is a story of second thoughts. The second thoughts relate to money and to fear. The state quite obviously began to think in terms of precedent and how many millions of dollars might be involved in moving people out of the Love Canal and Lord knows how many other miasmas. The people in the ostensibly "not-unsafe" areas were scared, but until last week they couldn't seem to get anyone's attention.

In the beginning, in the brochure-writing days, the state used that schoolhouse as a kind of command post. They took blood tests and checked everybody in the area for their health history, and, for the time being, decided that the health hazards were serious only for those first two rings of houses.

That was a conclusion the homeowners never bought. Further analysis of the study by the state revealed there was danger outside the first two rings. There were more miscarriages, birth defects and low-birth-weight babies than they had a reason to expect. So when Commissioner of Health Dr. David Axelrod reported these new findings but told them they didn't have any problems unless they were pregnant or under two years old, they reacted rudely.

DR. DAVID AXELROD: We have therefore brought to the governor our recommendation that pregnant women living in the canal area extending from 97th to 103rd Street be removed from the area. We have also brought to the governor our recommendation that children under two years of age be removed from the canal until such time as they are older than two or until such time as extensive — (negative audience reaction) — environmental data — (negative audience reaction).

REASONER: That, it seems, is when the second thoughts began. It looked, for example, that the state might have to deal with many more high-risk homes. The state gave the impression that it had made its last concession. The homeowners didn't think it was enough, and cancer research scientist Beverly Paigen shares their view.

DR. BEVERLY PAIGEN: You see, looking at human fetus — the baby before birth — is like looking at the miner's canary. You bring the canary down into the mine and, if the canary dies, then you know it's time to get the miners out. They looked at the canary — the human fetus — and when they saw that the human fetus was in danger, they said get the canary out. They didn't say get the miner out.

REASONER: Dr. Beverly Paigen has been the chief — and unpaid expert — working with the Love Canal homeowners — their advocate with state and federal officials.

DR. PAIGEN: Does EPA want to be seen as an agency who's out there doing something? Or is EPA ...

REASONER: And she helped them design and conduct their own health surveys. More than a year ago, she presented their results to a congressional committee. The homeowners had found more problems with pregnancy and birth than the state had, and they found additional problems the state had not identified: nervous breakdowns, asthma, urinary-tract diseases. Even then, she was calling for drastic action.

DR. PAIGEN: These studies have led me to conclude that a minimum of 140 additional families should be evacuated immediately, and evacuation may need to be extended to as many as 500 more families.

REASONER: Commissioner, I'm sure you're familiar with the Love Canal Homeowners Association.

DR. AXELROD: Oh, yes, I'm very familiar with them.

REASONER: They have conducted a number of studies themselves and follow-up studies and, in effect, they accuse you of minimizing adverse health information that the department has found.

DR. AXELROD: Well, I think that what you have to do is to assume and accept the information that they have as organized subjectivity, because that's the way it was collected. They're not experts. They're not trained in this area.

REASONER: Dr. Paigen, has anyone who might be described as disinterested looked at your information?

DR. PAIGEN: The top-notch panel of epidemiologists spent a day listening to me and my information and they spent a day listening to the Department of Health studies, and they came out and said that my data in — was substantial enough to warrant further studies.

REASONER: The fancy brochure came out in September, 1978, and it was in February, 1979, that Dr. Axelrod told the Love Canal residents they had nothing to worry about unless they were pregnant or very young. But in the many months since then, there's been an ongoing struggle to get the information on which that conclusion was based — the presumably exhaustive and scientifically defensible study of the residents' health story.

They've sealed up that study almost as tightly as they sealed up those homes in the first two rings. They haven't given the homeowners their own health data. They didn't give it to a congressional committee that wanted to see it. And it took a subpoena before they gave it to the Federal Department of Justice, which is suing Hooker Chemical and would like to look at Dr. Axelrod's study. Dr. Axelrod says he's not stonewalling; the only delay is the necessary care in preparing his raw data for release. And because the state is also suing Hooker Chemical, he, like practically everyone else in this horror story, has lawyer trouble.

DR. AXELROD: We are in the process of preparing properly documented scientific publications which will provide the basis for the kinds of recommendations that we have taken, and also provide an opportunity to independently evaluate all of the information that we have gathered. Currently, there is an additional problem that relates to the litigation which is underway, and so that I really do not control the flow of information at this point. My attorneys do, and my attorney in this case is the Attorney General of the State of New York.

REASONER: Dr. Axelrod has been saying that all his recommendations were reviewed by his own blue-ribbon panel. I asked Dr. Paigen why this didn't change her mind.

DR. PAIGEN: If the blue-ribbon panel had been open, if their recommendations had been written, if the blue-ribbon panel had been given tables of data, that would have been fine; then I would have said maybe I'm wrong. But the blue-ribbon panel is secret. The minutes of the meeting are secret. The recommendations are secret.

REASONER: Have you released the names of the blue-ribbon panel?

DR. AXELROD: No, we have not. That still is protected, is considered to be protected by counsel, by the canons of confidentiality under the public health law.

REASONER: We read the public health law and there's nothing in it about protecting the names of any members of Dr. Axelrod's panel.

The President's Commission on Organized Crime — which was certainly subject to a variety of harassment and possible worse — one of the whole points about it was the publication of the names — men of unimpeachable qualifications. This would be almost unique, wouldn't it, Doctor —

DR. AXELROD: Well —

REASONER: — to have a blue-ribbon commission with secret names?

DR. AXELROD: I don't think it would be unique. I believe that there have been panels in the past which have been convened. I can't cite them.

REASONER: And we looked for other examples to cite and we couldn't find them, either.

The people outside the fence, who can't afford to move and are afraid to stay, are unreassured by Dr. Axelrod's unpublished study and his secret panel. They are not even reassured by the $13½ million that has been spent to put a clay cap on the ditch and to install a system so that none of the chemicals could seep out. They are more impressed by statistics the Homeowners Association has assembled. Since the Love Canal story broke, 15 pregnancies occurred in families living outside the first two rings; only two resulted in normal births. Eight of the babies had birth defects, two were stillborn, three were either miscarried or aborted.

Two normal children out of 15 pregnancies would be substantially below what you would expect nationally.

DR. PAIGEN: That's terrible.

REASONER: I mean, I would —

DR. PAIGEN: You don't need statistics, you don't need science. Two normal children out of 15 pregnancies in anybody's book is a disaster.

REASONER: Though Dr. Axelrod admitted concern about pregnancy outcomes, he didn't feel the threat called for more evacuations.

DR. AXELROD: Those individuals who choose to remain there and do become pregnant — either voluntarily or involuntarily, as the case might be — they know what those risks are and they are remaining there with those risks.

REASONER: Aren't you very much thinking of the fact that there are maybe several dozen other potential hazards in Niagara County, several hundred in New York State, many thousand in the United States?

DR. AXELROD: Absolutely. It would be not — it would — it would — it would be facile for me to say otherwise. I think that I'm constantly concerned about it. But that would not change my policy with respect to proceeding to taking the best scientific information and making a recommendation on the basis of that scientific information.

REASONER: I'm not challenging your scientific procedure, but I am suggesting you don't operate in a vacuum. You are appointed by the governor of New York. Do you serve at his pleasure, or is it —?

DR. AXELROD: I certainly do.

REASONER: Serve at his pleasure. Have you ever had any hint from the governor or anybody in his staff or from anybody in the state that it would be extremely useful to them if it was determined that most of Love Canal is habitable?

DR. AXELROD: I have never had anyone tell me that.

REASONER: Or hint at it?

DR. AXELROD: Or hint at it? Perhaps I'm naive and perhaps there were hints, but that's a subjective evaluation. No one has hinted to me that I should do anything but provide them my best scientific judgment, rather than a political judgment.

REASONER: During the last several months, home appraisers had been working in the neighborhood. Even in the face of the federal government's suit, which claims there is a continuing health hazard and asks for either a total cleanup or a total evacuation of the area, and even in spite of the continuing conflict with the homeowners' studies, the State of New York committed $5 million to a local authority to "revitalize and stabilize" the area. The $5 million could be used to purchase the homes of people who wanted to leave. The appraisals sent to the homeowners totalled $18 million. Niagara Falls Mayor Michael O'Laughlin heads the task force that was working on the "revitalization and stabilization" effort. We asked him if he couldn't get in sudden money trouble.

Let's say half the families decide to move out, which is not im-

	possible, you're out of money then, aren't you? You haven't got enough money to do this job right?
MAYOR MICHAEL O'LAUGHLIN:	That — that's a — that's a real problem, and it was so different in the original purchases of the land. There you had a definite amount. You're going to move the houses in those first two rows, the first two rings, and here's the money to do it.
REASONER:	One obvious thing in — if you had to buy a lot of homes and ran out of money, would be to sell the homes to somebody else at a bargain or with a tax break. Is that in the cards?
MAYOR O'LAUGHLIN:	I would shy away from selling homes at bargain rates. I think they should be pretty much at the market value as appraised here. I would see, however, some kind of arrangement where they would have interest reductions on the mortgage that they would take over over a period of time. I would see that prob — po — possibly having some kind of tax abatement over a period of time.
REASONER:	Sir, with all the uncertainties, do you really think that anyone's going to buy a house in that neighborhood?
MAYOR O'LAUGHLIN:	I have to say that, under the right circumstances, yes. People smoke, and there are signs on the side of the cigarette package that says it's dangerous. And there are thousands of people in our country and in our city who would be looking for a place or a chance to be a homeowner. This may be one of them.
REASONER:	The mayor's opinion may now be moot. Certainly until it's decided how temporary is the current evacuation there aren't going to be any sales to new owners. Some health officials still say the new evacuation is justified only for psychological reasons. There is still no consensus, or apparently the basis for serious discussion to reach one, among the scientists involved. But the other element in the delay and the argument is clearer than ever. More than ever, governments are asking themselves and each other: Who's going to pay for all this and for all the others?

Courtesy of CBS News

The Minidocumentary

An increasingly popular program type in the early 1980s has been the early evening **magazine format**. This format reflects the success of "60 Minutes" and is similar in its coverage of a number of feature- and documentary-type stories. However, the magazine format's half-hour length cuts down the eighteen-minute segments of "60 Minutes" to segments of from five to seven minutes. The writer must write even more concisely. Shown at 7:30 P.M. E.S.T. in most markets, the magazine program bridges the period between news and entertainment and most magazine producers have tried to make it a combination of both.

Ron Blau, filmmaker and television producer, has written documentary films, full-length television documentaries, and dozens of minidocumentaries ranging from four to ten minutes each. He believes that the standard radio or television documentary and the minidocumentary are essentially the same except for the obvious difference: the regular length program has time in which to present more information and develop ideas.

Most minidocumentary writers work through the same chronological sequence. First is the topic or theme. This can come from many sources: the executive producer, the field producer, newspaper stories, and, less frequently, the free-lance writer-producer. After the topic is determined, the writer must do appropriate research; some of it can be done in libraries, some on site, some through interviews.

After the research an outline is prepared, something akin to a rundown sheet, but quite flexible because the writer does not yet know who is going to say what or what kinds of visuals will be available. The outline is the basis for shooting. Blau advocates the outlining of a fairly simple structure because there is not time enough in the minidocumentary for anything complicated. He states that there are three principal types of material to look for: voice-over, **bites** or quotes, and "breathing" visuals or film of background, actions, or persons without voice. Blau also suggests that room be left for music, if possible.

Following the shooting, the screening of all materials permits the writer to prepare the final script. Most writers, says Blau, structure the piece from the bites and the voice-overs. He advises that the piece be allowed to breathe; for example, a piece on dance could have dance itself shown without any voice-over, and a piece on housing could have film of the neighborhood or of interiors without voice. The latter approach is sometimes referred to as using the **B roll**, arising from the practice of putting interview material on one projector and noninterview visuals on the second or B projector.

Most documentary writers follow the basic principles of journalism by starting with a strong topic sentence giving the essence of the piece, following immediately with the five Ws, and then filling in the details in whatever time is left. Blau takes a little different approach, beginning with something attention-getting, of special interest, then filling in the basic structure with field materials, and finally adding the voice-overs. The usual practice is to structure a piece around voice-overs and fill in with the bites and breathing shots.

With a large number of minidocumentaries for a given program (sometimes at least three for a half-hour show) and limited time to produce them (sometimes less than a week per piece), one needs either a large staff or extra care to see that all the facts are straight. Be careful not to take liberties with the facts if you find that time and staff haven't permitted you to get them all. Write from what you have. Don't make up facts to fill in.

Many minidocumentaries essentially repeat what has been covered in full-length documentaries or in newspaper stories, and there is a temptation to embellish in order to give a new look to the story. Where do you draw the line between factual documentary and fictional documentary? *New York Times* critic John J. O'Connor has referred to the "questionable craft of 'docudrama'."

---○---

• *Following is a reproduction of one of Ron Blau's minidocumentary scripts, "The New Right," with the author-producer's notes and emendations to give you an idea of what happens to a script by the time it gets on the air. Analyze where and how it follows Blau's writing approach, as just described. The neat, clear script in a textbook is not necessarily the way a script looks in the real-life atmosphere of a pressured production office so one page of Blau's working script, typos and all, is reproduced exactly as he used it.*

───────────────────○───────────────────

TS 86 : Head: 23:01:30   (1)

Inauguration
N 556   10

Begin of film:
556
783
953
961

Begin with "God Bless America," etc: Tip O'Niell

59:23 Just two years ago when Ronald Reagan
assumed the Presidency, it was
counted a great victory for
conservatives. 59:28

N 556   Reagan Inauguration 1/20/81 Rin 4:21 in 0/

Singing America Great to begin on this: With Tip
mouthing the words.   "RESERVE PROTECT AND DEFEND
THE CONSTITUTION OF THE UNITED STATES"   (10 sec)
13:19:21: The government has no power except that
granted it by the people. It is time to check and
revrse the growth of government 19/30 which shows
sighns of having grown beyond the consent of the
governed 16/04 (OUT OF SYNC: MUST FIX)

9

"L+L" Banquet w/
Wagner + Phillips

59:28

14

Almost overnight, the New Right--
which had unquestionably contributed
to Reagan's victory--had become
a force to reckon with in American
politics. And the faces of its
leaders--men like Jerry Falwell and
Jesse Helms, were familiar images
on the news. 59:42

5

"L + L: 192
Jesse helms.
"I'll stand up
Jerry Falwell
any time,'
@ Capitol.

A reproduction of one page of Ron Blau's working script for "The New Right."

Begin with "God Bless
10 *America," etc: Tip O'Neill*

59^{23} Just two years ago when Ronald Reagan assumed the Presidency, it was counted a
5 great victory for conservatives. 59^{28}

Inauguration
N556

(N 556)   Reagan Inauguration   1/20/81
Rin 4:21 in 0/

Begin with file:
556
783
953
961

Singing America Great to begin on this: With Tip mouthing the words. "RESERVE PROTECT AND DEFEND THE CONSTITU- TION OF THE UNITED STATES" (10 sec)
13:19: 21: The government has no power
9   except that granted it by the people. It is time to check and reverse the growth of government 19/30 which shows signs of having grown beyond the consent of the governed
16/04 (OUT OF SYNC: MUST FIX)

"L+L" Banquet with 59^{28}
Wagner and Phillips

14

Almost overnight, the New Right — which had unquestionably contributed to Reagan's victory — had become a force to reckon with in American politics. And the faces of its leaders — men like Jerry Falwell and Jesse Helms — were familiar images on the news. 59^{42}

"L+L" 192
Jesse Helms — "I'll stand
5   *with Jerry Falwell any*
time." @ Capitol.

59^{43} The New Right had a well-defined agenda. Though each group within the movement had its own priorities, the fundamental aims were similar:

26
— To reduce government's role in solving the nation's social problems.
— To build up our defenses, especially against the Soviet Union.
— To promote moral living (which was often identified with Christian prin- ciples).
— To push for conservative legislation on issues ranging from abortion to gun

Montage

"L+L"
451 Ohio Parade —
good ftg.

"L+L" Technology:
christian Broadcast
N88 —

6

2↑   0:10

11

2↑

11

8

4

WIDE

23   T.D.

10

control, pornography, busing and school prayer. 0:09

"L+L"   ← *clistr*
31 Rev. James Robison.
Religious Roundtable "Time
for God's People to come out
of the closet and change
america"

Millions of Americans identified themselves with the New Right.

And their organizations were bringing in millions of **dollars** each months. These riches put a lot of **muscle** into the movement. 0:21

0:22

For example, before the 1982 elections, NCPAC, the National Conservative Political Action Committee, had the funds to produce and buy air time for many antiliberal TV spots. 0:33

0:36 *Sound up*
But the 19**82** (EMPHASIZE THE "TWO") elections proved a great disappointment. Republicans lost 26 seats in the House of Representatives. And conservative candidates and issues took a beating in state and local elections all over the country. 0:46

0:48
Terry Dolan, National Chairman of NCPAC. 0:52

Begin 13:51

13:54 Well, it was a moving away of .. ⌐ To be perfectly honest, if there was a referendum issue in the 1982 elections, it had to be ⌐Ronald Reagan. Ronald Reagan is perceived 14:04 as a conservative. To the degree that Reagan was repudiated, ~~and I think he was moderately repudiated in House elections~~ Yes, there was a moving away⌐ But to say that was a repudiation of Jerry Falwell or an embracement of, let's say for example, of the nuclear freeze movement, that's silly. That's ridiculous. 14:23 |

0:53
The New Right feels that conservative **principles** did not lose ground in '82. The voters, they say were simply reacting negatively to President Reagan. Howard Phillips, of the Conservative Caucus | 0:03

CU 7/41 I think the 1982 elections confirmed the predictions of those of us in the New Right who said that the Reagan Admin was on the wrong track 7/52 In a number of ways first of all, the R admin did no retain the pro-defense concensus which it inherited in 1980 8/01 (THEN LOTS OF STUFF ON DEFENSE) (SECOND, NOT BALANCED BUDGET … LOTS … LIBERAL ACTIVIST ORGS … PLUS SOCIAL SPENDING)

One of these two:

961 5/13/82 Re Unemploy 19/24/03 + defense Nothing special press conf setting ok shots. 20Z19 24/48 I do think there is one thing present now that was not present before. And that is the determination of the US to rebuild its national defenses 25/01 etc for sound under

just this
REAGAN

N 783 1/19/82 Reagan news conf on econ, discrimination, abortion etc. Run 2/32 In 29/50 Walking in, silent, etc. All silent except for bites. Fine quote, but 1983 better. Here: If we don't know, then shouldn't we morally opt on the side that it is life?" (9 sec)

In spite of the fact that Reagan appears to be quite conservative, the New Right faults him for speaking loudly and carrying a small stick about arms control, abortion, a balanced budget and other matters.

that it was a repudiation, I think it was a mild repudiation of Reaganism. Whether we care to admit it or not, we are associated with Ronald Reagan's administration, even though we have gross and tremendous disagreements. Reagan is the symbol of our cause. ECU And to the degree that he is disliked, we are going to be disliked. What you saw in 1982, if anything, was the year of the

| 27

Analysts who are less conservative, however, maintain that the New Right diminished in power because in these recessionary times Americans are interested not so much in MORAL issues, as in PRACTICAL ones. Syndicated columnist Ed Yoder. | 40

4/01   They have, or at least as far as I can see, they have not succeeded for example, having elected they supposed a president who was thought to be and is indeed sympathetic to their point of view on a lot of things, they have not been able to get their program, their agenda, executed, because the country has been busy with other matters and other problems. 4/23 (GOOD)

either this ↑ or this ↓

MS 8/15   ... the economy, the Fed deficit, int rates the control of inflation, they don't seem to have a program on these matters, and yet I think those matters that affect the pocketbooks are central 8/30 I may be making Am pol seem like a bland enterprise but fundamentally people are interested in very homely things 8/39 GOOD When it comes to the central issues of the pol process 8/43 That's why I think the NR is marginal on these matters 8/47

953   5/6/82 School prayer In 14.26.01 29/25 No one will ever convince me that a moment of voluntary prayer will harm a child or threaten a school or state 29/34 but I think it can strengthen our faith in a Creator who alone has the power to bless America 29/41 Said he would propose const amendment.

MCU 15/14   I think the Pres recognizes there are people out there who liked the themes he was emph. in 1980 The problem is rhet diff from pol of his govt. 15/31 And at some point that gap is going to be observable to more & more people 15/37

| 43

Organizations such as the Conservative Caucus and NCPAC are working overtime to make sure millions more Americans will be able to observe this gap ... | 50

NCPAC PHONE BANK

k6/14   First woman on phone, fine bite
16/33 wide, then CUs 16/50 I'm Chris; Spec
Asst good, cause she's black and it's clear
17/07 touchtone and man's face, just wait-

#3   ing. My name is Chris (ALL CHRIS) 17/41 4
shot and pan to thers (ESTAB) then touchtones, then same chris man … 18/35 ECU

8 →   touchtones . then CU woman pulls on ciga-
rette. 19/52 Terry wanted me to call you because he knows you are one of our loyal
supporters 19/55 and he knows you are just
as concerned about the Conservative Movement as we are here at NCPAC 20/01 (GOOD
INTRO TO THIS AND TO NOT CALLING IT
NEW RIGHT) and the 1982 elections prove
that there is still much work to be done in
the house and that there are many powerful opponents in the senate 20/12 (GOOD
FOR INTRO 1982) 20/22 pacman lady brief
20.35 touchtone and winden 21/24 Pacman
lady 21/43 list of addresses, some not too
visible, especially after ZO

4 |**52** The New Right claims their war on the Lib-
erals is, in fact, more popular than ever. |**56**

17³⁶ |**?** How's the money now? Fine. **MCU, then 20**
I just saw an income statement. I think we
had this last month $436,000. (glitche) This

T.D.   month. The month of January. Now, if we're
down for the count, $436,000 of income
17 2̶0̶ (?)   doesn't speak to that, I don't think. |**17⁵⁶** And our
goal is to multiply our activities, our involve-
ment in campaigns and bring new people
into our organization and we're on that goal
pretty much. 18:08 (lots of glitches in this
section)

Authtc
5¹⁵

Books, candidates supported by PACS. incl:
WIDE 12/27 There will be books published,
there will be hearings held, there'll be candidates supported by various PACs. And (ZI)

7   H.P.   we're going to move from the role that we
had during the Carter years of (BIG GLITCH)
critic, during the first 2 Reagan years of un-
welcome ally, to the new role of a group of
people who believe that our views represent
the centrist views of most Ams and that we

need to prep ourselves to govern 12/56
(GOOD FOR END OR NEAR END) (Q: YOU
SAY "CENTRIST?")

2⁰⁰ The New Right seems to be powerful enough
to put the President on the defensive. Recently, Ronald Reagan appears to have gone out
of his way to reassure these conservatives.
Just one week ago, speaking to a convention
of religious broadcasters, he spoke strongly
in favor of a Constitutional amendment to
return prayer to public schools ... *tax credits
for private school tuition ... and other matters dear to the hearts of the New Right. 2²²

20

also pickup,
so 2²² may not
be accurate

DEF for Monday, Jan 31, 1983 (NO TIME
CODE numbers for ref only) He's addressing
religious broadcasters: Christian Media. Talking in terms of a constitutional amendment
returning prayer to public schools. Tax
credits for private school tuition, Abortion

TAPE #5

REAGAN
23/16   We must go forward with unity of
purpose and will 23/20 And let us come together, Christians and Jews, let us pray
together, march lobby and mobilize every
force we have, so that we can end the tragic
taking of unborn childrens lives 23/32

12

Then more on balancing the budget through
using the Bible.

2⁴⁶ 2⁴⁸
In spite of these overtures, in spite of
Reagan's declaring 1983 the Year of the
Bible, many observers sense the President is
doing a balancing act: making sure not to
alienate conservatives too badly ... while at
the same time making sure not to be identified solely with a group so far from center. 3⁰⁴

being careful
the New Right

16

11/00   MCU It's true of any Pres 11/02
The Presidency is an office which to be successful has got to command the broad
middle ground in pol. And it means that
those on one fringe or the other who think
they own Pres going to feel a bit alienated
from him. It just takes a bit of time in any
admin for the recog to dawn on these people
that they don't own the President 11/26

E.Y.

28

EY

(pause pause)
↳11/28   And the New Right doesn't own
Reagan. It thought it did, but it doesn't
11/31⌡
Written and produced by Ron Blau
for *Chronicle*, WCVB-TV. Used by permission.

385 sec: 6²⁵

Process   As with radio, you don't need a major network in order to produce a first-rate television documentary. It does take more than a few audiotape recorders, but with careful planning and imagination local stations can produce dramatic and pertinent documentaries with a couple of ENG cameras. Though not usually controversial, the subject of libraries is a significant one in most communities, and Barbara Allen of WGAL, Lancaster, Pennsylvania, decided that it was pertinent to viewers in the many cities within her station's signal. Her approach was to take an ostensibly inanimate thing and humanize it. In doing so she captured many of the aspects of libraries that relate to human drama — in this case those of a worrisome nature that require action on the part of the viewers. Her approach was to dramatize the problem, but in the form of a factual statement, not a semidocumentary.

---○---

● *As you study the script, note the combination of approaches used: narration, interviews, on-site events. Note, too, the combination of visuals used. Make a list of all the visual techniques you can find. What are some of the interest-catching techniques used in the writing?*

---○---

LIBRARIES: BRUISED, BATTERED AND BOUND

VIDEO	AUDIO
CU ON INITIALS CARVED IN TABLES, WALLS, ETC., FOR EACH LOCATION	MUSIC UNDER — LOVE THEME FROM *ROMEO AND JULIET* BARB: This is a love story with an unhappy ending. In Harrisburg, R.P. loves B.L. In Lebanon, A.M. loves P.S. In York, it's M.O. and S.T. In Reading C.K. loves P.R. and in Lancaster, Brenda loves Bill. START TO FADE MUSIC
COVER SHOT OF TABLE TOP	But love is a very private relationship and these initials are written in very public places. MUSIC OUT
KEY TITLE OVER TABLETOP	They are your public libraries and they are Bruised, Battered and Bound.
DISSOLVE TO COVER OF BARB AND LIBRARIANS AT TABLE	Hello, I'm Barbara Allen. With me around this bruised and battered library table are five librarians from the Channel 8 area.
ZOOM IN TO BARB	They're not here to tell you about what your local library has to offer. They're here to talk about larceny, decay, suffocation and rape. These things are happening in

VIDEO	AUDIO
	your library right now. If you don't stop them the next time you visit your library, you may be greeted by this.
:05 TAPE, PERSON PUTTING CLOSED SIGN IN WINDOW BARB, THEN MR. DOHERTY	(INTRODUCE MR. DOHERTY, CHAT WITH HIM ABOUT CLOSED SIGN AT READING PUBLIC LIBRARY AND ASK HIM ABOUT THE PROBLEMS AT THE READING LIBRARY THAT YOU CAN SEE)
1:15 TAPE SHOWING EXTERIOR OF LIBRARY AND VISUAL PROBLEMS INSIDE MR. DOHERTY	MR. DOHERTY VOICE OVER TAPE (CHAT WITH BARB ABOUT ONE PROBLEM YOU CAN'T SEE)
BARB, THEN MISS YEAGLEY	(ASK ABOUT PROBLEMS YOU CAN SEE AT MARTIN MEMORIAL LIBRARY, YORK)
1:15 TAPE SHOWING EXTERIOR OF LIBRARY AND VISUAL PROBLEMS INSIDE MISS YEAGLEY	MISS YEAGLEY VOICE OVER TAPE (CHAT WITH BARB ABOUT ONE PROBLEM YOU CAN'T SEE)
BARB INTRODUCES MR. GROSS	(ASK ABOUT PROBLEMS YOU CAN SEE AT THE HARRISBURG PUBLIC LIBRARY)
1:15 TAPE SHOWING EXTERIOR OF HARRISBURG LIBRARY AND VISUAL PROBLEMS INSIDE MR. GROSS	MR. GROSS VOICE OVER TAPE (CHAT WITH BARB ABOUT ONE PROBLEM YOU CAN'T SEE)
BARB INTRODUCES MR. MARKS	(ASK ABOUT PROBLEMS YOU CAN SEE AT LEBANON COMMUNITY LIBRARY)
1:15 TAPE SHOWING EXTERIOR OF LEBANON LIBRARY WITH VISUAL PROBLEMS INSIDE MR. MARKS	MR. MARKS VOICE OVER TAPE (CHAT WITH BARB ABOUT ONE PROBLEM YOU CAN'T SEE)
BARB INTRODUCES MR. JENKINS	(ASK ABOUT PROBLEMS YOU CAN SEE AT THE LANCASTER COUNTY LIBRARY)
1:15 TAPE SHOWING EXTERIOR OF LANCASTER LIBRARY AND VISUAL PROBLEMS INSIDE MR. JENKINS	MR. JENKINS VOICE OVER TAPE (CHAT WITH BARB ABOUT ONE PROBLEM YOU CAN'T SEE ... COSTS OF WHICH THE PUBLIC IS UNAWARE ...)
:20 SHOWING ONE PILE OF BOOKS, THEN ANOTHER :45 TAPE SHOWING SIX OR SEVEN STEPS IN PROCESSING	(NUMBER OF BOOKS $100 BOUGHT TEN YEARS AGO AND WHAT IT WILL BUY NOW) (NUMBER OF PEOPLE IT TAKES TO SELECT AND PROCESS ONE BOOK)

VIDEO	AUDIO
BARB, THEN LIBRARIANS	(WHAT LIBRARIES ARE DOING TO HELP THEMSELVES. GENERAL CONVERSATION... THEN ASK MR. JENKINS ABOUT USE OF VOLUNTEERS AT LANCASTER LIBRARY)
:30 TAPE SHOWING VOLUNTEERS DOING THREE DIFFERENT THINGS	MR. JENKINS VOICE OVER BARB: How do you think the public would react if the libraries were closed?
LIBRARIANS	(GENERAL ANSWERS) BARB: We asked some of the users of public libraries that question, and some others. This is how they replied.
2:00 SOT, MAN ON STREET INTERVIEWED IN FRONT OF LANCASTER LIBRARY. AN-NOUNCER TALKING TO PEOPLE AS THEY COME OUT BARB AND LIBRARIANS	SOT Do any of these replies surprise you? (GENERAL ANSWERS) BARB: What can the public do or stop doing to help?
LIBRARIANS	(GENERAL ANSWERS) (FILL TILL 1:00 CUE) CLOSING BARB: We've been talking about larceny, decay, suffocation and rape...things that are happening in your library right now. You may prefer to call them petty theft, deterioration, shortage of funds and malicious mischief but they are leaving your library bruised, battered and bound...suffering slow strangulation. If you don't stop these things from happening, the next time you visit your library, you may be greeted by this.
DISSOLVE TO :30 TAPE STARTING WITH CU OF CLOSED SIGN BEING PLACED IN WIN-DOW AND ZOOM OUT TO LONG SHOT OF LI-BRARY AND WINDOW KEY TITLE AND CREDITS OVER ABOVE DISSOLVE TO BLUE	

Courtesy of Barbara Allen and WGAL-TV, Lancaster, Penna.

Writing the script alone is not the limit of the writer's contribution. As pointed out earlier, the writer and producer are frequently the same person. In the case of the "Libraries" documentary the producer required herself, as writer, to prepare other materials needed in the production of the program. In addition to "Questions for Man-on-the-Street Interviews" and "Tape Footage Needed — Chronologically According to Script," both of which follow as examples of such preparation,

Allen also prepared "Tape Needed — Geographically According to Location," "Additional Tape Needed for Promos," and "Official List of Names of Libraries and Librarians and Addresses." Further, each participant in the program was sent a letter describing the format and procedure in taping the show. This letter, reproduced here, is a good guide for the researcher-writer-producer in preparing any participants who will appear in the documentary.

Dear

Since we will not have much time to chat prior to the videotaping of Libraries: Bruised, Battered and Bound on Thursday, February 4, at 1:30 PM, I want to let you know how the program will proceed.

After introducing the subject, I will ask you to briefly describe the problems you can see in your library. We will use the tape footage here showing the exterior of the library and allowing approximately ten seconds for each problem.

Then I will ask you about one problem that is not visible, which you can describe in one minute. Mr. Jenkins will be talking about the high cost of books and the number of people and steps it takes to select and process one book. I would suggest that you think of several possibilities: the more startling, the better. Then, when you arrive at the station you can compare notes with the other librarians to make sure each of you mentions a different problem.

I will also be asking you what the library is doing to help itself and how the public could help.

There will be a brief taped "man-on-the-street" interview concerning libraries and I will ask for your reactions.

I know that there could be a whole series of programs on this subject, but since we are limited to thirty minutes it would be best to keep answers fairly brief and yet revealing for it is obvious that the public has no conception of the depth of the library crisis. It's up to us to create an impact.

Librarians participating are: Dean C. Gross (Harrisburg Public Library), Louisa Yeagley (Martin Memorial Library), Robert Marks (Lebanon Community Library), Edward Doherty (Reading Public Library) and Harold R. Jenkins (Lancaster County Library).

Would appreciate any advance promotion you can give the program in or out of the library. Air date and time is February 8 at 7 P.M.

Thank you for your cooperation.

Sincerely yours,

Barbara Allen

QUESTIONS FOR MAN-ON-STREET INTERVIEWS

Libraries: Bruised, Battered and Bound
(to be asked by reporter outside front and back doors of Lancaster Library of people
who are coming out of Library)

1. How would you feel if lack of money caused the library to close indefinitely?
2. What does the library mean to you?
3. How do you think libraries could meet rising costs?

TAPE NEEDED FOR LIBRARIES: BRUISED, BATTERED AND BOUND

CHRONOLOGICALLY (according to script):

:05	CU initials carved in Harrisburg Library
:05	CU initials carved in Lebanon Library
:05	CU initials carved in York Library
:05	CU initials carved in Reading Library
:05	CU initials carved in Lancaster Library
:15	COVER SHOT top of Lancaster Library table with carvings
:05	Person putting CLOSED sign in Reading Library window

:10	Showing exterior of Lebanon Library
1:00	Close-ups of visual problems inside Lebanon Library

:10	Showing exterior of York Library
1:00	Close-up of visual problems inside York Library

:10	Showing exterior of Harrisburg Library
1:00	Close-ups of visual problems inside Harrisburg Library

:10	Showing exterior of Lebanon Library
1:00	Close-ups of visual problems inside Lebanon Library

:10	Showing exterior of Lancaster Library
1:00	Close-ups of visual problems inside Lancaster Library

:20	Close-up of hands piling books that could be bought for $100 ten years ago, then pan to hands piling books that can be bought for $100 today
:45	Pan six or seven sets of hands showing the people and steps necessary to select and process one book at Lancaster Library

:30	Cover shots of three different volunteers doing three different things at Lancaster Library
2:00	SOT interview outside Lancaster Library ... some at front door, some at rear
:30	Start with close-up of CLOSED sign in Reading Library window and zoom out to cover on library and window

— consecutive footage

_____ For Application and Review _____

1. Write a routine sheet for a how-to-do-it *radio* feature. The subject should be one of importance to a professional or vocational group in your community.
2. Write a script for a behind-the-scenes human interest *television* feature. The purpose should be to persuade as well as to inform. Try a public health or social welfare subject.
3. Write a documentary script for television *or* radio, using one or a combination of the basic documentary types. The subject should be one that is vital to the welfare and continued existence of humanity, and that is of some controversy in your community as well as nationally.
4. Write a documentary script for the medium not used in 3, above. The subject should be one that is relatively unimportant and not of vital interest to humanity. Can you, even so, incorporate a point of view that makes the documentary pertinent in your community?
5. Apply the structure of the "Who Killed Michael Farmer?" documentary to an outline for a "60 Minutes" type of eighteen-minute television sequence and to a magazine program seven-minute sequence.

6

Talk Programs

alk programs is used sometimes as an all-inclusive term, encompassing the major program types that are not news, documentaries, drama, music, features, game shows, or commercials. Included in talk programs are interviews, discussions, and speeches. Audience participation and game shows were at one time included in that category, but have since become a genre of their own. Although some of the latter use routine sheets, veteran game show producer Dan Enright states that the principal prepared materials are the intro and outro; after the show is on the air for a while, the talent has learned the routine and scripts are unnecessary.

Speeches are, of course, fully prepared — or, at least, ought to be. Interview and discussion programs are outlined, either in rundown or in routine sheet form. A principal reason they cannot be prepared in complete script form is that the very nature of an interplay of ideas and, sometimes, feelings among people requires extemporaneity. Another reason is that the participants, excluding the interviewer or moderator, usually are nonprofessionals and cannot memorize or read a prepared script without seeming strained and stilted.

Nevertheless, the writer should prepare as much of the script as necessary — whether a detailed routine sheet or a simple outline — for the best possible show. Why take a chance with an unprepared question or sequence when the chances of success are better with prepared material? The rundown sheet is the key for most talk programs. As noted in an earlier chapter, the rundown sheet is a detailed list of all the sequences in a given program, frequently with the elapsed time, if known, for each item. Because broadcasting operates on a split-second schedule, the final version of the rundown sheet must be adhered to in the taping or live broadcast of the program. Some talk shows use the more detailed routine sheet, which includes as much of the actual dialogue and action as can be prepared.

Rundown and routine sheets sometimes include alternate endings of different lengths so that the extemporaneous nature of the program can be maintained and still end on time through the choice of the proper length sequence for the final item in the program.

The Interview

The interview on radio or television may be prepared completely, with a finished script for interviewer and interviewee; it may be oriented around an outline, where the general line of questioning and answering is prepared, but the exact words to be used are extemporaneous; it may be completely unprepared, or ad-lib. Very rarely are interviews either completely ad-lib or completely scripted. The unprepared interview is too risky, with the interviewee likely to be too garrulous, embarrassing or embarrassed, or just plain dull, and the interviewer likely to be faced with the almost impossible task of organizing, preparing, and thinking of appropriate questions on the spot. The prepared script usually results in a stilted, monotonous presentation except when both the interviewer and interviewee are skilled performers who can make a written line sound extemporaneous, a situation not often likely to occur.

Approach

Most interviews are set up in outline form. A broad outline of the purpose and form of questioning is prepared by the interviewer and staff and, on the basis of knowledge or research concerning the interviewee, a number of questions are prepared. In order to be ready to ask questions in a logical order, the interviewer must have an idea of the possible answers to the major questions already developed. For this purpose a preliminary conference or preinterview, if possible, is held with the interviewee who is briefed, sometimes lightly, sometimes fully, on the questions to be asked. The interviewee indicates the general line of answering. On the basis of this conference the interviewer is able to develop follow-up and probing questions and arrange the general line of questioning in its most effective order.

The written material for the extemporaneous interview is the rundown and/or routine sheet, a step-by-step outline of the program that includes a list of questions and content of answers as determined in the preinterview session. Sometimes, of course, the interviewee will not be available for a conference before the show, and the interviewer and staff must guess at the probable answers to their questions — based on thorough research of the interviewee, whose answers to certain questions, if consistent, can fairly accurately be anticipated. Sometimes the interviewee can be persuaded to appear at the studio a substantial time before the program, and a rehearsal will serve, in part, as a preinterview session. On some occasions the interviewee is not only available for a preinterview conference but also comes to a rehearsal, thus solidifying the show while retaining its extemporaneous quality.

In all interviews — prepared, extemporaneous, ad-lib — the writer, ideally, prepares at least the opening and closing continuity, introductory material about the interviewee and, for each section of the program, lead-ins and lead-outs for commercial breaks, and an outline of the questions and, if possible, answers. The closing continuity should be of different lengths in case the program runs shorter or longer than expected. The writer should be certain that the background of the guest is clearly presented. Except where the interviewee is very well known, it is sometimes helpful to begin with questions of a human interest nature so that the audience gets to know something about the personality of the guest before the interview is too far along. Even with a well-known guest this sometimes is advisable. In the strictly informational, news-type interview this approach could be distractive, although even in such programs the interviewer frequently asks personality questions.

Types
There are three major interview types: the opinion interview, the information interview, and the personality interview. Any given interview can combine elements of all three.

The opinion interview   Any interview that concentrates on the beliefs of an individual may be an opinion interview. However, inasmuch as many of the interviews of this nature are with prominent people, usually experts in their fields, such interviews are not only opinion, but also, to a great extent, information and even personality types. Even in the completely ad-lib street interview, the interviewer should have an introduction, a question, and follow-up questions developed in the light of possible answers. Prospective interviewees may be briefed before the program is taped or goes on the air live.

The information interview   The information interview usually is of the public service type. The information may be delivered by a relatively unknown figure or by a prominent person in the field. Because the main object is the communication of information, sometimes a complete script may be prepared. The interviewee may provide direct factual material, may deliver information oriented toward a cause or purpose, or may combine information with personal belief. If a script is written, the personality of the speaker should be kept in mind. If the interviewee is not likely to be a performer, that is, a good "reader," then it is better to prepare a detailed outline and rehearse the program as an extemporaneous presentation.

A news interview such as "Face the Nation," which follows, falls into the category of the information interview. When important personalities are the subjects, the information frequently is mixed with opinion — although what might be called opinion by some is called fact by others.

The personality interview   This is the human interest, feature story kind of interview. The format of the program may be oriented toward one purpose — to probe or to embarrass or to flatter — or it may be flexible, combining and interweaving these various facets. The most successful personality interview programs of recent years seem to be oriented toward a combination of probing for personal attitudes and revelation of personal beliefs and actions. To prepare pertinent questions for the personality interview, full background information on the interviewee must be obtained. The questions must be outlined and the interviewee must be talked with before the program in order to prepare the depth questions and the logical order of questioning.

Television Considerations
We usually think of the interview as static: two or more people talking at each other. However, even in the simplest question-and-answer process, some visual interest

can be injected. The visual movement may be of a subjective nature, with the camera probing the facial expressions and bodily gestures of the interviewee. The visual approach may be broader and more objective, with film, or photographs of places, events, or personalities referred to by the interviewee. For example, an interview with a college professor may have a film or tape of the institution where he or she teaches; an interview with a scientist may include visual material concerning his or her experiments. Shots of the interviewee's home town are sometimes effective. Because television is visual, the interviewer (and writer-producer-director) must be cautioned about misleading the audience, even unintentionally. One classic story is about the television interviewer who made much in preprogram publicity of a forthcoming interview with a famous stripper. Although the audience should have known better, many viewers were quite disappointed that she didn't do what she obviously couldn't do on television.

Technique

Format is paramount. Each interview program has its own organization and the writer must write for that particular format. Some interview shows open with an introduction of the program, introduce the guest, and then go into the actual interview. Others open cold, with the interview already under way, in order to grab immediately and hold the audience's attention, with a subsequent cut-in for the standard introductory material. The following scripts for ''Face the Nation'' illustrate the latter approach. Note the use of the term **tease** for this kind of opening. Note, too, the alternate closings prepared for edited and nonedited versions of the radio broadcast. Do you find any distinctive differences between the radio and television scripts? Should there be any special, different techniques used for each medium?

CBS RADIO

Face the Nation

12:30:00–12:58:55 P.M.   _____

(Date)

2:30:00–2:53:30 P.M.

(Edited Version)

OPENING:	Radio takes TV audio (Herman asks tease question, guest(s) answer(s)). Before TV announcer comes in, Radio cutaway as follows:
SOUND:	RADIO "PUBLIC AFFAIRS SOUNDER"
ANNOUNCER:	"From CBS News, Washington ... Face the Nation ... on the CBS Radio Network ... a spontaneous and unrehearsed news interview with Senator Henry Jackson (Democrat of Washington) Senator Jackson will be questioned by CBS News Diplomatic Correspondent Marvin Kalb, David S. Broder, National Political Correspondent for the Washington Post and by CBS News Correspondent George Herman. We shall resume the interview in a moment. But first, here is George Herman.

(2:00 Herman Tape)

ANNOUNCER:	"And now, we continue with Face the Nation."

INTERVIEW

CLOSING: Radio cuts away from TV audio on Herman's cue:
            (… "Thank you very much for being here to Face the Nation, a word
            about next week's guest in a moment.")

            (PAUSE: :02 PROMO: _____)

ANNOUNCER: "Today on Face the Nation, Senator Henry Jackson (Democrat of
            Washington) was interviewed by CBS Diplomatic Correspondent Marvin
            Kalb, David S. Broder, National Political Correspondent for the Washington
            Post, and CBS News Correspondent George Herman.
              Next week, (another prominent figure in the news)

            (_____)

            will Face the Nation.
              Today's broadcast was recorded earlier today in Washington and was
12:30 feed produced by Sylvia Westerman and Mary O. Yates. Robert Vitarelli is the
            director. Face the Nation is a production of CBS News.
            (CLOSING PUBLIC AFFAIRS SOUNDER)   (CRN CUE)
              Today's broadcast was recorded earlier today in Washington and was
2:30 feed   edited to conform to time requirements. It was produced by Sylvia Wester-
            man and Mary O. Yates. Robert Vitarelli is the director. Face the Nation is
            a production of CBS News.
            (CLOSING PUBLIC AFFAIRS SOUNDER)   (CRN CUE)

                                                              Courtesy of CBS News

CBS TELEVISION
Face the Nation

HERMAN TEASE QUESTION _____
SEN. JACKSON ANSWERS _____

(ANNCR: V.O.)

FROM CBS NEWS WASHINGTON … A SPONTANEOUS AND UNREHEARSED NEWS INTERVIEW
ON "FACE THE NATION," WITH SENATOR HENRY JACKSON, DEMOCRAT OF WASHINGTON.
SENATOR JACKSON WILL BE QUESTIONED BY CBS NEWS DIPLOMATIC CORRESPONDENT
MARVIN KALB, DAVID S. BRODER, NATIONAL POLITICAL CORRESPONDENT FOR THE WASH-
INGTON POST AND CBS NEWS CORRESPONDENT GEORGE HERMAN. "FACE THE NATION" IS
PRODUCED BY CBS NEWS, WHICH IS SOLELY RESPONSIBLE FOR THE SELECTION OF
TODAY'S GUEST AND PANEL.

BILLBOARD _____ 10 sec. _____
  (IMBB   1801)   (VTR)

COMMERCIAL _____ 1:40 _____
  (SRA MATH   IMSR   5112)   (VTR)

(HERMAN CLOSING)
I'M SORRY GENTLEMEN, BUT OUR TIME IS UP. THANK YOU VERY MUCH FOR BEING HERE
TO "FACE THE NATION."

COMMERCIAL _____ :36½ _____
 (THIRTY SECONDS   IMCO   3312FN)

(ANNCR: V.O.)

TODAY ON "FACE THE NATION," SENATOR HENRY JACKSON, DEMOCRAT OF WASHINGTON, WAS INTERVIEWED BY CBS NEWS DIPLOMATIC CORRESPONDENT MARVIN KALB, DAVID S. BRODER, NATIONAL POLITICAL CORRESPONDENT FOR THE WASHINGTON POST AND CBS NEWS CORRESPONDENT GEORGE HERMAN.

(BILLBOARD   IMBB   4806   6 sec.)

"FACE THE NATION" HAS BEEN SPONSORED BY IBM.

(ANNCR: V.O. CREDITS)

NEXT WEEK, ANOTHER PROMINENT FIGURE IN THE NEWS WILL "FACE THE NATION." THIS BROADCAST WAS PRODUCED BY CBS NEWS.
"FACE THE NATION" ORIGINATED FROM WASHINGTON, D.C.

Courtesy of CBS News

In the earlier Approach section, we noted what the writer ideally prepares. The interviewer's technique, configuration of the program itself, and the producer's and director's styles modify what is ideal. The script preparation becomes what is necessary and effective. For example, Duncan MacDonald was her own writer, producer, and interviewer for the program she conducted on WQXR, New York. After a while she did not need written-out opening, closing, and continuity preparation. Her concentration was on the content. One of her keys was to be certain that under each major question there were enough follow-up or probe questions, so that she was not faced with the possibility of getting single-phrase answers and running out of questions and topics in a few minutes. The following is the rundown outline used for one of her thirty-minute programs.

Today is the anniversary of the signing of the United Nations Charter in San Francisco. In observance of this anniversary our guest today is Dr. Rodolphe L. Coigney, Director of the World Health Organization liaison office with the UN in New York City.

Dr. Coigney was born and educated in Paris. His career in international health began in 1944. In 1947 he became director of health for the International Refugee Organization. In his present post at the UN he represents WHO — the World Health Organization — at Economic and Social Council meetings, the Committee of the UN General Assembly, and other bodies of the UN.

1) Dr. Coigney, as one of the 10 specialized agencies of the UN, what is WHO's specific function?
   a) Is it included in the Charter of the UN?
   b) Active/passive purpose?

c) Is WHO affected by various crises within UN?
Financial/political? Your own crises in health?
d) Do you have specific long-term goals, or do you respond only to crises in health? Earthquakes/Floods/Epidemics?

2) How does the work of WHO tie in with other UN organizations?
UNICEF/ILO/Food and Agriculture/UNESCO/International Civil Aviation/International Bank/
· Reconstruction and Development/International Monetary Fund/Universal Postal/International Communications/World Meteorological.

3) Background of WHO.
a) How started? Switzerland?
b) Headquarters for all international organizations?

4) How much would the work of WHO differ in a country medically advanced, such as Sweden, as opposed to developing countries: Africa, Far East?
a) Religious or social taboos?
b) Witch doctors?
c) Birth control?

5) Can you give an example of a decision made at Headquarters and then carried out in some remote area of the world?

6) What do you consider WHO's greatest success story in fighting a specific disease: malaria, yaws?
a) Ramifications of disease? Economic/Disability for work?

7) Your secretary mentioned on the phone that you were going to Latin America. What specifically takes you there now?

8) How does a country get WHO assistance?
a) Invited?
b) Matching funds?

9) We are aware of the shortage of doctors and nurses in the United States. What is the situation world-wide?
a) Do you think Public Health is an important career for young people? Now? For the future?

Courtesy of Duncan MacDonald

One of television history's most successful interviewers, Barbara Walters, has conducted interviews that, by the nature of the person being interviewed and the critical events of the world at the time, have reflected all three basic interview types: opinion, information, and personality. One of Walters' strengths is her ability to combine elements of all three in any given interview, although just one of the types may be the principal orientation of the program.

Neophyte interviewers and writers, when informed that the Walters shows have no prepared scripts, may incorrectly assume that there has been no preparation. On the contrary, the detailed research report and list of questions required by Walters entails more than the writer might do for many nondramatic programs with full scripts. For example, for an interview with Carol Burnett, Walters worked from a thirty-eight-page research report which not only provided chronological facts of Burnett's life, but quoted from various sources about her personal as well as professional background and attitudes. From the research report she developed a list of over one hundred probe questions, only a fraction of which could be used in the actual interview.

The following excerpts from the research report and question list provide an idea of the writer's contributions. Note especially the categories of questions; these and others not included in these excerpts cover all possible areas of thought and experience.

CHRONOLOGY

4/26/34	Carol Burnett born in San Antonio, Texas
1938 or 1939	Parents move to Los Angeles
1940	Carol and Grandmother move to Los Angeles
Dec. 1944	Sister Christine born
1946	Parents divorce
June 1952	Carol graduates Hollywood High School
1952 - 1954	Carol attends UCLA
1954	Carol's father, Jody, dies
August 1954	Carol goes to New York
1955	Carol appears 13 weeks, Paul Winchell's television show
	Marries Don Saroyan
Sept. 1956	Begins as regular on TV show "Stanley"
11/9/56	First appearance on Garry Moore morning show
March 1957	"Stanley" cancelled
July 1957	First nightclub appearance, Blue Angel.
	Sings "I Made a Fool of Myself Over John Foster Dulles"
Dec. 1957	Visits L.A. Brings sister back to New York
1/10/58	Mother dies
1958 - 1959	Regular "Pantomime Quiz," ABC
1959	Separates from Don Saroyan
May 1959	Off-Broadway show, "Once Upon a Mattress" later moves to Broadway

* * *

CHILDHOOD - FAMILY - EDUCATION

Carol Burnett was born in San Antonio, Texas, April 26, 1934.
"I'm a lot Irish, and I'm part Indian … we were Irish and English and there was Cherokee blood."
Esquire, June 1972

Carol's father, Jody Burnett, was a movie theater manager in San Antonio. She says that he was a charming man, but weak-willed, more interested in drinking than working.

> "He was a lanky six feet two and a half inches tall — and not un-
> like Jimmy Stewart in speech and mannerisms."
> Good Housekeeping, December 1970

Carol's mother's name was Louise Creighton Burnett.

> "Mama was short, fiery, quick-witted and quick-tempered, but
> basically kind."
> Good Housekeeping, December 1970

> "I got my sense of humor from my mother. I'd tell her my
> tragedies. She'd make me laugh. She said comedy was tragedy
> plus time."
> TV Guide 7/1/72

Sometime in the late 1930s, Carol's parents left her in Texas with her grandmother, Mae White, and moved to Los Angeles. In 1940, Carol and "Nanny" joined them.

Jody and Louise fought a lot and were frequently separated. Christine was born in December 1944, after one of their brief reunions.

* * *

CAREER

Carol used to say that she left California because

> "To succeed in the movies, you have to look like Marilyn Monroe or
> Tony Curtis. Unfortunately I look more like Tony Curtis."
> Current Biography, 1962

Carol arrived in New York, August 1954, and Don Saroyan followed a month later. Carol moved into the Rehearsal Club, a hotel for aspiring actresses, made famous in the stage play and movie, "Stage Door." Her first job was checking hats in a restaurant in the Rockefeller Center area.

> "The one thing I can tell (aspiring actors) is, Get a part-time job. So
> when you see a producer you don't have that desperate, starved,
> I'm-going-to-kill-myself look."
> Current Biography, 1962

She made the rounds of producers and agents and got the same old story, I can't give you a job until I see your work. Finally, one person suggested she put on her own show.

By that time, Carol was president of the Rehearsal Club, and talked 25 of the girls into chipping in to rent a hall. They badgered some writers they knew to put some material together for them and Don Saroyan directed. They invited every agent and producer in New York and a few showed up.

Carol's piece in the show was a spoof of Eartha Kitt's sexy song, "Monotonous." It got her an agent, Martin Goodman, and got Don a job directing an industrial show in Chicago.

* * *

MARRIAGES AND CHILDREN

Don Saroyan, a distant cousin of William Saroyan, was Carol's singing and acting partner in college and also received a $1,000 check from their secret fairy godfather. He followed Carol to New York a month after Carol had left, arriving in September 1954.

Don lived across the street from the Rehearsal Club, and because Carol's rent included board, she brought part of her dinner each evening to Don.

When they married in 1955, Carol was appearing on Paul Winchell's television show and Don was directing an industrial film.

Carol's career was going better than Don's in 1959, and she attributes their separation to their "ego problem."

> "We get along better now than when we were living together. It's
> hard on a marriage when the woman makes more money."
> Good Housekeeping, November 1960

The divorce was final in the summer of 1962. In 1963, Don was reported to be an actor and director in Los Angeles.

Garry Moore said of Carol:

> "She needs someone to love. I think she wants desperately to
> marry. But I don't think she realizes herself what a tremendous
> talent she has. The public will never let her go. A talent the size of
> Carol's is a terrible mixed blessing. She has a difficult life ahead."
> Ladies Home Journal, May 1963

Carol was seen at dinner with Bob Newhart and with Richard Chamberlain, but dating wasn't going well.

* * *

PERSONAL

Sometime in the early 1970s, Carol lost a lot of weight, going from a size 14 to a size 8. About the same time, she quit smoking, gave up coffee and became a vegetarian. She eats no red meat, but it goes further than that.

"I don't eat any canned foods, any frozen foods."
                        TV Guide 4/14/79

Carol had been having a lot of headaches and taking up to eight aspirin a day, when in 1974, a friend suggested she take up yoga.

"You don't have to meditate or worry about your soul unless you want to. There are no strings attached ... I don't have headaches anymore and I don't live on aspirin ... and I've never felt better in my life."
                        Good Housekeeping, February 1975

Later Carol did become interested in yoga meditation in addition to the exercises.

She changed a great deal during the 1970s. It was also the time she began attending production meetings and making her desires known to the writers and staff.

All her life, Carol was unhappy that she was not pretty.

"The first time I ever forgot I was homely was the first time I heard an audience laugh."
                        Life 2/22/63

* * *

QUESTIONS — CAROL BURNETT

1. Right now, this minute, how is your life?
2. If your life was a movie, can you give us a synopsis of the plot?
3. How would you describe Carol Burnett?

Childhood

1. What is your strongest childhood memory?
5. What kind of person was your mother?
5A. You've said that your mother "cuffed you around." Was it, although you may not have realized it then, a case of child abuse?
5B. Was your mother pretty?
6. Did you feel you were pretty? Did she?
7. What kind of person was your father?

* * *

Youth

22. From everything I've read about you, for much of your life you had little confidence, yet you became an enormous success. What kept you believing in yourself?
23. You were only 23 years old when you decided to bring your 12-year-old sister to New

York to live with you. Wasn't that a lot to take on then ... your career was barely under way ... then your mother died.

24. I read that you were able to go to UCLA because someone anonymously left the tuition money in an envelope for you. Is that true?

* * *

Career

30. You did the Carol Burnett Show for eleven years. Will you ever do another television series?
31. You used to invite your audience to ask you questions. What did they most want to know?
32. What was the most embarrassing question you were asked?

* * *

36. In 1970, Ronald Reagan appeared on one of your shows. What was he like? Are you a fan of his?
37. Do you have any political involvements?

* * *

Motherhood & Daughter Career

38. How did your own upbringing affect you as a mother?
39. What kind of a mother are you?
40. Were you very strict?
41. Were you ever torn between your work and the children?
42. Were you home enough?

* * *

View of Herself

48. Sometime in the 1970s, you changed quite dramatically. You said you began attending production meetings on your series for the first time, you began saying "no" ... even your looks changed. What happened to you and why?
49. Do you have confidence now?
50. In the early 1970s, you went from a size 14 to a size 8, totally changing the way you look. What made you do this?

* * *

Philosophical

60. You have performed for such a wide cross section of the American audience for so many years now. What changes do you see? Are these tough times? Do you feel optimistic? Fear for our future?

* * *

Marriage

66. Tell us about your husband, Joe Hamilton. What is special about him?
67. What has marriage meant to you?
68. When you were first dating your husband, Joe Hamilton, there were a lot of ugly rumors. He was still married. He had eight children already. How did you handle that?

* * *

Meditation Reincarnation

76. I understand you meditate. Do you do it regularly? What does it do for you?
77. Are you religious?
78. I read that you believe in reincarnation. Do you have any feelings about who you were in other lives?

Courtesy of Barbara Walters
and the American Broadcasting Company

Discussion Programs

Discussion programs are aimed toward an exchange of opinions and information and, to some degree, toward the arriving at solutions, actual or implied, on important questions or problems. They should not be confused with the interview, in which the purpose is to elicit, not to exchange.

Approach

The writer of the discussion program has to walk a thin line between too much and not enough preparation. It is not possible to write a complete script, partially because the participants can't know specifically in advance what their precise attitude or comment might be before they have heard a given issue or statement that might be brought up in the discussion. On the other hand, a complete lack of preparation would likely result in a program in which the participants would ramble; it would present the moderator with the impossible task of getting everybody someplace without knowing where they were going. To achieve spontaneity, it is better to plan only an outline, indicating the general form and organization of the discussion. This is, of course, in addition to whatever standard opening, closing, and transitions are used in the program. This might include opening and closing statements for the moderator, introductions of the participants, and general summaries to be used by the moderator in various places throughout the program.

The discussion outline should be distributed to all participants in advance of the program so that they may plan their own contributions in accordance with the general format. It will give them time to do necessary research and prepare specific information for use during the discussion. The writer should indicate in the format the issues to be discussed, the order in which the discussion will take place, and, where feasible, the time allotted for each point for each participant. If possible, the participants, in consultation with the writer (and/or producer and/or director) should prepare brief statements of their general views so that there can be a preprogram exchange of ideas and a coordination of all participants' contributions toward a smooth, well-integrated program. Just as too much preparation can result in a dull program, too little preparation may result in the participants being unable to cope with the needs of a spontaneous program. In addition, without preplanning with the participants, there may be an unnecessary duplication of material. A program in which everyone agrees on everything can become quite boring; preplanning should assure, for incorporation in the rundown or routine sheet, that all points of view on the given issue receive adequate representation — unless, of course, the program is deliberately oriented toward a particular, nonobjective viewpoint.

A decision should be made in the early stages of planning whether to use a controversial topic, certainly a good way to achieve vitality and excitement in the program, and whether to promote or avoid disagreement among the participants. The topics should be presented as questions, thus provoking investigation and thought. In addition, the topics should be broadly oriented, preferably in terms of general policy, and should not be so narrow that they can be answered with a yes or no response or with obvious statements of fact.

In the extemporaneous discussion program the same principles apply as in the interview. Opening and closing remarks and introductions should be written out. If possible, general summaries should be prepared for the moderator or master of ceremonies. In some instances, depending, as in the interview program, on format and approach, a brief outline or routine sheet consisting of a summary of the action of the program and a listing of the topics to be covered, or a rundown sheet, may be sufficient.

In television visual elements should be incorporated. The setting should, if possible, relate to the topic. Although the visual element may be relatively simple, it should help to convey a feeling of excitement and challenge in terms of the topic under consideration.

Types
There are several major types of discussion programs: the panel, the symposium, the group discussion, and the debate.

Panel   The panel discussion — not to be confused with the quiz-type or inter-view-type panel — is the most often used and the most flexible. It presents a number of people in a round-table type of situation exchanging ideas on some topic of interest. There is no set pattern or time limit on individual contributions and sometimes not even a limitation on the matters to be discussed. The participants usually do not have prepared statements and have done whatever background preparation each one individually has deemed necessary. A moderator, who usually does not participate in the discussion, attempts to guide it and to see that it does not get out of hand or too far from the topic. The approach is informal, with the participants offering personal comments and evaluations at will. On occasion the discussion may become heated between two or more participants. The moderator tries to see that the discussion is not dominated by just one or two persons. No solution to the problem being discussed is necessarily reached, although the moderator frequently summarizes in order to pull the discussion together and to clarify for the audience — and the participants — the point at which the panelists have arrived. A routine sheet usually consists of the moderator's opening remarks, introduction of the panel members, statement of the problem, flexible outline of subtopics to be discussed under the main topic (the outline should be given to each panel member sometime prior to the program, preferably in time for them to prepare materials, if they wish), and the closing.

As you read the following beginning and end of a script routine sheet prepared for a panel discussion program, note the careful and liberal insertion of subtopics. The complete script repeats the principal question-subtopics organization four times for a one-hour show.

_____○_____

● *Apply to this script the following questions (which you should apply to any discussion script that you may subsequently write). Do you feel that the phrasing of the subtopics provides the essentials for a good discussion? Is the development of the topic too limited or is there opportunity for the clear presentation of varied opinions, attitudes, and information? Does the organization of the program seem to move logically toward a climax? Does there seem to be a logical interrelationship among the various parts of the discussion? Are the participants properly introduced? Does the structure permit periodic summarizing?*

_____○_____

WUNC CAROLINA ROUNDTABLE

The Berlin Wall

Thursday, 7–8 P.M.

MODERATOR (OPEN COLD) West Berlin — to be or not to be? This question has been
(GEORGE HALL): reiterated thousands of times by the peoples of the world. The Berlin Wall has become a symbol of the ideological conflict between the East and West German regimes, between East and West Europe.

This is your Moderator, George Hall, welcoming you to another "Carolina Roundtable."

All of us are by now fearfully aware of the critical importance of West Berlin. Most of us recognize that the East Berlin limitations on inter-city travel and the West Berlin opposition to negotiation with and recognition of the East have created an impasse that demands a response from both sides. What is that reponse to be — not only that of the West and of the United States, but that of the Communist East and of the Soviet Union? How will the choice of a course of action determine not only the fate of both Berlins, but of Europe itself? Are there any areas of compromise that would be satisfactory to all parties?

This evening, with the aid of our guests, we will attempt to seek answers to these questions.

Dr. Charles B. Robson is a professor of Political Science at the University of North Carolina and an authority on Germany. Dr. Robson teaches in the fields of German government and in modern political theory. He recently spent a year in Germany studying that country's political affairs. Good evening, Dr. Robson.

ROBSON:	(RESPONSE)
MODERATOR:	Dr. Leopold B. Koziebrodzki is an associate professor of Economics and History at the University of North Carolina. His special field is Russian foreign relations in the twentieth century, and he has observed first-hand government policies of eastern European countries in relation to the Soviet Union. Good evening, Dr. Koziebrodzki.
KOZIEBRODZKI:	(RESPONSE)
MODERATOR:	Dr. Samuel Shepard Jones is Burton Craige Professor of Political Science at the University of North Carolina. His area of specialization is United States foreign policy and international politics. He has served as cultural attache with the U.S. State Department, and has lectured at the National War College. Good evening, Dr. Jones.
JONES:	(RESPONSE)
MODERATOR:	I'd like to remind our participants and our listeners that questions are encouraged from our listening audience. Anyone having a question for any or all of our panel members is invited to phone the WUNC studios at 942-3172. Your question will be taped and played back for our panel to answer at the first opportunity. That's 942-3172.
	In view of the growing power and influence of the small and uncommitted countries in the United Nations, what concessions, if any, should the West be prepared to make in the interest of peace in Berlin? Dr. Jones, would you start the discussion on this matter?
	(BRING IN OTHER PANELISTS ON THIS QUESTION. THROUGH PRE-DISCUSSION, DETERMINE TENTATIVE AGREEMENT ON SOME AREAS, AS BELOW.)
	(SUB-TOPICS, AS NEEDED)

1. Berlin to be a free city under U.N. jurisdiction, as proposed by Soviet Union?
2. Recognition of East German government?
3. Demilitarization with foreign troops withdrawn?
4. Admission and roles of West and East Germany in U.N.?

MODERATOR:	(REMINDER TO AUDIENCE ON PHONE CALLS)

* * *

MODERATOR:	(IF ABOVE TOPICS NOT CONCLUDED BY 8 MINUTES BEFORE THE END OF THE PROGRAM, SKIP TO FOLLOWING): Of all the possibilities discussed on the program, which, if any, do you think have the most chance of acceptance?
	(IF FEW OR NONE, ASK ABOUT ALTERNATIVES AND POSSIBILITIES OF WAR.)
MODERATOR:	(SUMMARY AT 3-MINUTE MARK)

1. Possible concessions by West.
2. Attitudes and actions of East Germany and the East.

3. Attitudes and actions of West Germany.
4. Future of Berlin.
5. Chance of war.

MODERATOR: (AT 1-MINUTE MARK) Dr. Charles Robson, Dr. Leopold Kozie-
              brodzki, and Dr. Shepard Jones of the University of North
              Carolina, we thank you for being our guests this evening on
              this "Carolina Roundtable" discussion of the possible solu-
              tions to the Berlin problem.

GUESTS: (MASS RESPONSE OF GOOD NIGHT, ETC.)

MODERATOR: We thank you all for listening and invite you to join us next
              week at this same time when "Carolina Roundtable's"
              guests, _____, and _____ will
              discuss _____.

              This has been a presentation of WUNC, the FM radio station
              of the Department of Radio, Television and Motion Pictures,
              in the Communication Center of the University of North
              Carolina.

Symposium   The symposium presents several persons who have prepared individual solutions to a given problem. Each of the participants is given an equal
period of time in which to present his or her ideas. First, each participant presents,
within equal time limits, a prepared statement on the question. The question should
be one which has at least two distinct sides, such as ''Should the United States
Adopt an Equal Rights Amendment?'' After the participants have presented their
prepared talks, members of the audience may direct questions to any or all members
of the symposium. During this question period the participants sometimes cross-
question each other and exchange ideas. After a specified time period, the questions
from the audience are ended and each participant is permitted an equal amount of
time for summing up his or her viewpoint. ''America's Town Meeting of the Air,''
on radio for many years, was an outstanding example of the symposium. The
typical routine sheet or outline contains the moderator's opening remarks, the
introduction of the participants, set time limits for the prepared statements, audience
question period and summaries, and the closing for the program.

Group discussion   Group discussion is a form of problem solving that has been
used very effectively in industry and in other professional situations. Although
rarely used in radio or television, it has the potential for arriving at objective
information and action for mutually beneficial purposes, not only among the participants, but for the audience as well. Group discussion differs from most other forms
of discussion in that it attempts to solve a problem by employing the objective,
cooperative thinking and research of all the participants. The participants do not
attempt to impose their own viewpoints and do not take opposing positions, but
attempt to examine all materials in an unbiased manner and, in common investigation and unanimous decision, reach a solution acceptable to and best for the entire
group. A moderator, who does not participate, guides the discussion and sees that it
remains objective, that all group members participate and that none dominates, and

that the discussion does not go off the track. A basic organizational approach for a group discussion would be a definition and limitation of the problem, a determination of the causes of the problem through objective research, and a determination of solutions based on the causes. Ideally, each participant is prepared with an outline containing facts pertinent to each step in the discussion process. The question itself should be a broad one, not answerable by a yes or a no, such as "Should Legal Penalties for Marijuana Use Be Abolished?" but necessitating analysis, such as "What Should Be Done about Legal Penalties for Marijuana Use?" The prepared material need be only an outline containing the opening, the introduction of the participants, some basic factual information under each step of the process, and the closing.

Debate   Another form of discussion infrequently seen on television or heard on radio, except during political campaigns, which offers many variations in format, is the formal debate. Yet, by the very nature of its form of dramatic conflict, the debate is a natural for broadcasting. A debate consists of two distinctly opposite sides of a question, one side taking the affirmative, the other side the negative. In the debate the participants devote all of their energies to disputing each other, to building up their own arguments, and to destroying those of the opponent. The debaters may be individuals or may be in teams of two or more on a side. The debate itself has a number of distinct forms of organization. In all forms, however, there are just two sides, and each side is given a specified time for presentation of an initial argument, for rebuttal of the opponent's argument, and for summary. Some forms utilize direct confrontation and cross-examination. The prepared continuity need be only the opening, introduction of participants, introduction and time limits for each phase of the debate, explanations and interviews, if desired, and closing.

Speeches
Most speeches are prepared outside the station and the staff writer usually has no concern with them except to write the opening and closing material for the station announcer, which may include introductory comments on the speaker, depending on how well known the latter is. It is improper to go beyond: "Ladies and gentlemen, the President of the United States." However, if the President is speaking at a special occasion or for a special public purpose, prespeech commentary would describe the occasion and/or purpose, with appropriate background material. Commentary and analysis may also follow a speech.

If the speaker is not well known — for example, a spokesperson responding to a station's editorial — information about that person's position and qualifications as a spokesperson on the issue should be presented, as well as a statement on the reason for his or her appearance. A good rule to remember is that the better known the speaker, the less introduction needed.

In some instances, usually on the local level, speakers unfamiliar with radio and television time requirements may have to be advised how and where to trim their speeches so they are not cut off before they finish. Speakers unfamiliar with television and radio techniques frequently do not realize the necessity for split-second scheduling and their speeches may run long or, sometimes, too short, leaving unfilled program time. In other instances it may be necessary to remind (or even help) the speaker to rewrite in terms of legal, FCC, or station policy concerning statements made over the air, including libel, obscenity, personal attack, and Fairness Doctrine considerations.

If a speech is prepared by the writer in the station, it must, of course, be done in collaboration with the speaker. First, the format should be determined. Will it be a straight speech? Will there be a panel or interviewer present? Will there be questions from an audience? Will the speech be read from a desk or lectern, be memorized, or be put on cue cards? At all times the speech style should fit the personality of the speaker.

Occasionally, the speech on television may be developed into more than a simple verbal presentation and may include film clips, tapes, photos, and other visual material. Such speeches are, however, essentially illustrated talks or lectures and would more likely be prepared as features.

A simple, basic format, containing intro, outro, and transitions, is the following, used for speeches during a political campaign.

ANNCR: In order to better acquaint Virginia voters with the candidates and issues in the upcoming general election ... the WGAY Public Affairs Department presents ... "Platform" ...

Now ... here is _____

(play cart)

You've just heard _____

Now ... here is _____

(play cart)

You've just heard _____

In the public interest, WGAY has presented "Platform" ... a look at Virginia general election candidates and issues. The opinions expressed are those of the candidates and do not necessarily reflect the feelings of WGAY or its sponsors. Stay tuned for other candidates and their views throughout the campaign. (PAUSE)

From atop the World Building ... WGAY FM & AM, Washington & Silver Spring. (WGAY-FM in Washington)

_____ For Application and Review _____

1. Prepare an outline, rundown, and routine sheet for an opinion interview, a personality interview, and an information interview. Each interview should be with a *different person* of local importance.
2. Do the same exercise, using the *same person* as the subject for all three interview types.
3. Prepare an outline, rundown, and routine sheet for a panel discussion program on a highly controversial subject, first for radio, then for television.

7
Music, Variety, and Comedy Programs

Except for some all-talk and all-news stations, radio programming today is music programming. Independent stations rely primarily on recorded music for program content, and network affiliates insert news and feature **feeds** into what is otherwise an all-music format. Since the 1930s, when Martin Block successfully developed the concept of a radio announcer playing records separated by comment and commercials, the disc jockey and the record show have become national institutions. Before television drew so much of the live talent away from radio, live studio musical programs featured symphony orchestras, popular singers, jazz bands, opera stars, and other musical soloists and groups. Virtually all such programs gradually disappeared from radio, although some of the quality shows such as the Texaco Opera series continued on radio in an age of television. Some radio shows with music made a transition to television, particularly the comedy and variety programs.

Television has not utilized the musical program to the same degree that radio did. There have been some successful series of musical personalities and orchestras, such as Liberace and Lawrence Welk, and occasional attempts at adapting the radio disc jockey program — in effect, on-the-air discotheques with local young people dancing to the television disc jockey's records and commentary. Dick Clark's success with this format in Philadelphia and then nationwide led to similar shows in many cities. Popular entertainers who are primarily singers have been successful with television variety rather than with strictly musical shows. Live or live-type taped popular musical groups have appeared on television as separate acts on comedy and variety shows such as "Saturday Night Live," although there have been occasional television specials featuring rock groups, particularly on late-night schedules and on local stations. In the early 1980s several music formats, especially rock, began to be popularized on cable systems. For example, MTV, a rock music cable television network, was available on a 24-hour basis as part of a basic cable subscription service, and was rapidly expanding to tens of millions of homes. Continuing series of music programs of special quality have proven popular with a segment of the viewing audience, particularly operas and Boston Pops concerts on public television.

The job for the scriptwriter in the area of music and variety is principally to prepare continuity for the television variety show, for an occasional music special, and for the classical music radio program. The variety program depends for its success on humor, and you will notice that the credits at the end of such programs frequently contain long lists of names of comedy writers. Comedy writing is a craft in itself and, according to most producers and writers in the field, can't really be taught. As with singing, there has to be some natural and early-developed talent and aptitude which can then be improved through practice. This book does not attempt to teach comedy writing, except to present some basic principles and to comment on the sitcom in the drama chapter. It does, however, provide an introduction to the format of the variety program for the staff writer who may also be the associate producer, or for the associate producer who may also have to prepare the basic continuity.

Music Programs on Radio

A musical program must have organic continuity. That is, there should be a central program idea, a focal point around which all the material is organized and from which the program grows and develops. That is not to say that all disc jockey programs have scripts. Very few have. Yet, very few disc jockeys are clever enough to grab a batch of records at the last minute and organize them spontaneously into a good program. Although virtually all disc jockeys are spontaneous with their continuity, most of their programs are planned and organized in terms of musical content.

The format preparation for each program reflects the format preparation for the station as a whole. The concept of specialization is the cardinal principle of most stations' programming and image. Most stations have a particular type of format, such as beautiful music, rock, contemporary, **MOR** (middle-of-the-road, combining popular and standard music), or AOR (album-oriented rock). Some stations combine several types of programming and an **American Research Bureau (ARB)** survey showed that those stations in the top fifty markets with the highest quarter-hour audience shares for the longest time were those that combined two or more types of music and included news, talk, and features. These so-called **full-service stations** have dominated their markets for many years. As the size of the market grows smaller, however, the music stations become the leaders. In the early days of FM, most listeners equated FM with "good" music, especially classical music. FM stations have programmed more and more for the young listener, however, and by the 1980s rock dominated FM formats.

Definitions of music are constantly changing and formats change accordingly. MOR, for example, has a different connotation today than it had ten years ago. Contemporary music means the music of living composers to some programmers, but is limited to current hit songs for others. Music both reflects culture and builds it. It is the dialogue of youth, providing a sense of psychological freedom for the listener and a sense of artistic freedom for the performer. Pop music is a socio-logical phenomenon, partly because it reflects the flexibility, growth, and change of society, particularly young society. The Beatles changed not only the face of popular music but also the attitudes and behavior of youth. The Beatles motivated an escape from the traditional formulas, and their music was not music alone of bodily rhythm, but music of ideas, the communicating of unspoken and spoken meanings that were vital and forceful to the young people who eagerly pursued them. The basic concept was not new, but the music was, and combined with the inexpensive availability of the transistor radio receiver it made radio the link between creative artistry and creative reception as never before.

Record companies and radio stations believe that radio record music is a demo-cratizing tool, serving the desires of the public. Occasionally the question may arise, of course, as to whether wants are the same as needs and whether the *democratic denominator* may be merely a euphemism for *lowest common denomi-nator (lcd)*. In any event, record companies and radio stations have found that the terms *democratic* and/or *lcd* are broad in scope and that a station cannot be all things to all listeners. Thus the trend toward specialization and development of a number of major formats, with individual stations in individual communities tending more and more to exclusivity within any given type.

Format Types
In the late 1940s radio needed a new approach. Postwar growth in the number of stations was almost completely local and local revenues began to exceed those of the networks. Music programs on local stations had affinity blocks — that is, fifteen-minute or half-hour segments devoted to a particular band or vocalist. Format was what was decided on each day by the program director, disc jockey, or music librarian; the latter frequently prepared actual continuity. In many local stations the disc jockey would sign on in the morning with piles of records already waiting, prepared for each show for that day by the music librarian the night before, and the disc jockey might not even know what the music for each show was before it was played. Then came top-40, an attempt to reflect and appeal to the tastes of the listeners by choosing records based on popularity as judged by sales charts, juke box surveys, and record store reports. Top-40, at its beginning, was eclectic, with a number of stations playing the same forty most popular selections and the disc jockey's personality providing the principal difference between station images. Soon, however, many stations began to seek specialized audiences and concentrated on certain types of top-40 music, such as country and western, rock and roll, and other forms. By the late 1960s many top-40 stations had become almost mechanical, with virtually no disc jockey patter, a play list of only the most popular records, and quick segues from record to record. From time to time top-40 stations rejuvenated themselves by bringing back emphasis on the disc jockey, providing "warmth" between the playing of records and more flexibility in format. When personality becomes important, deejays spend more time on continuity.

MOR is probably still the most popular sound. It is essentially "adult" music, programming without extremes in volume, rhythm, timing, or technique. Of course, the meaning of MOR changes. To one generation it is Frank Sinatra, Peggy Lee, and Nat King Cole. To another it is the Beatles and the Fifth Dimension; to a later one, the Rolling Stones and the Police. And to still another, The Kitchen Sink and the Electric Grater. Adult tastes are different because adults are different and, to some degree, even contemporary rock can be considered MOR. MOR is personality-oriented and announcer-deejays are likely to become local and even regional celebrities.

MOR is probably the least specialized of the specialized formats and includes one approach that is sometimes a complete station format or image in itself: "golden oldies." These are MOR records usually limited to popular music of some fifteen to thirty years' vintage. Its popularity is probably attributable to the same reason for all shifts to nostalgia: discontent of the people with the events of their time. Some golden oldies formats mix oldies with more current MOR.

Beautiful music sometimes is also called semiclassical or dinner music. This is the music of Mantovani, Andre Kostelanetz, and Broadway shows. It is chosen carefully to fit different moods and tempos of different times of the day. Some 20 to 25 percent of the radio audience listens to beautiful music. The format is usually standardized into quarter-hour segments, each segment cohesive and providing a consistent mood in itself.

Rock was easy to categorize when it was new. Hard rock, underground rock, and acid rock began to require flexibility and reorientation of rock formats. The socio-political nature of some 1960s rock lyrics, for example, required a soft sound, as opposed to the emphasis on tempo and sound alone some years back. Jazz and folk rock have led many artists into combinations of country and rock. Like the earlier music types, rock proliferated into specialized subtypes, such as punk rock and new wave. In the late 1970s and early 1980s some rock music again reflected political overtones, but this time the sound was louder and harder.

Country music became one of radio's major formats in only a few short years in the 1970s. Country music is represented by three principal types: modern or "soft" country, standard country and western or "hard" country, and the popular Nashville sound. A growing number of sophisticated professionals — bankers, lawyers, scientists — boast about their conversion to country music, perhaps seeking escape from the increasing stresses of their everyday urban world. Country music stations vary in format: some emphasize one of the three major types; others cross types but, as do some MOR stations, concentrate on the oldies mixed with traditional-sounding new songs; some find excellent audience reaction to a combination of one country and one pop or to a mix of country with soft rock.

In the late 1970s and early 1980s many stations adapted their formats to the revival of jazz, from Dixieland to contemporary, and others began to reflect an unexpected interest in the Big Band sound. As you read this, tastes may have changed again, by the year or by the month, and religious, soul, ethnic, rhythm and blues, or one of the other major formats may be currently popular. And even within each of these types there are endless variations and adaptations to the individual station's market and listening audience.

Theme
Some music programs, in addition to being made cohesive through a type of music, are developed around a central theme: a personality, an event, a locality — anything

that can give it unity. The writer — that is, the person who prepares the script or rundown sheet continuity — can find ideas for central themes in many places: special days, national holidays, the anniversary of a composer's birth, a new film by a popular singing star, a national or international event that suggests a certain theme such as love, war, the jungle, adventure, corruption, drugs, and so forth. The musical selections themselves should have a clear relationship to each other, and the nonmusical transitions should indicate this relationship.

The following program, one of a series sent to RCA Victor subscriber stations, is illustrative of continuity for the classical recorded music program built around a theme. Note that a listing of records according to catalogue number and according to playing time precedes the script, thus providing a simple rundown sheet.

MUSIC YOU WANT

LM-6026	Catalani: LORELEI: DANCE OF THE WATER NYMPHS NBC Symphony Orchestra, Arturo Toscanini, conductor	
SIDE 3:	Band 4	6:23
LM-1913	Delibes: COPPELIA: EXCERPTS Boston Symphony Orchestra, Pierre Monteux, conductor	
SIDE 2:	Entire	25:31
LM-2150	Stravinsky: SONG OF THE NIGHTINGALE Chicago Symphony Orchstra, Fritz Reiner, conductor	
SIDE 2:	Entire	22:13

GO7L-0783	AIR FOR G STRING (fading after 20 seconds)
ANNCR:	(Sponsor or) His Master's Voice is on the air with THE MUSIC YOU WANT WHEN YOU WANT IT, a program of RCA Victor High Fidelity Red Seal records.
GO7L-0783	AIR FOR G STRING (Up 5 seconds and fade out)
ANNCR:	Today's program is devoted to musical works that deal with the supernatural. One of the three selections is from an opera, one is a suite from a ballet, and the third — from a new RCA Victor album — is a symphonic poem, later used for a ballet. The supernatural has always had a strong hold on the imagination of man. The unknown and the unusual, with the laws of nature in a distorted or sus-pended state, has occupied story-tellers from their earliest days. It is only natural that this strong impulse, throughout time and all races, should attract composers as suitable subject matter. Our three works today deal with three separate types of the supernatural: mythological creatures who are por-tents of evil for mankind — a mechanical doll with complete but superficial resemblance to living beings — and animals with human characteristics and traits.

We open with a selection from Catalani's opera *Lorelei*. The opera deals with maidens who inhabit a rock in the middle of the Rhine River and lure sailors to destruction. We hear the "Dance of the Water Nymphs," in a performance by Arturo Toscanini and the NBC Symphony Orchestra.

LM-6026
SIDE 3:
Band 4   Catalani: LORELEI: DANCE OF THE WATER NYMPHS   8:05

ANNCR: We have opened today's program with the "Dance of the Water Nymphs" from the opera *Lorelei* by Catalani. Arturo Toscanini led the NBC Symphony Orchestra in our performance.

Our second selection devoted to the supernatural in music is the suite from the ballet *Coppelia* (Coe-pay-lyah), or the Girl with the Enamel Eyes, by Leo Delibes (Lay-oh Duh-leeb). *Coppelia*, one of the most popular of all evening-length ballets, had its first performance at the Paris Opera in May, 1870. The dominant figure in the story is Coppelia, an almost human mechanical doll. The youth Frantz falls in love with her, much to the chagrin of his lively fiancee Swanhilde. But all ends happily, and in the final act the betrothal of Frantz and Swanhilde is celebrated. The selections we are to hear from *Coppelia* are as follows: "Prelude" — "Swanhilde's Scene and Waltz" — "Czardas" — "The Doll's Scene and Waltz" — "Ballade" — and "Slavic Theme and Variations." We hear *Coppelia* in a performance by members of the Boston Symphony Orchestra under the direction of the veteran French composer, Pierre Monteux. Selections from the ballet *Coppelia* by Leo Delibes.

LM-1913
SIDE 2:
Entire   Delibes: COPPELIA   34:52

ANNCR: Members of the Boston Symphony Orchestra under the direction of Pierre Monteux have just been heard in selections from the ballet *Coppelia* by Leo Delibes.

Animals with human traits and emotions are at least as old as Aesop. Igor Stravinsky, before composing his ballet *The Firebird*, wrote the first act of an opera, *The Nightingale*, which — for a number of years — remained unfinished. The opera was to deal with a nightingale who, moved by pity, returns to save the life of a man who previously rejected it. Stravinsky was prevailed upon to finish his score after the composition of his revolutionary *Le Sacre du Printemps*. Naturally, he was a different composer at that time, disparities of musical style resulted, and Stravinsky remained dissatisfied with the opera. He took the later selections of *The Nightingale* and turned them into a symphonic poem, changing the title to *The Song of the Nightingale*. Like most of his works, this symphonic poem became the basis for a ballet.

The Song of the Nightingale concerns the Emperor of China who shifts his affection from a live nightingale to a mechanical one, a present from the Emperor of Japan. He falls ill and is on his deathbed. The real nightingale, contrite at having deserted the Emperor after his change-of-heart, returns to sing to him and restores him to health.

The Song of the Nightingale, a symphonic poem by Igor Stravinsky, in a new RCA Victor recording by Fritz Reiner and the Chicago Symphony Orchestra.

LM-2150 SIDE 2: Entire	Stravinsky: THE SONG OF THE NIGHTINGALE	58:33

ANNCR: Fritz Reiner and the Chicago Symphony Orchestra have just played Stravinsky's *Song of the Nightingale*, a new RCA Victor recording. The other side of this album, Prokofieff's "Lieutenant Kije" (Kee-gee), will be played at a later date.

STANDARD CLOSE
Next Program (Premiere) — Monteux interprets Tchaikovsky's
Sleeping Beauty Ballet.

G07L-0783   THEME UP TO END OF BROADCAST PERIOD.

[Examples of further types of central themes are evident in the following excerpts:]

ANNCR: The three greatest masters of the Viennese classical school are Ludwig von Beethoven, Wolfgang Amadeus Mozart and Franz Joseph Haydn. Today we will hear works by each of these three masters.

ANNCR: Our program today offers Russian music of the 19th century. We open with Borodin's atmospheric orchestral sketch, "On the Steppes of Central Asia." Leopold Stokowski leads his orchestra in this performance.

Organization and Technique

It is important to get variety into any musical program, which should reflect the elements of any good entertainment program. Open with something that gets the attention of the audience, relax a bit, then build to a climax. Offer the listener a change of pace throughout; after each high point give the audience a rest and then move on to a higher point.

The deejay-producer-writer must analyze the potential audience — just as do the producers and writers of commercials. Though the audience is given the music that interests it — the station format and image are created for a particular audience — the program should not play down to the audience, should not pander to a low level of taste. The deejay-producer-writer, to a great degree, molds and determines the tastes in popular music. No matter what type of music is used, the best of that type should be presented.

Never forget that the audience tunes in to a program because it likes that particular musical format. Its reasons for listening may differ: for relaxing, for thinking, for learning, for dancing, for background while working, for reinforcement while playing, or for many other purposes. This suggests an adherence to a single type of music. Although there are exceptions, the mixing of Beethoven with country or of rock with string quartets is not likely the most effective way to reach and hold an audience. At the same time, the program organization and continuity should fit the personalities of the performers, whether an orchestra, a vocalist, or a disc jockey.

Continuity always seems to be limited to orchestras that "render," singers who give "vocal renditions of" or pianists who always have "impromptu meanderings" and are always playing "on the eighty-eight," and to songs that are "hot," "cool," "mellow," "explosive," "ever-popular," or "scintillating." The trite joke or play on words for transitions and lead-ins has become an overused device. Phrases such as "For our next number," "Our next record," and "Next on the turntable" have long ceased to serve a worthwhile purpose. Perhaps that doesn't leave much choice? If it is impossible to think of something new and fresh and not trite, the best approach is to keep it simple.

The timing of the show has to be exact, with the combination of musical selections, continuity, and commercials coming out to the length of the program. You do this by outlining all these elements on a rundown sheet. Each record or tape cut has a specific time length indicated. Each commercial is written for a specified time. Don't forget to leave time in between for transitions and lead-ins. Rundown sheets such as the following are frequently used:

THE JIM LOWE SHOW

August 28, 10:10–10:30 A.M.

1. S'WONDERFUL   SHIRLEY BASSEY   MGM
      LIVE: COMMERCIAL (60)
2. PUT AWAY YOUR TEARDROPS   STEVE LAWRENCE   COL
      LIVE: COMMERCIAL (30)
3. VOLARE   ELLA FITZGERALD   VERVE
      LIVE: PROMO, NEWS (15)
4. THE JOLLY PEDDLER   HARRY SOSNICK   MERCURY
      ET: COMMERCIAL (60)
5. I LOVE PARIS   ANDY WILLIAMS   CADENCE
6. COMIN' HOME BABY   JACK LAFORGE   REGINA
      OFFTIME: 29:55

Courtesy of WNBC-AM/FM, New York

Rundown or format sheets such as the following may be prepared for an entire evening's schedule, containing the timing for each musical piece and the listing of nonmusical program segments.

9:00   yes we can can/pointer sisters   6:00
        half moon/janis joplin   3:50
        water song/hot tuna   5:17
news   #21 roller coaster/bs&t   3:25
        brandy/looking glass   3:07
        sylvia/focus   3:32
9:30   something so right/paul simon   4:34
        let's get together/youngbloods   4:39
        so what/monty alexander   10:29   (FADE)
*news   #14 too high/stevie wonder   4:35
        out in the country/three dog night   3:08

```
10:00    hollywood/chicago  3:53
         ooh la la/faces  3:35
         jessica/allman brothers band  7:00
news     #2 angie/stones  4:30
         dolly/nicky hopkins  4:42
10:30    brandenburg/walter carlos  5:05
         aquarius/ronnie dyson & company  2:55
         aubrey/grover washington, jr.  3:40
         lady honey/pan  4:07
**news   #9 all i know/art garfunkel  3:50
         super strut/deodato  8:55
*BACKGROUND REPORT #1
**EDITORIAL
```

Courtesy of WMAL-FM, Washington, D.C.

The pop music program   Although very few of the pop music deejay shows have written continuity, it doesn't mean that preparation is not done. There may be some personalities who can recall, organize, interrelate, and present ideas correlated with musical numbers with speed and fluency. Unfortunately, too many deejays who think they can, actually can't. Ad-libbing off the top of the head usually becomes boring and repetitious or embarrassing. Successful deejays rarely take a chance with complete ad-libbing. Why be half-safe when you can be more sure with some preparation?

Harold Green, as general manager of WMAL, Washington, D.C., detailed the kind of preparation required for his music programs, including the gathering and development of material to be used as continuity:

> The day of the ''limited'' announcer is about over. Just a beautiful voice, or just a snappy, witty or attractive personality is not enough for today's successful radio station. All the tricks, gimmicks, formats, points of view have been tried in one form or another. Some are quite successful in a limited way. The danger that the individual suffers is the strong possibility that he will remain submerged or anonymous. This is particularly true in a station that depends strongly on a particular ''format.'' We feel that the stations that matter in the community don't limit themselves to a format or other gimmick. The key is community involvement — information with a purpose — and a continuity of sound (in music and personality) that will continually serve, and please, the audience that particular station has cultivated.
>
> Our announcers go on the air each day with a thick folder of clippings, personal observations, letters from listeners, and tears from all the news and sports wires. By the time our announcers go on the air each day, they are fully briefed on all that is happening that is significant in the news, in sports, special events in the community, special broadcasts of more than routine interest scheduled for that day and week, or anything else that amounts to information *with a purpose*. They have spent a minimum of two hours in the music library. Generally, each day's music preparation time amounts to approximately 50% of air time. A four-hour program re-

quires about two hours to prepare musically. This is for one who is thoroughly familiar with the library. Otherwise it becomes a 1:1 ratio, or even longer. This is because the music list must reflect variety and balance: up-tempo music, boy vocal, lush orchestral, girl vocal, combo or variety, group vocal, and back around again. Specialty, novelty, or other types that break the pattern must be showcased by the D.J. There must be a reason for playing these "extras," and it must be explained.

It is safe to say that when a person does a smooth, informative, professional four-hour show — and one that teased the imagination and piqued the curiosity — he or she did an equal four hours of preparation. If they don't, they'll know it in about an hour. I'll know it in about an hour and a half, and the listener will know it before noon the next day. Without preparation, background, genuine interest in the world, . . . and diligent attention to getting informed and staying informed, broadcasters sink instantly into mediocrity. They are then relying on tricks. . . . They are ordinary. . . . They are short-changing the audience.

They won't last long.

The music library is of great importance. Know its content. Records should be auditioned, timed, and catalogued when received. Cross-indexing is desirable, with separate indices for theme, performer, composer, and any other area that may be a determinant in the organization of a program. Be conscious of the changing fads and fancies in popular music. Do not assume that because popular music is not in the same artistic league with classical music that it is not serious music to its listeners. In specific pop music forms, such as hard rock, jazz, and new wave, the deejay is expected to be highly knowledgeable.

The classical music program   As noted earlier, very few radio music programs have prepared scripts, and these are usually limited to classical shows. The classical music audience expects more than a cursory introduction, and more continuity is needed than in the pop program. The listener is likely to know something already about the music to be presented and to expect intelligent and informational background material and, frequently, aesthetic comment and interpretation. The expert analysis must be presented thoroughly. It is not sufficient to say, "This is the finest example of chamber music written in the twentieth century." The writer should give the reasons why.

Classical music continuity may be oriented toward special areas. There may be a concentration on symphonies, or on chamber music, or on operatic excerpts, and so forth. Note how the program outlined earlier in the chapter dealing with the supernatural is able to combine opera, symphony, and ballet within its central theme.

Examine the following scripts for examples of continuity in another classical music area, the complete opera.

● *Determine the degree to which the following continuity presents expert information and to which it serves the other requirements for a musical program script.*

MUSIC YOU WANT

LM-6025   Beethoven: FIDELIO: ACT ONE
Bampton, Steber, sops.; Laderoute, ten.; NBC Symphony
Orchestra, Arturo Toscanini, conductor

SIDES 1
and 2:   Entire   58:09

G07L-0783   AIR FOR G STRING (fading after 20 seconds)

ANNCR: (Sponsor or) His Master's Voice is on the air with THE MUSIC YOU WANT WHEN YOU WANT IT, a program of RCA Victor High Fidelity Red Seal records.

G07L-0783   AIR FOR G STRING (Up 5 seconds and fade out)

ANNCR: We are to hear today and tomorrow Beethoven's opera *Fidelio*, interpreted by Arturo Toscanini. The story of Act One, which we hear today, concerns Florestan, a political prisoner unjustly imprisoned by his enemy Pizarro, governor of the state prison. Florestan's wife, Leonora, disguises herself as a boy and — using the name of Fidelio — becomes assistant to the jailer Rocco. Pizarro decides to kill Florestan upon learning that the Prime Minister is to visit the prison, and bids Rocco dig a grave. Rocco balks, however, at murder and Pizarro decides personally to kill Florestan. Rocco allows the prisoners access to the courtyard, but Leonora, scanning the faces, is unable to find Florestan. She rejoices when she finds she is to accompany Rocco to the dungeon. Arturo Toscanini conducts the NBC Symphony and the following soloists: Rose Bampton — Leonora; Herbert Janssen — Pizarro; Sidor Belarsky — Rocco; Eleanor Steber — Rocco's daughter; and Joseph Laderoute — Rocco's assistant. The Overture and Act I of Beethoven's *Fidelio*.

LM-6025
SIDES 1
and 2:
Entire   Beethoven: FIDELIO: ACT ONE   59:38

ANNCR: You have just heard Act I of Beethoven's *Fidelio*, in a rendition conducted by Toscanini. Listen tomorrow at this same time for the conclusion of *Fidelio*. STANDARD CLOSE

MUSIC YOU WANT

LM-6025   Beethoven: FIDELIO: ACT TWO
Bampton, Steber, sops.; Laderoute, ten.; NBC Symphony
Orchestra, Arturo Toscanini, conductor

SIDES 3
and 4:   Entire   53:54

G07L-0783	AIR FOR G STRING (fading after 20 seconds)
ANNCR:	(Sponsor or) His Master's Voice is on the air with THE MUSIC YOU WANT WHEN YOU WANT IT, a program of RCA Victor High Fidelity Red Seal records.
G07L-0783	AIR FOR G STRING (Up 5 seconds and fade out)
ANNCR:	Yesterday we brought you the Overture and Act One of *Fidelio*, an opera by Ludwig van Beethoven. We conclude our playing today of this RCA Victor complete opera recording, an album taken from Arturo Toscanini's NBC Symphony broadcasts for December 10th and 17th, 1944. Our artists include Jan Peerce, Rose Bampton, Nicola Moscona, Eleanor Steber and Herbert Janssen.

Beethoven had long wanted to write an opera because — more than any other musical medium — opera was an art of and for the people. He also knew it was lucrative — a consideration one should never rule out in Beethoven's case. He searched for a suitable libretto for many years. Finally he decided on an old French story and hired a German versifier to make a libretto of it. The original title was "Leonora, or Conjugal Love."

The German composer's efforts on his opera were titanic, even for him. His sketch-books reveal no fewer than eighteen different beginnings for Florestan's second act aria, and ten for the final triumphant chorus.

Similar uncountable revisions figure throughout the score. Perhaps the quintessence of this desire for perfection is illustrated by the four overtures Beethoven wrote in his obsession to find just the proper mood with which to begin his opera. Because the opera was originally entitled *Leonora*, the first three overtures retain that title. The lighter, less heroic *Fidelio* Overture was finally chosen by Beethoven as being more in keeping with the emotional mood of the opera's opening scene.

The premier of *Fidelio* took place in 1805. It was a failure. Beethoven, prevailed upon by friends, compressed the opera into two acts and cut three whole numbers from the opening parts of the score. The second production was on its way to becoming a success when Beethoven, in one of his typical, unreasonable rages, withdrew *Fidelio* from the boards. The opera's third production, in May of 1814, was the last during Beethoven's lifetime.

The story of the second — and last — act of *Fidelio* is as follows: Florestan, the husband of Leonora (now disguised in man's attire as Fidelio, the jailer's assistant), is chained to a wall in the prison dungeon. He sings of his miserable plight. Leonora and Rocco, the jailer, appear. Upon seeing her husband, whom she recognizes with difficulty, she says nothing and assists Rocco to dig the grave, intended for Florestan and ordered by Pizarro, governor of the state prison. Pizarro appears and tries to stab the defenseless prisoner. Leonora rushes to shield Forestan. "Kill his wife first," she cries out. Enraged, Pizarro attempts to kill them both; Leonora defends herself and Florestan with a concealed pistol. At this point the long awaited Prime Minister arrives and releases all the political prisoners unjustly held by Pizarro, who is arrested and led away.

The cast includes Jan Peerce as Florestan — Rose Bampton as Leonora — Nicola Moscona as Don Fernando, the Prime Minister — Herbert Janssen as Pizarro — Sidor Belarsky as Rocco, chief jailer — Eleanor Steber as Marcellina, Rocco's daughter — and Joseph Laderoute as Jacquino, Rocco's assistant, in love with Marcellina. The choral director is Peter Wilhousky and Arturo Toscanini conducts the NBC Symphony Orchestra. Act Two of Beethoven's opera *Fidelio*.

LM-6025
SIDES 3
and 4:
Entire | Beethoven: FIDELIO: ACT TWO | 57:35

ANNCR: We have just brought you the second act of Beethoven's opera *Fidelio*, as recorded from Arturo Toscanini's NBC broadcasts for December 10th and 17th, 1944. Yesterday we brought you Act One of this score, Beethoven's only opera. Included in our cast were Rose Bampton as Leonora — Jan Peerce, Florestan — Nicola Moscona, the Prime Minister — Herbert Janssen, Pizarro — Sidor Belarsky, Rocco — Eleanor Steber, Marcellina — and Joseph Lauderoute, Jacquino.
STANDARD CLOSE
Next Program (premiere): Presenting "Tozzi" (TOT-see), a program of nine bass arias by Mozart and Verdi by Giorgio Tozzi ... of the Metropolitan Opera.

G07L-0783 | THEME UP TO END OF BROADCAST PERIOD

Music Programs on Television

One of the reasons that music programs have not been especially popular or successful on television is that music, obviously enough, is not a visual art form. Attempts to make visual action the focal point of musical programs on television often have defeated the purposes of musical presentation and have resulted in unfulfilled aural and visual goals. The action must remain secondary to the sound. Yet, the action must be of sufficient interest to make worthwhile the audience's full attention and time to the television screen. Otherwise, the listener might just as well hear the music on radio or from a stereo record or tape.

The success of the rock specials on television illustrate the importance of visual action. Most viewers see for the first time, close up, performers whom they previously saw only from the cavernous recesses of stadiums — if they could get tickets.

The first thing the writer must ask is: "What will the picture add to the sound?" Avoid gimmicks, strange angles, and bizarre shots that may be exciting in themselves, but have no integral relationship to the music. If you first develop a central theme, such as a relationship to a locale, an interpretation or representation of a situation, or the conveying of a mood, it will be easier to find the specific visual elements for the program.

The most common approach, and in its simplicity perhaps the most effective, is the direct presentation of the performers on camera. This is the principal form of the disc jockey show on television, where the disc jockey, the guest performer, or a studio audience dancing to the music is the usual visual ingredient.

Different sections or members of the orchestra, band, or other musical group may be the focal points. This permits a visual concentration on and an examination of the different aspects of the performance, such as the brass section, the first violinist, the drummer, or the conductor. The same approach may be used with vocalists. Elements of the variety show may be incorporated with this visual emphasis on the performers. For example, the antics of a country band in costume may provide effective visual action.

Abstract representations also may be used effectively. These abstractions, or visual symbols conveying the meaning and mood of the music, may be drawings or paintings, free forms, architectural compositions, or a kaleidoscope of any of the elements of the plastic arts. Color combinations can be used to great advantage.

Other art forms, specifically pantomime and dance, may provide interpretive visualizations of the music. Inanimate objects and forms, such as photographs and paintings, can also illustrate realistic and nonrealistic interpretations. Landscapes, people, places, actions, and events may be shown, indicating various environmental and psychological meanings and moods of the music.

_____O_____

- *The following is the script for one of the "Evening at Pops" programs on public television. The educational and aesthetic interest level of the audience is likely to be fairly high. What techniques would you add to make the program visually informative as well as entertaining? Note how this program emphasizes both the music and the personalities, the latter consisting not only of the singer but also the conductor.*

_____O_____

EVENING AT POPS

Tonight, Broadway and film star Bernadette Peters. With music from Broadway and Hollywood, movie star and entertainer Bernadette Peters joins John Williams and the Boston Pops, tonight on Evening at Pops.

And now to get this evening's concert started, here is John Williams for Leonard Bernstein's Divertimento for Orchestra. The Divertimento is in 8 parts and tonight John Williams has made a selection of four — Sennets and Tuckets, Waltz, Mazurka, and March: The BSO Forever.

out by:	THE DIVERTIMENTO
	The Divertimento for Orchestra by Leonard Bernstein. John Williams conducted the Boston Pops. The Divertimento was commissioned by the Boston Symphony in celebration of its centennial year.
cue:	And now tonight's guest Bernadette Peters.
	Ms. Peters has chosen a program that includes a medley "We're in the Money" and "Pennies from Heaven," "If You Were the Only Boy," "Broadway Baby," "Other Lady," and a medley of Harold Arlen tunes. (pause)
	Here is Bernadette Peters with John Williams and the Boston Pops. To start — "We're in the Money"
out by:	PENNIES FROM HEAVEN
	IF YOU WERE THE ONLY BOY
	BROADWAY BABY
	OTHER LADY
	HAROLD ARLEN
	A medley of Harold Arlen tunes with tonight's guest Bernadette Peters; John Williams conducted the Boston Pops. With Miss Peters were pianist Marvin Laird and Cubby O'Brien on drums. Bernadette Peters' first starring part was in the off-Broadway musical "Dames at Sea." That part led to starring roles in the Broadway musicals "George M," "On the Town," and "Mack and Mabel." Her movie appearances include "The Longest Yard," "Silent Move," and most recently, "Pennies from Heaven" and "Annie."
	In just a moment John Williams and the Boston Pops for *Overture to Candide* by Leonard Bernstein.
out by:	CANDIDE
	Overture to Candide by Leonard Bernstein. John Williams conducted the Boston Pops. In just a moment "Tara's Theme" by Max Steiner from the film "Gone with the Wind."
out by:	TARA
	Tara's Theme by Max Steiner from the film "Gone with the Wind." John Williams conducted the Boston Pops. And now another tune from the movies, "Raiders of the Lost Ark March" composed by Boston Pops conductor John Williams.
out by:	RAIDERS OF THE LOST ARK
	"Raiders of the Lost Ark March," composed and conducted by John Williams. And now to close this evening's program, from the film E.T. the "Flying Theme" composed by John Williams.
out by:	E.T.
	"The Flying Theme" from E.T. by John Williams.
	This brings us to the end of tonight's Evening at Pops with John Williams and the Boston Pops Orchestra. Tonight's special guest was Bernadette Peters. Major funding for Evening at Pops was provided by Public Television Stations. Additional funding was provided by Digital Equipment Corporation. This is William Pierce inviting you to join us again for our next Evening at Pops.

Courtesy of William Cosel Productions

The following is the sole prepared written material — the final production routine sheet — for a contemporary music program on a variety series, ''Nightshift,'' on a commercial station in Boston. Produced by broadcasting majors from colleges in New England, "Nightshift" consists of drama, music, variety, and interview shows.

NIGHTSHIFT #_____ TAPE DATE <u>12/12</u>   AIR DATE <u>12/14</u>
PROGRAM TITLE <u>"AN EVENING WITH THE RON GILL AND MANNY WILLIAMS TRIO"</u>
SCHOOL <u>EMERSON COLLEGE</u>
PRODUCER <u>RICHARD BUXENBAUM</u>
DIRECTOR <u>ISAAC LAUGHINGHOUSE</u>

ITEM #	VIDEO	AUDIO	SEGMENT TIME	RUNNING TIME
	SLIDE 1,2,3,4,5,6 (OPENING)	"WHEN THE MORNING COMES"	:30	00:00
	SLIDE ¢ w/EFFX (mix, card)			
	SLIDE 7 – 24			
	SLIDE 25			00:30
	DISSOLVE TO EXCU (cymbal, matching shot) STUDIO		5:30	
	ZO – CS (wide shot)			00:32
	FILM CART I	w/sound, MUSIC UNDER	00:47	06:00
	LONG CS (with Ronnie's back facing camera)	"WONDER WHY"	03:00	06:48
	MA (MANNY)	(PIANO INTERLUDE)	01:00	09:50
	M2S (RONNIE, MANNY)	"SADNESS"	05:05	10:50
	FILM #2	w/sound MUSIC UNDER	00:42	15:56
	KNEELING HAND CAM LOOKS UP RONNIE	"PHOTOGRAPH"	04:00	16:38
	EXCU RON, CU PIANO KEYS MIX	"RAINING OUTSIDE"	04:40	20:38
	2S BASS DRUMS	"WAY OUT THERE"	03:00	25:18
	FILM #3	MUSIC UNDER w/sound	01:33	28:18
	SLIDE: WRITE …	Cart #7	00:09	29:51
	BLACK			30:00

Joe Chapura, who produced the series while a student at Emerson College, Boston, offers the following advice to young writers from the point of view of both student and producer:

1. Be conservative in the amount of words used. As a rule, both TV and radio formats allow little time for extensive extrapolation. Be direct and to the point, choosing your words carefully.

2. Television and radio techniques and devices limit the attention span of their audiences. It is therefore essential to remember the power of the spoken word. Some people in the business say "don't worry about the dialogue; animation, squeeze boom and sound effects will take all of the audience's attention." Don't believe it.

3. Never talk down to your audience. The late television writer Rod Serling advised that if you underestimate the intelligence of your audience you've lost the battle before it even started.

4. Use colorful words. All writers should be lifelong students of semantics. It is the tool of your craft.

Variety and Comedy Programs

Reading a chapter of a book or reading a dozen books will not give a writer the craft of comedy of a Goodman Ace, a Carl Reiner, a Norman Lear, or a Neil Simon. But there are some basic approaches to the organization of the variety program, which includes elements of comedy, drama, and music, that the writer can learn.

Program Types

The term *variety* implies a combination of two or more elements of entertainment and art: a singer, a dancer, a stand-up comic, a comedy skit, a Shakespearean actor, a puppeteer, a ventriloquist, a pianist, a rock group. Depending on the personality who is the principal figure in the program, several of these elements would be incorporated in a manner that shows off the star to the best advantage. Catchall, nonstar variety shows are rare.

The basic variety show types are the vaudeville show, the music hall variety, the revue, the comic-dominated show, the personality (usually singer or dancer) program with guests, the musical comedy approach, and the solo performance. Although all of these forms have been on television from time to time over the years, they vary according to audience reception and interest.

The variety show is not a haphazard conglomeration of different acts. Even the vaudeville show — exemplified in television history by the "Ed Sullivan Show" — carefully integrates and relates its various acts and frequently is focused on a clear central theme. Vaudeville and music hall variety are basically the same, oriented around specialty acts of different kinds. The revue is organized primarily in terms of music and dance, however, with comedians frequently providing the continuity and transitions between musical numbers.

The comic-dominated show may consist of a comedian as the central performer, with various guests and/or standard acts, as in a Bill Cosby or Bob Hope special. A singing personality may mix his or her songs with participation in comic skits (a comic could add the songs), with contributions from guests, creating what is in essence a revue centered on one performer. When such shows have a thread of continuity, no matter how thin, they become musical revues. The thread may be any kind of theme: the songs of a particular composer, a national holiday, a historical happening, the biography of a famous entertainer, a locale — almost anything can serve.

When more than a thread, but a plot line (even a meager one) is used, we have the makings of a musical comedy. Some musical comedies on television pretend to that category in name only, however, and may be little more than thinly connected series of songs and dances by popular entertainers.

An adaptation of the vaudeville variety show has been successful on American television, substituting a host or hostess who rarely participates in the overt performing and who introduces and interviews various guest entertainers. Because most of the program is banter between host and guest (and in these segments the host or hostess is a principal entertainer), these are frequently called talk shows and have been most notably exemplified by "The Tonight Show" with Johnny Carson, the "Dick Cavett Show," the "Merv Griffin Show," and the "David Letterman Show." The solo performance of a star performer is a frequently used format. The content ranges from the innocuous and frivolous to the relevant and searching.

There may, of course, be combinations of various types of performances and variety forms in any given program.

Approach and Organization

The most important thing for the writer of the variety show to remember is that there must be a peg on which to hang a show. You must develop a clear central theme, capable of being organized into a sound structure, with a unity that holds all the parts of the program together. Otherwise, each number will be a number in itself, and unless the audience knows what the next act is and especially wants to watch it, it would feel free at any time to tune in another station at the end of an act. The theme could be a distinct one or the continuity factor could simply be the personality of the host or comedian or singer. An exception to the need for strong continuity is the vaudeville or music hall type of presentation. In these shows the audience is held by frequent reminders of the special act still to come.

Within each separate type of variety show there are distinct orientations that must be determined by the writer. Will the musical portions stress popular or novelty numbers? Will the dances be classical in style? Modern? Presentational? Representational? Interpretive? The comedy must be written to fit the personality of the comic, and it must contain a sufficient amount of ad-lib material to forward the public concept of the comic's spontaneous talents. What kind of comedy will be emphasized? Simple good humor? Wit? Satire? Slapstick? Will it combine elements of several types? Will it go into special areas of farce, of sophisticated humor, of irrelevancy, or irreverence? Does the comedian's style require material oriented toward broad, physical gags? Toward sophisticated wit? The intellectual approach? The irreverent type of satire? "Laugh-in" and later, "Saturday Night Live," started with satire, but ultimately overlaid it with other forms of comedy to fit the personalities of the particular performers.

When planning a variety show, consider the intrinsic meaning of the term *variety*.

There must be a differentiation between each successive number and among the various segments of the program. Contrast is important — not too great a contrast to disturb the viewers, but enough so that there can be no feeling of sameness, a feeling too easily transferred into boredom. Musical number should not follow musical number, comedy routine should not follow comedy routine — except for the special formats of a purely musical program, as with a solo singer, or of a total comedy program such as "Second City" or "Saturday Night Live." The suspense created by a juggler who balances an unbelievable number of fiery hoops on the end of his or her nose should not be directly followed by the similar suspense of a group of acrobats balancing one another on each other's noses.

In programs that use outside acts — that is, those that cannot be scripted and timed exactly, as with vaudeville or with late-night talk or variety programs — the final number or act should have two versions, a short one and a long one. The proper one can be called for, depending on the time remaining when that act is about to begin.

───○─────────────────────────────

● *Compare and contrast the following rundown sheets for two of tele-vision's most famous variety shows — "The Carol Burnett Show" and "The Tonight Show."*

● *(1) How would you classify each of these shows in terms of variety show "form"? (2) Are the acts or sequences so arranged that there is enough variety in each succeeding one? (3) Is there a preponderance — in number, in appearances, or in allotted time — of any one type of act? If so, is it helpful or harmful to the particular program? (4) Are the commercials well placed? Considering the exigencies of commercial television, could or should they have been placed any differently? (5) What are the major similarities as well as the major differences between the two programs?*

───○─────────────────────────────

THE CAROL BURNETT SHOW

PRODUCTION #717	TAPE: FRIDAY, JANUARY 18
AIR SEQUENCE #19	AIR: SATURDAY, FEBRUARY 2
RUNDOWN (a/o 1/16)	GUESTS: TIM CONWAY, STEVE LAWRENCE

1. QUESTIONS & ANSWERS (Carol)	(1)
2. SHOW FILM (Lyle V.O.)	(1)
3. THE OLD DRESSER (Harvey, Tim)	(2)

 4. OPENING COMMERCIAL BB   (11)
    (FIRST HALF)
    (Lyle V.O.)

 5. COMMERCIAL #1   (12)

 6. INTRO & "HERE'S THAT   (13)
    RAINY DAY"/"RAINY DAYS
    AND MONDAYS"
    (Steve, Carol [V.O.])

 7. COMMERCIAL #2   (15)

 8. BACHELOR PARTY   (16)
    (Carol, Steve, Lyle,
    Boy Dancers)

 9. COMMERCIAL #3   (22)

10. INTRO & THE AD MEN   (33)
    (Carol)

11. CLOSING COMMERCIAL BB   (34)
    (FIRST HALF) & INTRO
    STATION BREAK
    (Lyle V.O.)

12. STATION BREAK   (34)

13. OUT OF STATION BREAK   (34)
    (Lyle, V.O.)

14. COMMERCIAL #4   (35)

15. DAY SHIFT — NIGHT SHIFT   (36)
    (Carol, Tim)

16. COMMERICAL #5   (40)

17. KITCHEN COMMERCIALS   (41)
    (Carol, Harvey, Vicki,
    Lyle, Steve, Tim, Dancers)

18. COMMERCIAL #6   (50)

19. FINALE: GERSHWIN SALUTE   (51)
    (Carol, Steve, Vicki,
    Harvey, Dancers)

20. GUEST BB & GOODNIGHT   (67)
    SONG
    (All)

21. CLOSING CREDITS   (68)

22. PROMO FOR PROD. #717   (71)
    AIR SEQ. #19

Courtesy of CBS Television

THE TONIGHT SHOW
TAPED: Thursday, May 9
AIRED: Friday, May 10

6:00:00   (12:00:00)

GUESTS: JACK PALANCE (PAPUSH) JOANNA CASSIDY (SAM) JOSE MOLINA (DOLCE) ORSON BEAN (DOLCE)	4. MATERIAL

GUESTS: JACK PALANCE (PAPUSH)
        JOANNA CASSIDY (SAM)
        JOSE MOLINA (DOLCE)
        ORSON BEAN (DOLCE)

4. MATERIAL

5. COMML: VICK/SIMMONS — LCI
   (VT/VM — MTC SL)

HOST: JOHNNY CARSON
ANNCR: ED McMAHON

6. ORSON BEAN

7. COMML: NO. AMERICAN SYSTEMS/
   J & J — LCI
   (VT/VM — MTC SL)

NOTES:

7A. CONTINENTAL SL

8. STATION BREAK

9. STARRING SL

9A. ANNOUNCE UPCOMING GUESTS

10. ORSON BEAN

5:30:00   (11:30:00)

11. COMML: SUNBEAM/ROCKWELL —
    LCI
    (FM/VT — MTC SL)

1. THEME AND OPENING TAPE

2. JOHNNY MONOLOGUE

12. JOANNA CASSIDY

3. COMML: DUPONT/CLOROX — LCI
   (VT/RM — MTC SL)

13. COMML: WAMSUTTA/SIMMONS — LCI
    (VT/FM — MTC SL)

14. JOANNA CASSIDY

15. COMML: SEARS — LCI
   (FM — MTC SL)

16. STATION BREAK
   6:30:00   (12:30:00)

17. STARRING SL

18. JACK PALANCE

19. COMML: WINTHROP/GLENBROOK —
   LCI
   (VT/VT — MTC SL)

20. JACK PALANCE

21. COMML: KENTUCKY FRIED CHICKEN
   — LCI
   (CHICKEN BUCKET) (VT — MTC SL)

22. JOSE MOLINA (Dance to Panel)

23. MTC VT & NET FILL & LOGO SL

24. PANEL

25. DISC SLS & LOGO SL / STATION
   BREAK

Comedy Techniques

Although there are many books containing hundreds of comedy situations and thousands of one-liners, there are few books that do more than give you ideas for comedy or overviews of comedy approaches. But, you can't learn to be a comedy writer from a book. Each comedian has his or her own "shtick." You can learn individual techniques by watching them. And some books delve into principles of comedy writing that you may be able to apply, depending on your own type of humor.

Comedy writer Hal Rothberg, writing in *Audio-Visual Communications*, stated that "to write funny, you have to think funny." He gave several guidelines for the comedy writer:

1. "Understand your audience." Are they the type who will laugh at slapstick or prefer more sophisticated humor? Situation comedy or one-liners?

2. "Make the humor spring from the characters or situation." As with writing any action, as analyzed in the drama chapter in this book, the characters and the situation must first be believable to the audience before you can move into comedy, satire, or farce.

3. "Use all your tools." Don't forget that humor can be presented both aurally and visually. On television, you can use films, cartoons, and other visuals alone or with live performers. On radio, sound effects (as in the old Jack Benny script in Chapter 2) have always been useful tools.

4. "Watch the budget." Neophyte writers sometimes think that far-out situations that are very expensive to produce automatically will be funny. A relatively low-budget show like "Saturday Night Live" demonstrates how creativity is more effective than costliness alone.

5. "Keep it clean." In some situations blue humor may fit, but on television one must be careful while also being clever. Most nightclub stand-up comedians have visions of being Lenny Bruce or George Carlin and resort to sophomoric

bathroom humor and four-letter words as substitutes for comic ideas. Too many young comedy writers take their cues from these would-be comedians and substitute shock for stimulation.

6. "Don't beat a joke to death." Except for the running gag, don't repeat something, even if you think it's good. It works only once.

7. "Mix 'em up." Use a variety of ways to get laughs. Surprise your audience. Varying camera perspective or the music mood can be just as effective as a punch line.

8. "Keep it fun." In most situations, the audience wants to see only the bright side of life. Heavy or black humor is risky for the mass television and radio audience. That doesn't mean meaningful humor will not work. Mark Twain and Will Rogers were superb satirists of society. Mark Russell has been successful on television. Richard Pryor and Dick Gregory, from gentle to sharp satire, have shown how serious comedy can win audiences.

9. "Try it out, but don't be discouraged." Before you sell or give it to your agent or client, try it out on friends, strangers, anyone from whom you can get a reaction; then cut, fix, and rewrite.

10. "Don't expect to be loved." The people you sell your comedy writing to are likely to be skeptical; until your material is getting laughs from an audience, don't expect much applause.

11. "Read a little." To write humor, you have to keep up with what is happening to people and the world. Find out what other comedy writers are producing and what is working.

12. "Are you communicating?" What is the purpose of your humor? Is there a goal besides simply making people laugh?

As Rothberg says, "first and foremost, communicate."

_____ For Application and Review _____

1. Prepare rundown sheets for three different local disc jockey pop music radio shows, each with a different music format.

2. Write the complete script for a half-hour radio classical music record show, to be distributed on a national basis to local stations.

3. a) Watch a television variety show. Analyze and evaluate the following: theme, if any; organization of the acts; general approach to the material (kinds of dances, comedy, music); freshness of writing; special use of visual techniques.

   b) With other members of a writing team (i.e., other members of your class), write a half-hour variety show for television, each member of the team concentrating on a special part of the program and all cooperating in the overall planning of the show. State your central theme for the show; the special organization of the material; the reasons for the placement of each act; the reasons for the approaches used in the dance, music, and comedy sequences.

8

Children's, Women's, and Minority and Ethnic Programs

In the 1970s, responsiveness by the FCC and other government agencies to the concerns of children, women, and minority and ethnic groups led to a sudden increase in programs that served these populations. Some network and station development of such programs resulted from FCC regulation, some from congressional pressures, and some from lawsuits filed by organizations representing these various groups.

One important factor in prompting attention to the needs of previously neglected large segments of our population was the FCC's requirement for yearly ascertainment of community needs and proof of programming designed to meet those needs. Deregulation not only eliminated the ascertainment requirement, but also established a milieu, in which other compunctions on stations to serve these constituencies were gradually lessened.

The needs, however, have not lessened. Although there is relatively little opportunity for writers to work in these program areas in commercial or public broadcasting, some local stations do try to serve as many as possible of their varied audience groups. Cable companies that provide programming for or access to a cross section of groups in their communities are in the vanguard of new areas of opportunity for work with children's, women's, minority, and ethnic programs.

With an eye on future changes in broadcasting and on developing opportunities in cable, these special program types are presented here.

Children's Programs

The high-quality, concerned children's television programs in the 1970s turned into the quick-buck, business-as-usual deregulated children's fare of the 1980s. The Children's Television Workshop, producers of "Sesame Street" and "The Electric

Company,'' and the national organization Action for Children's Television (ACT) survived. But Captain Kangaroo was cut down to weekends, the FTC abandoned attempts to protect children from harmful advertising, and FCC policy statements clarifying broadcasting's responsibilities to children in programming and advertising were not implemented.

Before the public pressures on behalf of children in the 1970s, the writer's principal aim was to develop a good action program that could keep kids at home on the edges of their seats, glued to the violence and, not incidentally, to the hard-sell commercials of programs that were mostly cartoons. The children of that era, the students now reading this book in the 1980s, will find by looking at children's programs today that television has come full circle to their early viewing experiences.

The writer of the children's program should, first and foremost, keep in mind the effect of the program on the vulnerable minds and emotions of young viewers. The writer should be socially aware and, one would hope, have a social conscience. Even *unintended* violence, prejudice, and sexism are inexcusable. Nevertheless, all three dominate children's programming. For example, studies have shown that television's Saturday morning cartoons contain virtually no females who are principal characters; the females generally are used to support males in the latter's tasks, they are subservient or submissive, and are usually the victims of actions initiated by male characters.

Ideally, writers of children's programs will exercise their consciences and at least test out new program ideas on child experts and child advocates before writing treatments of scripts that may prove harmful to children.

Approach

Imagination is the key in the preparation and writing of programs for children. The imaginations of children are broad, exciting, stimulating. It is only when we approach adulthood that we begin to conform, to restrict our minds and thoughts, to dry up that most precious of creative potentials.

A young friend of mine, when three years old, one day placed strips of transparent tape across the dials of his family's television set, stepped back to look at what he had done, and then seriously observed, ''Now I control the world.''

And in a sense he was right. For it is through television that much of the world first makes itself known to the small child. Writing for children offers an excellent opportunity for creativity, as children are open and willing to receive what the world has to offer. At the same time, because what comes to them through the television set has such meaning and importance, they are not willing to accept commercial television's usual narcotizing program content as easily as are most of their parents.

Some advertisers, producers, and writers think that children will believe anything. Yet, because their imaginations are so sharp, they are sometimes more critical than adults. They can release themselves to be led into almost any fantasy, *provided there has been a valid, believable base to begin with*. Therefore, the approach to writing the children's program approximates the approach to writing the adult farce or comedy. As long as characters, situation, and environment are initially believable, and as long as what has been established is developed logically and in terms of the characters' motivations, the subsequent actions and events will be accepted within the context of the play.

The writer must be consistent in the format and execution of the program idea. The writer should assume the place and attitude of the viewing adult — a task of some proportion for some writers, judging by some of the programs on television and radio. If an adult watching a children's program finds it dull and tasteless and not worth the time, then quite likely that program is not going to enrich the child's day, develop taste, or be worth watching. One must differentiate between audience ratings and value to the child. The child may "love" the program. But that is not the only criterion of its value, entertainment-wise or otherwise. The child may "love" candy, too, but a responsible parent — and writer — will not allow the child to subsist on it during all the waking hours. The child may release some aggressiveness by throwing mud pies in the park, but the responsible parent — and writer — will not permit the child to be exposed constantly to participation in or observation of aggressive violence.

Format and Content
Some years ago at the FCC hearings on television, Melvin Helitzer, the advertising director of a toy manufacturer that spends 90 percent of its advertising budget on television, gave some advice, to which most television producers, unfortunately, paid no attention. He stated that one of the reasons for the failure of some shows written for children was that "the intelligence level of the writing was below that of the children." He said that "children are more intelligent than most adults believe" and that a program produced by people "who have no respect for children" was doomed to failure.

The best format is, indeed, of a level of intelligence that respects the child who is watching. Traditionally, in theater as well as in the mass media, certain age levels have responded best to certain kinds of content forms. Age levels have been used as a primary determinant in the approach to individual programs for children. Given programs of intellectual and emotional stimulation on a high plane, children of certain age levels will respond in a positive manner to certain approaches.

For example, in the first edition of this book, in 1962, we wrote: "For the preschool child the activity program featuring some elements of fantasy, such as Mother Goose rhymes, as well as the use of things familiar to the child's world, is common." That such a format works is shown in the most successful application of this concept since this quote was written, in examples of both fantasy and the familiar: Big Bird and a street called Sesame.

The child in the first few grades of elementary school is able to relate to material containing beginning elements of logical thinking. Sketches with simple plots and fairy tales are usually successfully appealing. Activities with which the child can get involved, if not too sophisticated or complicated, are effective.

The child over eight or nine years of age is able to respond readily to the activities and accounts of the outside world. At this age drama begins to be very effective, particularly stories of adventure and individual action in which the child can identify with the heroine or hero. The mid- and upper-grade elementary school child is ready for elements of reality developed through drama, discussion, documentary, and participatory and observational activity. These chidren have begun to read many parts of their daily newspapers and have watched news and documentary programs on television. The reality may relate to political and social events of the world about them or it may deal with scientific and environmental history and happenings. The writer should be careful, however, to avoid sensationalism and to ensure that the elements of reality used are not disturbing or exciting out of context.

The best children's program is not that which is written exclusively for a certain age level. Though the specific format of the program may appeal more to one age level than another, the good program should be meaningful to and be enjoyed by all ages on different levels. For example, a nuclear science program may be too advanced for the preschooler; however, if the preschooler's program seems silly to the elementary school child and vulgar to the adult, it is not because it is below their level of understanding. It probably is because it *is* silly and vulgar. A dramatization of *Winnie-the-Pooh,* for example, can be seen by the preschooler, the elementary school child, the teenager, and the adult, and if it is well done it will appeal to all these groups, although on different levels.

Writing Techniques

The child should be reached in the most direct manner. The presentational approach is most effective, with the narrator or character relating to the viewer candidly. The children must be able to understand the ideas presented. Be simple and be clear. This does not imply that children should be talked down to. On the contrary, avoid patronizing children; they are only too aware when this is happening. Too much dialogue is not advisable in either dramatic or nondramatic programs. Action and vivid, colorful presentation of ideas are most effective. This implies an adherence to a simplified plot in the dramatic story. Too much should not be presented at one time and the story should not be drawn out; children have neither the practice of holding many ideas at once nor the sitting patience of adults. Material of a light nature should be featured on children's programs or, if the material is serious in content, it should not be morbid and it should not contain the sometimes disturbing psychological probing often found in the better adult programs. This is especially true of programs oriented primarily to younger children. The resolutions should not be ambiguous and the characters, though not necessarily real, should be believable.

The child identifies to an extraordinary degree with those dramatic elements that are within his or her own realm of experience and understanding. The zeal of the sheriff or the detective — or their writers — to beat up or shoot as many bad guys as possible in the course of a half-hour or hour may stimulate latent tendencies toward violence and sadism in some children, although the story and the characters may have little or no lasting effect on the well-adjusted child (any suggestion of violence as a way of life is unacceptable, of course). Lassie, however, has had a continuing impact because to so many children she is the "dog next door"!

If you wish to present a program of an educational nature, avoid the simple repetition of material that children viewing the program may have gotten in school. Known material may be used in the educational program, but it should be used to stimulate the child to participate in the program through thinking and applying the knowledge already learned, and to learn more. Some programs go beyond the schools in quality and teach what most schools never taught but capable parents have always taught — self-esteem and self-ego and a relationship of self to the social, political, and environmental ideas and happenings of the real world.

The writer should not pad the children's program. Determine the purpose of the program and stick to it. Don't try to fool or confuse the children hoping that they won't be aware of a bad piece of writing. If a moral is to be presented, make it definite and clear, at the same time stimulating the children to think more about it.

Several techniques have been especially successful in the story or drama for the child audience. First, there must be suspense. Children, like adults, should be caught up in a conflict, no matter how simplified, and should want to know what is going to happen. Children should be let in on a secret that certain characters in the play do not know. And, finally, children always love a good chase no less than the adults who assiduously followed the Keystone Kops in silent films and who follow the adventure and police shows on television today. Keep in mind, however, that there must be a believable base and that slapstick for slapstick's sake usually ends up as low-level violence, as evidenced in too many of the Saturday morning cartoon programs over too many years!

Television techniques   The visual element of television can be used very effectively in children's programs. On any show, in any format, the writer can use people, special set pieces, puppets and marionettes, tape, film, interesting makeup and costumes, attention-getting camera angles and movements and, particularly enjoyable for children, special electronic devices and effects.

The presentational approach mentioned earlier is important. On television the performer can play directly to the camera and to the child viewer. Care must be taken not to overdo this because children know when the performer is fawning or condescending.

Television is particularly good at illustrating visual elements and experiences in society and involving children in some kind of activity. Preschool programs frequently use this approach, emphasizing painting, construction, dancing, cooking, and other arts and crafts and visual action games. Television also can introduce ideas and sights beyond the games and art activities through showing such things as visits to museums, demonstrations by artists, an inside view of a fire station, the backstage of a theater, the dressing room or playing field at an athletic event, the assembly line at a factory, a courtroom — the possibilities are unlimited.

Drama, however, continues to dominate the children's market. Much of it — many of the cartoons and animated programs, some of the old movies, some of the lowest-common-denominator made-for-adults situation comedies, for example — is not suitable for a child's intellectual and emotional growth. Some of it does provide visual experiences and relationships to reality that would not be possible if the same drama were to be seen on the stage or heard over radio. It should be noted, however, that radio's greater freedom and stimulation of the imagination permits a child's own psyche to provide bases for interpretation that sometimes is too explictly and inflexibly spelled out on television, bound by the literal nature of the television picture. It is sometimes more difficult for the child to screen out undesirable elements from the television drama than from the radio or theater presentation.

Radio techniques   With their orientation to the visual element of television and the need to bring almost nothing to much of the entertainment they receive, children who have grown up in the second half of the twentieth century have not exercised the disciplines of imagination or concentration developed by those a bit older who grew up with radio. The radio writer today must consider this lack of concentration and short attention span, and at the same time should be aware of the need and opportunity to rejuvenate the creative imaginations of our children. How many children do you know who surreptitiously stay up late to hear the "Radio Mystery Theater," discovering something new that excites their imaginations more than do most television dramas?

The Manuscript

Many children's shows are written out completely. That is, the complete dialogue and directions are presented, as in the "Sesame Street" script found later in this chapter. In many situations, particularly for nondramatic programs that use a live-type production approach, it is difficult to prepare complete scripts. Usually, detailed outlines or routine sheets are written, from which the performers are able to develop the informal content extemporaneously. The following excerpts are from the combination script and routine sheet of "Captain Kangaroo."

───────────────────○───────────────────

● *As you examine this script, analyze it in terms of the principles for good children's program writing. Discuss the following, evaluating the reasons for your answers.*

(1) Is the action simple and clear? (2) Is there sufficient action? (3) Are there elements of comedy? Of a chase? (4) Is the presentational approach used effectively? (5) Does the show build, with suspense for individual sequences as well as for the program as a whole? (6) Are there educational values in the script? (7) Does the production make use of special visual elements? (8) Does the program attempt to raise the viewers' standards of artistic and cultural appreciation?

───────────────────○───────────────────

CAPTAIN KANGAROO
February 12

ITEM	PROPS AND MUSIC
1. OPENING "CK" Telop.	gobo
2. OPERA BIT (TBA) Bob dances off the gobo and turns off theme at the desk. Greeting. He asks the boys and girls if they would like to hear a story. "There are many ways to tell a story, this is one way (takes book from pocket). Ballet is a story told in dance. Opera is a story told in song. This morning Mr. GJ, Mr. Moose and I are going to tell a story in song, we're going to present an Opera. The name of our Opera is 'The Happy Magic of Mr. Moose', and it's all about a King who learns that everyone in his Kingdom	Book, cue cards for lyrics, Moose flower cart COSTUME: King's crown and robe (Bob), Court Jester costume (GJ), Robin Hood hat (Moose) MISC: curtain telop "the end" telop

ITEM	PROPS AND MUSIC

is happy all day long. The King is delighted that his people are so happy but
he can't help wondering what has made
them so. He thinks perhaps his Court
Jester has gone thru the streets making
everyone happy and gay, and as the
Opera begins the King is in his castle
waiting for his Court Jester. Mr. GJ plays
the Jester, Mr. Moose plays himself and I
play the King."
DISSOLVE TO CURTAIN TELOP, "TBA"
CLASSICAL UNDER. DISSOLVE FROM
TELOP to Bob wearing crown and robe,
he is pacing the floor in deep thought.
"TBA"- OUT. Bob paces, stops and sings:

"This news is grand!" (He paces then
stops)
"Throughout my land!" (He paces then
stops)
"Everyone is happy and gay
But what has made them that way? — "
(He paces floor.)

(GJ enters wearing Court Jester costume.
Bob goes to him and sings:)

BOB (TUNE: "THE MUFFIN MAN")

"Oh have you heard the latest news
The latest news, the latest news
Oh have you heard the latest news
Thank you Jester mine"

GJ:
"Oh yes I heard the latest news
The latest news, the latest news
Oh yes I heard the latest news
But thank good Mister Moose"

(Bob delivers an "aside" to camera: "A
Moose? Did he say a Moose?")

BOB:
"Oh did you say thank Mister Moose
Thank Mister Moose, thank Mister Moose
Oh did you say thank Mister Moose
For this our Happy Land?"

The song continues for several verses.

ITEM	PROPS AND MUSIC

(Bob and GJ join hands and dance in circle as they sing:)

"Yes yes we found the Magic Moose
Yes yes we found the Magic Moose
Yes yes we found the Magic Moose
Hurry with us if you care"

(Bob and GJ tiptoe to garden where GJ points out the flower cart)

(Bob tiptoes to the cart and inspects it carefully before giving this aside:
"My Jester has done his job well for the Magic Moose lives here
And perhaps the Moose will tell us the secret of spreading good cheer")

(The Moose pops up CUT TIGHT on him as he says:
"Magic? ... Me a Magic Moose?
I spread good cheer without magic I fear
But lend an ear and my secret you'll hear")

MOOSE: (TUNE: "LONDON BRIDGE")

"Be-ing nice to every-one, every-one, every-one
Be-ing nice to every-one is my secret

Be-ing kind to every-one, every-one, every-one
Be-ing kind to every-one is my secret

Be-ing good to every-one, every-one, every-one
Be-ing good to every-one is my secret (Moose Call)."

Bob gives this aside:
"Here is a lesson we must learn well
Join in the singing, the whole world we'll tell")

Verse is repeated.

DISSOLVE TO TELOP: "THE END," "TBA"
MUSIC UP AND UNDER

ITEM	PROPS AND MUSIC

3. TAG OPERA BIT (LEADS CARTOON) DIS-
SOLVE TO BOB AT DESK sans costume.
Bob: "And so the 'Happy Magic of Mr.
Moose' was nothing more than being nice
to everyone and only those who have tried
this magic know how well it really works."
Bob leads cartoon per content.

4. CARTOON

5. POCKETS (LEADS "BLING BLANG")
Bob empties pockets at desk. As he
finishes playing the last pocket prop (SE:
AXE CHOPPING WOOD). Bob: "That's Mr.
GJ, he's splitting some logs to make a new
fence, in the old days that's the way they
used to make houses. They'd split the logs
and then pile them on top of one another
until they had a log cabin. Do you know a
log splitter who later became the President of the United States? ... Abe Lincoln,
that's right. Did you know that today is his
birthday? Mr. GJ and I are going to talk
about President Lincoln in just a little
while but right now let's pretend we've
split a whole pile of logs and we're going to
build a log cabin." HIT RECORD

3 mechanical toys

SOUND:
axe chopping wood

6. RECORD: "BLING BLANG BUILD A
HOUSE FOR BABY" Bob panto's while a
log cabin, in three sections, is matted
from limbo (GUS). Lincoln logs are
sprayed with UV.

Lincoln logs sprayed with UV

7. LINCOLN EXHIBIT
On hand RESEARCH gives short incidents covering Abe's kindness, his home,
his education, his honesty and his first
law book. Extended RESEARCH to cover
dates of office, birth, death, etc. As "Bling
Blang" tags GJ enters with a picture of
Lincoln and puts it on Goat. Bob invites
the boys and girls to the Goat where
the exhibit is set. They follow his
life from cabin to President.

covered wagon (oxdrawn if possible), log
cabin, one room school house, ½ lb. of tea, 6
pennies, law book (Blackstone's "Com-
mentaries" if possible), a picture of Lincoln,
model Capitol building

8. and 9.:
Lead in and Record, "Swinging on a
Star."

ITEM	PROPS AND MUSIC
10. PLAYTIME	shirt cardboard, scissors, pencil, tape

10. PLAYTIME
Bob makes a log cabin from shirt cardboard. Cut strip of shirt cardboard approx. 4 inches wide, fold three times to shape of house and tape. Add cardboard roof. Draw on logs.

11. CLOCK "KNOCK KNOCK" BIT
The sequence involves the studio audience and the viewers.

12. DRUM BIT (LEADS "NOISY FAMILY")
GJ comes in with bass drum strapped to his back. Grange Hall Parade next week. Bob asks if the drum is easier to play with it strapped on the back. GJ: "You know I was wondering about that, Captain. I only put it there so I could see where I'm going." Bob suggests GJ try to hit the drum with the drumsticks. GJ tries but can't. Bob tries to loosen the strap but it won't come off. "That's a shame Mr. GJ, I thought maybe we could march around the T.H. and play the drum." GJ suggests that Bob take the drumsticks and follow him around. Bob agrees and panto's blowing whistle (SE: POLICE WHISTLE). Bob: "Fooowarrd maaarrch!" HIT RECORD.

(Props and Music for item 12:) large bass drum (straps) and drumsticks

SOUND: police whistle

COSTUME:
2 Shako hats

13. RECORD: "THE NOISY FAMILY"
Bob and GJ march around the T.H. Relief shots in limbo of the various musical instruments are supered into drum.

(Props and Music for item 13:) small bass drum, toy snare drum, cymbals, triangle, and striker

14. BAND BIT — TBA
At tag of record GJ still cannot remove drum from his back.
The sequence involves playing of record.

(Props and Music for item 14:) 2 tablespoons, 2 whisk brooms, toy piano

15. LEAD IN TO CARTOON
Per content.

17. HIDE AND SEE BIT
Sequence in which Bob tries unsuccessfully to find Bunny Rabbit.

(Props and Music for item 17:) two dinner bells, two carrots

ITEM	PROPS AND MUSIC
18. LEAD IN TO "WINTER WONDERLAND" Bob comes to sandbox where model houses, trees and cars are set. Bob "asks" the boys and girls about the placement of buildings, etc., as he makes a village. GO TIGHT on village when it is finished. Bob drops snow on it saying, "Now if we drop some 'Wonder Snow' on our town what will we have? ... That's right, a Winter Wonderland." HIT RECORD, DISSOLVE TO LIMBO.	houses, cars, trees, large box of "snow"
19. RECORD: "WINTER WONDERLAND" Limbo. Entire table is set as a snow covered village (end to end). Table is covered with snow and has snowmen and candy canes strewn about. Snow crawl.	entire plasticville town, 2 small snowmen, 6 candy canes, large box of "snow" MISC: snow crawl
20. CLOSING CREDITS	
21. SONGTIME: "MARY HAD A LITTLE LAMB" Bob does songtime to allow GJ time for costume change. Bob at desk tells the boys and girls the song he is going to sing and calls BR "so he can act as the lamb." BR is not to be found. The Moose pops up at door and Bob asks him to play the part. Moose agrees. HIT RECORD. Moose keeps giving his call instead of Lamb imitation. At tag Bob explains and demonstrates lamb's "Baaa" to Moose. Moose catches on. Bob: "Now say goodbye to the boys and girls." Moose: "Baaa baaoys aan girls, basa you tomorrow."	
22. SIGN OFF	

Although it has been frequently criticized on many grounds — including that of being oriented toward rote learning and of using materials more familiar to children of white middle-class backgrounds than to economically deprived minority children, at whom it was supposed to be aimed (special committees of the BBC examined and evaluated it and found it seriously wanting) — ''Sesame Street'' has nevertheless become the most acclaimed children's program in the United States.

Setting aside the relevance of its content and its impact on children's creativity, it has been highly successful in helping children learn information and skills more effectively and quicker. It has also been helpful in shaping positive humanistic attitudes in relation to children of different backgrounds and conditions. In part, "Sesame Street" is an entertainment program that includes cultural materials. Its highly innovative use of the television medium employs techniques that motivate and hold the audience's interest. Principally, it is an instructional program and, along with "The Electric Company," is watched not only at home, but also as part of school curricula. We are not dealing with "Sesame Street" here as an instructional program, however; writing the formal instructional program is discussed in Chapter 9.

As you examine the following script excerpts of "Sesame Street," note that it doesn't talk down to children. The writing presents the material in noncondescending terms, using varied forms of audience persuasion and motivation. For example, some segments are in variety show form; others are in audience participation show form; still others use the dramatization or skit. Comedy, ranging from gentle satire to farce, is also used. Drawing on the persuasive impact of commercials writing, "Sesame Street" frequently captures and holds its audience's attention by adapting the form of the commercial.

Another effective writing approach used is the continuing segment and the continuing characters, not only providing in some instances the suspense that causes an audience to tune in from day to day, but in this case providing familiar approaches that do not require the child to readjust every day to a new format and that permit the child to react more easily to the learning stimuli. It provides the child with character identification or empathy that also motivates watching and facilitates comfortable and friendly openness to the materials presented by those characters.

"Sesame Street" is outstanding in its use of the kinds of television techniques noted earlier: its combination of various elements such as puppets, settings and performers, presentational approach, expert use of electronic effects — its total "visualness." It is an excellent example of how children more effectively can learn print — that is, how to read — through the proper use of the visual medium rather than the print medium.

---○---

• *As you examine the script, list the different types of television program formats used, and analyze each one for its potential effectiveness on a child audience.*

• *List, as well, the various production techniques used, such as animation, puppets, and so on. Do you find any that seem to be more effective than others?*

---○---

CHILDREN'S TELEVISION WORKSHOP

S E S A M E   S T R E E T

AIR: MARCH 15
Final Air Version

VTR: DECEMBER 7

1. Film: Show Identification   :15

2. Film: Opening Sesame Street Theme   :50

3. DAVID IS STUDYING (SOCIAL ATTITUDES)   2:02

HOOPER DRESSED IN DAY OFF OUTFIT ENTERS NEAR FIXIT SHOP. HE GREETS AND
THEN GOES INTO STORE. DAVID IS BEHIND COUNTER. HE IS READING A BOOK AND
TAKING NOTES.
HOOPER: Hello David.
DAVID: Oh hi Mr. Hooper. What are you doing here? This is your day off.
HOOPER: I know but I just happened to be in the neighborhood and I thought I'd drop by.
(NOTICES DAVID WAS READING) Reading huh?
DAVID: Uh ... yeah I was.
HOOPER: (LOOKS MIFFED) Reading on the job?
DAVID: Hey wait a minute. I know this looks bad ... but there were no customers in the
store and I just ...
HOOPER: (CUTS HIM OFF) Yes I know ... but the floors could use a sweeping ... and
shelves could be straightened. I don't know ... in my day when I was young like you ...
when I worked ... I worked.
DAVID: (A LITTLE MIFFED) Listen Mr. Hooper. I know I shouldn't be reading when you're
paying me to work, but I wasn't just reading. I was studying.
HOOPER: Studying?
DAVID: Yeah, I have a big law school test tonight.
HOOPER: A test? Why didn't you say so? Studying is very important. It's a good thing I
came by. You shouldn't be here in the first place. (STARTS USHERING DAVID OUT OF
THE BACK INTO THE ARBOR) Come on come on. You gotta study. I'll work today.
THEY GET TO ARBOR ...
DAVID: Wait, Mr. Hooper. That's not fair to you. It's your day off.
HOOPER: So you'll work on your day off and make it up. You want to be a big lawyer
some day no?
DAVID: O.K. If you say so. Thanks a lot, Mr. Hooper, I appreciate it. (SITS AND STARTS TO
READ, AT TABLE)
HOOPER: My pleasure, Mr. Lawyer, my pleasure.

SCENIC: Street, Arbor, Store
TALENT: David, Hooper
PROPS: Constitutional Law Book, note book, pencil
COSTUMES: Hooper in regular clothes

4. VTR: BEAT THE TIME-TRAIN (GUY, CM, AM) (446) (33a)   3:03

5. BB STUDIES WITH DAVID   3:03

BB ENTERS ARBOR AREA CARRYING A SCHOOL BAG. DAVID IS STUDYING. THERE IS A
STOOL AT TABLE OPPOSITE DAVID.
BB: Hi David. Do you mind if I study with you?
DAVID: What are you gonna study BB?
BB: (REACHES INTO SCHOOL BAG AND TAKES OUT LETTER "U" AND PUTS IT ON
TABLE) The letter "U." It takes a lot of study you know.

DAVID: O.K. BB go ahead. (GOES BACK TO READING)
BB: (GETS CLOSE TO LETTER) U ... U ...
DAVID: (LOOKS UP) BB quietly.
BB: Oh sorry David. (TAKES A UKULELE OUT OF SCHOOL BAG, PUTS IT NOISILY ON TABLE THEN DOES THE SAME WITH AN UMBRELLA.
DAVID: BB what now?
BB: Oh these are just some things that begin with the letter "U." A ukulele and an umbrella. See it makes it easier to learn a letter if you know a word that begins with that letter.
DAVID: I know ... I know. But listen BB. You can't be putting all kinds of things on the table. It bothers me.
BB: Oh sorry Dave. Well then how about if I do something that begins with the letter "U"?
DAVID: (WILLING TO AGREE TO ANYTHING BY NOW) O.K. Sure. As long as you're quiet.
BB: I'll be quiet.
DAVID GOES BACK TO READING.
BB: (GETS UP AND TIPTOES TO SIDE OF TABLE ... BENDS OVER AND PUTS HIS HEAD UNDER THE TABLE AND TRIES TO GO UNDER IT ... POSSIBLY KNOCKING IT OVER)
DAVID: BB what now?
BB: I was going under the table. Under starts with the letter "U."
DAVID: BB you're driving me crazy.
BB: Gee it's not my fault the letter "U" is a noisy letter to study. Well anyway I'm finished studying it.
DAVID: Good.
BB: Are you finished studying your law book?
DAVID: No.
BB: Well don't feel bad. Not everybody is as fast a learner as me. (STARTS GATHERING HIS STUFF TOGETHER)
DAVID: (BURN)

SCENIC: Arbor
TALENT: BB, David
PROPS: BB school bag, letter "U", a ukulele, umbrella

6. FILM: U IS FOR UP   :34

7. FILM: DOLL HOUSE #2   1:32

8. FILM: U CAPITAL   :46

9. BB AND SNUFFY STUDY WITH DAVID   2:57

BB AND SNUFF NEAR 123. BB HAS A #2.
BB: O.K. Mr. Snuffleupagus, are you all set to go study with David?
SNUFF: Sure Bird. I'm ready. What are we gonna study?
BB: The number two. (HOLDS UP NUMBER)
SNUFF: Oh goody, let's go.
BB: O.K., but be very quiet. Don't make a sound. We mustn't bother David.
SNUFF: O.K. Bird. I won't even say a word.

THEY GO TO ARBOR ... SNUFF SITS IN BACK OF DAVID WHO IS READING INTENTLY ...
BB GOES TO STOOL OPPOSITE DAVID.
DAVID: (LOOKS UP) Oh no, BB. I thought you were finished studying.
BB: I was finished studying the letter "U" ... now we're gonna to study the number two.
(PUTS "2" ON TABLE)
DAVID: BB you've got to be quiet.
BB: Oh we will. We won't make a sound. We promise.
DAVID: Good. (GOES BACK TO READING THEN LOOKS UP) Who's we?
BB: Me and Mr. Snuffleupagus.
DAVID: You and Mr. Snuffle ... ? Oh not again with that imaginary friend.
BB: He's not imaginary. He's right behind you.
DAVID: O.K. ... I don't have time. Just be quiet. (GOES BACK TO READING)
BB: We will. O.K., Mr. Snuffleupagus. Let's study the number two.
BB AND SNUFF STARE INTENTLY AT NUMBER 2. SNUFF GETS AS CLOSE BEHIND DAVID
AS HE CAN.

SCENIC: Arbor
TALENT: David, BB, Snuff
PROPS: #2

10. FILM: FALL DOWN   :16

11. BB AND SNUFF STUDYING TAG   1:21

BB AND SNUFF STILL IN SAME POSITIONS STUDYING #2. DAVID IS READING.
BB: Well I guess that's all the studying of the #2 we're gonna do for now.
DAVID: (WITHOUT LOOKING UP) O.K. BB.
BB: (GOES TO SNUFFY LEAVING #2 ON TABLE) Come on Mr. Snuffleupagus. Let's go. (HE
TAKES SNUFFY'S TRUNK AND THEY WALK TOWARD CONST. DOORS)
IF POSSIBLE CUT TO SHOT OF DAVID WITH BB AND SNUFF EXITING IN BACKGROUND.
DAVID: (LOOKS UP) Snuffleupagus? Man that BB has some imagination. (TO AUDIENCE)
What? What did you say?
BB AND SNUFF SHOULD NOW BE GOING THROUGH DOORS OR SIMPLY OFF CAMERA ...
DAVID: Oh I see BB forgot his #2. (PICKS UP #2 AND TURNS AROUND) Oh he's gone.
Well, he'll get it later. (GOES BACK TO READING)

SCENIC: Arbor, Street
TALENT: BB, David, Snuff
PROPS: Per bit

12. FILM: ONE BUMP   :17

13. Deleted

14. FILM: (LA) ANIM PARTS OF BODY   2:14

15. FILM: ROCKING U   :23

16. FILM: (LA) KIDS, ANIMAL PAIRS   :55

17. FILM: MAN AND FROG   1:30

18. VTR: THE COUNT-MAILBAGS REVISED   (420) (14)   2:56

19. FILM: HENSON #2   1:14

20. VTR: COUNTING EGGS AND CHICKENS (Kermit)   (282) (30)   1:56

21. FILM: (LA) U — UNDERPASS   :42

22. FILM: DRUMMER — STREET   :55

23. VTR: SONG: GONE WITH THE WIND   (34) (4)   2:17

24. MARIA STUDIES WITH DAVID (DIFF. PERSP.)   3:21

     DAVID STILL STUDYING ... MARIA ENTERS CARRYING A SHOULDER BAG CONTAINING
     BOOKS, A BAG OF POTATO CHIPS AND A PORTABLE RADIO.
     MARIA: Hi David.
     DAVID: Hi Maria.
     MARIA: You studying?
     DAVID: Yeah. I have a big test tonight.
     MARIA: I was just going to the park to study ... but I'd rather study with you if you don't
     mind.
     DAVID: Sure. Sit down.
     MARIA: Thanks. (SITS AND TAKES OUT SOME BOOKS)
     THEY BOTH START TO STUDY THEN ...
     MARIA: (TAKES OUT RADIO AND TURNS IT ON)
     MUSIC
     DAVID: (DOES A TAKE THEN) Uh Maria?
     MARIA: Yeah?
     DAVID: Do you mind turning off the radio? I can only study when it's real quiet.
     MARIA: Really? Gee I'm just the opposite. I love music when I study. Oh well.
     (TURNS RADIO OFF)

29. Deleted

30. VTR: ERNIE IS THIRSTY (B/E)   (459) (4)   2:25

31. Deleted

32. VTR: FRACTURED LETTER "U"   (416) (12)   1:09

33. VTR: SONG: I'M COLD   (368) (40) (AM GIRL)   1:22

34. Deleted

35. MARIA CLASSIFIES (FUNCTION)   1:22

MARIA AT ART CARD AS FOLLOWS: CAR, PLANE, TRAIN, IN ONE GROUP. ... BUS AND
TEAPOT IN ANOTHER GROUP. MARIA SINGS CLASSIFYING SONG ... EXPLAINS.

SCENIC: Street
TALENT: Maria, Kids
GRAPHICS: Per bit
MUSIC: Classification song

36.	VTR: GANGSTER CARROTS #1	(255) (23)	1:16
37.	FILM: 2-2 TRAIN		:24
38.	VTR: GANGSTER CARROTS #2	(255) (25)	:58
39.	FILM: ROCKING U		:23
40.	VTR: GANGSTER CARROTS #3	(255) (27)	:43
41.	FILM (LA) RIVER		1:58
42.	VTR: HARVEY KNEESLAPPER "U"	(468) (31)	:35
43.	VTR: HANGING UP THE WASH (LUIS, DAVID)	(438) (14)	1:29
43A.	VTR: THE DOCTOR (B/E)	(124) (24)	3:08
44.	VTR: CITY SHAPES II RECT. CIRC (WILD)		1:10
44A.	FILM: LETTER Q		:38
45.	Deleted		
46.	GOODBYE — DAVID THANKS HOOPER FOR TAKING OVER FOR HIM AND LETTING HIM STUDY ... THEY SAY GOODBYE ...		1:07

SCENIC: Street
TALENT: David, Hooper

47. COMMERCIAL CREDITS

48. PACKAGE CREDITS

49. BACKER CREDIT AND OFF

58:36

For Application and Review: Children's Programs

1. Watch several hours of commercial network Saturday morning programming for children and several hours of public broadcasting programming for children (such as "Sesame Street" and "Vegetable Soup"). In separate lists for the commercial and noncommercial children's programs note the particular formats, approaches, and techniques that you, as a responsible writer, think are good and worth incorporating or adapting for children's programs you might write. What are the major differences, if any, between the commercial and noncommercial programs?

2. Individually or as part of a team (with other members of a writing class, for example) prepare: (a) a fifteen-minute script for a children's program series already on the air; (b) a fifteen-minute script for a new children's program; (c) a rundown/routine sheet for a new half-hour children's program.

Women's Programs

Minority status is not measured by numbers. More accurately, *minority* refers to the lack of the same opportunity, power, and prerogative afforded the majority in any given society. Although women constitute a numerical majority in the United States, they do not have the prerogatives or opportunities that men have and in that sense are a minority group.

The growth of media to communicate visually and verbally for women the subjugated nature of their roles in society, and the availability of communications to reach out to society in general and to organize women to take action to free themselves, have both worked the same way as for racial minorities. The self-directed Black revolution for human dignity and freedom provided impetus for a similarly self-directed revolution by women. It should not be forgotten, however, that it is really a re-revolution, a resuming of the women's rights and suffrage movements of one hundred and more years ago that ultimately resulted in some of the more humane and progressive laws enacted in this country and that provided background and impetus for subsequent efforts of other minority groups. The lack of ratification of an Equal Rights Amendment in 1982 does not lessen the effort or the need.

The negative images of women in television and radio are legion. From the soap opera to the dramatic series the woman usually is portrayed as either incompetent or overbearing. Even in programs where women behave in adult, responsible, re-spected ways, there is always the tragic (or, more accurately in terms of media practice, "comic") flaw that makes the woman less than the ideal image presented of the male. (This is not to ignore the countless "father-knows-worst" kinds of programs that show the male, as well, as an incompetent bumbler.)

Perhaps the most flagrant area of antiwoman media practice is in commercials. A study by the National Organization for Women (NOW) of 1,241 television commercials showed women's place as in the home in almost all. In 42.6 percent of the commercials women were doing household work; in 37.5 percent their role was to provide help or service to men; and in 16.7 percent their main purpose was for male sex needs. In only 0.3 percent of the commercials were women shown as independent individuals. It is not surprising that a *Good Housekeeping* survey found that one-third of the women surveyed have at one time or another turned off commercials because they found them offensive.

Changes in media programming for women clearly are tied to the women's liberation movement's campaign to abolish negative images of women and its worldwide recognition that the media not only reinforce and create attitudes toward women but also serve as a direct means for women to change their life-styles. Romy Medeiros de Fonseca, women's rights movement leader in Brazil, stated that television "is the first means of education from which Brazilian men have not been able to bar their women. They stopped them from going to school, stopped them from studying, kept them at home and cut off all contact with the world. But once that television set is turned on there is nothing to stop women from soaking up every piece of information it sends out. They soak it up like a sponge, and they don't need to be able to read a word."

For decades the so-called women's programs were those that primarily attracted women viewers and listeners because of the time of day they were presented and that carried content traditionally deemed of interest primarily to women. These programs, particularly on radio, largely have been local programs consisting of noncontroversial material such as announcements of club meetings, advice on interior decorating, information on fashions, cooking hints, and interviews with local personalities. Depending on the intelligence, perception, and motivation of the writer-producer, they also have contained material relating to youth problems, consumer needs, environmental affairs, civic development, and similar subjects. Many of these programs have reinforced campaigns of interest to the principal listening target, the homemaker, such as promoting higher budgets for schools and referenda for better municipal services. More recently women's programs have included topics even more vital to women and society, such as equal opportunities, job training, pollution, nuclear development, rape, abortion, birth control, financial dependence, and legal discrimination. Some of these programs have served as consciousness-raising tools for women and men both.

Barbara Walters, who established the acceptance of a woman interviewer-commentator on the "Today" show, believes that information-education programs that appeal to both women and men should be developed on daytime television. "To say a show is just for women is to put down women," Walters is quoted in *Broadcasting*. Also in *Broadcasting*, Robert Howard, as president of NBC, is quoted as stating that the key to portraying women in stronger roles is "getting more women into writing."

The following guidelines for women's programs on radio, developed by broadcasters Barbara Peterson, Elaine Prostak, Mary Roman, and Marion Watson, stand as a model for all media:

1. Topics such as cooking, sewing, child care, housekeeping and food shopping should be considered of general interest and not, as traditionally, materials stereotyped for women.

2. The audience listening at home includes, along with housewives, the infirm, the elderly, the retired, and the unemployed.

3. There are topics of particular interest to women, such as legal rights for women.

4. Community awareness should be increased as to what women have done and are doing in politics, art, sciences, and technology.

5. Women's awareness should be increased as to what it means to be a female, through such topics as female physiology and sexuality, female perspectives in public affairs, and female sensibilities in the arts.

Essentially, writing the women's program is not any different from writing other program types, as far as basic form is concerned. The news program or panel discussion or feature that considers the needs of women does not change in its essential technique. What it does is to be sensitive to the needs of the women, to the kind of content and words that reflect women's achievements and aspirations and are not insulting to or stereotyping of women.

The following example of a women's program series carried not on broadcast stations but on a number of cable systems follows the standard format of the interview show. However, the program's approach deals with issues relating principally to women or featuring women, and the program's content generates discussion related principally to women's concerns or perceptions.

TELEVISION BROADCASTING FROM THE WOMAN'S POINT OF VIEW
Segment of WOMEN ALIVE

Hostess: Ina Young; **Guests:** Marsha Della-Giustina, free-lance news producer and professor of mass communication, Emerson College, and Debby Sinay, vice-president of sales, WCVB-TV, Boston.

Feature	Time Segment	Total Time
Introduction by Ina Young	01:00	01:00
Two Commercials (1 minute each)	02:00	03:00
Interview with Marsha Della-Giustina	10:30	13:30
Two Commercials (1 minute each)	02:00	15:30
First Part of Interview with Debby Sinay	05:30	21:00
Two Commercials (1 minute each)	02:00	23:00
Second Part of Sinay Interview	05:00	28:00
Thanks and Outro by Ina Young	01:00	29:00
Credits	01:00	30:00

INTRODUCTION:

INA: This is WOMEN ALIVE and I am your hostess, Ina Young. Television is considered to be a very glamorous, often high-paying profession. One successful series can make instant stars of previous virtual unknowns. Yet, for every Barbara Walters, Jessica Savitch and Suzanne Somers, there are thousands of women working industriously behind the cameras in television offices and studios.

Today on WOMEN ALIVE we will be looking at "Television Broadcasting from the Woman's Viewpoint" and our two guests are two talented TV women. Marsha Della-Giustina is a free-lance news producer and director of broadcast journalism and associate professor at Emerson College, Boston. Debby Sinay is vice president of sales at Channel 5, WCVB-TV, in Needham, Massachusetts. So stay with us here on WOMEN ALIVE and we will be back with a behind-the-scenes look at "Television Broadcasting from the Woman's Viewpoint."

COMMERCIAL BREAK

INA: Today on WOMEN ALIVE we are going to take a look behind the glamour and the glitter of television. We are all familiar with the high-paid, highly visible news anchorperson. But what do we know of the men and women who ferret out the news and prepare it for television delivery? We know the stars of popular series, but are we aware of the television sales staff that keeps each station a productive and flourishing business? Our first guest is Marsha Della-Giustina, free-lance news producer and professor at Emerson College. Welcome to WOMEN ALIVE, Marsha.

[The initial questions relate to the process of news gathering, processing, preparation, and reporting, regardless of sex. After the credentials and knowledge of the interviewee are established, again regardless of sex, questions relating to women are introduced, such as the following.]

INA: Marsha, at Channel 5, where you do free-lance producing, how big is the news staff? How many men, how many women? What are the approximate ages? Which seem more appreciated by management?

*   *   *

When a station changes ownership, such as recently happened at Channel 5 when Metromedia purchased it, there is a great turnover, staff leaving, fired or replaced. Is there any pattern now at Channel 5, in relation to women and minorities?

*   *   *

What kinds of advantages and obstacles can a woman with a career behind the camera in TV broadcasting expect? What do you foresee in the immediate future for women — and men — in this profession?

[The second interview, with Debby Sinay, followed the same format.]

INA: We are back again with WOMEN ALIVE and our second guest today is Debby Sinay, vice president of sales at Channel 5 in Needham, Massachusetts. I am delighted to have you on the show, Debby.

*   *   *

As vice-president of sales at a major television station, could you give our viewers an idea of what that entails?

* * *

How big a staff do you have? How many males, how many females? Do females bring different qualities to the job than males? Is one sex better at sales than the other? Which responds better to taking orders from you, a female boss?

* * *

Do you think that being female helped or hindered you in your climb up the corporate ladder?

Written and produced by Ina Young, Essex Video Enterprises, Inc.

For Application and Review: Women's Programs

1. Listen to a women's program on a local radio station. Using the same basic format, rewrite it to the extent you think necessary to make it more responsive to the needs of the listening audience.

2. Develop a format for a television broadcast or cable women's program that provides a service to both men and women not now seen on network television.

3. Of the next few television commercials you see featuring women performers, pick the most sexist and rewrite it so that it does not degrade women and at the same time sells the product.

Minority and Ethnic Programs

The truism that a writer writes best out of his or her personal experience is particularly applicable to minority and ethnic programs. This applies to all program types, whether news, documentaries, features, talk, drama, or commercials. The orientation of the materials must be in terms of the feelings and attitudes of the minority audience — which are to greater or lesser degrees different than those of the majority audience, for whom almost all other program materials are written. It is not simply a matter of "thinking" what a particular minority group may be interested in or affected by. It is a matter of "knowing" and "feeling." Unless the writer has been part of the minority experience, there can be only the superimposition of understanding, no matter how sincere or talented the writer.

The principal problems minority groups have had with the media are the same as those described for women earlier: denigrating, stereotyping, or unrealistically sympathetic or condescending portrayals. What is significant about the prejudicial portrayals of minorities in media is that they are not, except on rare occasions, done deliberately; they are done out of insensitivity. Writers who mean well but who do not have the understanding and feeling of the minority experience, with the best will in the world, frequently turn out materials that to the particular minority group are stereotypical and harmful.

Writer Donald Bogle stated that "the television industry protects itself by putting in a double consciousness. They take authentic issues in the black community and distort them.'' *Washington Post* critic Joel Dreyfuss, reviewing a new television series about a Black family, summed up his evaluation by stating that if the producer ''gets some black input into the writing end of the program, it might move away from the brink of absurdity and develop into a pretty good television program.''

The same basic problems pertain to all minority and ethnic programming, including those serving Hispanics, Native Americans, Asian-Americans, and people of different language and nationality backgrounds, as well as Blacks. In many urban areas where there are relatively large first- or second-generation immigrant populations, radio stations have for many years presented foreign language programs and programs oriented toward the ethnic considerations of foreign backgrounds. When done well, these programs are not merely copies or translations of standard majority-oriented broadcasting, but are especially designed and often conducted by people from the particular minority or ethnic group. Nationality and religious groups, too, often take issue with portrayals in the media. The stereotypes frequently reflect those that have been used by bigots in real life, and rather than correct the stereotypes, television and radio have sometimes, albeit unwittingly, reinforced them.

The approaches and techniques in this section apply to all minority and ethnic groups, although the examples and principles used may be predominantly Black-oriented because more has been written and produced about Blacks in recent years.

Program Types

Consideration of and sensitivity to minority and ethnic needs in writing applies to all formats and program types. In commercials, for example, minorities have served as convenient stereotypes for humor for decades. The fact that the portrayals are meant to be funny and that one presumably should have a sense of humor and overlook the stereotyping for the laughs does not eliminate the derogation and negative impact.

Cecil Hale, former president of the predominantly Black National Association of Television and Radio Artists, states that there must be an understanding among the writer, announcer, and audience that is based on common feeling. He says that the writer must understand and find the common relationships among the character of the product, the character of the listener, and the character of the occasion. Commercials for the same product need to be different for different audiences because they see the product differently. Two Black-oriented stations in the same community may deal with significantly different audiences, just as would two majority-oriented stations.

Caroline Jones, as creative director of the Black Creative Group, advising ad agencies dealing with the Black market, stated in Joel Dreyfuss' *Washington Post* article ''Blacks and Television,'' that ''they are getting blacks in ads, but they are not doing black ads. It's not black lifestyle. I'm talking about why they use a product, why they buy it.'' Referring to studies showing that Black women cook foods longer and add spices to them, stressing taste rather than speed, Jones adds that a Black-oriented commercial ''instead of saying, 'You can cook it in a minute,' they should say 'you will have more time to spend with your family.' I'm talking about why they use a product, why they buy it. They haven't researched it.''

A most important concern of minority and ethnic groups is the lack of adequate news coverage pertaining to their special needs. Many of the complaints to the FCC concerning failure of stations to serve community needs relate to the quantity and quality of news, features, and public affairs items that affect or are about minorities in the stations' coverage areas. Television news executive Robert Reid stated in Dreyfuss' story that minority-group reporter-writers make a difference by providing a perspective that the majority-group reporter doesn't have. "Blacks in television tend to accord a more even treatment. How often do you see a man-in-the-street interview and no blacks are interviewed? The black reporter is more likely to come back with some blacks among those interviewed."

From the minority viewpoint, therefore, the approach is twofold: there should be equal opportunity for reporter-writer jobs for all kinds of stories; however, a member of a particular minority group is more likely to bring a sensitivity and perspective to covering a story relating to that group than would a reporter-writer not a member of that group. Like the writer of commercials, the newswriter must be aware of the special needs, attitudes, feelings, and motivations of the minority/ethnic newsmakers and viewers as well as those of the nonminority audience. Impact of a particular news event on minorities — and such impact, by the nature of our society, is frequently different than it would be on the majority — is usually ignored, except where the happening directly and strongly includes a minority issue.

Application: Black Programs

The 1970s saw a growth in Black-oriented programming and Black-owned radio stations, largely because of pressures from the minority community and FCC responsiveness to complaints about broadcasting's responsibilities. Deregulation helped diminish such programs in the 1980s. One of the services that remained on the air is the National Black Network (NBN). The following excerpts from two of its newscasts illustrate how a general news story can be given special emphasis for the special needs of a particular audience.

November 5 — 8:00 P.M. — King
The Reagan administration's attitude toward Black unemployment is "cruel, cynical and vicious ..."
I'm Ron King with World Wide News from the National Black Network in New York.
That biting and descriptive assessment of Reagan policies toward Black unemployment was given today by Black Maryland Congressman Parren Mitchell. Speaking before the Joint Economic Committee of Congress in Washington, following today's release of new unemployment figures, Mitchell blasted the administration for policies which have increased unemployment. Today's figures show a nationwide jump from 10.1 to 10.4 percent, with Black unemployment remaining at a staggering 20.2 percent. Congressman Mitchell says that's unconscionable.

CART: #27   runs: 27   out: unconscionable

President Reagan reacted to today's new unemployment figures by saying he is "sympathetic and concerned about the difficulties of those who are unemployed," but he reiterated that his programs have laid the foundation for economic recovery that will alleviate joblessness.

Other reactions include a proposal by Parren Mitchell for a seven-million-dollar public works bill, and a call by Henry Reuss of Wisconsin for a shift in funds from defense to housing and public works projects.
This is NBN, World Wide News.

November 5 — 10:00 P.M. — King
Several lawmakers and national labor leaders are calling on Congress to approve programs that will create jobs.
I'm Ron King with World Wide News from the National Black Network in New York.
The call was made today after the government announced that the unemployment rate in October was at a 42-year high, 10.4 percent. House Speaker Tip O'Neill, AFL-CIO leader Lane Kirkland and the chief economist for the National Federation of Independent Businesses were among those predicting even higher unemployment. And they urged Congress to approve a public works program to create jobs in the wake of today's unemployment figures. The Reagan administration says, however, it remains opposed to such action. Massachusetts Senator Edward Kennedy went even further and urged Congress to act in the lame duck session, instead of waiting until the new Congress convenes in January. With Black unemployment hanging at 20.2 percent overall, Maryland Congressman Parren Mitchell also joined the call for new jobs programs. Said Mitchell:

CART: #30   runs: 17   out: every one percent.
This is NBN, World Wide News.

Application: Native American Programs

The question of language and terminology is a critical one in writing minority and ethnic programs. Loraine Misiaszek, director of Advocates for Indian Education and a producer of radio and television programs by, about, and for Native Americans, stresses this point as a part of the understanding and sensitivity the writer should have. She finds that non-Indian writers frequently use words such as *squaw* and *breed* and similar terms, perhaps not realizing how derogatory they are. She feels that writers are sometimes deliberate in their prejudicial attitudes. She cites, for example, news programs that almost always are "put-downs to Native Americans. Their very manner of presenting the news is editorializing. They influence listeners into drawing conclusions that whatever it was that the Indian did was 'bad,' although from the Indian point of view and from an outside objective point of view the action may have been 'good.' Anyone concerned with script writing for radio or television," Misiaszek says, "ought to be very aware of this problem. It is not necessarily intentional, but it happens because of the general conditioning in our society that causes people to think of Indians in terms of stereotypes."

Thomas Crawford, writer-producer of Native American-oriented programs, endorses Misiaszek's approach to writing. "In considering writing and producing scripts with/for/about Native Americans," Crawford states, "one must first of all become familiar with the idioms, patterns of expression, turns of thought, and pronunciations of the particular Indian community with which one is dealing. This kind of background will enable a scriptwriter to deal with the subject in a way that will interest and be appropriate to the people. The writer must also be willing to shift the topic to one that has more immediate interest and appeal.'' Crawford also stresses the need for personal experience and empathy on the part of the writer. ''The complexities of writing a program for or about Native Americans on a national level would be nearly prohibitive for the non-Indian. An Indian writer/producer can present his own idioms and viewpoints as a valid part of the Native American scene in the United States. Such an effort would probably relate to some degree to nearly every Native American community throughout the U.S., unless it were very extreme in tone or content.''

These concepts are illustrated in excerpts from the beginning and end of one of Crawford's scripts, a public affairs program entitled ''Who Has the Right?''

SCRIPT FOR "WHO HAS THE RIGHT?"

By Tom Crawford, Advocates for Indian Education and KPBX-FM, Spokane
and Tony Grant, Kootenai Communications, Elmo, Montana
Broadcast on KOFI-AM, Kalispell, and KUFM-FM, Missoula

Begin with Intro music (stick-game song played and sung with guitar). Fade into Narrator: Who has the right? The first in a series of programs on The Kootenais: Their Political Power in Northwestern Montana.

The Kootenai people have occupied northwestern Montana since "time immemorial." Before white men came the Kootenais hunted bison, deer and elk, and thrived on the local berries and herbs which at that time were abundant. Aside from occasional conflicts with the Blackfeet, they lived peacefully and controlled their own lives.
Today it is a different story. The United States Government has included them in the Confederated Salish and Kootenai Tribes of the Flathead Reservation; the Kootenais number roughly 1/10 of this confederation. Of the ten members of the tribal council, the Kootenais have one representative. They also find themselves heavily outnumbered by the non-Indian people of Lake County, where most of the Kootenais live. Even in Elmo, a town on the northern end of the Flathead Reservation which is 90 per cent Kootenai, the two stores, the grade school and the water commission are all run by non-Kootenais. This situation existed for many years, and has created a certain amount of frustration among Kootenai people. Lyllis Waylett, tribal development specialist of Pend d'Oreille descent, put it this way:

> "I would say that the Kootenai area people have been isolated or remote from the focal point of our tribal government and I think that they've been disadvantaged because of it. I don't think that they've seen good things — if indeed there have ever been any good things flow from the government to the Indian people, the Kootenais and their primary area of residence on our place. I feel that this has strained relationships."

NARRATOR: Residents of the Elmo area express their difficulties with the present situation:

> "It seems like so many other people around here try to run the place. They don't give us minority a chance to really speak our piece." (G. Crew)

"Do you think the Kootenais have a strong voice in council affairs?
No, because of the fact that we, the Kootenais, have only one
Kootenai in the council." (B. Kenmille)

"Well, we went across to that island, we circled the island. We
found ten deer — ten deer dead. Whoever killed them or whatever
killed them took the head. It was sawed off, we could tell it was
sawed off. ... I think it must be the white guys did it because they
wanted the head and the horn. If an Indian did it, they would
have took the whole deer. An Indian would have took the whole
deer. They use every part of the deer." (F. Burke)

"When the people come out from Washington, D.C. and ask how
the Indians been treated they take them to these new houses
where these people are well off. They don't take them around to
these lower grades of Indians, or show the all tore-up house. ...
They really should take them around right here in Elmo here.
Because I know there's a lot of people that really need help."
(L. Stasso)

* * *

Within a social structure, one can often tell which group feels in control and which group
feels that it has no power by asking the simple question, "What are the needs of this area?"
Those who feel in control will probably see few if any needs. Kootenai Communications found
that while non-Kootenais by and large saw no great needs in the Flathead Valley area,
Kootenai people saw some very immediate ones.

* * *

To understand the wisdom of the Kootenais, one must first understand their history. This history goes back many centuries. It begins with the Kootenai as a plains people, occupying
much of the land now held by the Blackfeet, the Assiniboine, and other present-day tribes of
the northern plains.
Maulouf, 395 ("Going back ...") to 487 ("other side of the divide")
The Kootenai organized themselves into regional bands, each with its chief and subchiefs,
each with its own government, yet all sharing the Kootenai blood, language, and way of life.
Malouf, 20 ("Of course, the Kootenai had ...") to 70 ("one of their
most ancient important centers")
When the Kootenais were invited to join the Salish and Pend d'Oreille at Council Groves to
make a treaty with the whites, they saw no reason to come. They had seen few of the whites
and were certainly not threatened by them.

* * *

Throughout the century following Council Groves, this question would plague the Kootenais:
What right, after all, did the whites have to make decisions for them, to control their lives?
Next week we will historically trace some of the economic and social problems which resulted
from the decision to place the Kootenais on the Flathead Reservation.

(Fade-in with theme music)

NARRATOR: This program was produced by Kootenai Communications with the help of a grant from the Montana Committee for the Humanities. The views expressed here do not necessarily reflect those of the Committee.

Written by Anthony Grant and Thomas Crawford

Application: Asian-American Programs

The special background and history as well as the immediate needs of a particular minority or ethnic group help determine the writing approach to a radio or television script. Russ Lowe, producer-member of the Dupont Guy Collective, Chinese for Affirmative Action Media Committee, described a weekly radio program, "Dupont Guy," as a combination of news, commentary, and satire. The writers were scholars of Chinese-American history and people in the arts as well as reporters and media experts. The materials reflected the perspectives and viewpoints of the Chinese-American that are not otherwise usually heard on the air. As an example, Lowe cites an historical skit that tells of the tax collectors during the Gold Rush days going through the mining camps for the $2.50 monthly tax on miners — but trying to collect it only from the Chinese miners. Lowe also notes that the script writers chose words especially carefully, with the vocabulary frequently referring to different parts of the community or to certain events or actions that may have explicit meaning only to the Chinese-American listener.

As do many minority scripts, in order to take advantage of the relatively sparse airtime available to minorities, "Dupont Guy" takes a strong point of view. This is clearly implied in the standard opening:

STANDARD OPENING FOR THE DUPONT GUY RADIO SHOW

NARRATOR: Welcome friends and tourists to DUPONT GUY, a listening trip through Chinese America. Brought to you by the DUPONT GUY COLLECTIVE of Chinatown Saaan Fraanciscooooo.

The name DUPONT GUY comes from the original name of Grant Avenue, Dupont Street. After the 1906 Earthquake, City redevelopers decided to take over Chinatown and changed Dupont Guy to Grant Avenue. Of course, when the Chinese returned to claim their homes, they continued to call their main drag Dupont Guy.

In this spirit of truth and defiance, we commence our program of community news and commentary, of music, poetry and satire.

The following rundown sheet for a Dupont Guy program indicates the variety of formats used and, even in the terms describing the program segments, the spoof approach to making a political-social point. In examining sections of the program script itself, note the satire and "in" language, beginning with the "Chonk Amer-ca" nonstandard opening, which counterpoints the historical information and current events commentary.

DUPONT GUY #14   pilot: HEADHUNTER
                                 copilot: JOHN

1) NON STANDARD OPENING   Out: "Art Gilham,
     TAPE + LIVE MIC   1913"   2:45
     CUT 1

2) SPORTSMAN MARCH CART
     CURTIS: And now the NOOS!
     F.O. CART   Out: 1:30
     MABEL: (Asian American Studies)

3) COLLEGE BOWEL SKIT   LIVE MICS
     Russ, Breen, Connie   Out: "... they never
                                      taught me dat at
                                      Podunk U."   2:00

4) BOOK REVIEW   LIVE MIC
     Kathy   Out: "... screaming
                                      vengeance to
                                      uncover their his-
                                      tory in America"   2:00

5) DICTIONARY DAY LESSON 3
     LIVE MICS   Out: "... check your
     Curtis, Kathy   dictionary"   1:30

6) THREE KINGS   LIVE MICS
     Breen, KING 1, KING 2   FADEOUT on 2nd singing
     Connie   "... bearing gifts
                                      we traveled afar"   :30

7) KUNG FU FIGHTING REVISITED
     LIVE MICS + TAPE
     (cut 2 - track 2)
     Curtis

     Chris   TAPECUE: "it's an olden golden &
                                      kinda scratchy"

                                 TAPEOUT: grunt at slow
                                      speed FADEOUT   3:30
8) STANDARD CLOSE   CART

NON STANDARD OPENING

"Chinatown, My Chinatown" in BG

CURTIS: Welcome friends and touresses, to DUPONT GUY, a listening trip through
            Chonk Amer-ca.

            That was "Chinatown, My Chinatown" by The Whispering Pianist, Art Gilham,
            1913.

NEWS

From the University of California in Berkeley, the question is: Will Asian-American Studies wither and die or will it be absorbed into the traditional white-dominated humanities program?

Survival seems tenuous for Asian-American Studies, which began in 1969 after the Third World Strike. After a lot of protest by minority students that they were being whitewashed with middle-class values and that they were not learning about themselves and their roots, a Third World College was promised. There were to be four divisions: one for Black studies, one for Chicano studies, one for Native American studies, and one for Asian-American studies.

Today, Third World College remains a dream, and a broken one at that. There is no Third World College in sight; but there is a lot of disunity around. Black Studies wants to join the College of Letters and Science, the traditional humanities college of U.C. Asian-American Studies does not want to. It wants to retain its autonomy. But budgetary considerations make things difficult.

Says Asian-American Studies coordinator Germaine Wong, "White liberals don't think there is a need for ethnic studies. They hope it won't be necessary in the future because we'll all be one big happy family."

COLLEGE BOWEL

RUSS: And now we bring you the KOW BEE SEE Network brain show, College Bowel. On today's team we have Mr. Cally Flower of Podunk U. facing Yu Fong of Choy-Lai's School of Chinese-American history. Before we begin, let me offer my regrets to you Yu Fong on the impending threat of your school's obliteration. I know there has been activity prevailing in some of our great universities to eliminate Asian-American studies. But let us see if you can show us what you've learned in today's match of COLLEGE BOWEL.

Are you ready Calley Flower?

BREEN: Uh, yeah, sure.

RUSS: Yu Fong, are you ready?

CONNIE: SHR!

RUSS: All right, tell me the answer to this question. ... When did the first Chinese arrive in the United States?

BREEN: Oh that's easy! Everyone knows they came after the California gold rush in 1849.

RUSS: That is absolutely ... WRONG! Yu Fong, do you have an answer?

CONNIE: In 1785, three Chinese, Ah Sing, Ah Chyun, and Ah Coun were in Baltimore. Their presence was noted by the Continental Congress.

In 1796, five Chinese were brought to Philadelphia to be servants for Andreas Evardus Van Braan Houckgeest.

In 1807, Pung-hua Wing Chong arrived in New York to collect his father's debts.

In 1815, Ah Nam, the cook to Governor de Sola of California was confirmed a Christian at Monterey.

In 1818, Wong Arce attended the Foreign Mission School at Cornwall, Connecticut, with Ah Lan and Ah Lum and Lieau Ah See.

In 1847, the Chinese junk "Ke Ying" sailed into New York harbor with an all Chinese crew.

In 1847, Yung Wing, Wing Foon and Wong Sing enrolled at Monson Academy at Monson, Massachusetts. Yung Wing went on to Yale and became the first Chinese to graduate from a U.S. university, in 1854. In 1852, Yung Wing became a citizen.

BREEN: Gee whiz, they never taught me that at Podunk U.

Dupont Guy Collective, Chinatown, San Francisco

Application: Hispanic Programs

Dr. Palma Martinez-Knoll, as director of Project: Latino, in Detroit, wrote and produced an hour-long series for Spanish-speaking Americans. She states that "too many writers, because of lack of understanding, are either prejudicial or condescending. When writing about Hispanics, or creating Hispanic characters, make them a part of everyday society, not an excluded group." She advises that when depicting the unique problems Hispanics face, the writer should show the Hispanic as a responsible person who is an integral part of the community.

Knoll-Martinez's program, "Mundo Hispano," consisted of a variety of formats including cultural presentations, interviews, different kinds of music, information for women, news, features, documentaries, commercials, and PSAs — similar to the formats of many other minority and ethnic programs. "Mundo Hispano" also included a weekly editorial. "Like the rest of the program," Martinez-Knoll says, "the editorial shows that the American Hispanic community is an offshoot of the Spanish-speaking community all over the world. It is not a Chicano here, a Puerto Rican here, but an entire linguistic community who face a common problem. It is the entire community that must communicate with the majority society."

The following example of the beginning of one program's editorial illustrates this approach.

Nearly one of every 20 Americans has a Spanish-speaking heritage. In other words, there are approximately 10 million Americans with a Spanish-speaking heritage in the mainland United States representing 5 per cent of the population. They are the country's second largest minority group.

Yet, the Spanish-speaking have had a long-standing problem in the area of equal employment opportunity, which only recently has become the focus of national attention and action. In addition, the Spanish-speaking population has had to face problems of social and economic deprivation as well as their own particular problem of a language barrier.

Working to help the Spanish-speaking peoples is not as easy as it may appear. The reason for the difficulty is that those with Spanish heritage are a heterogenous group despite their shared Spanish-language background. In fact, they represent a microcosm of American ethnic diversity.

Interestingly, not all those with Spanish heritage speak Spanish, although most of them do, and all have ancestors who did. Some of these people are recent immigrants or are first generation citizens while others come from families that were living in the Southwest or

Puerto Rico. But by far the largest group — well over 5 million — are of Mexican origin or descent. The next largest group would be those from Puerto Rico followed by a large group from Cuba. Others can trace their families to Central or South America. Thus, it is evident that the Spanish-speaking community is made up of groups from different areas with different backgrounds and cultures.

These groups are located in different parts of the country. For example, most Mexican-Americans live in the Southwest; the Puerto Ricans live largely in New York City and the majority of Cubans live in Florida. Of course, there are smaller concentrations of these various groups in large metropolitan centers such as Detroit.

Within these metropolitan centers, many of the Spanish-speaking have moved into distinct, close-knit neighborhoods, either by choice or because they cannot afford or are barred from housing elsewhere. Unfortunately, these neighborhoods are sometimes in city slums or in poverty stricken "barrios" on the fringes of metropolitan centers.

Partly because of these concentrations of Spanish-speaking peoples into separate urban areas, they continue to have English language problems. At times, the language barrier may not even be overcome during the second generation. There is also the frequent movement of people back and forth between Puerto Rico and the mainland which tends to reinforce the language barrier.

All of these factors have had the effect of culturally isolating the Spanish-speaking from the mainstream of the population. Of course it hasn't helped that ethnic prejudice and discrimination exist in some communities, creating additional barriers to the assimilation of the Spanish-speaking into the community.

In addition, for Spanish-speaking adults there is often a lack of education along with the lack of knowledge about the English language. Both work toward preventing the individual from obtaining a well-paying job. However, the relative number of Spanish-speaking youth with a high school education or better has been rising.

* * *

The problems of the Spanish-speaking in this country are not going unnoticed. Manpower and related programs have been developed to deal with the problems of joblessness and low-level employment. The goal of these programs is to help Spanish-speaking workers qualify for and enter more skilled occupations, offering both higher wages and promise of steady work.

These programs will not lead to any overnight successes, but they are part of a mounting effort to help the Spanish-speaking and all other minority groups.

Courtesy of Palma Martinez-Knoll, ''Mundo Hispano'' Latino Hour

The approaches and examples presented here clearly do not represent all the points of view concerning writing for minority and ethnic programs. Even within individual minority and ethnic groups there are differences of opinion about purpose, content orientation, and technique. Many diverse minorities need to be served by television and radio. Special interests of comparatively small audiences may range from planning herb gardens to making leaded glass to learning Sanskrit to protecting water environments to listening to Kabuki performances, and include racial, religious, nationality, cultural, and similar concerns. Groups such as the aged and the mentally and physically handicapped constitute minorities who have been largely neglected by the media. The key for the writer is sensitivity to

minority needs as a whole and understanding of and empathy with the specific group being written for or about.

For Application and Review: Minority and Ethnic Programs

1. If you are not a member of a minority or a nonmajority ethnic group, select one such group and prepare a fifteen-minute radio or television news broadcast for that group. Your daily newspaper will provide content materials. Arrange for a colleague (a member of your class, for example) who does belong to that minority or ethnic group to do the same exercise. Compare scripts and discuss the differences. Participate in the exercise below.

2. If you are a member of a minority or distinct ethnic group, participate in the exercise above. In addition, prepare a radio or television documentary, feature, or interview program relating to the arts and culture or to a political, social, or economic problem of your group. Arrange for a nonminority colleague to do the same. Compare scripts.

9

Education and Information Programs

Education and information programs are usually differentiated from other types of radio and television shows by being categorized as nonentertainment. Unfortunately, the designation too often is true: education and information programs frequently are dull, boring, pedantic and not at all entertaining. Too many are little more than *talking heads* — that is, the head or voice of a lecturer simply reciting things that could be read in a book or heard in a classroom lecture. Writing a good, effective education or information program requires as much creativity, skill, and knowledge of the medium as does writing a good, effective news show, commercial, documentary, or play. Indeed, an education or information radio or television program may use these and other writing formats.

Of course, not all education and information programs are dull. In fact, a good many are considerably more stimulating and enjoyable than many entertainment programs. Their purposes and settings, unfortunately often linked to traditional concepts of education and teaching and therefore stereotyped and prosaic, frequently give them a dreary quality. As the field of education and information program writing grows, however, more and more writers with a background in television and radio and with creative motivation are going into it — and the product gets better and better.

Education and information programs cover many areas: formal instruction to the classroom, informal education to adults at home, technical updating to professionals, vocational preparation, industry training, and many others. Some of the programs are purely or principally instructional in nature. Others are primarily informational. Still others, with elements of education and information, are public relations oriented. The percentage of station time devoted to education and information programming is relatively low.

A principal form of the education or instruction program is the formal lesson designed for classroom use. Another important form is the training program, principally for government and industry use. Also prominent are programs updating professionals in their fields, particularly in the health sciences. Public information programs that at the same time promote an organization, product, or idea — in essence, public relations — are a staple with both government and industry. Four major types, which should serve as examples of virtually all forms of educational and informational radio and television writing, are covered here: the formal education script for the classroom, the training script for both government and industry, the professional updating medical script, and the public information script.

Formal Education Programs

The writer of the formal education program is, above all, a planner. The writing of the program begins with the cooperative planning of the curriculum coordinator, the studio teacher, the classroom teacher, the educational administrator, the producer, the television (or radio — though formal instruction on radio has, except for a comparatively few stations, been largely neglected) specialist, and the writer. The writer must accept from the educational experts the purposes and contents of each program. The writer should stand firm about the method of presentation; educators, by and large, are too prone to use television as an extension of the classroom, incorporating into the television program the outmoded techniques of teaching in most classrooms. Try, with the producers, to prevent the programs from being used as reinforcement of poor teaching and learning practices. The most important thing to remember is to avoid the talking head. Indeed, inasmuch as effective use of television and radio in the classroom depends on the cooperation of a good teacher who knows how to use the media, the video or audio material coming into the classroom should implement the purposes outlined by John Dewey: bringing the classroom into the world and the world into the classroom. To do this it is not even necessary to present a teacher in the television program. Unfortunately, the insecurity of many teachers and administrators makes that prospect frightening, and you'll have to fight hard and long to keep out some superfluous, but traditional, elements of the formal educational process.

After determination of learning goals and contents, the length of individual programs and of the series is determined and the programs are outlined. The outline should carefully follow the lesson plan for each learning unit as developed by the educational experts. The important topics are stressed, the unimportant ones played down. The educational program does not have to be fully scripted, however. It may be a rundown or routine sheet, depending on the content and whether you use a studio teacher — and to what degree that studio teacher is a professional performer. Many instructional television (**ITV**) practitioners over the years have seriously proposed that professional performers be hired as the on-camera teachers for instructional programs.

Even in the outline stage you should explore the special qualities of television that can present the content more effectively than in the classroom, even when there is a competent classroom teacher. Infuse creativity and entertainment into the learning materials. Though most ITV programs are designed to convey information, reflecting the noncreative purpose and practice in most classrooms, ITV writers and producers are becoming more aware of the need to stimulate the viewer-learner and to orient the material toward the practical past, current, and future life experiences of the student.

The television lesson can use humor, drama, and suspense and borrow liberally from the most effective aspects of entertainment programs. "Sesame Street," probably the most successful program in motivating young people to learn, uses a combination of the best television techniques and forms, from animation to commercials. Go beyond the mundane approaches to learning you were subjected to in most of your school experiences.

Don't be afraid of a liberal infusion of visuals for television and of sound effects for radio. On television, for example, even with limited budgets you can use tape, slides, live actors, close-ups of graphics, photos, demonstrations, detail sets, and other techniques discussed in Chapter 2. Good use of visual writing permits more concrete explanation of what is usually presented in the classroom. The classroom teacher frequently presents principles and explains with examples. Through television the examples can be infinitely more effective than the usual verbal descriptions. You can, in fact, show the real person, thing, place, or event being discussed.

Even discussion may be utilized in the ostensibly one-way ITV technique. In many schools with closed-circuit television or the Instructional Television Fixed Service (**ITFS**), unlike broadcast television, two-way audio is used between the studio teacher and each classroom. Even with one-way television, discussion can be built into the program. Discussion between students and classroom teacher during the program — and there should never be a case where the classroom teacher is not an active participant in the television communication process — can be planned, and appropriate times set aside in the script. Evaluations (testing, for example) can follow the same procedure. The studio teacher and the educators planning the program should know the kinds of questions the students will ask during and following the program and should anticipate and answer them within the program. Professional broadcasters have an inordinate fear of dead time, and many ITV people have accepted this commercial dictum. Yet, some of the best ITV programs have gone to black for appropriate periods to permit effective interaction within the classroom.

The classroom teachers do not work in vacuums. Each ITV series has a teacher's guide that details the purposes, level, content, approach, and evaluation of each program, among other things. The guide usually includes preparatory and follow-up suggestions. Sometimes the guide is prepared after the series has been made. Sometimes the person working on it develops it as the series develops. The writer should note that in the latter case the guide provides an excellent outline base for the full script or routine sheet.

The sequences in the script follow a logical order, usually beginning with a review and preparation for the day's material and concluding with introductory elements for follow-up in the classroom, including review, research, field projects, and individual study. Before you begin your script and before you incorporate all the imaginative visual stimuli and the attention-getting experiences, you have to know what is available to you in terms of the program's budget. If you're preparing a lesson on China, you may find that it is not financially possible to send a film crew to Beijing for a week. It may come as a shock to you to find that you can't even use the excellent tape on China you saw on STV the other day because the producer can't find the $100 to get rights to it.

The word *motivation* is mentioned so often in education that we have become inured to it. Yet, it is still the key to television watching and to learning. The better a show you have, the better the student will learn. To make learning exciting, the material must be pleasurable and stimulating. Teaching is a form of persuasion. The instructional script should be developed as much as possible for a target audience: Is the program designed for one school, one city school system, a county school system, a state? For national distribution? Who are the students who will watch? Their backgrounds? Their interests? Be carefully guided by the educational experts you are working with as to the degree of complexity of concepts you can present, what you can presume is already known, and the language level that the students in the particular grade the program is designed for require for comprehension. Even though for different persuasive purposes, the instructional program may follow the organization of the commercial: Get the students' attention, keep their interest, impart information, plant an idea, stimulate thinking about the subject, and, most important of all, motivate the students to create something new through their own thinking.

The instructional program, like the good play, should increase in interest and intensity. If we start too high, we have no place to go. There is exposition and background, followed by the conflict or suspense of what will happen to the idea, characters, or situation. The complications are the problems and methods of what is being learned. We reach a climax when either an answer is found and the lesson element learned or, as in Brechtian drama, when the student has been presented with all the alternatives and must seek a solution through deductive or inductive thinking on his or her own in order to satisfy hunger for knowledge on that given subject. Now, that is education! Remember that the dramatists of the world have educated us with deeper insights and feelings about the relationships among people and between people and their environment than have the historians and social scientists.

One of the simplest and most-used ITV formats is the direct presentation of views and sounds of people, places, and things that otherwise would not be available to most students. Science experiments, biographical interviews, and geographical descriptions are among the topics that fall into this category. Often the television presentation may physically resemble a travelogue, with the television teacher, voice-over, commenting on the filmed or taped material. The material, its sequence, and the descriptive information are, of course, carefully planned in terms of curriculum and learning requirements. An example of this kind of script is the following beginning and ending of one lesson from a series designed for fourth-grade social studies — which, because of the great variation in curriculum levels throughout the country, is actually being used from the third through eighth grades.

———————————————————O———————————————————

• *Given the economic considerations of producing an ITV series and the broad purpose of this particular lesson, would you have written this script any differently? If so, what approaches and techniques would you have used?*

———————————————————O———————————————————

LANDS AND PEOPLE OF OUR WORLD

Lesson Number: 29   Lesson Title: Japan

FILM — 1 min.

MUSIC — 1 min.

MAT — "Lands and People
     of Our World"

MAT — Donna Matson

Legend says that the Sun Goddess founded the islands of Japan, and for many years only tribespeople inhabited the land of the rising sun. Then Chinese traders and other foreigners began visiting Japan; they brought new ideas and culture. But the rulers of Japan didn't want any changes, so they closed their gates, allowing no one to enter and no one to leave. For nearly 200 years Japan and her people remained isolated from the outside world.

Then, in 1853, Commodore Perry of the United States Navy sailed his warships into Tokyo Bay and persauded the Japanese to open two of their ports to U.S. trade.

The Japanese quickly learned the ways of the modern world, and today they are one of the greatest industrial nations in the world.

ON DONNA

Hello, boys and girls. Our lesson today is about Japan, one of the most amazing countries in the world today.

PIX #1 MAP — ASIA

Japan is a group of islands, located in Asia, off the East Coasts of Russia, Korea and China, in the Western part of the Pacific Ocean.

Japan consists of four main islands: Hokkaido, Honshu, Kyushu, and Shikoku, plus about 3,000 smaller islands. All together they about equal the size of the State of California. The islands of Japan stretch from North to Southwest for a distance of about 1200 miles.

FILM — 3 min.
MUSIC

Mount Fujiyama, a volcanic mountain, over 12,000 feet high, is the highest point in Japan. The islands of Japan are actually the tops of mountains which are still growing.

Japan is located in the Pacific Great Circle of Fire, and has about 1500 earthquakes each year, but most of them cause little damage.

Japan has a wide variety of climate ranging from tropical on the southern islands to cool summers and snowy winters on the northern islands.

Tokyo

More than 104 million people live on the islands of Japan, and two out of three live in cities.

Tokyo, Japan's capital city, is the largest city in the world, with a population of more than 11 million people. Osaka, Kyoto, and Yokohama are also large cities, with populations of more than two million each.

The city of Tokyo has been rebuilt twice in the last 50 years, once after an earthquake, and again after the air raids of World War II.

Today it is very much like an American city, with wide paved streets, tall modern buildings, and heavy traffic. Tokyo has been able to grow so fast mainly because of its very modern railroads that carry more than one million people into work each day.

Most Japanese homes are made of wood panels and sliding doors. They stand earthquakes well, but not fires. Many homes have beautiful gardens. The floors of the homes are like thick cushions and the Japanese people kneel on the floor while eating off low tables, and they sleep on the soft floors, in comforts and blankets that they roll up during the day. And to keep these floors clean, they always remove their shoes before entering their houses. The Japanese are some of the cleanest people I've ever met in the world.

Students

In Japan, all boys and girls must go to school for nine years. That's grade one to nine. And they have at least two hours of homework each night, and homework assignments all summer long. All students in Japan are required to study English. There are more than 50 universities and colleges in Tokyo.

Mother and Child

Japanese children are very respectful and polite to their parents and grandparents, and try very hard to never bring shame to their family in any way.

Harbor

Japan is an island nation, and island nations need ships. Japan is first in the world in ship building, second in plastics, and fourth in auto making. Yet, only about 3 out of every 100 Japanese have automobiles. Japan imports much steel from us, manufactures trucks, autos and machinery, and exports it to the United States and other countries.

People travel mainly on electric trains and buses. There just wouldn't be enough room if many people had cars. Space is a problem. . . .

Film Ends (3 min.)

Japan is also the world's largest exporter of ceramic tableware, cameras, lenses, electronic equipment and motorcycles.

ON DONNA

As a matter of fact, here are some of the things I own that are manufactured in Japan. My camera, tape recorder and ceramic tableware.

FILM — 7½ min.

The textile industry is another important industry in Japan. Japan produces more than half the world's supply of raw silk. Silk, remember, comes from cocoons, of the silkworms.

Fishing

Japan is one of the world's greatest fishing countries. It has over 400,000 fishing boats. That's more than any other nation.

*   *   *

FILM

For over 1,000 years Japan was ruled by an Emperor who had great powers over the people. Today his duties are mainly ceremonial. Here we see the Emperor of Japan greeting his people on New Year's Day at the Imperial Palace Grounds in Tokyo.

After World War II, the United States helped Japan set up a democratic form of government, and the head of their government is the Prime Minister, who is chosen by the Diet. The Diet is like our Congress, with a House of Representatives and a House of Councilors which are elected by the people of Japan.

ON DONNA

Hibatchi, food, toys, dolls, kite.

MUSIC — 15 sec.

Closing

ON KITE

MAT — Consultant
MAT — Western ITV

As noted earlier, some ITV programs are not scripted, but use rundown or routine sheets. Here is an example from a series on music designed for the second and third grades. Note how the writer has the studio teacher — in this case a professional performer — bring in the active participation of the students watching in the classroom. Writing a rundown sheet such as this takes just as much time as writing a complete script for a ''Lands and Peoples of Our World'' lesson, says Donna Matson, producer and writer of both programs. She states:

> You have to think and organize and plan every move in order to keep it as simple and flowing as possible. For example, if you teach the verse, will you sing the song through first? After you have taught the verse, will you follow up with a repeat, or will you have another song or an instrument as a transition between segments? What techniques of involving the classroom student should be used? Will you go out with the theme, so that the child keeps on singing after the program has ended? What is most important in the program: the song? the use of instruments? These are only some of the considerations the writer has to keep in mind. The script may be short, but the work time that goes into it is long.

LET'S ALL SING

Lesson Number: 17   Lesson Title: Magical Food

Theme — Live — Guitar

MAT — "Let's All Sing"

MAT — Tony Saletan

ON TONY   There are many songs about food such
                                        as ...

                                        But today we're going to sing a song about
                                        mystical magical food. And it goes like
                                        this ...

                                        TEACHES REFRAIN

                                        SINGS ENTIRE SONG

                                        SHOWS FOODS

                                        SINGS SONG — LISTEN TO RHYMING
                                        WORDS

                                        SINGS SONG — Children fill in rhyming
                                        words

ON BELLS	BELLS — 4 tone refrain + 2 = 6
ON PIX — Malvina Reynolds	MALVINA REYNOLDS
	SING "LET IT BE"
	SING "MAGICAL FOOD" — make up verses
	CLOSING
	MAGICAL FOOD
MAT — Saletan MAT — Reynolds MAT — Western ITV	

Courtesy of Western Instructional Television

Government Training Programs

Writing educational scripts for government training purposes varies with the size and production budgets of each agency. Some, like the Department of Defense, have superb facilities for writing and producing training programs for radio and television. Other agencies have no facilities and do virtually nothing at all. Still others attempt to do good jobs with barely adequate resources. But whether a high-budget or a low/no-budget situation, the basic element of the program, the script, has got to be as good as possible.

Eileen T. McClay was the writer-producer-director of ITV training materials for the FTC, which is typical of agencies with limited budget and resources. The budget and resources limitations on the producer-director impose limitations on the writer. Some of McClay's experiences are specifically applicable to such a situation; others of her experiences are typical of the writer's concerns in all situations and in all agencies. One of the important considerations to the writer, McClay has said, is multiple clearances:

> You may find that your product must be reviewed (for content, format, policy, security) by so many layers of authority that you despair of ever getting a program out on a timely basis. Also — and this may be one of the most substantial differences between you and your counterparts in commercial or public television — the persons who will rule on your product may have little knowledge about either the limitations or the special capabilities of audiovisuals and may, in fact, have little sympathy with the concept of instructional television. To many people, television is associated with, and thereby ineradicably tainted by, "show biz."

Another problem for the ITV writer in government is the lack of opportunity to preplan. McClay explained:

A great many elements must be coordinated to bring a production together. Good programs take advance planning. Workers in the world of the
small audiovisual operation often listen wistfully to their more affluent colleagues talk about an insistence on total control, pre-planning, and righteous
refusal to uncap the lens of a single camera until a full script has been
written. More typical may be the phone call that informs you that Supervisor John Smith is on his way with an urgent message of indeterminable
length on a cloudily outlined subject, which must be taped, duplicated, and
sent out to regional offices by sundown. You arrange props, set lights, test
sound, and sit down to wait for Smith — who arrives two hours late with
an armful of graphs and charts on $8\frac{1}{2}$ x 11 sheets, and accompanied by two
or three members of his staff who would like to share the camera with him.
All express great surprise at the time involved in rearranging all the equipment to accommodate to the new situation. As for preparing a script. . . .

McClay divides an agency's needs into two categories: communications and
training. "Each, of course, may well contain elements of the other. The first,
however, is usually an information-carrying vehicle: a news briefing, a back-
grounder to explain agency action or policy, an interview with a new bureau or
division chief that will acquaint regional offices with his or her operating philosophy. The second kind of program should be precisely geared to the training needs
of the agency's personnel."

One training script written and produced by McClay related to educating supervisory staff personnel on the problem caused by careless filling-out of a standard
government form. The FTC at first planned to send only a memorandum to the staff,
then decided to supplement the memo with a videotape on the subject. One of the
requirements was that the television program retain large portions of the language of
the memo. A second requirement was that the project — conception of format to
writing of script to final taping — be completed in two working days. McClay
started with the memorandum:

Executive Director Notice

Subject: Timely Reporting of Personnel Actions

The agency recently converted to a computerized payroll system which
is operated for us by the Treasury Department in Philadelphia. Since the
new system has been in operation, we are constantly receiving complaints
from the Treasury people that our personnel actions are getting to them
too late. The result is that some employees are not getting paid on time,
while others are being overpaid and checks are having to be cancelled.

Specifically, the problem relates to Standard Form 52, Notification of Personnel Action. This form is the medium through which operating officials
communicate to the Division of Personnel what is happening in their organizational units. It is also the basis from which the employee is ultimately paid. The
52's are not coming in from the operating bureaus on time. This is the primary
reason why our actions are getting to Treasury too late.

Treasury has given us an absolute deadline of the second Wednesday of the pay period (the day after payday) for getting actions to them for that pay period. They want to receive actions on a gradual, day-to-day basis, not all at one time on the deadline date. Therefore, the maximum deadline that the Division of Personnel can accept personnel actions is the second Tuesday of the pay period in which the action is to be effective. Actions received after this date may not be made effective until the following pay period. It is absolutely necessary that you

- Send your 52's in by the beginning of the pay period.
- Don't hold resignations — submit them as soon as you are aware of an employee's intention to leave.
- Advise the personnel processing section by phone of any actions that will be coming in late — be prepared to justify the reasons why they will be late.
- On appointments in the field offices, air mail the oath of office, withholding forms, and 52 (if not previously submitted) on the morning of the day the employee enters on duty, and monitor very closely the status of employees requiring follow-up actions, e.g., not-to-exceed dates, expiration of leave without pay, changes in tour of duty, etc.

Each operating official should delegate the responsibility for preparing 52's to a competent, reliable person, and should designate an alternate for that person so that delays will not occur because of absence. The same is true of Timekeepers — this is an important function and should be assigned to a responsible person and an alternate. The Timekeeper and the person responsible for 52's should be in close communication with each other and with the Personnel Processing Section, so as to alert each other regarding impending personnel actions. You, the operating managers, are responsible and accountable for insuring that all personnel actions are submitted on time and are accurate.

A film is being prepared on this subject to be shown to all Timekeepers and persons responsible for preparing 52's. The matter is being called to your attention prior to releasing the film so that you will be aware of the urgency of this situation, and can make immediate efforts to correct the problem. We must make this new system work, since our own payroll staff has been practically disbanded. The only way it can work is if personnel actions are reported on a timely basis.

The approach taken by McClay:

I decided to make a 15-minute tape, the nuclei of which would be three short skits dramatizing the major difficulties the Personnel Office was having as a result of errors in the completion of the forms. Because of the time pressure, I decided not to write complete scripts for these particular scenes, but to use improvisational techniques and to schedule short but intensive rehearsal periods with staff members who were directly involved in the kinds of situations to be dramatized and who would, therefore, be able to talk spontaneously and knowledgeably on the subject. Also, because of lack of time, I made no attempt to use music or graphics. The script I wrote was more of a detailed routine sheet, in which I prepared as much of the introductory, ending and transitional continuity as possible, but left the analyses and discussion of specific problems in the improvisational form. Also, as writer-director I prepared the video portion of the script, as well. The completed tape — which was basically a dramatized interoffice memorandum — was well-received by the supervisory staff audience for whom it was directed and was generally deemed to have achieved its goal of focusing attention on a problem of some urgency.

———————————————————◯———————————————————

● *As you examine the following script, compare its purpose, language, and effectiveness with the memorandum that prompted it. Note that even with improvisational elements made necessary by lack of time, the script is prepared as fully as possible, following the principle that the more you know about where you are going and how you want to go, the better chance you have of getting there. Would you have written it any differently? How? Note, as well, that the writer, as producer, put in complete video directions, similar to what the writer of the film script would do.*

———————————————————◯———————————————————

Title: STANDARD FORM 52:
Notification of Personnel Action

VIDEO	AUDIO
Fade up from black	
Camera 2 LS form 52, slow Zoom to CU of title: hold 3 secs.	
Dissolve Camera 1 MCU Marie _____	MARIE: This is Marie _____ of the Personnel Office at Headquarters. I want to discuss with you a very serious problem. You all know we recently converted to a computerized payroll system, operated for us by the Treasury Department in Philadelphia. Ever since the new system has been in operation, however, we've been receiving complaints from the Treasury people that our personnel actions are getting to them too late for timely action. The result is that some employees are not getting paid on time, while others are being overpaid and their checks are having to be cancelled.

VIDEO	AUDIO
	MARIE:
Take Camera 2	Specifically, I am talking about Standard
LS Marie	Form 52, Notification of Personnel Action.
	This form is the medium by which operat-
	ing officials communicate to the Division of
	Personnel what is happening in their orga-
	nizational units. It is also the basis on
	which the employee is ultimately paid. The
	fact is, the 52s are not coming in from the
	operating bureaus on time, and this is the
	primary reason our actions are late getting
	to Treasury.
Take Camera 1	Even when a form is correctly filled out, it
MCU Marie	takes time for Personnel to process the
	action. All too often, however, vital informa-
	tion is incorrect, or is missing altogether.
	When that happens, more time is wasted
	while we return the form to you and then
	wait for you to send us the correct informa-
	tion. Meantime, the personnel action is
	held up and the change in the employee's
	status can't be reflected in his paycheck.
Take Camera 2	Let me show you some examples of forms
CU Form 52 as Marie uses pointer to indi-	that have been incorrectly filled out. In this
cate 2 different items. Camera follows	instance … (Marie states what is incorrect
pointer.	and explains consequences.)
Take Camera 1	**MARIE:**
LS Marie at desk, Joyce sitting beside her.	Errors like these cause problems for us
Slow Zoom to MCU as they talk. (Zoom to	almost every day. In fact, Joyce has just re-
CU Marie at conclusion)	ceived a Form that is missing some very
	important information.
	JOYCE:
	Yes. This Form doesn't give us enough in-
	formation about an employee's resignation.
	(Marie and Joyce discuss the problem,
	stressing these points:
	a. If the effective date is not given, em-
	ployee continues to draw pay after he
	has resigned.
	b. If no forwarding address is given, em-
	ployee cannot be mailed his final check.
	c. A Federal regulation requires that em-
	ployee fill in the reason for leaving.)

VIDEO	AUDIO
Camera 1 holding CU Marie	MARIE: I want to show you another example of what can happen when Regional Offices fail to give us complete information. (Marie outlines problem.)
Take Camera 2 CU Form 52 as Marie again uses pointer to indicate a problem	
Take Camera 1 CU Marie	MARIE: This morning Julie had to call one of our Regional Offices because ... (Marie states problem.)
Dissolve Camera 2 LS Julie; slow Zoom to MCU as she speaks	JULIE: (Julie carries on telephone conversation with RO supervisor, discussing problems caused by his not getting Form in on time, or not having it correctly filled out.)
Dissolve Camera 1 CU Marie	MARIE: When the Forms are properly filled out, the process of a change in employee status goes very smoothly. But I think you're beginning to see that errors can be very time-consuming. Also, and I want to emphasize this point, mistakes can cause real hardship for an employee. Right now, for example, Karen is trying to help an employee discover why he didn't receive his last paycheck.
Dissolve Camera 2 LS Karen and John. Slow Zoom to John at conclusion; soft focus out on John still talking	(Karen and John discuss the fact that he didn't receive his last paycheck.)
	Audio out on John, up on Marie
Dissolve Camera 1 LS Marie	MARIE: The Treasury Department has informed us they must receive all actions on a gradual, day-to-day basis, not all at the same time. Therefore, effective immediately, the maximum deadline we can accept personnel actions is the Friday before the beginning

VIDEO	AUDIO
	of the pay period in which the action is to be effective. Actions received after this date may not be made effective until the following pay period. The only exceptions to this are appointments in the Regional Offices, which should be air-mailed to the Division of Personnel on the day the employee reports for work.
Take Camera 2 CU Marie	It is absolutley necessary that you: —Send your 52s in by the beginning of the pay period. —Submit resignations as soon as you are aware of an employee's intention to leave. —On appointments in the Regional Offices, air mail the oath of office, withholding forms, and 52s (if not previously submitted) on the morning of the day the employee enters on duty, and — Monitor very closely the status of employees requiring follow-up actions like: not-to-exceed dates, expiration of leave without pay, changes in tour of duty, and so forth.
Take Camera 1 LS Marie	Most of you who are viewing this tape are responsible for preparing 52s in your organizational unit, or are Timekeepers. The fact that you have been assigned these important functions indicates that you are competent and reliable employees. We, therefore, look to you for your cooperation in getting 52s in on time.
Holding Camera 1 Zoom to MCU Marie	Timekeepers and persons responsible for preparing 52s should work in close communication with each other and with the Personnel Processing Section so as to alert each other regarding impending personnel actions.
Holding Camera 1 Slow Zoom to CU Marie	Remember, our own payroll staff has been practically disbanded, so we must make this new system work. And it won't work unless every Form 52 is filled out accurately, completely, and on time.

VIDEO

AUDIO

At the beginning of this tape, I told you I wanted to discuss a serious problem with you. I hope you see now just how urgent it is.

Dissolve Camera 2
CU LOGO; hold 3 secs.

Fade to black

Written by Eileen T. McClay for the Federal Trade Commission

Industry Programs (Corporate Video)

Probably the most sophisticated use of media in instruction is in the business and organizational field. Industrial television (or, as it has become more widely known, corporate media), has combined motivation with resources and developed some highly effective training programs, offering growing opportunities for young media writers and producers. Although the basic concept of the television script remains the same, time, objectives, and techniques differ from those of the formal instruction or government training program. Donald S. Schaal, as television producer-director for Control Data Corporation Television Communications Services, stated in *Educational and Industrial Television* that "when you come to grips with scripting for industrial television, for the most part you might just as well throw all your preconceived ideas about creative/dramatic and technical writing in the circular file." Schaal said that attempts to transfer the classroom teacher to television have failed and that "unfamiliarity with what television could or could not do . . . resulted in a product which left just about everything to be desired. It lacked organization, continuity, a smooth succession of transitions and, in many cases, many of the pertinent details. . . . Since we think so-called 'training' tapes should *augment* classroom material and not supplant it, we soon realized that we could gain little but could lose everything by merely turning an instructor loose in front of the tube to do exactly what he does in person in the classroom. . . . The videotape he needs for his classroom *must* provide something he cannot conveniently offer his students in person."

Schaal's solution to the problem was to use professionals to do the voice tracks describing electromechanical and electronic equipment. He found, however, that this created a further problem: although the teacher who knows the equipment doesn't usually know how to present it effectively on television, the professional who can make a good presentation doesn't usually know much about the equipment. Schaal said that "the solution, of course, is the professional must *sound* as though he invented every part of the machine and painstakingly handtooled it out of solid gold. To accomplish this effect, you must contrive what I like to call a 'shadow' script."

The shadow script, according to Schaal, is a transcription of the classroom teacher's presentation of a particular subject and a minimum rewriting of the transcription for smoother continuity and subsequent voice-over recording by a professional. Schaal found two distinct difficulties because the classroom instructor tended to reflect the classroom teaching approach: a lack of concise, clear continuity and the accidental omission of pertinent material. Schaal wrote:

> Now an instructor who comes into our shop to make such a tape arrives with at least a very detailed, topical outline prepared with television in mind. In many cases, he is actually provided with a detailed rough shooting script from which he reads for the benefit of the audio track. These outlines and scripts are provided by the curriculum people of the school and tend to confine the instructor to an orderly and complete description of the equipment. . . .
>
> Had we gone the route of preparing formal scripts in the technical writing style (which would have been the most appropriate in this case), dropped the instructor out of the loop completely by telling him he was a clod on television and showing him the door, and refused to cooperate with the curriculum people because they didn't think in terms of television at first, we not only would have alienated a lot of people, but also I doubt if we would have produced a compeletely usable tape. . . .
>
> The moral, as I see it, is that industrial television scripts must be tailored to meet the situation. I have talked of only one aspect of industrial scripting — the description of equipment for training people on how to use and maintain it. For this type of script, I feel it is very important to retain the credibility of the person who knows the equipment the best, even though his voice does not appear on the finished product.
>
> For this reason, I confine my rewrites to removing bad grammar and clarifying hazy or badly worded description. I make no attempt at restructuring mainly because the pictures are already on the tape. If I do see continuity problems, however, I call them to the attention of the curriculum people involved and let them make the decisions. I do make every attempt to keep the narrative as conversational as possible without lapsing into the creative/dramatic vein. All such scripts must be straightforward, sound natural, and contain a minimum of slang. Rarely is anything flippant allowed to survive the waste basket. Cliches and stylized narrative are avoided like the plague.

Roger Sullivan, director of education of the Commercial Union Assurance Companies, offered the following advice for the effective development of corporate video scripts:

> It is very important that business video program writers understand the objectives of the particular video being produced. For example, when we develop a video for the business adult education community we have, in truth, two audiences: the organization for which the video is being developed, which wants a program that provides employees with the practical knowledge and skills they need to carry out successfully one or more particular predefined performance functions on the job; and the employee, who seeks personal growth and the ability to carry out a performance function as confidently and competently as possible. Both audiences want

to have the learning completed in as a short a time as possible and within reasonable cost limits. The business video production begins with a detailed agreement about the objectives, the performance which the employee can be expected to demonstrate as a result of the learning. The completed scenario is a series of interrelated modules of skills or knowledge leading to the final ability to perform the objectives. The most effective visual presentation for each module is developed. The emphasis is on the practical — how to do it. The theoretical — why — is secondary. Insofar as possible, the environment, the dress, and the language of the actors should simulate the workplace. Effective techniques include methods such as 1) explanation followed by a "wrong-way" demonstration or role playing, then a "right-way" demonstration or role playing; 2) a close-up step-by-step demonstration by the leader followed by a close-up of a student carrying out each step during an exchange of questions and explanations. The employee must feel that the knowledge is learnable. Once your audience and objectives are well-defined and the modular building blocks assembled, then the scenario may be fleshed out. Work closely with subject matter experts and rely on their comments, as well as on your own imagination.

Industrial video presentations have moved strongly into the area of drama, creating a suspense that holds an audience and a conflict whose solution achieves the objective of the presentation — comparable to the principle of the dramatic commercial (see Chapter 3) and as close as possible to the play itself (see Chapter 10). In the *Audio-Visual Communications* journal, Thomas C. Hunter offered some advice from one of the most successful industrial film writers and directors, Richard Bruner. One of Bruner's important contributions was the effective use of dramatic dialogue and action as differentiated from the voice-over narration and lecture-type dialogue that dominates too many corporate video programs. Bruner concedes that when the purpose of the programs is simply expository explanation, narration can do a good job. But he prefers the dramatic format. "For a film to have dramatic impact," he stated, "the audience must be convinced that something important is at stake. The protagonist must have a stake in the outcome of the conflict. So must the other major characters. And, obviously, there must be conflict. That's where an industrial client sometimes gets uneasy, because to have a conflict, everything can't be rosy." While endorsing the cinema verité approach that is used frequently in corporate video, Bruner cautions that it has become an overworked device, as have a profusion of special effects and "razzle-dazzle."

An example of the corporate video script is one written, produced, and directed by Frank R. King, director of video training for the John Hancock Mutual Life Insurance Company. The occasion for this particular program, "The Hantel Advantage," was the introduction to agents in 430 locations throughout the country of a new company-wide computer system, HANcock TELecommunications. The video program was to lead off day-long meetings in which agents were to be introduced to HANTEL. King described his objectives for this script: to kick the meetings off with a positive feeling, and to convince managers that if they did not use the computer system the company wouldn't save the money that prompted its installation. To achieve the second objective King decided he had to make clear the benefits of the new system to each individual manager.

He chose a dramatic format for the program as lending itself more easily to humor than would a narrative or discussion format. To provide realistic identification for the viewers, the show was shot on location. He used professional talent in the lead roles and carefully chosen John Hancock people in minor parts. He boiled his informational objectives down to four: to show as well as to tell managers and agents how HANTEL would be used to (1) train agents, (2) facilitate sales, (3) create a more efficient sales proposal system, and (4) strengthen administrative processes. As you study the following script excerpt, note how it reflects some of the approaches discussed earlier by Roger Sullivan, including the contrasts between the wrong way, as shown in the practices of the fictional insurance company without a computer, and the right way, as shown in the HANTEL operation of John Hancock. King sticks to the play format, concentrating on motivated dialogue rather than on expository monologue. The contrasts between the new and the old are exaggerated sufficiently to provide visual humor and entertainment for the viewer. Here is the first half of the actual shooting script.

HANTEL ADVANTAGE

AUDIO	VIDEO
	JHVN LOGO
	Fade up: Opening Title:
	THE HANTEL ADVANTAGE
	Fade to Black
NARRATOR: (Music under):	Fade up on: LS
	Aerial photo, small town.
Our story takes place in a small town. Like any other American town, there are a number of businesses here, including two life insurance companies.	Slow zoom in.
Now, most people think that life insurance companies are all the same. But there's one person in this town who knows better. That's Bob Shields. Bob's brother is an insurance agent himself, and now Bob's decided to become an agent too. He's made plans today to learn a little bit about how the 2 companies in town operate.	Dissolve to: Exteriors:
	Olde-Fashioned Life and John Hancock, with signs. The first is old, decrepit; JH is modern, clean.
	Cut to: Pan and follow one pedestrian, Bob Shields, walking through light crowd. Late 20's, well-dressed, whistling tune.
	Bob walks into door of Olde Fashioned Life. Zoom into sign.

AUDIO	VIDEO
(MUSIC OUT)	
BOB: Er … excuse me …	Interior, reception area. Receptionist, a short, fat woman is sleeping in her chair. She is snoring.
Uh … miss …	Bob tries waking her, getting louder and louder, finally succeeds with a shout.
HELLO?!!?	
RECEPTIONIST: (Waking suddenly) OH! What … what is it? (She looks around anxiously) (Sees Bob. Angrily:) Who are you? What do you want, anyway?	
BOB: Sorry, miss. My name is Bob Shields, and …	
RECEPTIONIST: (Interrupts) Well, Bob Shields, do you always shout at people? Can't you see this is a place of business?	
	Bob peers over her shoulder into clerical area. We see about three women, all sleeping in their seats.
BOB: Well, I'm really very sorry. I have a 10:00 appointment with Mr. Hindenburg.	
RECEPTIONIST: Well, just find a seat over there and he'll be with you soon.	
	Bob finds waiting area, sits down. Looks around for reading material. Finds a copy of *Liberty* or other defunct magazine, circa WWII. Reacts with surprise. Starts to read.
	A kindly, frail woman about 40 enters office and goes to receptionist. Bob watches …
RECEPTIONIST: (Gruff tone) Yeah!	
WOMAN: (Taken aback slightly) Uh … How do you do? I wonder if someone can help me?	

AUDIO	VIDEO
RECEPTIONIST: Could be. What's your problem, honey?	
WOMAN: Well, my husband and I just moved here a few weeks ago from Minnesota ... You see, our moving expenses were a bit higher than we expected, and we were hoping we might be able to get some money out of an Olde-Fashioned policy my husband bought in 1959?	
RECEPTIONIST: Well, it's not that easy, you know. We can't do that *here*. First, you've got to fill out these change of address forms. (She slaps on the counter a pile of papers.) Then you've got to complete these "Intent to Raid the Nonforfeiture Value" forms (more papers). After that, there's this one: "Declaration of Anticipated Financial Status for the Next 35 Years" (more papers). And if the amount you want is over $15, we need your fingerprints, passport information, police record, and grammar school history on these (a last huge bunch of papers).	From receptionist's viewpoint: only the very top of woman's head now shows above the huge pile of papers.
WOMAN: Thank you. How soon will I get my money?	
RECEPTIONIST: (Looking at calendar) Well, this is November ... with any luck around Easter.	
WOMAN: THANK YOU.	As she struggles to take the papers off the counter, dropping many ...
Fade to Black	
(MUSIC UNDER)	TITLE: That afternoon ...
	Wipe to: Bob enters *JH* office. Goes to receptionist. Office is bright, neat, receptionist is attractive young woman.
(MUSIC OUT)	
RECEPTIONIST: Hello, may I help you?	

AUDIO

VIDEO

BOB: Yes, thanks. My name is Bob Shields.
I have a 2 o'clock appointment with
Mr. Davis.

RECEPTIONIST: Oh yes, Mr. Shields.
Mr. Davis is expecting you. If you'll have a
seat I'll tell him you're here.

BOB sits, notices a small sign on end table
or wall that reads:

ASK US ABOUT
THE HANTEL ADVANTAGE!

Same woman enters office, goes to receptionist. She looks haggard from her ordeal
that morning.

RECEPTIONIST: Yes, Ma'am. What can I
do for you?

WOMAN: I *hope* you can help me.
It's about a John Hancock insurance policy
my husband has. I'd like to get a loan
through the policy … if that's not asking
too much?

RECEPTIONIST: I'm sure we can help.
Let me get one of our representatives to
take care of you.

DAVIS: Mr. Shields?

DAVIS enters waiting area. Walks over to
Bob.

SHIELDS: Yes.

DAVIS: I'm Herb Davis. Glad you
could make it today.

SHIELDS: It's nice to meet you, Mr. Davis.
I appreciate your taking the time for me today.

DAVIS: My pleasure.

SHIELDS: I've got a lot of questions — but
first of all, tell me — what's this (pointing
to sign) about a HANTEL advantage?

DAVIS: Well, before we talk about your aptitude test or anything else — that's a pretty

AUDIO

good place to start, because HANTEL has really become the *heart* of our agency. If you'll come with me, I think I can *show* you what HANTEL's all about.

AGENT: Mrs. Bingham, by any chance do you know the number of the policy?

WOMAN: No, I'm afraid not — but I think I have the last bill John Hancock sent me. Would that help? (Goes into purse.)

AGENT: Yes, that'll give me just what I need.

WOMAN: (Hands bill to agent)

AGENT: (Writing it down) OK. Now the 1st thing we should do is make sure we get that new address.

WOMAN: Oh, yes. It's 506 Whitman Rd.

AGENT: Fine (writing). Now if you'll be kind enough to wait here for just a moment I'll be right back.

DAVIS: You see, Bob, HANTEL stands for *HANCOCK TELE*COMMUNICATIONS. Right here in this office, we have a direct link to the computer system in our Boston Home Office. It's really a whole new way of doing business in the insurance industry.

DAVIS: (V/O)

For example, Bob, with HANTEL our agents have instant access to a wide range of information contained in literally millions of John Hancock policies. We can do a lot of things in just seconds now that used to take us days through the mail. We can make necessary changes in policy information ... and we can find out policy values that are up-to-the-minute!

DAVIS: The machinery is something, Bob, but I'll tell you — Hantel's *real* value is the

VIDEO

DAVIS & BOB peer into agent's office. We see AGENT, about 45, with WOMAN.

Agent exits, DAVIS & BOB watch him go.

AGENT arrives at clerical window ... Gives request, info to HANTEL operator ...

HANTEL operator, on terminal: changes address to 506 Whitman Road. Calls up value screen and points to Cash Value, Accumulated Dividends figure and writes these down. Gives to Office Manager. CU: Check being written by OM (young male).

AUDIO	VIDEO
better service our clients get — and it sure helps the agents sell!	DAVIS & BOB
	AGENT'S OFFICE. Agent returns.

AGENT: OK, Mrs. Bingham, here's that money you needed (hands her check). We took it out of your dividends. You had plenty to spare.

WOMAN: So soon? That's marvelous! *Thank* you *very* much!

AGENT: Not at all. We're happy to help. While you're here, Mrs. Bingham, tell me about this new house of yours. Have you and your husband taken any steps to protect your mortgage?

WOMAN: Well, I don't think we've done anything about that, no.

AGENT: The biggest single investment most people make is in a home. Don't you agree?

WOMAN: Oh, definitely.

AGENT (V/O): Your home is important to your husband and yourself. I'd like the chance to talk to both of you together about making sure your options are left open ...

CU, BOB, nodding in appreciation at this scene.

(fade out)

WIPE TO:
(FAST-MOVING SCENE)

Waiting room of Olde Fashioned Life. Bob reading magazine. Hindenburg enters. He is about 45 or older, short, rotund, smokes cigar, conservatively dressed, looks old-fashioned: belt and suspenders, hair parted down center & slicked back, handlebar moustache, 1890's look.

HINDENBURG: Shields?

BOB: Uh — yes.

HINDENBURG: Harry Hindenburg's the name — insurance is my game! How ya doin!

BOB: Pretty good, thank you ...

AUDIO

HINDENBURG: (Slaps Bob on back, knocking him over) That's great! Glad to hear it! You wanna be an agent with us, right!

BOB: Well, I'd like to become an agent, yes, but I haven't decided which company to go with quite yet.

HINDENBURG: (Blowing smoke in Bob's face as he talks) Oh, a comparison shopper eh? Very smart, kid. I like your style.

BOB: (Coughing) Uh ... thanks. Where do you think we should start?

HINDENBURG: Well ... (thinking; suddenly, he grabs Bob's shoulder, startling him). Come with me! We've got the very latest in *communications!* State-of-the-art stuff, you know what I mean? Josephine, would you send that letter I gave you to the Home Office now?

JOSEPHINE: Sure, Mr. H.

HINDENBURG: (to Bob): Our company uses *only* the fastest birds.

BOB: Oh. Where's your Home Office?

HINDENBURG: Ottawa.

BOB: How long will it be before you get an answer?

HINDENBURG: Well, usually about two months, but this is the mating season. Might take a little longer.

WIPE TO:

DAVIS: You know, Bob, *we* try to

VIDEO

Josephine takes letter on her desk, folds it into tiny square, opens bottom drawer of desk, removes carrier pigeon, attaches letter to leg, and throws bird out window.

Clerical area, JH. Bob & Davis talking. Davis holds folder.

AUDIO	VIDEO
organize our office to accomplish two things: to help our agents sell insurance, and to give our clients the quickest, most courteous service possible. Believe me, HANTEL has really made that easy. The basic things are much simpler — like getting in touch with our Home Office. Before, it was either wait for the mail to go to Boston and back, or try to get through by phone. *Now* — well, watch this ...	
(TO HANTEL OPERATOR) Kathy, will you send this message? (Takes paper from folder, gives to her.)	2S: Davis and operator
	Operator sends message: (CU, HANTEL CRT:)
	"TO: MARKETING/EDUCATION: PLEASE SEND FIVE COPIES OF CLU material 'Getting Started' and 'Action Information.' Needed by the 24th. Please confirm."
(V/O): In a sense, HANTEL is really like having our own private telegram system, but it costs much less. We can even communicate with any other Hancock office across the country. (Pause). That's it! They've heard me in Boston!	
It's a funny thing — I guess old habits are hard to shake. I still like to have a hard copy of my messages. Kathy, would you mind?	DAVIS & BOB.
	Operator has printer deliver printed copy of message.
If things go as usual, I'll have a response to this late today or first thing tomorrow.	Davis rips it off.
BOB: Hey, that's really something!	

[The end of the program describes the actual working of HANTEL as it relates to specific insurance operations and procedures.]

"The Hantel Advantage" written by Frank King, Director, John Hancock Video Network, John Hancock Companies

Writer-director-producer Ralph J. De Jong concentrates on the information and education program; his principal awards have been for industry and government productions. De Jong stated:

Industrial films offer the writer an opportunity to bring into play any one or a combination of several conventional storytelling approaches and techniques. But unlike the typical entertainment film, the industrial film demands that the writer be acutely aware of the relationships between people, procedures, processes, equipment and institutional philosophies and goals.

Most industrial films are relatively short, running anywhere between 10 and 30 minutes, with an average running time of 15 minutes. Since industrial films are proprietary, the scriptwriter needs to determine a client's objectives and purpose of the film and then conduct sufficient research on the subject so that the final product will convey its message succinctly and with authority, credibility and integrity.

In addition to running-time constraints, most industrial films have tight budgets and protracted deadlines. Since the scriptwriter is very often the first person to be involved with a film project, it is essential that he or she have a thorough understanding of production techniques in the three basic audiovisual formats: film, video and slide-sound. Armed with this knowledge the scriptwriter can utilize various aspects of these formats to create a production that can be completed within budget and on time while meeting its objectives in an interesting, informative and entertaining way. Where the typical entertainment film is geared for a general audience, most industrial films are designed for a specific viewership. To ensure that the film meets its objectives the scriptwriter must identify the target audience and develop a profile of its interests and familiarity with the subject matter so that the film will satisfy both the needs of the audience and the client.

The following excerpts from one of De Jong's industrial film scripts illustrates how some of the concepts he discusses have been integrated. This twenty-eight minute videotape was designed to inform and instruct cardiovascular radiologists on the uses of a medical device while at the same time serving as a promotional vehicle for the product. Note that although the production was video, it combines techniques associated with film and with slide-plus-sound.

———————————————————O———————————————————

● *What principal differences in form and technique do you find between this script and the John Hancock script?*

● *"An idea I had," De Jong states, "was to include a 3-minute segment that could be lifted in toto and put into a continuous loop for screening in a convention display booth." Do you find this loop complete in itself? Does it maintain the continuity of the larger script?*

———————————————————O———————————————————

THE MINI-BALLOON APPROACH TO INTRAVASCULAR OCCLUSION

VISUAL	AUDIO
TEASE	
Angiography–Catheter Lab area: Johns Hopkins Hospital, Baltimore.	

VISUAL	AUDIO
	(SFX: AMBIENT SOUNDS/VOICES.)

VISUAL

LS: Personnel coming and going through double entry doors. A patient or two being wheeled in/out of lab area. Elevator to right in middle distance.

Elevator doors open and several passengers emerge. Among them are a man and a woman.
(Man is patient coming in for a varicocele procedure using the B-D MINI-BALLOON.)

Man and woman take a few steps and encounter Robert White, MD, who has entered scene walking from behind camera-left. White is dressed in surgical gown, mask loose around neck. He is on his way to cat lab.

Patient and woman walk off-camera. White heads for cat lab.

Camera follows as White passes through entry doors. White full frame.

White joins several other MD's who are examining radiographs depicting a pulmonary arteriovenous fistual-malformation or other condition suitable for MINI-BALLOON occlusion.

Close in slowly on MD group.

AUDIO
(SFX: AMBIENT SOUNDS/VOICES.)

(SFX: WHITE, PATIENT, WOMAN EXCHANGE A FEW WORDS OF GREETING. WHITE ASKS PATIENT HOW HE FEELS, ETC. WHITE TELLS PATIENT HE WILL SEE HIM SHORTLY.)

(SFX: CONVERSATION AMONG MD's IS HEARD MOMENTARILY AS THEY DISCUSS MEDICAL PROBLEM SEEN, THEN FADES UNDER AS NARRATOR SPEAKS.)

NARRATOR V/O
These radiologists are discussing a nonsurgical technique for occluding blood vessels — a technique that can be performed with local anesthesia — and, generally, with less patient risk than that associated with the injection of particulate embolic material.

VISUAL	AUDIO
Continue moving in, focusing on pulmonary AVM radiograph displayed on light box.	
	The procedure about to be performed on this patient is also suitable as the therapy of choice for other vascular conditions that may exist in various parts of the body ...
Begin series of cuts of diagnostic radiographs, matched to narrative.	
Carotid cavernous fistula.	... carotid cavernous fistula ...
Bronchial pulmonary artery fistula.	... bronchial pulmonary artery fistula ...
Hemobilia.	... hemobilia ...
Renal traumatic aneurysm.	... renal traumatic aneurysm ...
Varicocele.	... varicocele ...
Show two or three other conditions suitable for MINI-BALLOON occlusion; i.e., vascular head and neck neoplasm/ hepatic artery branch/ traumatic fistual or aneurysms of non-essential branch/ or dry field surgery. Shots should be tight enough and on long enough for relatively experienced eye to identify problem.	... and others ... (NO COMMENTARY)
Final diagnostic radiograph serves as freeze-frame which becomes live-action cine of MINI-BALLOON procedure in progress: dye being injected and balloon catheter coming on-screen — for positioning. [LOOP SECTION BEGINS]	(SFX: FADE IN MUSIC LOW, THEN UNDER.) NARRATOR V/O This is balloon embolotherapy — a proven technique for transcatheter vascular occlusion. The procedure seen here centers on the use of a detachable balloon system — a system that provides control, reversibility and precise placement at the desired point of occlusion.
Cine continues: MINI-BALLOON seen being reversed, positioned, inflated and detached as Main Title crawls.	

VISUAL	AUDIO

MAIN TITLE

THE MINI-BALLOON
APPROACH TO
INTRAVASCULAR
OCCLUSION

Presented by
BECTON-DICKINSON AND COMPANY

Cine continues briefly after titles, then go
to brief lap dissolve of slightly elevated,
moderate wide-angle pull-back revealing
preceding cine on portable viewer screen:
angled OTS of radiologist's POV. (RADIOL-
OGY LIBRARY) Radiologist seen at portable
viewer, looking at screen.

(SFX: CROSSFADE TO RADIOLOGY LIBRARY
AMBIENCE.)

Continue pull-back to reveal radiologist and
narrator in library.

During pull-back, narrator, with medical
journal in hand, walks from bookstacks to
portable viewer, glances at screen, then
speaks on-camera. (Narrator dressed in
casual attire: somewhat tweedy jacket, tie,
etc.)

NARRATOR (ON-CAMERA)
Until the 1930's, surgical ligation was the
only technique available for occluding a
specific blood vessel.

MS.

Then, in that year, a minute particle of
muscle tissue was implanted percu-
taneously to embolize a carotid cavernous
fistula.

MCU.

While the procedure was successful, it was
not until the early 1960's that advances in
medical technology made it possible for
intravascular occlusion techniques to be explored and developed more extensively.

Camera follows as narrator walks to library
table.

Since then different types of particulate
material and mechanical devices have
been injected — by way of a catheter — to
promote vascular occlusion.

VISUAL	AUDIO
Cut to CU L-R pan: assorted embolic/occlusion materials and devices, ending with B-D MINI-BALLOON system.	(NO COMMENTARY THROUGH PAN.)
Cut to table-top MS: Narrator in background, half-seated at end of library table top. Embolic/occluding devices in foreground. MINI-BALLOON system closest to narrator. Narrator gestures toward materials while speaking.	Today, each of these is used for intravascular occlusion. When they are used and how they are used depends on the medical problem involved, the condition of the patient, and the skill and experience of the physician.
Move slowly over devices toward narrator, stopping as narrator picks up MINI-BALLOON catheter.	Of these, only one provides permanent vessel occlusion where you want it — when you want it.
Cut to OTS: MINI-BALLOON catheter in narrator's hands.	NARRATOR (ON-CAMERA) This is the Becton-Dickinson detachable MINI-BALLOON system.
Slow zoom toward MINI-BALLOON, going to out-of-focus and dissolving to:	When the MINI-BALLOON is injected into a vessel by way of a catheter ... it becomes flow-directed.
ANIMATION: Flow-direction feature of MINI-BALLOON.	(SFX: FADE OUT LIBRARY AMBIENCE TO DEAD AIR.)
ANIMATION: Positioning of MINI-BALLOON in vessel.	And, because it is tethered, the MINI-BALLOON is completely controllable — it can be guided forward or backward so that it can be placed precisely at the desired point of occlusion.
ANIMATION: MINI-BALLOON inflation and detachment.	Once in position, the MINI-BALLOON is inflated ... and detached.
ANIMATION: hold momentarily on detached balloon in vessel.	
[LOOP SECTION ENDS]	
Dissolve to MLS: cat lab corridor.	(SFX: FADE IN CAT LAB AREA AMBIENCE.)
Move in to MS, then to MCU of White and two other physicians seen at left studying radiographs of varicocele.	WHITE AND COLLEAGUES (PICK UP BRIEFLY ON CONVERSATION AMONG WHITE AND COLLEAGUES DIS-

VISUAL	AUDIO
	CUSSING VARICOCELE CONDITION SEEN ON RADIOGRAPH. COMMENTS CENTERING ON PROBLEM AND WHAT NEEDS TO BE DONE.)

* * *

VISUAL	AUDIO
XCU: Syringe in hand, smooth injection.	WHITE Once you have blood back and a good seal, then we simply give a nice smooth injection . . . until the balloon catheter is well beyond where you want to send it.
Dissolve to cine: balloon injection. NOTE: From here, visuals are combo of live action and cine. Included are: balloon positioning, flow-directability, reversibility, inflation, deflation to reposition, reinflation and final positioning, detachment and catheter removal. During this sequence, use modified split-screen with circular cine inserted with live action.	(PAUSE)
	(NOTE: WHITE'S COMMENTS FROM HERE TO INCLUDE BALLON MANIPULATION, FLOW DIRECTION, REVERSIBILITY, INFLATION, DEFLATION TO REPOSITION, REINFLATION AND FINAL POSITIONING, BALLOON DETACHMENT AND CATHETER REMOVAL. ALSO INCLUDE TEST INJECTION TO SEE BRIDGING COLLATERALS.)
Final cat lab sequence: circular cine inserted with live action. Cine shows balloon in position. Slowly expand cine insert to full-screen, then slowly dissolve to CU of White removing catheter and begin lazy pull-back to MLS of procedure wrap-up. White, tech(s) and patient; then patient being wheeled out of lab. White and tech(s) having conversation, relaxed.	WHITE (AFTER FINAL COMMENTS REGARDING PROCEDURE, TALKS BRIEFLY CITING PERSONAL EXPERIENCE WITH MINI-BALLOON PROCEDURE (STRAIGHT, NO HARD SELL) AND THE TECHNIQUE, GIVING SUGGESTION ON APPROPRIATE MEDICAL CONDITIONS TO BEGIN WITH AND SOME TO WORK UP TO, THEN SHIFTS TO BRIEF CHAT WITH PATIENT, WITH PATIENT RESPONDING.)

VISUAL	AUDIO
	(CONVERSATION WITH TECH(S) UP MOMENTARILY, THEN SLOWLY CROSS-FADING TO MUSIC LOW AND UNDER, COMING IN WITH RADIOGRAPH REPRISE.)
MLS: White and tech(s) talking, patient being wheeled out of cat lab.	NARRATOR V/O MINI-BALLOON embolotherapy — a non-surgical approach to intravascular occlusion.
Insert dissolve cuts: reprise of opening diagnostic radiographs.	A proven technique suitable as the therapy of choice for a wide range of vascular conditions ...
Dissolve in complete ANIMATION sequence.	... a procedure that centers on the use of a detachable balloon system — a system that provides control ... reversibility ... and precise placement at the desired point of occlusion.
Dissolve to full-screen cine: reprise of footage appearing behind Main Title as end credits crawl.	(SFX: MUSIC UP THEN FADE OUT.)

Courtesy of Ralph J. De Jong, President, WORDSYNC, Silver Spring, Md.

Professional Updating Programs

In providing an example of instruction and information programs in the various professions, Dr. Sandra W. Bennett, associate director of the Ohio Nurses Association and former writer-producer for the Ohio Medical Television Network, stressed the need for writers of health education programs to work very closely with the health professionals. Her comments are applicable to virtually all professional areas:

> Most health professionals involved with television production require the assistance of a television writer. Depending on the format and objectives, the health professional may be supplying the largest percentage of the content for the production. That health professional must be made to understand and appreciate the limitations as well as the boundless opportunities television offers.
>
> That's where television writers combine their skills with health professionals. All the principles of television writing still apply. Good television writing should not be compromised. (The pressure to abandon what you know to be good writing, however, may be great, especially if you are working with people inexperienced in television.)

Writing for health education requires a few other basic principles:

(1) Give yourself twice as much lead time. Too many health professionals are not at all concerned with your time or television's deadlines. Even those who are knowledgeable about TV have patients whose health care needs take priority over your time schedule. Allow for it.

(2) Identify your intended audience and the specific objectives at the outset. Television writing for closed-circuit or VTR distribution is different from open-channel commercial broadcasting.

(3) References to patients need to be carefully screened for public viewing. While this may seem obvious, TV writers must double check to be sure that the information they've been given has protected the privacy of the health care consumer.

Health and medical programs on radio and television range from presentations to lay persons on elementary home sanitary measures to highly detailed surgical procedures such as — to note the title of one program of this type presented by the Ohio Medical Network — "Emergency Closed Tube Thoracostomy." Critical in writing the professionally oriented program are the technical level and content, clearly requiring for the writer who is not a professional in the given field the research, advice, and editing of people in that field. As pointed out by Bennett, the intended audience and whether the program is for closed-circuit distribution or for public viewing or hearing also affect what can be presented.

A script example is the beginning of "The Breast Fed Child," written for broadcast over local commercial stations to the general public as well as for viewing by physicians in hospital centers over a special network.

THE BREAST FED CHILD

VIDEO	AUDIO
	(ANNOUNCER) :30
SUPERS over film — (CCME logo) (College of Medicine logo) (Title) (Doctor credits)	The Ohio State University Center for Continuing Medical Education and The College of Medicine presents "The Breast Fed Child" with Dr. Willard B. Fernald, Pediatrician; Dr. James C. Good, General Practitioner, specializing in Obstetrics; and Dr. J. Douglas Veach, Obstetrician and Gynecologist.
STUDIO — Dr. Good	Whatever the reasons that the Womanly Art of Breast-feeding has been relegated to a lesser position in the field of infant nutrition during the past few generations, the consensus seems to be that breast-feeding *is* the best for baby and for mother during

VIDEO	AUDIO
	the baby's early life. As physicians, we are frequently consulted by mothers concerning feeding problems of the newborn and the young infant.
Dissolve to CAM on bottles	Many physicians feel more at ease with bottle formulas and recommending how to change various ingredients and foods to bring about the desired effect in the child. This trend toward the "bottle" has been fostered by the commercial development and advertising of various formulas which are said to be "nearly like mother's own."
Dissolve to FILM rolling	At the same time, medical education has done little to instruct the student or the practitioner on the physiology of lactation or the advantages of breast-feeding over other methods. However, in recent years there seems to be a definite trend back toward "nature's way" of nursing babies. It now becomes necessary for the interested physician to fill in the gaps in his education and to lend support and encouragement to these very sincere mothers trying to nurse their infants in a sometimes hostile world.
STUDIO — Dr. Good	This program is intended to present a view of breast-feeding from the baby's standpoint, with emphasis on some of the advantages, some points about technique and what to do with a few of the problems encountered.
STUDIO — Open — Dr. Veach	For the most part successful breast-feeding rests upon the motivation of each individual mother, since almost any woman has the physiological abilities to produce enough milk for 3 or more babies, if necessary.
Dissolve to VTR (simulated office visit)	During even the first office visit while taking the medical history, there is a natural opening to discuss, among other important things, reasons for support of breast-feeding. During subsequent pre-

VIDEO	AUDIO
	natal visits, after having as much information as possible, she must choose the feeding method for her needs. The infant's needs remain the same. When she chooses breast-feeding, at about 7½ months, she needs instruction on the techniques of nipple preparation because the usually protected and often immature nipple needs toughening to withstand the demands of nursing. This is a demonstration of a simple maneuver which accomplishes this when done once or twice daily.
	As you can see, these motions of stripping between finger and thumb anticipate the action of the baby's nursing as pictured here.
Dissolve to CAM CARD #1	(Pause) The nipple and areola are surrounded.
CAM CARD #2	(Pause) The tongue slides forward and grips them.
CAM CARD #3	(Pause) The nipple is pulled against the hard palate by backward action of the tongue and suction of the tongue and
CAM CARD #4	cheeks. Here, the gums press on the areola pushing milk against the roof of the palate. Milk flow continues because of the higher pressure and activities of the milk ducts themselves.
CAM CARD #5	This last diagram shows the problems associated with bottle feeding. The rubber nipple holds the lips open and causes gagging because it touches the soft palate and interferes with tongue action.
	In order to try to control the gush of overflowing formula, the baby's tongue pushes against the gums. The cheek muscles are not used and remain relaxed. Therefore, if this baby is offered the breast it becomes confused.
Dissolve back to VTR or STUDIO (Dr. Veach)	In most hospital situations this struggle starts within 12 hours, even for those

VIDEO	AUDIO
	babies whose mothers desire to nurse. Human babies are the only infants who are given supplementary water in the belief that they should not have the normal 10% weight loss.

*　*　*

Produced by the Center for Continuing Medical Education, Ohio State University College of Medicine

Public Information Programs

Sid L. Schwartz, as motion picture and audiovisual officer for the Department of Energy, likened the government public information message to the PSAs discussed in Chapter 2:

> The writer's primary task is to find the kernel of the message so that when produced as a PSA it can be compressed to fit a very brief period of time and still make a point in the show-biz presentation that will make more than a mere statement. That is why the successful PSA script must be producible as an entertaining, interesting, startling or beautiful moment for the radio ear or the television eye and ear — otherwise the effort will be a failure.
>
> Writing a PSA is like designing a billboard and reducing it to seconds of sound or seconds of sight and sound. Catching an audience's attention, holding their interest and imparting a message in 30 seconds is like a billboard that succeeds in imparting a message to traffic passing at 55 miles per hour.

Schwartz noted that one popular type of PSA mainly urges the audience to write for more detail. Here are radio and television examples of this type:

ENERGY I
TV Public Service Announcement
30 Seconds

VIDEO	AUDIO
1. CU hand with quill pen, period coat and cuffs, signs Declaration of Independence.	(FX: Room noise ... crowd murmurs, etc.)
	ANNOUNCER: PHILADELPHIA ... JULY 4TH ... 1776! A REVOLUTION TAKES PLACE THAT CHANGES THE COURSE OF THE WORLD.
2. Dissolve to traffic montage.	(FX: Traffic noise)

VIDEO	AUDIO
	TODAY, 200 YEARS LATER, ANOTHER REVOLUTION ... THIS ONE CONCERNING ENERGY.
3. Dissolve to scientist in lab with test equipment.	(FX: Fade traffic)
	THE NEW BATTLEFIELD IS THE LABORATORY ... THE PRIMARY WEAPON, THE HUMAN MIND! WE'RE WORKING HARD TO DEVELOP NEW ENERGY SOURCES.
4. Dissolve to logo: WASHINGTON, D.C. 20545	TO LEARN HOW, WRITE: DEPARTMENT OF ENERGY WASHINGTON, D.C. 20545.

Written by Jack Moser, Department of Energy

ENERGY II
Radio Public Service Announcement
30 Seconds

(FX: Sound of jet taking off ... cross-fade to traffic montage ... cross-fade to train with diesel horn ... all under after establishing)

ANNOUNCER: ENERGY ... THERE'S ALWAYS A NEED FOR JUST A LITTLE BIT MORE. UNFORTUNATELY THE SUPPLY IS LIMITED ... IT WON'T LAST FOREVER ... AND THE SOLUTIONS ARE A LONG WAY DOWN THE ROAD.

(FX: Cross-fade to clock ticking)

WE'RE WORKING HARD TO MAKE SURE CURRENT ENERGY SOURCES AREN'T EXHAUSTED BEFORE NEW TECHNOLOGY IS READY TO TAKE OVER. TO LEARN HOW, WRITE: DEPARTMENT OF ENERGY, WASHINGTON, D.C. 20545.

Written by Jack Moser, Department of Energy

Although common in practice, Schwartz said, this type of ''write-in'' PSA is not a preferred one:

> More popular and effective are those PSAs that carry the burden of the entire message in their brief exposure. For example, the U.S. Forest Service campaign where Smokey Bear says: ''Matches don't start forest fires — people do. Next time think before you strike.''
> Once the kernel of the message is attained or agreed to, the writer's job is to reduce the idea to words as in a slogan or to conceive it as a visual. Ideally it may be words and a word picture as in the cases of two competitive airlines advertising slogans: ''the wings of man'' and ''navigators

of the world since it was flat.'' These appeared and were heard during the same broadcast season.

PSA script writing should relate to the client's current campaign or herald the next one. The script should develop empathy and involvement by signalling the audience to use its memory, understanding, ambitions and fantasies. The writing of TV PSAs, for government or nongovernment information purposes, generally follows a written concept, a treatment, a shooting script and, in many cases, a story board. The radio PSA follows the same steps except that the radio story board, rather than a series of thumbnail visual sketches, is a ''scratch'' track with the voices, sound effects and music mixed in a rough presentation.

The government public information or public relations program, therefore, is not different in execution than that for the private sector — except, as described by Eileen McClay earlier in this chapter, it is subject to different kinds of constrictions and administrative requirements. As Sid Schwartz said, ''We turn it out to fit the form of the particular program type — the same as any other writer and producer.''

_____ **For Application and Review**_____

1. Go to your local public television station, ITFS system, or closed circuit television operation (this is easy if you are reading this book as part of a course and are within an educational institution using instructional television in some form) and volunteer to work as a writer with one of the ITV series. If this is not possible, obtain a lesson plan for any subject or level (it could be for a television and radio writing course!) and prepare a script for one television program that will be of special value to the students in that course.

2. Do the same for radio, with a public radio station, a campus carrier-current station, or for a course.

3. Obtain a memorandum relating to some internal problem or process at the place where you work or study and prepare a television and/or radio script from it, similar to the example in the section on government training scripts in this chapter.

4. Choose a business or industry or organization in your immediate area that is large enough to benefit from a media training program. Discuss with its training, sales, or human resources executive some of its current needs and prepare a half-hour video script designed to solve a specific problem.

10

Drama

Brander Matthews, who was one of the theater's leading critics, wrote in his book *The Development of the Drama* that "dramaturgic principles are not mere rules laid down by theoretical critics, who have rarely any acquaintance with the actual theater; they are laws, inherent in the nature of the art itself, standing eternal, as immitigable today as when Sophocles was alive, or Shakespeare, or Molière."

The rules of playwriting are universal. They apply generally to the structure of the play written for the stage, film, television, or radio. The rules are modified in their specific applications by the special requirements of the particular medium.

Don't assume, merely because there are rules, that playwriting can be taught. Genius and inspiration cannot be taught, and playwriting is an art on a plane of creativity far above the mechanical facets of some of the phases of continuity writing. America's first and foremost playwriting teacher, George Pierce Baker, stated that what can be done, however, is to show the potential playwright how to apply whatever genius and dramatic insight he or she may have, through an understanding of the basic rules of dramaturgy. That is all that can be done and that is all that will be attempted here.

Yet, even this much cannot be taught in one chapter or in several chapters. Any full discussion of playwriting technique requires at least a complete book, a number of courses, and endless practice. What will be presented here is a summary of the rules of playwriting and some new concepts of playwriting in terms of the special needs of the television and radio media. If you seriously wish to write television (and radio) drama, first explore as thoroughly as possible the techniques of writing the play for the stage. Only then will you have a sound basis for the television play.

Remember that a play is a play is a play. Do not confuse the means of transmission with the medium. Whether presented over the airwaves (television broadcasting) or through cable or by satellite or via laser beams, the play is the same — a dramatic presentation reaching people seated in front of an oblong box with a small screen usually ranging from thirteen to twenty-five inches.

Therefore, when you see the term *television* used in this chapter, don't say "But I'm going to write for cable." It's the same thing. The differences in form and content are determined by the elements discussed in Chapters 1 and 2.

The principal differences in technique are between the continuous-action taped television play and the filmed-for-television play. And even here differences have become more and more blurred as the styles developed separately in New York (the live television drama) and in Hollywood (the treatment of the television screen as a miniature extension of the traditional film screen) have gradually come together to utilize the most effective approaches of both.

Sources

Before the actual techniques of writing can be applied, the writer must be able to recognize and exploit the sources out of which the ideas for the play can be developed.

The writer may find the motivating ingredient for the play in an event or happening, in a theme, in a character or characters, or in a background.

Many times a playwright has witnessed or experienced an incident or series of incidents that contain the fundamentals for good drama. From this event or happening the playwright can build character, situation, theme, and background. Remember, however, that what is exciting in life is not necessarily good drama. Drama is heightened life. It is a compression of the most important elements of a situation and requires a rearrangement, revision, and condensation of life to make it drama and not merely human interest reporting. It is difficult for the beginning playwright to understand this, particularly when he or she has been a participant in or an observer of an interesting life situation. What may seem to be the most tragic, most humorous, most exciting thing that has ever happened to the writer may actually be hackneyed, dull, and undramatic in play form. Because something seems dramatic in real life does not mean that it will be dramatic if put into a play. Such transposition requires imagination, skill, and, to no small degree, the indefinable genius of playwriting. For example, many of us have seen a situation where a destitute maiden aunt has come to live with a sister and brother-in-law, and in her psychological need has become somewhat of a disturbing factor in the marriage. To the participants, or even to a close observer, such a situation might have provocative and electrifying undertones. To someone not connected with the situation, it appears, and understandably so, dull and uninspiring. To the imaginative playwright, in this case to Tennessee Williams, it could become *A Streetcar Named Desire*.

The writer may initiate the preliminary thinking about the play from a theme or an idea. Although censorship often hampers the television and radio playwright, the writer can find basic concepts such as loyalty, independence, and self-realization as motivating factors upon which to develop a drama. The theme must be translated into specific and full-blown people and concrete situations. Under the theme of loyalty, for example, there is the ever-present son who won't marry because his psychologically motivated notion of loyalty is one that says that he cannot leave his mother. Under independence, there are any number of variations of the wife who leaves her husband because she is not accorded the freedom or respect she feels she needs. Under self-realization, there is an endless supply of potential plays oriented around the artist who prefers living on bread and beans in a cold-water flat to accepting the lucrative advertising agency job. The writer must be wary of attempting to develop a play around a theme alone. As can be seen from the examples above, the results can be uninteresting and trite. The theme serves merely as the germ of the idea for the play.

Another source for the play may lie in a background. The backgrounds of war, of high society, of a ghetto environment, of the business world, have provided the settings and motivations for many plays. The college student could do worse than to use the background of the campus environment as an initiating factor for the play.

A final source for the play may come from a character or several characters, either as a group or rolled into one. In modern dramaturgy, character motivates action; that is, the plot develops out of the characters. For this reason, the choice of character as a source provides a potentially stronger foundation for the play than do the other sources. The writer must be cautious, however, in using this source independently of the others; it is difficult to build a play solely around a character or combination of characters taken from real life. For example, how trite is the idea of a salesman getting fired from a job because he is getting old and cannot make as many sales as he once did! Even if his character is enlarged by adding pride, self-deception, and despondency leading to suicide, the dramatic potential is not yet fully realized. But work on the character, develop his many facets, beliefs, psychological needs, physical capabilities, and relationships to other people, clarify a theme and background, and one might eventually get to Willy Loman of Arthur Miller's *Death of a Salesman*.

The sources of the play — situation, theme, background, and character — individually are only germs of ideas. To be valuable to the initial development of the play, each of these factors must be explored, expanded, revised, then developed in relationship to the other sources, and finally re-examined in its complete form to determine if the idea has any dramatic value at all. If it has, then the playwright is ready for the next step. Too many beginning writers think that once the source, the motivating factor, is clarified, the play can be written. Inexperienced writers — and lazy writers — sometimes believe that all they have to do is to have a pretty good idea of where they are going, and then to sit down and write the play. Unfortunately, this is not the case. The actual writing of the play is the dessert of the playwright's art. The hard work is devoted to the planning of the play and, later, to the revisions of the manuscript. After deciding on the theme, situation, character, or background as a base for the play, clarify in your mind and on paper the various elements that develop from the base. For instance, if you choose to work from a background, determine the characters, the situation, and the theme to go with that background.

The writer should, ideally, write out of personal experiences or knowledge so that the play may have a valid foundation. However, if the writer is too close, either emotionally or in terms of time, to the life-ingredients of the play, it will be difficult to heighten and condense and dramatize — the writer will tend to be a reporter rather than a dramatist. The playwright should never be part of the play, but should be able to write it objectively. Feel and understand every moment of it, but do so as a third person. Don't use the play as personal therapy. It is a good idea to be several calendar years and several emotional light years away from the play when you start to write it.

Structure

Until the eighteenth century, with the exception of works by only a few playwrights (notably Shakespeare), plot or action was the dominant element in the play. The plot line was the most important factor, and the characters and dialogue were fitted into the movement of the action. Modern drama has emphasized character as most important. The actions that determine the plot are those the characters *must* take because of their particular personalities and psychological motivations. The dialogue is that which the characters *must* speak for the same reasons. The three major elements in the play structure — character, plot, and dialogue — all must be coordinated into a consistent and clear theme. This coordination of all elements toward a common end results in the unity of the piece, a unity of impression. The characters' actions and the events are not arbitrary, and the audience must be prepared for the occurrence of these actions and events in a logical and valid manner. *Preparation* is the term given to the material that thus prepares the audience. The background and situation also must be presented; this is the *exposition*. Another element the playwright must consider is the *setting*, which the playwright describes in order to create a valid physical background and environment for the characters.

After you are certain that you understand and can be objective about the characters, theme, situation, and background, you can begin to create each of them in depth. Do as much research as necessary — or, perhaps, as much as possible — to acquaint yourself fully with the potentials of the play.

Each character should be psychoanalyzed. This should be done on paper, so that you have the characters' complete histories and motivations in front of you at all times. Develop a background for each character, not only for the duration of the action of the play, but extending back much before the opening of the play (even going back to ancestors who may not appear in the play but who would have had some influence on the character's personality). A complete analysis of the character also will provide an indication of the kind and form of dialogue the character should use. Test out the dialogue on paper, putting the character into hypothetical situations with other characters. It cannot be repeated too often that dialogue is not an approximation of real life speech; dialogue must be heightened and condensed from that of real life.

After the characters have been created, you are ready to create the situation, or plot line. This should be done in skeletonized form. You need, first, a conflict. The conflict is between the protagonist of the play and some other character or force. A conflict may be between two individuals, an individual and a group, between two groups, between an individual or individuals and nature, between an individual or individuals and some unknown force, or between an individual and the inner self. The nature of the conflict will be determined largely by the kinds of characters involved. After the conflict has been decided upon, the plot moves inexorably toward a climax, the point at which one of the forces in conflict wins over the other. The play reaches the climax through a series of complications. Each complication is, in itself, a small conflict and climax. Each succeeding complication complicates the situation to a greater and greater degree until the final complication makes it impossible for the struggle to be heightened any longer. Something has to give. The climax must occur. The complications are not arbitrary. The characters themselves determine the events and the complications because the actions they take are those, and only those, they must take because of their particular motivations and personalities.

George Pierce Baker wrote in *Dramatic Technique* that the "situation exists because one is what he is and so has inner conflict, or clashes, with another person, or with his environment. Change his character a little and the situation must change. Involve more people in it, and immediately their very presence, affecting the people originally in the scene, will change the situation."

British playwright Terrence Rattigan wrote similarly in a *Theatre Arts* article, "The Characters Make the Play":

> A play is born — for me, at any rate — in a character, in a background or setting, in a period or in a theme, never in a plot. I believe that in the process of a play's preliminary construction during that long and difficult period of gestation before a line is put on paper, the plot is the last of the vital organs to take shape.
>
> If the characters are correctly fashioned — by which I do not mean accurately representing living people but correctly conceived in their relationship to each other — the play will grow out of them. A number of firmly and definitely imagined characters will act — must act — in a firm and definite way. This gives you your plot. If it does not, your characters are wrongly conceived and you must start again.

Once the preliminary planning, gestation, research, and analysis are completed, the writer is ready. But not for writing the play. Not yet. Next comes the scenario or detailed outline. The writer who has been conscientious up to now will learn from the scenario whether or not he or she has a potentially good play, if any play at all. Through careful construction and analysis of the scenario, the writer may eliminate the bad points and strengthen the good points of the play before it is written.

Before writing a detailed scenario, however, the writer must have a knowledge of the concepts of dramaturgy — of the basic rules for the play regardless of whatever medium it is written for, and of the modified rules for the television and radio play, concepts determined by the special characteristics of these media.

Concepts of Playwriting

Unity

One of the essentials that applies to all plays, regardless of type or style of production, is the unity of action or impression. There should be no elements within the play that do not relate in thorough and consistent fashion to all the other elements, all moving toward a realization of the purpose of the playwright. Not a single extraneous element should detract from the unified totality of impression received by the audience. The so-called unities of time and of place are completely flexible in modern dramaturgy.

Plot

The plot structure of a play is based on a complication arising out of the individual's or group's relationship to some other force. This is the conflict, the point when the two or more forces come into opposition. The conflict must be presented as soon as possible in the play, for the rest of the play structure follows and is built upon this element. Next come a series of complications or crises, each one creating further difficulty in relation to the major conflict, and each building in a rising crescendo so that the entire play moves toward a final crisis or climax. The climax occurs at the instant the conflicting forces meet head on and a change occurs to or in at least one of them. This is the turning point. One force wins and the other loses. The play may end at this moment. There may, however, be a final clarification of what happens, as a result of the climax, to the characters or forces involved. This remaining plot structure is called the *resolution*.

The elementary plot structure of the play may be diagrammed as follows:

Character

Character, plot, and dialogue are the three primary ingredients of the play. All must be completely and consistently integrated. In modern dramaturgical theory character is the prime mover of the action, and determines plot and dialogue. The character does not conform to a plot structure. The qualities of the character determine the action. The character must be revealed through the action, that is, through what the character does and says, and not through arbitrary description or exposition. Character is delineated most effectively by what the individual does at moments of crisis. This does not imply physical action alone, but includes the concept of inner or psychological action. The character must be consistent throughout the play in everything done and said, and must be plausible in terms of life and reality. This does not mean that characters are copies of real life persons; they must be dramatically heightened interpretations of reality.

Dialogue

There is some difference of opinion as to whether dialogue should be realistic or poetic. In either case, however, it must be "dramatic." Inasmuch as the play does not duplicate real people or the exact action of real life but heightens and condenses these elements, the dialogue also has to be heightened and condensed rather than duplicated. The dialogue must truly conform to the personality of the character speaking it, it must be completely consistent with the character and with itself throughout the play, and it must forward the situation, the showing of the character, and the movement of the plot.

Exposition

Exposition, the revelation of the background of the characters and situation and the clarification of the present circumstances, must not be obvious or come through some device such as the telephone conversation, the servant, or the next-door neighbor. It must come out as the action carries the play forward and must be a natural part of the action. The exposition should be presented as early as possible in the play.

Preparation

Preparation, too, must be made subtly. Preparation, or foreshadowing, is the unobtrusive planting, through action or dialogue, of material that prepares the audience for subsequent events, making their occurrence logical and not arbitrary. Proper preparation validates subsequent actions of the characters; it is presented throughout the play.

Setting

Setting is determined by the form of the play and the physical and mechanical needs of the play structure. Setting serves as locale, background, and environment for the characters of the play; it is a psychological and aesthetic presentation of the purpose of the play and of the author.

This summary of the basic rules of dramaturgy is applicable to the writing of any play; it should serve as an introduction to the special techniques of writing the television and radio play.

The Radio Play

Although plays have almost completely disappeared from radio, the occasional broadcast drama and the use of drama as a training ground for student writers warrants an overview of writing the radio play. The writer of the radio play should interrelate the basic rules of dramaturgy with the special characteristics of the radio medium. First, review the basic elements and technical aspects of radio in Chapters 1 and 2.

Radio rightly has been called the "theater of the imagination." There are no limitations except those of the human mind. The radio playwright has no restrictions on place, setting, number of characters, kinds of actions, or movement of time. In radio, the writer can take the audience anywhere and make the characters do anything. The writer can create mental images of infinite variations, as long as these images are within the realm of the imagination of the listeners. The special characteristics of the radio medium, as indicated in Chapters 1 and 2, result in the following modifications of the basic rules of dramaturgy in writing the radio play.

Unity

There are no unities of time and place in radio. The radio script may take us 20,000 years into the future and in the twinkling of a sound effect transport us to an age 20,000 years in the past. Radio may present a character in a living room and in a split second place the same character (and place us, the audience, who are in the position and place of the characters who are on mike) in his or her office in another part of town. Radio may move us from a polar ice cap to the moon to a battlefield to a jungle to the depths of Hades, creating without restriction the settings for our imaginations. Radio has no visual limitations. In writing for radio, don't restrict your own imagination by what you can "see." Radio has no physical space limitations. It can present a rally at the Washington Monument with a million people and, within seconds, a dozen similar rallies throughout the world with as many more millions.

Don't forget, however, that no matter how loose the unities of time and place, the radio play must have a unity of action; that is, it must have a consistency and wholeness of purpose and development within the script. Each sequence must be integrated thoroughly with every other sequence, all contributing to the total goal or effect you wish to create.

Plot

The plot structure of the radio play is essentially the same as that for the stage play. Exposition, a conflict, complications, a climax, and, if necessary, a resolution must be set forth clearly. The radio play must have a rising action that creates suspense and holds the interest of the audience. The limitation of time modifies some of the rules concerning these elements. Exposition may be revealed as the action is progressing, with the presentation of the conflict at the very opening of the drama. The limitation of time also makes it necessary for the writer to concentrate on only one simple plot line and to avoid subplots.

Character

The characters in the radio play must be as valid as those in the stage play, and the rules for their creation and development apply just as fully to radio as to theater. The time limitation of radio makes it impossible, however, to deal with the characters, even the most important onces, in depth. In much radio drama, therefore, character is not the motivating force; plot is. The writer should attempt to develop a concomitant effect of one upon the other. The characters must be consistent with themselves and appropriate with reality, although heightened from real life. It might be expected that the lack of visual perception in radio would change the revelation of a character from what he or she says and does solely to what is said. This is not so. Character is revealed through what the character does. The difference between radio and the stage and television is that, in radio, what characters do is not shown visually, but their actions are presented through sound and dialogue. Because too many voices may become confusing to a radio audience, the number of roles in the play should be limited. For the same reason, the writer should limit the number of characters in any one scene.

Dialogue

Dialogue in the radio play must be consistent with itself and with the characters; it must be appropriate with the situation and the characters; and it must be dramatically heightened. Even more than on the stage or in television, dialogue in radio serves to forward the situation, reveal character, and uncover the plot line. Everything on radio is conveyed through dialogue, sound effects, music, or silence. The use of sound and music is more important in radio than in other media. The use of dialogue similarly is more important. Dialogue must clearly indicate all of the action taking place. Dialogue must clearly introduce the characters; presented naturally, such dialogue not only must tell who the people are, but must describe them and, if possible, tell something about them. Dialogue often may be used to describe movement and places of action, but not in an obvious manner. For example, how trite for the character to say, ''Now, if you'll excuse me, I'll push back this chair I'm sitting on, and go. My coat is hanging on that clothes tree right inside the front door, isn't it? I can get it. It's only a few steps from here.'' Or: ''Now that we're in my sixth floor bachelor apartment with the etchings on the wall, the stereo speakers in the corners by the windows, the waterbed on the red plush carpet in the center of the room. . . .''

Exposition

Exposition is difficult in radio because it must be presented solely through dialogue and sound. Because of the short time for the play, exposition should be presented as soon as possible, but preferably through the action, not through description. Inasmuch as the audience can't see the characters or the settings, the writer must clarify these elements of the play before any important action takes place. To solve this problem, radio has employed a technique used much less frequently in the other media: the narrator. The narrator can either be divorced entirely from the play or can be an integral part of it.

Preparation

Preparation functions in the radio play in the same way as in the stage play. It must be valid and it must be made subtly. Because the radio writer cannot present the preparation visually, with all the subtle nuances of the visual element, you must be certain that just because you know what the character motivations are you do not fail to let the audience know. If anything, the radio play requires an overabundance of preparation rather than too little.

Setting

Radio offers the writer limitations and advantages in the matter of setting. One drawback is that the writer cannot present a visual setting that, at one glance, can provide an environment and atmosphere for the characters. You have to do it all through dialogue and sound. On the other hand, the radio writer is limited only by the imaginative potential of the audience; you can put the audience into almost any setting you wish. Be wary of using this facility too freely, however. Do not be tempted into creating an imaginary setting that is invalid. The mental picture you create for the audience must be the right one for the play. The locale and environment must be believable for the characters and the situation, and must forward the psychological and aesthetic purposes of the author.

Movement from setting to setting may be accomplished through silence, fading, narration, a music bridge, or sound effects.

As indicated in Chapter 1, one of the great advantages the radio playwright has over the stage playwright is that the former can control and direct the attention of the audience much more effectively than can the latter. The radio audience cannot select the elements of the play by which it is to be stimulated, but the theater audience can pick out any part of the action on the stage it desires. Radio facilitates a much greater subjective response, and the writer can deal with elements that strike close to the emotional needs and desires of the audience. These emotional stimuli can also be used to activate the intellectual concerns of the audience. If you use the medium correctly you can hold a tight grip on the feelings and minds of the listeners.

In creating the play for radio, keep several special technical considerations in mind. Don't skimp on sound effects or music; these elements are needed to clarify movement, setting, and action. While not overdoing it, be certain that you use sound effectively and sufficiently for the purposes of the play. Be certain that the script contains the proper devices for transitions of time and place and has enough music, fulfilling all the needs indicated in Chapter 2. The exits and entrances of characters should be made clear through sound. The sound effects and music should be integrated with the action of the play, and each of these effects should be indicated clearly in relation to the specific need of the script at the precise moment the effect is used.

The play should be of a proper length for the time period, and within the play the scenes should be neither so short as to lack clarity nor so long as to be repetitious and boring. Nor should individual speeches of characters be too long. In any play, character development should be revealed through action, though the soliloquy may be effective in certain kinds of plays. The plot, dialogue, and characters should, of course, follow effective dramaturgical form and relationships, and the exposition and preparation must be clear, sufficient, and not obvious.

The Television Play

Television's Special Characteristics
The television audience and some problems of censorship are analyzed in Chapter 1. Arbitrary censorship has hampered television's potentially high level of dramatic production, and the television playwright must deal with these restrictions.

The special characteristics of the television audience require a special approach on the part of the playwright. You may combine the subjective relationship of the viewer to the television screen with the electronic potentials of the medium to create a purposeful direction of the audience's attention. You may direct the audience toward the impact of the critical events in the character's life and toward the subjective manifestations of the character's existence. The ability to focus the viewer's sight, attention, and even feeling so specifically permits the writer to orient the consciousness of the audience closely to the inner character of the person on the screen.

All of the preceding should be in your conscious consideration at the very beginning of the creative process, when you are choosing the subject and planning the basic development of the play. In the so-called golden age of television the slice-of-life play dominated, quantitatively and qualitatively, because the play-wrights utilized to advantage, rather than fighting to their disadvantage, the small-screen, limited-time aspects of the medium. In more recent years, longer time periods and television filmed plays have expanded settings, plots, and characters, particularly in two- and three-hour specials and in multiepisode series. Yet, the good plays on television, whether one-shot or in series, do continue to reflect the new principles of playwriting that marked the early years of television drama in depth of character analyses and presentation. Even in continuing series — whether situation comedy, police, or adventure shows — the good programs stress character. In many of these, the approximately twenty-one-minute (for the half-hour show) and forty-two-minute (for the hour program) scripts reflect the same time restraints for any given happening in the continuing characters' lives as did the early half-hour television dramas. Time and space limitations, the censorship of controversial material, and the ability of the medium to control and direct the audience's objective and subjective attention still make the intimate, probing, searching slice-of-life play the logical candidate for television success.

The direct relationship of the television performer to the audience suggests a further kind of orientation: a presentational approach that is possible at the same time as the illusionistic, and that permits an exciting combination of intellectual and emotional stimulation for the audience.

Chapter 2 points out how the writer should develop the script in terms of television's technical potentials and incorporate these potentials into the action of the play. Perhaps the most important contribution of the mechanical and electronic devices of television is to enable the writer to direct the audience toward the intimate, toward an examination of the inner character in a manner not possible on the stage or in radio. The ability of television to capture significant details through the camera implies a greater concentration on the visual than on the verbal elements (the latter, of course, dominate the stage and radio play). Indeed, television's most effective means for capturing the intimacy of its presentation is the close-up, which permits physical action to substitute for what sometimes would have to be done through dialogue or sound on the stage or in radio.

The Hollywood-style taped or filmed television play permits a great expansion of action over the stage play and can include a greater number of transitions. Television is not bound by the conventions of the theater. Because of cuts, dissolves, fades, and other electronic devices there are no restrictions of time and place. Television does not need a curtain or blackout convention, but can signify a change of time or place with an effect lasting only a second or two. Other techniques, such as the split screen, the wipe, and the matte also permit excellent fluidity.

Time and space are two more special characteristics of the television medium that the writer must understand and apply. One of the most important problems of all for the television playwright is that of time. The hour drama is really only about forty-two minues long, the half-hour drama twenty-one minutes in length. Even the hour-and-one-half dramatic program permits only about sixty-three minutes for the play. The television play should be extremely tight; it should have no irrelevancies. It should have as few characters as possible and one main, simplified plot line, containing only material relating to the conflict of the major character or characters.

These limitations often result in characters who are stereotyped figures with little richness of human personality. The writer sometimes may concentrate on plot at the expense of character, or stress character without including any valid action. Neither approach makes for good playwriting.

Space limitations are of two major kinds in television. First is the physical size of the studio. Second is the decreasing smallness of the objects in a picture picked up by an increasing camera distance, and viewed over the narrow and constricting viewing area of the relatively small television screen.

The limitation of space suggests two major considerations for the writer: the number of characters on a screen at any one time, and the number and scope of sets. In order to avoid a situation where the small television screen is choked with a mass of humanity, the writer must be sure that only a few characters are on camera at the same time. Stage convention permits ten people to represent a crowd. Except in the filmed play, ten people on television (in sitcoms, for example) are likely to appear too jumbled.

The limited number of sets in a taped studio production and the limited size of a given set imply the need for short scenes, although the fluidity possible through television's electronic devices and through taping and editing permits frequent change from set to set and easy reuse of sets. Long scenes may require movement to avoid monotony, which may not be possible under some studio space restrictions.

The space and time limitations combine to indicate an effective approach for the television play: an intimate probing of a short span of the subjective life of the character. This approach is reflected in the following analysis of the special drama- turgical concepts for the television play. (The emergence of the miniseries — that is, the presentation of a drama in two or more parts, anywhere from two to twenty-six or more hours — has largely eliminated the time restriction.)

Dramaturgical Concepts for Television

Unity   The most important changes in the unities as applied to television relate to time and place. Television can transcend boundaries of time and place that even the most fluid stage presentation cannot match. In representational theater a scene cannot be changed every other minute; television can present many realistic settings in relatively few minutes or even seconds. In the theater, the movements of time and place often are aural as well as visual; television transitions are more visual because of the utilization of mechanical and electronic techniques. Film and tape permit a wider scope of time and place in television than can be achieved in even the most flexible theater form. Television has been able to achieve what August Strindberg, in his Author's Note to *A Dream Play,* hoped for in the theater: a situation where "anything may happen: everything is possible and probable." Strindberg looked for dramatic presentation where "time and space do not exist," where "imagination spins and weaves new patterns: a mixture of memories, experience, unfettered fancies, absurdities and improvisations." In television one not only can change setting and change time as on the stage, but also can change time without changing setting and change setting without changing time — and do so much more quickly and easily. The unities of time and place are completely loose and fluid in television.

The unity of action or impression is as vital to the television play as to any other form of drama, and the television writer should be certain that this most important unity is present.

Plot   The dramaturgical rules relating to plot apply to the television play as to the stage play. The problem of time, however, necessitates a much tighter plot line in the television play and a condensation of the movement from sequence to sequence. The art of drama is selective. In brief minutes we must present what life may have played out in days or years or centuries. Life is unemphatic, whereas drama must be emphatic. The short time for the television play requires the plot to be the essence of reality, to contain only the heightened extremities of life. Aim for the short, terse scene.

Although the emphasis on plot, because of the time factor, seems to make this the motivating factor in the television play, the exploration of television's intimacy and subjectivity potential enables the writer to delve into character and to use it as a plot-motivating element.

In condensing the play structure to conform to the time and space requirements, consider several of the approaches presented by George Pierce Baker in *Dramatic Technique*. First, the dramatist may "bring together at one place what really happened at the same time, but to other people in another place." Second, episodes happening to a person in the same setting, but at different times may be brought together. Third, events that have "happened to two people in the same place, but at different times may . . . be made to happen to one person." Finally, "what happened to another person at another time, and at another place may at times be arranged so that it will happen to any desired figure." Baker concluded: "The essential point in all this compacting is: when cumbered with more scenes than you wish to use, determine first which scenes contain indispensable action, and must be kept as settings; then consider which of the other scenes may by ingenuity be combined with them."

The dramaturgical rules relating to conflict also are modified in the television play. Because of the shorter running time, the conflict must come much sooner than in the stage play. The television play may open immediately with the conflict, with the exposition cut virtually to nothing. The point of attack in the television play should come quickly and should bring with it the first important moment of pressure. The television play cannot show that pressure slowly developing, as can the stage play; therefore, the writer should include the basic expository elements, if possible, in this moment of conflict. Tell who the people are, show where they are, place the time of the story, and reveal what actions or events have caused the conflict.

The kind of conflict in the television play differs from that in the stage play. On the stage almost any conflict may be successful. Because of the intimacy and subjectivity of television, the conflict between individuals usually is more effective than are those between people and nature or between groups or between any large bodies of forces.

The use of complications in the television play follows their use in the stage play. Although television's time limitation permits fewer complications, include a sufficient number to validate and build the actions of the major characters. Each complication should move the characters and the action closer to the climax. The final complication should be the crisis, and should reach a valid and inescapable climax that is the result of the conflict reaching its peak.

The modern playwright, influenced by the plays of ideas, has put less and less emphasis on the resolution. Television often dispenses with the resolution entirely, unless some doubt remains about the moral principle involved. Indeed, time frequently does not permit the inclusion of a resolution. Sometimes the resolution can be incorporated as a part of the climax.

Character The character in the play is not the person one sees in life. The playwright cannot validate the actions of the character by saying ''but that's what they did in real life.'' Drama is heightened life. The playwright reveals the character by showing the character's actions in moments of crisis. The television writer should be especially attentive to this. Not only concentrate on the action that strikingly reveals the individual character, but concentrate as well on the few characters whose actions strikingly reveal the purpose of the play. Do not use unneeded people. A character who does not contribute to the main conflict and to the unified plot line does not belong in the play. If a character is essential, put it in the script. If there are too many essential characters, then rethink the entire approach to the play. This principle does not necessarily apply, of course, to the continuing series, where the continuity of characters over many weeks or months permits longer time for exposition and for many featured characters.

The presentation of depth, of the intimate, inner character, is one of the advantages of television. Mechanical and electronic devices permit physical and psychological closeness and empathy that are not possible in the theater. The television writer can direct the audience's attention to the details relating to the inner character; the television camera can focus the audience's eye on the elements which most effectively project the character's feelings. Good visual action presented through script directions and effective camera work can often present exposition that, on the stage, would have to be explained verbally.

Although plot is the motivating factor in most television plays today, writers of quality plays understand more and more that the relationships among characters are the basic factors in drama: byplay between character and plot, with character determining incident and vice versa. The concentration on the subjective and the intimate, while applying the basic dramaturgical rules for television, leads to the emergence of character as the motivating force in the well-written television play.

Dialogue The principles of dialogue for the television play are the same as for the stage play. The dialogue must forward the situation; it must be consistent with the characters, the situation, and with itself; it must be dramatic and heightened in comparison with the dialogue of real life.

Television requires one significant modification in the use of dialogue to forward the situation and to provide exposition. The visual element can often substitute for the aural. If you can show the situation or present the expository information through action instead of through dialogue, do so. The long shot as well as the close-up has made it possible to eliminate time-consuming dialogue in which the character describes things or places. You can concentrate not only on action but also on reaction, keeping the dialogue at a minimum and the picture the primary object of attention. Anything that can be shown on television through a close-up should not be described, as it might have to be on the stage. Be careful, however, not to go too far in substituting visual action for dialogue. Pantomime and the close-up should be used cautiously and only when they are the most effective ways of presenting the material. On the intimate screen they can become awkward and melodramatic.

The condensing and heightening of real-life dialogue is of great importance in television. Television dialogue should avoid repetition; it should condense the ideas presented; it should be character-delineating; it should be written so that the purpose of every exchange of speeches is clear to the audience and so that the sequence carries the plot line forward; it should contain the necessary exposition and background for the characters even while presenting the continuing action of the play.

Exposition   The short time allotted to the one-shot television play permits only a minimum of exposition. It is difficult to present sufficient background material necessary to characterization and to present exposition subtly or as a natural part of the action because of insufficent time for a slow unfolding of the situation. Because the conflict should be presented almost as soon as the television drama begins, the exposition must be highly condensed and presented with all possible speed. The problem here is that although film and theater audiences generally have some foreknowledge of the drama they are about to watch, the television audience often has no preparation for what it is going to see. The reverse is true, of course, in the continuing television series, where a large part of the audience already knows the setting, the characters, and the background, requiring exposition only for the particular plot of the particular program.

Preparation   The principles of preparation apply equally to the television play as to the stage play. The writer should prepare the audience in a subtle and gradual manner for the subsequent actions of the characters and the events of the play. Nothing should come as a complete surprise. The audience should be able to look back, after something has taken place, and know that the action was inevitable because of the personality of the character who performed the action or because all of the circumstances leading to the event made it unavoidable.

Setting   There are many physical kinds of dramatic settings in theater: the Greek open stage, the Italian spectacle and painted backdrop, the cluttered stage of the naturalistic play, the use of light and shadow in expressionistic staging, and the Appia-influenced plasticity of modern production. But the physical areas of the television set are different from those of the stage. Television drama essentially conforms to the play of selective realism in content and purpose, and realistic settings usually are required. Both the limitations and the potentials of television have combined to modify the realistic setting, however. The studio television setting frequently must be smaller than the writer might wish it to be. On the other hand, the fluidity of television achieved through film and tape makes up for these restrictions by permitting a greater number of changes of setting and a considerable broadening of setting, with frequent changes of time and place.

Be certain that all of your scenes, background and set descriptions are carefully integrated with the forward action of the drama and that they serve as valid and delineating locales, environment, and atmosphere for the characters and for the plot.

Play Structure: Application

Putting together all of the principles thus far discussed into a complete whole is both the first and the last task of the playwright. It is the be-all and end-all. In between are the techniques, the restrictions, the orientations, the media requirements — all of the things that make that particular play fit exactly the format of the program for which it is intended. But, in the final analysis, it is still the basic play that counts.

The Scenario

It is called the **scenario,** the **treatment,** the outline, the summary. What it does is give the producer and/or script editor a narrative idea of what the play is about: the plot line, the characters, the setting, and maybe even bits of dialogue. Most producers and editors can tell from this narrative if the play fits the needs of the particular program. The scenario and treatment are usually longer than the outline and summary, perhaps as much as a fifth of the entire script (i.e., ten pages for a fifty-page script). The summary and the outline may be only two or three pages, in effect providing an additional preliminary judgment to the scenario. Some producers and editors want to see a summary or outline first, then a scenario or treatment, and, finally, the complete script. With some submissions, you are asked to include all three at the same time. The scenario or treatment not only helps the prospective buyer, but also can be of immeasurable help to the writer. As a detailed outline, it can tell you whether or not you've got a good play. Careful construction and analysis of the scenario can help you eliminate weak places and strengthen the good points. The scenario not only provides you with a continuous series of way stations in your construction of the play, but by using its checkpoints you can save exhausting work and valuable time by catching problems before they are written in, thus avoiding complete rewrites to get them out.

As already noted, the scenario or treatment you submit to the producer or editor is generally narrative in form. The scenario that you develop to help you construct the play may be more complex. It should contain, first, the purpose of the play, its theme, background, characters, basic plot line, and type of dialogue. You should include case histories for all your characters. Prepare plot summaries for each projected scene in chronological order. Note the elements of exposition and preparation. As you develop the plot sequences, insert important or representative lines of dialogue. The result of this kind of scenario, even in its simplest form, will be at the very least a clarification of all of the structural elements of the play.

Dramaturgical Analysis

Following the first working scenario and as many subsequent scenarios as necessary to make your preparation as complete as possible, you'll arrive at the point where you feel ready and confident to flesh out the play. This is where the pleasure of accomplishment comes in. For most playwrights, this is the fun part of writing. If you've planned well, the play will virtually write itself. If you find that some radical departures are needed from the scenario, then your preparation was not as good as it could or should have been. Go back to the scenario and shore it up, even if you have to start all over. Otherwise you will find that though you may complete most or all of the first draft of the play, you'll need many more extra drafts to repair all the holes, in the long run requiring much more time and effort than you would have needed with proper scenario preparation.

The following working scenario is one example of how one writer develops and checks the script. Two columns are used. The one on the left is the detailed outline — that is, an action summary. (It is this action summary that could serve, incidentally, as the narrative scenario or treatment for submission to a producer or editor.) On the right is a functional analysis. The play, *With Wings As Eagles,* is simple in format, transitions, and settings. Because of space this scenario is condensed; it could contain more precise analysis of character, additional dialogue, and more plot detail. Following the scenario and functional analysis is the first act of the play itself, so you may note how the writer filled out the structure.

● *Analyze the first act of the script in terms of the principles of dramaturgy. Match the scenario and functional analysis with their realization in the script and determine whether the playwright achieved what was intended. This script was written for live production, much like the play you might write in a college television writing class for production by the directing class.*

WITH WINGS AS EAGLES

ACTION SUMMARY	FUNCTIONAL ANALYSIS
The time is the early 1960s. The setting is a Jewish ghetto in an unnamed Near East country. The camera opens on a muddy village street and pans one wood and mud-baked hut to another. A Narrator sets the time and place, describing the poverty of the inhabitants, and how their history shows that though they live in hunger, sickness and oppression, they will find the promised land.(1) The Narrator mentions that few have ever seen an automobile and few would believe that such a thing as an airplane exists.(2) He stresses that in all their ignorance and poverty the people have hope of going to the promised land.(3)	(1) Exposition: the place, time, situation, the background and the needs of the people. (How effective is this semi-documentary approach to exposition, coming through a narrator as well as through visual action?) (2) Preparation: for their eventual departure for Israel and for the climax involving the airplane flight. (3) Preparation for the conflict: the stress on the hope of going to a promised land subtly suggests the conflict: will they or will they not be able to go?

ACTION SUMMARY	FUNCTIONAL ANALYSIS
	(4)
Reb Simcha goes from house to house, calling the people to a meeting. He does so stealthily, undercover.(4)	Exposition: shows the kind of existence of the people: fear, oppression.
	(5)
At one house, that of Simon and his son, Aaron, Reb Simcha encounters opposition to the meeting. At Aaron's insistence Simon finally agrees to go. We see that Simon's house is well-furnished, unlike the others.(5)	Preparation: for Simon's opposition, and for Aaron's opposition to his father.
	(5)
	Exposition: shows another aspect of the village life: someone in comparatively good circumstances.
	(6)
We follow Simcha to his own house. The house is fixed up as a small synagogue. He prays: "Please, God. This time, make men's words truth."(6)	Conflict: Without a clear statement yet, we learn something may be in opposition with something else. This is preparation for the revelation of the conflict.
	(6)
	Exposition: Reb Simcha's environment and profession.
	(7)
His daughter, Leah, enters. Reb Simcha complains about his tired feet.(7)	Preparation: The tired feet play a humorous part throughout and are particularly important for comic pathos at the end of the play.
	(8)
Leah says she saw some of the people, and that Aaron saw the rest, and that all are coming.(8)	Preparation and complication: We are prepared for Aaron's break with his father through the revelation that he is working on Reb Simcha's side. We are prepared for the relationship between Leah and Aaron in that they are working together. This preparation ties in with the later complications: Aaron vs. his father; Aaron's and Leah's love.
	(9)
Leah sees her father is worried and gets him to tell what it is. He says he hopes the words he heard from the government representative are true. His people are sup-	Conflict: It is made clear here. The people are supposed to go to the promised land. The doubts set up the conflict: the people against the government powers.

ACTION SUMMARY	FUNCTIONAL ANALYSIS
posed to leave for the promised land the next morning; but from an open field and without belongings.(9)	Will they or will they not reach the promised land?
This worries him. He does not know how they will go, from an open field. "How do we go?" he asks. "We fly, maybe, like a bird?"(10)	(10) Preparation: Again, the reference to flying, preparing the audience for the climax.
He doubts that his people will believe him and be ready, and if they are not ready they will not be able to leave again. He doubts, himself, for such promises have been broken for centuries.(11)	(11) Preparation for complication: the dissension among the people themselves, which might prevent them from achieving their goal, is foreshadowed here.
	(6–11) In the revelation of Leah's and Reb Simcha's actions, we get their characterizations.
Aaron comes for Leah. Leah and Reb Simcha talk about her intended marriage to Aaron. Leah is worried because his father, Simon, is friendly with the authorities and makes money as the official merchant in the ghetto and may not want to leave. He may prevent Aaron from leaving. Reb Simcha tells Leah that when they go to the promised land, she and Aaron will go hand in hand.(12)	(12) Preparation for complication: Will Simon stop Aaron and Leah; will this result in a delay or complete betrayal of all of the people?
	(12) Exposition: Simon's background and profession is revealed more clearly.
	(12) Reb Simcha's need to assure Leah prepares the audience for trouble in this respect.
The next scene, in the Police-Military office in the town. Dr. Ezam, the diplomat, arranges with the Lieutenant in charge for transportation and clearance. The Lieutenant does not want the people to go because they are helpful to the town. "They stay in their place," he says. They work for the town's businessmen at low wages.(13)	(13) Exposition: We see the attitude of the officials toward these people and the people's place in the community.
	(13) Preparation: We are prepared for the attempt of the town to keep them from going; the motivation: cheap labor.

ACTION SUMMARY	FUNCTIONAL ANALYSIS
	(14)
Dr. Ezam insists that they be permitted to leave, citing a United Nations ruling. The Lieutenant says he will agree to that, but if they are not ready and at the open field on time, he will not let them leave. He says a lot of people in the town would not like them to go. He intimates that they may not leave, anyway. They verbally fence with the political, moral and practical considerations.(14)	Preparation for complication: It is clear that the Lieutenant will try to stop the departure.
	(13–14)
	The discussion and action reveal character.
	(15)
The next sequence is in Simon and Aaron's house, where Simon and Aaron argue. Aaron is disturbed because his father cooperates with the authorities. Simon explains that he must do it to live well and to keep his promise to Aaron's dead mother that he would provide for him. Simon doesn't want to go to the meeting, fearing trouble from the authorities. Simon also wants his son not to see Leah again. They argue bitterly, and Simon decides to go to the meeting to stop Reb Simcha's foolish plans.(15)	Complication: The conflict is complicated by Simon's avowal to stop the proposed exodus, to fight Reb Simcha. It is further complicated by the avowed intention to step between Leah and Aaron. The rising action, moving toward an inevitable clash, is apparent.
	(15)
	Exposition: We have further understanding about Simon and Aaron's background and motivations.
	(15)
	Preparation: Simon's reasons for what he does are understandable, if not acceptable, and we see he is not a one-dimensional tyrant, thus preparing the audience for his actions at the end of the play.
	(15)
	The sequence is character-delineating.
	(16)
The next sequence is in the Lieutenant's office. The Lieutenant makes plans with one of the town's merchants, Rasin, to stop the departure. They decide to detain one of the villagers. "They're a thick people. If one were detained they wouldn't leave without him." Because of Dr. Ezam, they look for legal grounds for detention, such as one of the villagers "leaving" the ghetto without permission.(16)	Complication: Another block in the way of the people's exodus, thus heightening the conflict.
	(16)
	Preparation: We learn what the probable trick will be for detention and for stopping the departure.

WITH WINGS AS EAGLES

Act I

| Open FS Map of Middle East | NARRATOR (VOICE OVER): This is a map of the Middle East: Egypt, Syria, Iraq, Jordan, Israel. Of Arabs and Jews. Of cities and deserts, of camels and motor-cars, of hopes and fears, but mostly of people. This is the city of Mabbam. In what country? It doesn't matter. Like in many other of these towns outside of Israel there are small Jewish populations. Hebrew might be a better term, for these people are the direct descendents of Isaiah and Abraham, those who were led by Moses through the wilderness to the promised land, who fell by the waysides. The waysides grew into sections and streets ... |
| Pan across map, picking no special spot, dolly in, dissolve to a miniature of a small city, several new white buildings and off, at one side, a dingy, dirty-looking section, with mud huts and shacks. | |

Key in ext. of the town, showing the street of the mud huts and shacks.

... like that one. Tikvah Street, it's called. Tikvah means hope. That is about all they have, these Hebrews — hope. There is no special industry, no principal occupation — unless one can call hunger, fear, sickness and poverty occupations.

Pan down street, show dirt streets, wood and mud-baked huts.

It is not easy for the Hebrew these days. The new state of Israel has been steadily growing and the other countries hold no love for these people whose kinsmen they have fought and continue to fight. The Hebrews are beaten, jailed and starved. Everything the centuries have visited upon their brethren has not stopped because they are suddenly thrust into the middle of the 20th century. And that is an odd thing, too, for although the calendar of the Western world reads in the 1960's, the environment of these people is that of centuries before. No newspapers, no movies, no automobiles. Few have ever even seen an automobile. And as for airplanes, why none in this out-village of Mabbam would believe you if you told them that such a thing exists. But whatever else may be lacking, they have a rich heritage of spiritual inspiration. They have a Rabbi. They have hope — the hope of a promised land. Poverty ... hope ... fear ...

Dissolve to CU of a fist knocking on a door. The door opens revealing a small, cluttered room. Several small children cower in the back. Hannah, a woman of about 40, but looking tired and worn and much older, in tattered clothing, is at the door.

VOICE (OF KNOCKER, REB SIMCHA): (Reb Simcha is not yet on camera.) Half-an-hour after sundown. Tonight. At my house. (THE DOOR CLOSES.)

CU feet moving along the dirt street. CU fist knocking again. Door opens. A man, Schloem, the street-washer, old and wizened, stands in back of the door. Esther, his wife, stands in back of him. They are both in their late sixties.

VOICE (REB SIMCHA; OFF-CAMERA): Half-an-hour after sundown. At my house. Tonight. (SCHLOEM CLOSES THE DOOR FURTIVELY.)

CU feet moving again. This time they reach a small concrete patch in the street. The fist knocks on a door, ignoring the knocker there. The door is opened by a good looking young man of about 25. This is Aaron.

VOICE (REB SIMCHA; OFF-CAMERA): Your father? You haven't told him?

AARON: No. A moment, please.

(AARON RETURNS A MOMENT LATER WITH A LARGE, PORTLY MAN OF ABOUT

FIFTY. THIS IS SIMON, HIS FATHER, THE MERCHANT OF THE GHETTO. THE INSIDE OF THE HOUSE CAN BE SEEN. THERE IS SOME FURNITURE, INCLUDING A BED WITH A BEDSPREAD, TWO COMFORTABLE CHAIRS, A TABLE WITH A CANDELABRA. IT IS POOR, BUT WEALTHY IN COMPARISON WITH THE HOMES OF HANNAH, THE WIDOW, AND SCHLOEM, THE STREET-WASHER. SIMON IS DRESSED IN A SUIT, NOT IN RAGS LIKE THE OTHERS.)

SIMON: What? What do you want?

VOICE (REB SIMCHA; OFF-CAMERA): To-night. At my house. At a half . . .

SIMON (INTERRUPTING): Again? More trouble-making?

VOICE: It is important.

SIMON: Always it is important. And always it causes trouble. I've no time. I have to see about some goods.

AARON: We should go, father.

VOICE: (INSISTENT): It is most important.

SIMON: Well . . . all right.

VOICE: Half-an-hour after sundown.

SIMON: (ANGRILY) All right! (HE SLAMS THE DOOR.)

CU feet again, walking down the street. They stop in front of a door. This time the fist doesn't knock, but the hand opens the door, instead. The feet go in, past two humble cots, an old table and two rickety chairs, to a corner of the room where a shelf is seen, with several old and tattered books, two brass candlesticks. In the wall

there is a recession, the "Ark," in which
is seen a rolled up scroll. This is the
"Torah." CU of the Torah as a face bends
toward it and kisses it. Zoom out and see,
finally, the person of the feet and the
voice. It is Rabbi Simcha, a man of about
50, dressed in a black gown, wearing a
"yarmulka," the black skullcap. He is
bearded, a gentle face, worn, but with
eyes bright with hope.

REB SIMCHA: Please God. This time,
make men's words truth. (HE BEGINS TO
PACE BACK AND FORTH ACROSS THE
SMALL ROOM. THE FRONT DOOR SLOWLY
OPENS. A PRETTY YOUNG GIRL, ABOUT
23, A SOFT FACE AND LARGE EYES, HER
HAIR LONG BEHIND HER BACK, COMES
IN. SHE IS UNHEARD BY THE RABBI.
SHE WATCHES HIM A MOMENT. THIS IS
HIS DAUGHTER, LEAH.)

LEAH: Father, your feet will wear off
before the floor will.

REB SIMCHA: (COMING OUT OF DEEP
THOUGHT) Oh, Leah! (HE LAUGHS,
LOOKS AT HIS FEET.) Oh, of course. The
head sometimes pays not enough atten-
tion to the feet. (SITS DOWN ON ONE OF
THE COTS, RUBS HIS FEET.) They hurt.
These feet will be the death of me yet.
(AFTER A MOMENT) Did you tell them,
Leah? About tonight?

LEAH: Those I was supposed to. Aaron
saw the rest.

REB SIMCHA: They're coming?

LEAH: Yes.

REB SIMCHA: Good. (HOLDS HIS HEAD
IN HIS HANDS, AGAIN IN WORRIED
THOUGHT.)

LEAH: (SITS DOWN NEXT TO HIM.) You can tell me, father.

REB SIMCHA: (SMILING) Tell? There is nothing to tell.

LEAH: Mother used to say — may she rest in peace — "When your father says he has nothing to tell, it is a sure sign he is bursting to talk."

REB SIMCHA: (FONDLES HER FACE, WIST-FULLY) You are like your mother. (AFTER A MOMENT) I am worried.

LEAH: About the meeting?

REB SIMCHA: About the meeting, about the authorities, about our people, about whether what my ears heard today was really true or just another one of their stories.

LEAH: But you said it was a government official, a diplomat in a dark suit and bright shoes who told you.

REB SIMCHA: And since when is it that diplomats don't lie?

LEAH: Do you remember exactly what he said?

REB SIMCHA: He said, "Be at the field in the north of the city with all of your people and without belongings at nine o'clock to-morrow morning. If you are there, you will go to the 'promised land.' If you are not, you will not go." That's all he said. Not one word more.

LEAH: Somehow I don't feel it's a lie. Not this time.

REB SIMCHA: Last time, you said not last time. Next time, you'll say not next time.

But how do we go, if we go? We fly, maybe, like a bird? And with no belongings. Perhaps ... they want to loot the few pitiful things left in the ghetto?

LEAH: Perhaps?

REB SIMCHA: Leah, will our people believe me this time? Will they take the chance and come to the field? If we're not there, we won't go, he said.

LEAH: Aaron thinks they'll come. I think so.

REB SIMCHA: So long now I have been promising the people. Soon you will go to the promised land, I tell them. Days? Years! Centuries! Every day it is the same. Naaman, the carpenter, comes to me and asks, "Reb Simcha, when is it? Today? Tomorrow?" I smile and say, "not today, maybe tomorrow." Schloem, the street-washer, says "tell me when it is, Reb. Today?" And his eyes shine for a moment and I answer "maybe tomorrow" and he is sad again. For how long now this has gone on. Why should they believe me now, just because a diplomat has told me "tomorrow"? I begin to doubt. Is there a tomorrow?

LEAH: Don't doubt yourself. You can't take them on a magic carpet. You can only give them faith and lead them.

REB SIMCHA: Faith! Words from a book. I should find a magic carpet for them. (GETS UP, GOES TO THE DOOR, LOOKS OUT.) A ghetto: mud, dirt, barefoot people. (TURNS BACK) What if they ask me how do we go? What do I tell them? On the wings of an eagle, like Isaiah prophesied? Or do we walk for forty years, like Moses? We have walked and wandered enough, they will tell me.

LEAH: The authorities did bring us here from the desert to get ready for the promised land.

REB SIMCHA: For cheap labor they brought us here. To use our shoemakers and carpenters. How long now? Two — three years.

LEAH: We must keep hoping and trying. Fifty-four are left, father. Of all those from the desert, only fifty-four left.

REB SIMCHA: So, I ask you, why should we believe the authorities now?

LEAH: We have no choice.

REB SIMCHA: Simon has a choice. He will try to convince the others not to go.

LEAH: Aaron will try to make him understand.

REB SIMCHA: And how could we go, Leah? Do we walk? Do we ride a camel? They will not give us camels. What other way is there? One of the machines with wheels that spit poison? I have seen some of their automobiles in the city. How many can there be in the whole world? Not enough for us, at any rate. Besides, the people are afraid of them.

LEAH: If we stand together and have faith, we will find a way.

REB SIMCHA: (SLOWLY LOOKS UP, SMILES) My daughter is wiser than her father. I can read from the Holy Book, so they say I am wise. (SHAKES HIS HEAD) Wisdom comes from here (POINTING TO HIS HEAD) and here (POINTING TO HIS HEART). (GETTING UP) I feel better.

(LEAH GOES TO THE DOOR, LOOKS OUT, COMES BACK)

REB SIMCHA: Is there someone?

LEAH: I hoped.

REB SIMCHA: Aaron?

(LEAH NODS HER HEAD)

REB SIMCHA: A good boy. An honest boy.

LEAH: You don't mind me seeing him so often?

REB SIMCHA: Should I mind?

LEAH: Some of the people say a girl should not see a young man until they know they are to be married.

REB SIMCHA: So? There is something wrong in seeing a young man? Your mother used to see a young man. (POINT-ING WITH PRIDE AT HIMSELF.) Me! (AFTER A MOMENT) But Aaron's father, that's another matter.

LEAH: You think he'll try to stop the people from going tomorrow?

REB SIMCHA: Simon has worldly goods here. He's friendly with the authorities. They let him do all the selling in the ghetto. About Simon I don't know. But when we go to the promised land, you and Aaron will go hand in hand.

SLOW DISSOLVE TO POLICE-MILITARY OFFICE OF MABBAM. The Lieutenant, dressed in a military uniform, about 35, hard-looking, authoritative, is seated at his desk, going over some papers. Standing in front of the desk is the diplomat, Dr. Ezam, about 50, dressed well, immaculately. He is distinguished-looking, with a gentle, yet determined manner.

DR. EZAM: They'll go, Lieutenant. They'll all go.

LIEUTENANT: It's your idea, Dr. Ezam, not mine. A lot of people in this town don't like the idea of you people coming from the government and changing the way we do things here.

DR. EZAM: Perhaps. But this is an official agreement made with Israel through the United Nations. And the Americans are providing the transportation.

LIEUTENANT: There are people in this town who do all right by these Hebrews. They stay in their place. They work for us when we want them. It saves us money, and they don't need so much to live on. You know the way they live.

DR. EZAM: I have heard that there have been many deaths in the ghetto here.

LIEUTENANT: (STARTING TO SAY SOME-THING, THEN IGNORING THE LAST RE-MARK) All right. You gave me the orders. (NODS TO THE OFFICIAL PAPERS) I'll grant them free passage to the field at the north of town at nine in the morning. But I don't approve of this whole idea.

DR. EZAM: Approving is not your job, Lieutenant.

LIEUTENANT: I will do my job, Dr. Ezam. But if they're not ready, then they don't go. They stay in the ghetto. The orders say tomorrow at nine and nothing else.

DR. EZAM: It's been a long time they've been searching for the promised land. They'll be ready.

LIEUTENANT: You almost seem to feel sorry for them.

DR. EZAM: Sorry? No. A little envious, perhaps.

LIEUTENANT: Envious? Of Jews?

DR. EZAM: Why are you so bitter against Jews, Lieutenant?

LIEUTENANT: Why? Well, because ... well ... because ... they're Jews!

DR. EZAM: It must be a good feeling for them, Lieutenant, to be living the fulfillment of a prophecy. Think for a moment. For five thousand years there has been prophecy, expectation and hope. The greatest thing, you feel, that history has to offer mankind. Then, suddenly, in your lifetime, in your generation, in your year, your minute, it happens, and you are part of it.

LIEUTENANT: You don't have to preach to me.

DR. EZAM: (QUIETLY) I didn't intend to. You are an officer. Your job is duty. I am a diplomat. My job is understanding.

LIEUTENANT: If I had my way, we military would be the diplomats, too. Diplomats! Talk, talk, talk! Sometimes I wonder whether you ever accomplish anything.

DR. EZAM: So do I. But, then, when I look back, I know. Civilization lives by talk. It dies by force.

LIEUTENANT: Well, I suppose we both have a job to do.

DR. EZAM: (HALF TO HIMSELF) And I wonder where the balance lies ...

LIEUTENANT: (SIGNING AND STAMPING SOME PAPERS) Hmmm?

DR. EZAM: Nothing.

LIEUTENANT: Here are your papers. Clearance for them. I tell you again, Dr. Ezam. They're scheduled for nine in the morning. If they're not ready they don't go. That's my duty. A lot of people in this town would like to keep them here.

DR. EZAM: That's the second time you've said that, Lieutenant. Why?

LIEUTENANT: No matter.

DR. EZAM: (AUTHORITATIVELY) Why?

LIEUTENANT: (SMILING, CONFIDENT) Some of those Jews know when to be good Jews. There are some ... who like it here.

DR. EZAM: I've told their Rabbi. He'll have them ready.

LIEUTENANT: The Rabbi's a troublemaker. They know it. They're poor people, with no education, your Jews. A wrong word here, a wrong word there ... well, you'll see.

DR. EZAM: I think they'll be ready. It's their only chance.

LIEUTENANT: (STILL SMILING) We'll see ... you don't know those Jews! You don't know that ghetto!

DISSOLVE TO SIMON'S HOUSE. SIMON AND AARON ARE ARGUING.

AARON: You don't know this ghetto, father. You sell them goods, you take their money. But you don't know them.

SIMON: I know them well enough, Aaron, my son, to know they're not so stupid as to keep following that Reb Simcha. Another meeting. For what? To pray?

To tell stories? To cry about how bad things are? To make more promises about a promised land?!

AARON: It gives them hope. It gives me hope.

SIMON: A false hope. He promises, so they depend on him. I have the goods. It's me they should depend on.

AARON: (PLACATING) They need your goods.

SIMON: They need his promises more, it seems. (MUSING) If it weren't for him, I could control them all, work closer with the authorities and really be wealthy.

AARON: Wealth, goods, money. I am ashamed for my father. Simon, the merchant, seems to have no concern for people, only wealth.

SIMON: I have concern for you, Aaron, my son.

AARON: Not for my feelings. Not for my thoughts. If you did you would help our people, not live off them.

SIMON: For you, Aaron. I do it for you. (AFTER A MOMENT, QUICKLY, BUT STRONGLY) I promised myself that what happened to your mother will not happen to you. When there is hunger, you will eat. When authorities want tribute, you will have enough to buy your life. (SADLY AND SOFTLY) They took your mother because I was too poor to pay tribute. Thin and weak and hungry, they took her as a work-slave because I did not have enough money. I fought them. And two months later they let me come out from jail to get her body and bury her. (SHOUTING)

Because I did not have enough money for tribute! No more! No more! Not in my lifetime! Not to my child!

AARON: If our people stand together, they could not hurt us.

SIMON: Did our people stand with me? Did our people stop the authorities from taking your mother? You can't fight the authorities, my son. You can only buy them or cooperate with them. (AFTER A MOMENT) I'd do well to stay away from this meeting.

AARON: This one is important. You have to go.

SIMON: Important? Have to go? You know more about it than you let on.

AARON: I know that it's important.

SIMON: You have a hand in it, too. Again. When the authorities threw you into jail before, it wasn't enough. So much money it cost me to get you out. Now you have to get mixed up with that troublemaker Rabbi and his daughter again.

AARON: That's my business. With the Rabbi. With his daughter.

SIMON: And I, your father? It's not my business? Understand me, my son; I know what is happening.

AARON: What do you know?

SIMON: You and that girl, Leah. You think you are in love with her.

AARON: Have I told you that?

SIMON: You don't have to tell me. I am your father. (AFTER A MOMENT) She is like her father. Headstrong. Foolish. She has caused you trouble already. (AARON STARTS TO SPEAK, BUT SIMON SILENCES HIM) By seeing her you will only learn more trouble. I ask you to stop seeing her.

AARON: And what if I told you I really were in love?

SIMON: Then I would tell you that it is not love. In this world one loves only his own, and himself.

AARON: Then you don't know what love is. You couldn't know what love is.

SIMON: (SLOWLY) With more than my life, I loved your mother.

AARON: I'm sorry.

SIMON: Then understand what I say.

AARON: I understand. But you do not. Father ... let me tell you this ... soon, maybe very soon, we will be in the promised land. There we will live like human beings.

SIMON: Idle dreams. Troublemaking. Is this what the meeting is tonight? Some more stories about the promised land?

AARON: This time it's true. We will leave for the promised land tomorrow morning.

SIMON: Tomorrow morning! More foolishness from that Rabbi. I'll go to that meeting and I'll put an end to this troublemaking foolishness.

DISSOLVE TO THE POLICE-MILITARY OFFICE.

The Lieutenant is talking with a large, portly man, a leading citizen of the town.

He is dressed well and looks much like
Simon, except big-jowled, prosperous and
well-dressed from the proceeds of his clothing establishment. His name is Abd-Rasin.

RASIN: (EXCITED) This is true, eh? They're
going, eh? Whose idea? Your idea? Not your
idea … ?

LIEUTENANT: You take me for a fool … ?

RASIN: (INTERRUPTING) I take you for a
fool!

LIEUTENANT: Now, look here, Abd-Rasin …

RASIN: (INTERRUPTING) You look here! I
have a clothing establishment, eh? It costs
a great deal for workers nowadays. They
read too much. They want more money.
But now I have these Jews working, eh?
Good workmen. I'll say that much for
them. And they cost me practically nothing. My neighbor, Hezaf, the pottery-maker.
Six Jews in his factory. Good potters. The
blacksmith. With the Jews to work he's
opened another shop. If the Jews go, it
doubles our costs, it reduces our business,
eh?

LIEUTENANT: What do you want me to do?
It's an order. From the government.

RASIN: We have done well by you, Lieutenant, eh?

(THE LIEUTENANT NODS)

If this ghetto is allowed to leave … well …
the citizens of this town won't have it.

LIEUTENANT: You think I want it!

RASIN: Then do something. (AFTER A
MOMENT) Listen to me. I have one of their

carpenters, a fellow called Naaman, working for me today. I'm building an addition,
you know. Now, they're a thick people. If
one of them were detained ... this
Naaman, for instance ... they wouldn't
leave without him, eh? And if they don't
leave tomorrow morning ...

LIEUTENANT: This Dr. Ezam is on their
side. I'd have to find legal grounds.

RASIN: Then find them.

LIEUTENANT: Now, if one of them left the
ghetto, without permission, or committed
some similar breach of the law ... (SMILES
AND BEGINS TO NOD HIS HEAD TO RASIN,
AS ...

FADE OUT, END OF ACT I

The Manuscript

Although manuscript forms and specific writing techniques differ, the general
writing approaches are basically the same whether the play is taped live or filmed.
The play is being produced for viewing on the small screen, with the same restrictions, for the same general audience, and under the same limitations of subject
matter. The plot structure and the creation of characters and dialogue are the same.
The technical elements differ, but both styles are oriented toward the extensive use
of the close-up, the moving camera, and fluid transitions in place and time.

The television manuscript should have all the characters clearly designated, the
dialogue, the stage directions, the video and audio directions and, in the filmed
play, the shot designations. Ordinarily, producers and directors frown upon writers
including directions they believe only they are capable of creating, but many
writers indicate sound, music, camera, and electronic effects they consider vital to
the action and character delineation. This is particularly true when the visual effect
in television (or the sound effect in radio) serves in place of dialogue to move the
action forward. In addition, the writer also indicates any change of time or place,
and may state whether the desired effect is achieved through a fade, dissolve, wipe,
musical bridge, or other device.

The radio manuscript form, as noted in examples earlier in this book, uses the full
page, with the character's name in capital letters at the left-hand margin or in the
middle of the page. There should be double spaces between lines of dialogue and
between speeches. All sound and music directions should be indicated in capital
letters.

The final manuscript is the one that the writer may have nothing to do with: the production script. This script contains all the revisions that may have been made after the play has left the writer's hands (unless the writer's contract gives him or her the right to do or approve of revisions) and includes the producer's and director's notations for all technical effects.

Whether the production manuscript will have a direct relationship to the writer's original manuscript is a matter of chance as well as contract. Changes in content, style, and form may have been made of which the author may not even have been informed. The writer usually has no say in casting or production. After a script has run the gamut of script editor, screening, agency or network approval, production planning, rehearsal, and final editing for performance, the writer might have a difficult time recognizing it. As a writer, all you can do is offer a script of the highest artistic merit of which you are capable, and then fight to keep it that way. You may take comfort in the feeling that no matter what anyone else has done, you, at least, have done your best. And if worse comes to worst, you can always request that your name be taken off the credits, an occurrence not unheard of in television.

The Live-type Taped Play

As described earlier, some productions follow a continuous action approach and are taped in front of a live audience, coming as close as television usually gets to the continuity of the stage play. The play is performed and taped in sequence — that is, following the chronological order of the plot line of the script. Through editing, of course, certain sequences can be retaped and, in that respect, even the live-type show can be produced somewhat out of sequence, like the filmed play.

In terms of the arts of writing and performance, however, *live-style taped* should not be considered the same as *live*. The late Rod Serling, one of the few successful television writers who stayed with the medium throughout his entire career, was once asked on the "Merv Griffin Show" what we have gained and what we have lost with the advent of videotape. He answered, "We've lost spontaneity and the sense of living theater. We've gained polish and perfection."

The most frequently used form for the live-type taped play is the two-column approach noted frequently in this book: the right-hand column containing all of the audio — that is, the dialogue plus the character's movements — and the left-hand column containing the video — that is, the mechanical and electronic effects. The left-hand column may also contain special sound effects and music. In some cases, the right- and left-hand columns are reversed.

Another manuscript approach is to place all of the material, video and audio, together, right down the center (similar to the stage play form), or solely in a left-hand column or right-hand column, leaving the other side free for the director's notes. The names of the characters should be typed in capital letters in the center of the column, with the dialogue immediately below. Video and audio directions and author's stage directions are usually differentiated from the dialogue by being in parentheses and/or in capital letters and/or underlined. Script editors prefer that dialogue be double-spaced, with double-spacing between speeches.

An example of the live-type taped script form is the following opening excerpt from one of the programs of the "Good Times" series.

————————————————○————————————————

• *''Good Times'' was considered one of the better, more successful television series. Note the compactness of the writing and how in the first few
minutes of the opening scene (1) the background for the characters and
general plot line is established, (2) the characters begin to be delineated
and character relationships are shown, (3) the exposition for this particular story is established, and (4) the conflict begins to be introduced.
Identify where and how all four of the above are accomplished.*

————————————————○————————————————

GOOD TIMES
The Dinner Party

ACT ONE
FADE UP:
INT. EVANS' APARTMENT — DAY
(JAMES IS GOING OVER SOME BILLS AT THE TABLE. MICHAEL IS DOING HIS HOMEWORK.
THELMA IS COOKING. J.J. IS AT HIS EASEL PAINTING. FLORIDA ENTERS FROM BEDROOM)

FLORDIA:	Anybody seen my pin cushion?
J.J.:	I hope you don't mind, Ma, I used it for a still life of a bowl of fruit I just painted.
FLORIDA:	(REACTS — CROSSES TO J.J.) You used my pin cushion in a bowl of fruit?
J.J.:	It is a prime example of ghetto artistry. You make the most of what you got. Your pin cushion as the apple, Michael's basketball as the pumpkin, Dad's socks as the avocados and Thelma's face as the lemon.
THELMA:	Just bend a little and you can throw your body in as a banana. (THEY HASSLE)
JAMES:	Hey, you two, knock it off. I'm trying to figure out these bills.
FLORIDA:	(CROSSES TO CHEST) What's our financial position this month, James?
JAMES:	Well, we ain't in a position to threaten the Rockefellers ... but we ain't heading for the poor house either. For once we are in the black.
J.J.:	(LOOKS AROUND) What do you mean, for once?
FLORIDA:	J.J.! (PUTS PIN CUSHION DOWN — CROSSES TO SINK TO WASH HANDS) Is everything paid for, James?
JAMES:	(INDICATING ENVELOPES) Everything ... rent ... utilities ... and luxuries.
MICHAEL:	Dad, you didn't mention food.
FLORIDA:	(CROSSES TO JAMES WIPING HANDS ON TOWEL) These days that comes under luxuries.
	(JAMES COUNTS A FISTFUL OF DOLLARS)

The Filmed Play

The filmed play is more the director's creation than the writer's; the live-type taped
play, despite revisions and editing, is more the writer's play. Film permits more
sophisticated and detailed editing than does tape, and even after the script is shot,
the director can virtually rewrite the play in the editing room.

Screenwriter William Goldman, in a dialogue with writer Mal Karman in *Film-*

makers' Newsletter, described screenwriting as a craft.''It's carpentry. I don't mean that denigratingly. Except in the case of Ingmar Bergman, it's not an art.'' He added that ''a screenwriter's most important contribution to a film is not dialogue but structure . . . you try to find something cogent that will make it play as a story; that will take us from A to Z.'' As a novelist, Goldman found the screenplay form ''short, the camera insists that you hurry, you have little time for detail . . . it's a craft of pacing and structure.''

The filmed play permits a looser unity of time and place than does the taped continuous-action play. The filmed play has a break at each cut or transition. That is, the sequence may last two seconds to two minutes or longer. Between sequences the director can change sets, costumes, makeup, reset lights and cameras, and even reorient the performers.

The action itself may seem to be jerky. The actual sequences are shorter than in live-type television because they are shot separately. It is through editing that a number of sequences are fitted together into what appears to be a smooth-flowing continuous scene. The filmed play is not shot in chronological order. All the sequences taking place on a particular set or at a particular locale, no matter where they appear in the script, are shot over one period of time. Then the entire cast and crew move to the next set or locale and do the same thing. It is difficult to achieve a clear and concrete unity of impression in producing the filmed play; editing is, therefore, an extremely critical part of the process.

The filmed play requires a different manuscript form as well as different writing techniques. Instead of writing scenes, write shots. Each shot is set in terms of a picture rather than in terms of character action, although the latter should, in all plays — filmed or taped or live — be the motivating factor. As described in Chapter 2, the writer states the place, such as interior or exterior, and the shot, such as full shot or close-up. The writer also describes the setting, states the characters' physical relationships to the set and their proximity to each other, and then presents the dialogue for that shot. The dialogue (and scene) may be only one speech long. For example, the description may read:

1   INT. JOE'S LIVING ROOM — JOE AND MABEL are seated on the couch, quarreling.
    FULL SHOT Joe and Mabel.

> JOE
> This is the end, Mabel, do
> you hear? This is the end.

2   CLOSE-UP — MABEL

> MABEL
> I hear, Joe. I hear.

The individual shots are numbered in consecutive order so that the director may easily pick out any sequence(s) desired for initial shooting, retakes, or editing.

An example of the television film script form is the following opening excerpt from one of the programs of ''The Waltons'' series.

———————————————O———————————————
● *"The Waltons" was one of television's most successful series and its writing served as a model for similar programs. In addition to analyzing the differences between the film-style and the tape-style play, note how the flexibility of time and place are used in the opening to establish background and exposition. Analyze the degree to which (1) the characters begin to be delineated, (2) the dialogue begins to establish mood, and (3) the basic conflict in the plot begins to be revealed.*
———————————————O———————————————

THE WALTONS
The First Day

ACT ONE

FADE IN:

1 EXT. WALTON'S MOUNTAIN — DAY   1

It is dawn — the first gray light — and there's the suggestion of autumnal crispness in the air, the first blush of fall colors in the underbrush.

> JOHN-BOY (v.o.)
> (as a man)
> When you're growing up, Septembers
> have a special feeling. Another carefree
> summer is too quickly ended and a new
> school year is about to begin.

2 EXT. WALTON HOUSE & YARD — DAY   2

In the dawnlight, we make out the faintly yellow glow of a lamp burning in John-Boy's room.

> JOHN-BOY (v.o.)
> (as a man)
> There was an extra excitement for me
> in the September of 1935. My years at
> Miss Hunter's school on Walton's Moun-
> tain were over and I was ready to take
> those first faltering steps into the
> strange world outside.

3 INT. JOHN & OLIVIA'S ROOM — DAY   3

In the dim light, we see OLIVIA lies beside JOHN, who appears to be asleep.

> JOHN-BOY (v.o.)
> (as a man)
> How vividly I recall the edgy excitement,
> the awful exhilaration of preparing for
> my first day at college.

Olivia reacts to a MUFFLED BUMPING SOUND.

                    JOHN-BOY (v.o.)
                      (as a man)
            A day which showed me how little I
            knew about some things ...

Olivia begins to get up. John reaches out and stops her. She looks at him, surprised.
She didn't know he was awake.

                    JOHN-BOY (v.o.)
                (continuing: as a man)
            ... and how well my parents had pre-
            pared me for others.

Olivia kisses John and reaches for her bathrobe.

                      JOHN
            Where you going?

We HEAR the muffled sound again, coming from John-Boy's room.

                      OLIVIA
            John-Boy's up.

                      JOHN
            I hear. I guess he's anxious to get
            going.

                      OLIVIA
            It's so early ... maybe he doesn't feel
            well, or something.

                      JOHN
            I think he feels fine ... probably feels
            the same way we do.

                      OLIVIA
            How's that?

                      JOHN
            Nervous ... a little scared.

                      OLIVIA
            You want to go in and talk to him?

JOHN

Yeah. But you do too and I don't think
we all oughta go walking in there ... as
if he was starting kindergarten ... instead of starting college, like he is.

He kisses Olivia.

JOHN
(continuing)

Go on ... you go.

She smiles at him, draws her robe on, and moves softly out of the room. John watches
her go. He gets up and moves to the dresser. He catches sight of himself in the mirror.

JOHN
(continuing)
... starting college ... your son.

He nods at himself.

CUT TO:

4   INT. UPSTAIRS HALL — DAY   4

Olivia knocks lightly on John-Boy's door. After a moment, the door opens, revealing
JOHN-BOY fully dressed in his graduation outfit. He steps back and Olivia moves into his
room.

5   INT. JOHN-BOY'S ROOM — DAY   5

OLIVIA
(sotto)
What in the world are you doing up and
dressed at this hour?

JOHN-BOY
I was too excited to sleep.

He shuts the door as Olivia moves over to his bed. It is made and on the spread lie the
various cards, papers, schedules, pencils, pens — all the paraphernalia John-Boy must
take with him for his First Day.

From ''The First Day'' by John McGreevey — ''The Waltons''

The Soap Opera

The daytime adult dramatic serial, or soap opera, was described by Gilbert Seldes in
The Great Audience as ''the great invention of radio, its single, notable contribution

to the art of fiction.'' Although the radio soap opera is no longer with us, the television soap opera has become at least its equivalent in art, interest, and impact. Fergus Bordewich, writing in the *New York Times,* stated:

> Although soap opera aficionados would seem to be a minority among college students, there are nonetheless thousands of young people around the country who daily put aside their Sartre, Machiavelli and Freud — not to mention such obsolete writers as Fanon and Debray — to watch the moiling passions of middle-class America as portrayed on daytime TV. What is it about these slow-moving melodramas with their elasticized emotions that today's college students find so engrossing? . . . The fact is that in recent years the subject matter of daytime TV has changed and become much more relevant to the interests of young viewers. . . . The ''generation gap,'' abortion, obscenity, narcotics and political protest are now commonly discussed and dealt with on the soap operas of TV.

A phenomenon of the late 1970s and early 1980s was the remarkable success of prime-time soap operas, such as ''Dallas'' and ''Dynasty,'' which became the most popular television programs in the United States and Europe. Though of the same genre as the daily daytime soaps, their once-a-week evening presentation made them closer in pace to the weekly series program, although they retained the content and style of the daily soap.

Most soap opera viewers seek in the soaps a vicarious excitement through experiences the television characters have that they do not have, and the perverse, even unconscious satisfaction that we all get by seeing people with problems a little worse than ours, making our lives a little more tolerable. In addition, by dealing with real problems of society, soaps provide direct information, education, and even psychological assistance to viewers. Many of the afternoon dramas deal with real-life problems that are rarely treated as fully in prime-time television — topics such as women's liberation, child abuse, alcoholism, careers, abortion, environmental pollution, corruption, and the life-styles of married versus unmarried couples. Some hospitals have group therapy sessions that use soap operas as models, in which the patients relate the characters' problems to their own. Viewers frequently identify to the degree that they call in to the network or station as if the characters' situations were real (going to a psychotherapy clinic, finding an abortion clinic, seeking help for alcoholism) and ask for the names and addresses of the places involved so they can seek the same help.

Like life, soap operas that maintain their ratings just go on and on; there are no endings after an hour or a year; there are no dramatic climaxes, but just — as in life — a series of continuing complications. Sometimes soaps seem a little too clear-cut; good is good and bad is bad. The writer should find appropriate median areas. Sometimes the answers to problems are oversimplified. The lives of soap opera characters are more chaotic than those of real people; this does give the audience the satisfaction of knowing that their own lives are not quite so full of chaos and disruption. The important thing for the writer to remember is that the soaps offer the audience identification and diversion at the same time, entertaining and educating simultaneously; therefore, the soap opera plot lines and characters always have to be changing, meeting the audience's needs, and breaking new ground in terms of television drama content.

Approach and Technique

The setting should be familiar: the household, the doctor's office, the school, the small town, the large city, presented so that viewers anywhere can have some clear interpretation of their own of the background and environment.

The characters should be familiar, not necessarily in a detailed way, but in the kinds of persons they are and the problems they encounter. Thus every viewer can say, "That person is really like me, or like Amy or Bill or the plumber . . ." — like some person they know in real life. Every viewer should be able to identify to some degree with the main characters, whether they happen to be housewife, accountant, librarian, cheerleader, police officer, oil baron, architect, explorer, or even playwright. You can achieve this by developing the characters, no matter what environment they are in, on simple and obvious levels, with clear, direct motivations.

Though they may be similarly motivated, characters should be distinct types. One way to avoid confusion among characters is to limit the number. The dramatic serial should have the heroine and/or hero; the other woman and/or other man; the young woman and/or young man (or teenagers or children); the villainess and/or the villain; the interested and well-meaning relatives or friends, including the judge, the aunt and uncle, and their counterparts.

Perhaps the most important thing the writer must keep in mind in the creation of characters and situation is that the characters must be provided with the opportunity to get into an infinite variety of troubles. They must face problems that are melodramatic, basically real and valid but exaggerated beyond the real-life involvement of most of the listeners. This gives the listener the opportunity to commiserate with people who are worse off. Soap opera viewers usually consider themselves to have similarly infinite amounts of troubles. At the very least, specifically for daytime soaps, viewers should be able to find a mutual kind of commiseration with the characters so they can feel that they are not the only ones with these kinds of troubles and that somewhere they have "friends" and "compatriots" who come and visit for a while each day. As stated earlier, the soap opera serves many people as a kind of makeshift therapy, a counterpart of Aristotle's purgation. The characters should be very emotional and this emotion must be conveyed to the listener. They should face obstacles of the most difficult sort. Particularly if the protagonists are young people, they must face seemingly insurmountable odds.

At the same time, the characters should have some experiences that are different in some degree from those of the audience. They should meet situations and find themselves in environments that are, to the listener, exciting or exotic or both. The characters' experiences should serve, in some part, as means of escape for the listener who, through empathy, transports herself or himself to wherever the characters are and to whatever they are doing. The characters should do some things that the viewer would like to do, but can't.

Because the most important purpose of the soap opera is to establish viewer identification and empathy with the characters, character is the principal motivating factor in creating the script. Soaps usually require an eight-week story projection, so most writers are constantly working on the program, carrying a dozen or more characters in their heads at the same time. Some soap opera writers do as much research and planning with characters as do the writers of Pulitzer Prize-winning plays. They know the characters' intimate lives from the day they were born.

The plot, unlike that of the straight television drama, should contain a number of subplots, all bearing on the major conflict. They should complicate matters almost beyond endurance for the protagonist. The only limitation is that the complications should stop short of confusion for the viewer.

Because the viewer may not be able to give full attention to each episode, day in and day out, the plot line cannot always be brisk and sharp, nor constantly contain elements that demand the full attention of the viewer. In addition, the viewer may miss a number of episodes and should be able to go back to the story without missing anything of appreciable importance. The plot should move as slowly as possible. The soap opera never reaches a final climax, but holds interest for a number of rising action complications — such as the shooting of J. R. in "Dallas." The conflict is clear and ever-present and unfolds imperceptibly, particularly in the daily daytime soap. It develops with one very minor event at a time. An unexpected knock at the door can be built up into a minor complication lasting for weeks or even months. In each episode only a minute segment of action takes place, and there is little change. The time of the drama sometimes moves as slowly as the time of day. Rather than being a heightened and condensed interpretation of life, as is most drama, the soap opera is a slow, drawn-out, detailed report of life. Over a period of days or even weeks the action in the drama may cover only an hour's time. The viewer wants to believe that the characters are real, and that the events are happening as they are seen. The events, then, should happen as they do in the lives of the audience: slowly, unemphatically, even undramatically, but to the individual they should be of critical and extreme importance, no matter how minor the event. This implies that the dialogue must be like that of real life: slow and nondramatic, barely moving the action along, or excessively melodramatic. Listen for dialogue in the subways, on street corners, in supermarkets.

Start each episode at a peak — the crisis of what seems to be a complication. In each episode, the particular complication should be solved or should take another turn and the drama should level off. Before the program is ended, a new element of complication — and remember, these complications may be the most insignificant happenings — should be introduced. A critical point should be reached just as the episode ends. Like the serial of the silent film days, it should be a cliff-hanger, making it necessary for the audience to tune in the next episode to learn what will happen.

The basic technique of writing the television soap opera is somewhere between that of the live-style taped play and the completely live production. For a long time soaps were done live, broadcast simultaneously as they were performed. One of the advantages of tape in terms of the special dramaturgical character of the soap opera, is that you can make even better use of simultaneous action. Instead of continuous action, which would move the story along too fast to permit the slow development of subplots, you can switch frequently during the program to different scenes involving different characters, all of these actions ostensibly occurring at the same time. The daytime soap is still essentially continuous action; the evening soap follows the television film form.

The lack of time for much rehearsal or preparation for a five-times-per-week drama means that you should keep setting and special effects to a minimum, keep the characterizations well within the patterns already established for the roles, and make no sudden or drastic changes in the form of the plot or dialogue. It also means that you have to adapt to the real-life activities and problems of the performers. Because the characters appear in a continuous action situation, if someone in the cast goes skiing and breaks a leg, for example, you will have to rewrite the script to justify their having a leg in a cast or their absence from the scene for a time.

Beginning with the second episode, you need a **lead-in** — that is, a summary of the basic situation and of the previous episode. The script also needs a **lead-out.** This is the aforementioned cliff-hanger, where the narrator sets up suspense by asking what will happen to the characters in the precarious situation in which they are left until the next episode — as well as the closing scene visually conveying that question. For the daytime soap, the most intense cliff-hanger should be at the end of the Friday episode, providing that much more suspense to keep the audience interested over the weekend and eager to tune in on Monday.

The Adaptation

Adapting a short story, novel, or play to television is in some respects more difficult than creating an original. The greatest problem is in getting away from the original work. When adapting a short story or novel, the writer is in danger of attempting to follow the original's action sequence and even the dialogue, which are usually undramatic, repetitious, and introspective when compared with the heightened and condensed structure and dialogue of a play. The author of a prose work can describe people, explain their feelings, and clarify the situations, motivations, and even the action through examples or illustrations. The playwright cannot do this. She or he can *explain nothing,* but must *show everything.* The adapter of the short story or novel must therefore get away from the craft of the original and create anew, using as a base the essence of the theme, background, characters, and plot of the original.

It is advisable for the adapter to read the original work enough times to become thoroughly familiar with it, and then lay it aside. There should be no need to take it up again. From a thorough knowledge of the material, the adapter should be then able to create the television or radio script. From the short story or novel the adapter takes only the elements of character, plot, theme, and background, and maybe a hint of the dialogue style, although nondramatic dialogue frequently sounds ludicrous when read aloud.

Adapting the stage play is somewhat easier. The adapter has the basic elements of content and construction already at hand. The primary problem is one of condensation. The application of the special characteristics of time, space, audience, subject matter, and mechanical and electronic devices, and the rules of dramaturgy for the television play as modified from the dramaturgical rules of the stage play, should result in an effective adaptation.

The adaptation of the stage play has contributed importantly to dramatic fare on television (and, in the past, on radio). As an adapter you may approach the task from one of two major viewpoints. One is to consider the original inviolate and attempt to keep it as intact as possible, cutting and condensing only where necessary to comply with a time limit, and changing the original work only in the most dire emergency. The other is to consider the play a peg on which to hang your own creative ability, select the barest essence of the original, and write what may be virtually an entire new or different play. The approach of most adapters seems to be somewhere between the two extremes: to attempt to get the essence of the play in scenario form and then, selecting parts of the original that could be used intact, to round out the script with original work.

In adapting any form of literature you should retain the original author's intent and the essence of the story. Keep the basic character motivations and delineations. Attempt to capture the style, feeling, and mood of the original. Over and above all this, however, add, subtract, change, and modify so that the original work is translated most effectively in terms of the techniques of the medium. The adapter frequently has to delete some sequences, add scenes, combine two or more sequences into one, transpose scenes, delete and add characters, combine several characters into one, change characterizations, and introduce a narrator.

You must choose the approach to adaptation best suited to your own abilities. Some writers are better at working with characters and plots already created. Others are better at working from a basic theme or outline and creating their own characters and plot lines. Writer-adapter Irving Elman analyzed some of the pitfalls as well as the advantages in these two approaches to adaptation. He wrote:

> The tendency with the first type is for the writer's creative urge, with no outlet through original creation of his own, to use the material he is adapting merely as a point of take-off, from which he attempts to soar to heights of his own. If he happens to be a genius like Shakespeare those heights can be very high indeed. But if he is not a genius, or even as talented as the man whose work he is adapting, instead of soaring to heights, the adaptation may sink to depths below the level of the material he "adapted."
>
> The second writer, with sufficient outlet for his creativity through his own writing, is less tempted (except by his ego!) to show up the writer whose work he is adapting, proving by his "improvements" on the other man's material how much better a writer he is. But if he genuinely likes and respects the material he is adapting, he will restrain himself to the proper business of an adaptor: translating a work from one medium to another with as much fidelity to the original as possible, making only those changes called for by the requirements of the second medium, trying in the process not to impair or violate the artistry of the original.

The Miniseries

Although the miniseries seemed to be new to many American television viewers in the early 1980s, public television viewers became acquainted with a number of excellent British-made miniseries, such as "Upstairs, Downstairs," a decade earlier.

As already noted, the time length for miniseries, ranging from a few hours to literally dozens of hours over many days, permits bypassing some of the special quantitative limitations of the standard half-hour, hour, or even two-hour television play, including time, space, plot, and characters. For example, depending on length, the miniseries permits many subplots with many characters — a play structure not possible in the fifty-one-minute script of the hour program. One of the longest miniseries on commercial television when it was produced in 1983, "The Winds of War" accommodated a number of subplots with complications and rising action for each.

The writer should not let these greater freedoms also bypass the special qualitative potentials of the medium, however. One of television's most significant attributes, for instance, is the intimacy possible between performer and viewer. This can and should be maintained by combining the performer-audience relationship of the live theater with the close-up and moving camera of the film. In some cases this intimacy — and do not forget that the performer is coming to the viewer in his or her own living room — can be heightened by the use of the presentational techniques of the stage, as was so effectively done in the 1983 miniseries adaptation of the theater production of *Nicholas Nickleby*. Remember that the medium is still television, with the psychological set of the audience at home, the relatively small viewing screen, and the medium's own unique artistic and technical elements.

The abundance of time allowed for a miniseries sometimes lures a writer into losing track of a major principle of good playwriting: a tight, consistently developing, rising action. Some miniseries end up written at a soap opera pace, attempting to be literal with the fictional or semifictional time of the events or with the events of the time. Writers of drama based on history cannot excuse poor writing by saying "Well, that's the way it was." Real life seldom is dramatic. Drama is a condensation and interpretation of the crises of life. The 1982 eight-hour miniseries "The Blue and Gray," despite the obvious dramatic conflict inherent in its content, was considered by a number of critics to have been written at too slow a pace, resulting in dullness, and with too much melodrama and not enough historical drama.

The made-for-television movie is the principal production approach taken for the miniseries. Unfortunately, the approach of the traditional Hollywood feature film too often dominates and ignores the special qualities of the television medium. For the creative writer, the miniseries is very attractive, offering the opportunity for a play of almost unlimited length. Be careful of the temptation to pad. Few well-written plays can be sustained for a drawn-out period of time. And, although miniseries seem to be growing in popularity in the 1980s, the best practical vocational bet for the writer remains the continuing weekly series, with its stock plot, characters, and dialogue, presenting a weekly challenge for something new and exciting.

Comedy — Sitcoms

The situation comedy has dominated American commercial television drama. Some of them are excellent, using the best elements of comedy writing not only to make people laugh, but to make them feel and think at the same time.

Whether comedy writing can be taught or learned is questionable. Books on writing comedy present certain formulas; compendia of comedy materials provide situations and one-liners. At an early age some of us are inculcated with the wit, outrageousness, sensitivity, absurdity, incongruity, incisiveness and other elements of psyche and temperament that constitute humor, which we then combine with an irreverent look at the sacred cows of the society in which we live. If you've got the gift of comedy, you know it. The best learning is practice.

Good comedy has always related to the seriousness of life. Molière, for example, understood that serious dramatic essays on the hypocrisies and foibles of his time would not be acceptable to the establishment in seventeenth-century France that controlled the means by which ideas could reach the masses. He knew as well that the public, conditioned and intimidated by perceptions of what they were led to believe was acceptable political and social thought, would have been afraid to accept his ideas if they were presented in sober forms.

A modern example of the same approach is that of Norman Lear, who understands that serious television plays on the hypocrisies and foibles of our time are not often acceptable to the networks and advertisers who control the means by which the masses are reached now. He knows, too, that the public has demonstrated its fear of controversial ideas by its acceptance of the McCarthy-period blacklisting and by its tolerance in the 1980s of the television industry's capitulation, through self-censorship and the firing of controversial performers, to the pressures of self-styled moral majorities.

Molière wrote comedies, farces, and satires in order to express his ideas in a form palatable to the establishment and attractive to the citizenry, and took them to the public in the village squares and in the theaters of the cities throughout his country.

Lear, joined by painfully few other producers, expresses his serious ideas in comedies and farces so attractive to the people that the networks and advertisers entreat him to let them present them to the public.

Look at the difference, next time you watch sitcoms on television, between those that leave you laughing, thoughtful, and stimulated, and those that narcotize your brain and feelings as well as your tired feet. Too many of the latter are poorly written sophomoric farces, depending on surface characterizations that are little more than stereotypes exploiting the physical, mental, or emotional misfortunes of people around us.

The good situation comedies are the ones that are good plays, with believable characters who are consistent and who motivate the action. Archie Bunker, George Jefferson, Maude, Barney Miller and company, Hawkeye and B. J. and crew are among the too few. When the characters are too broad (as they are in most sitcoms, including some with high ratings) they become cartoons. You can write characters with comic flaws or you can write comic stereotypes — the two major genres of sitcom characters on television (this is the difference between Charlie Chaplin and the Three Stooges, for example).

If you've studied drama you know that sitcoms are not new. We can go back to Aristophanes with his comic satire, or to the ancient Roman farces of Plautus, or to the French farces of Scribe and Sardou. Adapt their plots and characters and you've got every sitcom on television today; all have been borrowed from, some with skill, some without.

Remember that it is character and situation that are most important. For television the plot has to be squeezed into twenty-five minutes for a play, or, in series with cliff-hangers or plot lines that carry over several episodes, twenty-five minutes for each scene or act. Once the characters have been established, the dialogue and plot action emanating from them also have been established and the trick is to find something new or different each week.

Problems and Potentials

Thus far television has not often enough lived up to its potentials. Radio did, at times, but ultimately sacrificed its achievements for a common denominator. Television drama, as well as most other forms of television production, seems to have fulfilled the dire prediction made by Gilbert Seldes as early as 1931. Television, Seldes wrote in the *New Republic,* will be as bad as or worse than the most mediocre aspects of radio: "Each new form of entertainment drains off the cheap and accidental elements of its predecessors." The commercialization of television is a great fault, he warned, for although it is a magic miracle, it will be used as "a miracle made for money."

This need not be so, of course. Television, like radio, has the potential to be a most effective art form as well as to contribute a great deal to entertainment and culture. Whether it will or not depends not alone on a handful of writers or producers or directors or critics. It does not even depend alone on the advertisers. A concerted effort by responsible members of the audience, by the public at large — through letters, phone calls, and other communications on the part of each individual viewer and listener — can most effectively influence a change in the programming practices of the mass-oriented and product-controlled media.

Rod Serling, who was one of television's most articulate as well as prolific writers, called television a medium of compromise for the writer. He was concerned that the writer cannot touch certain themes or use certain language. In an article by D. B. Colen in the *Washington Post* he criticized television because of "its fear of taking on major issues in realistic terms. Drama on television must walk tiptoe and in agony lest it offend some cereal buyer." Despite these restrictions, he felt, as he said on the Merv Griffin Show just several months before he died, that "you can write pretty meaningful, pretty adult, pretty incisive pieces of drama."

Tom Swafford, when vice-president for program practices at CBS-TV, said in *Broadcasting* magazine: "Society is changing. If a television network doesn't reflect those changes, it's going to turn off the audience it's trying to reach." Robert Kasmire, when vice-president for corporate affairs at NBC, stated in *Broadcasting*: "Even though we're moving into subjects that are more relevant and topical, more sensitive, we're still not lowering our standards bars. Our standards have to be far stricter than those of other media because we go directly into the home, and the network has no way of policing who's sitting in front of the TV set."

With little likelihood that either public attitude and action or those of the broadcasters will change drastically in the near future, we must operate in the framework we now have for television playwrights. Although there may be a future large market for playwrights in public television and in cable television, as a writer today you are still principally dependent on the commercial mass media for your existence; yet, you can take comfort in the fact that despite the restrictions put upon you by sponsors, networks, and production executives, your play is still the prime mover, the one element upon which all other elements of the production must stand or fall. With a script of high quality, with writing of ethical and artistic merit, you may at least take pride in knowing that you have made a significant effort to fulfill some of the mass media's infinite potentials.

11

Professional Opportunities

So you want to write for television!'' could be an advertising headline to entice glamour-struck young people into schools, correspondence courses, or books all but guaranteed to make them next year's Emmy Award winners.

I am convinced — after many years of teaching television and radio writing, writing for television and radio, and knowing television and radio writers — that good creative television and radio writing cannot be taught.

Putting together words or visual images that conform to specified formats can be taught. In that sense, many people can learn to write rundown sheets, routine sheets, and scripts that are usable for television and radio programs.

That's not a bad thing. If one accepts a certain format and approach as ethical and contributory to a positive effect upon the viewers, then there's nothing wrong with being a competent draftsperson of television and radio scripts. You can attain great success in this role of interpretive writer — that is, taking a format already created by someone else and putting it into a form that best presents it to the audience. Like an actor, a dancer, a musician.

Writing in its highest sense, however, is not copying or interpreting. It is *creating*. The ultimate aim of the writer is to be creative in the sense that the composer, the painter, or the choreographer is creative.

That cannot be taught in a classroom. It comes from a combination of motivated talent and experience. There are certain forms, techniques, and approaches that can and should be learned. Just as it is necessary for the painter to learn what is possible with color, form, line, and texture, so the writer must learn what is possible with the tools available to him or her. That is what this book tries to do.

The *creative* art of writing requires much more. It is a synthesis of one's total psychological, philosophical, physical background, heightened into expressiveness through a knowledge of form, technique, and approach. I have rarely found a person in any of the classes I have taught who was not able to write a rundown, routine, or script satisfactorily in each television and radio program genre. But too infrequently have I found a person who was able to go beyond the basic format and create a script that truly fulfilled the potentials of television or radio in affecting, in a humanistic, positive manner, the minds and emotions of the audience.

I hope that you who are reading this and contemplating a career in writing for television and radio are capable of the highest level of creative writing. But even if you are not, there are career opportunities. Indeed, sometimes the creative writer has less of an opportunity for gainful employment because of difficulty in lowering his or her artistic plane of writing to conform to the formulas of the particular program or script type.

In presenting some views on careers and the opportunities for writers in various areas of television and radio, I am making no judgment on what you should accept in terms of your particular talents, skills, and ambitions. How far you should go or how limited you should let yourself be is a matter only you can decide. But do know just what you are capable of and what you can be happy with.

The combinations of potential and restriction, of opportunity and responsibility, of creativity and compromise pertain to virtually all writing jobs for all levels and types and for all broadcast stations and other producing organizations. As stated in a flyer by the Lilly Endowment, Inc., in instituting a Humanitas Prize for television writing, "the writer of American television is a person of great influence, for the values projected on the TV screen begin in his or her mind, heart and psyche. Few educators, churchmen or politicians possess the moral influence of a TV writer. This entails an awesome responsibility for the TV writer. But it also provides a tremendous opportunity to enrich his or her fellow citizens. How? By illuminating the human situation, by challenging human freedom, by working to unify the human family. In short, by communicating those values which most fully enrich the human person."

Whether or not the writer is always or ever permitted to do this is another story. Barbara Douglas, whose executive position at Universal Studios included finding scripts, packages, and properties for film and television, acknowledged the frustrations of the writer within the commercial requirements of broadcasting, but at the same time believed there is hope for creative talented people who are able to write alternative scripts that large companies might be able to produce. She stated, in *Media Report to Women,* that integrity can be retained within an area of compromise, in which a script has mass commercial value but is not a sellout. "It's this fairly narrow area of quality which I wish our promising young people would consider, instead of either leaping to low-grade imitations of what appears to be a way to turn a fast dollar, or alternatively coming from a place that's so far from the mass mind that the script turns the studio people off before they get to page five."

Barbara Allen, writer, producer, and teacher of television and radio, offers some additional basic considerations for those who wish to write successfully for the broadcast media. She suggests that you should be:

Creative enough to turn out bright ideas fast and
Self-disciplined enough to watch others "improve" on them;
Organized enough to lay out a concise production script and

Unstructured enough to adjust to last-minute deviations;
Persistent enough to be able to research any subject thoroughly and
Flexible enough to be able to present it as a one-hour documentary or a 30-
    second spot;
Imaginative enough to write a script that can be produced at a nominal cost and
Practical enough to have a second plan for doing it at half that cost.
P.S. It also helps if you can spell, punctuate and type.

Where are the jobs in broadcast writing? Allen breaks down the categories as follows:

Network radio: news, editorials, features

Network television: soap operas, game shows, stunts for quizzes, comedy writing, preprogram interviews, research, children's programs, series writing, news, promotion, continuity

Local radio and television: news, promotion, continuity, documentaries, special programs

Related areas: cable systems, independent film production and syndication companies, advertising agencies, free-lance commercials, department stores, national and state service groups, safety councils and charity enterprises, utility companies, farm organizations, religious organizations, government agencies, educational institutions and organizations

Writer's Digest, which provides continuing analysis of markets for writers, including radio and television, has summarized opportunities as follows:

Opportunities at local stations and networks include news writing, editing, continuity writing, commercial and promotion writing, and script and special feature writing.

News writers and editors collect local news and select stories from the wire services, often editing and rewriting them for local audiences. News men may also serve as reporters, covering local stories and interviews along with a cameraman. Continuity writers develop commercials for sponsors that don't have advertising agencies, write station promotional and public service announcements and occasionally program material. Both news and continuity writers are able to get across the essentials of a story in simple, concise language. Most script work is done on a contract or freelance basis, but some staff writers are employed. Special feature subjects are generally sports and news stories, usually written by a staff writer in one of these areas. However, stations are always eager to listen to new feature ideas from staff writers or outside writers.

A good broadcast writer has all the basic writing skills at his command and, since he frequently doesn't have time to rewrite, develops his speed and accuracy. A college education in liberal arts or journalism is desirable, but a good writer who has other talents such as announcing is also well-qualified. As always, the writer with talent and original ideas will get the job.

It is best to approach a broadcast company through an employment agency. If you prefer not to do this, submit a resume with some of your best writing samples to the station or personnel manager and ask for an interview. Apply first at a small station and get that priceless experience that you can list on your work record, then contact the larger organization.

In their book, *Your Career in TV and Radio,* George N. Gordon and Irving A. Falk stated:

> Programming departments of relatively large stations can use people who have developed skills as writers to create continuity, commercial announcements, and other material read over the air in the course of a day. Major stations and networks also have work for people with a bent for research. They provide background for feature programs and interviews.
>
> Television *alone* (and let us consider only *network* television) is responsible for some *twenty thousand hours* of programming per year. True, some of it is made up of replayed Hollywood films, but a scribe writes each one of those commercials you see, each news broadcast, and all the "ad-lib" remarks that your favorite master of ceremonies produces so glibly. Not all the material broadcast on our more than 5,000 radio stations is written out in script form; many disc jockey and interview programs are ad-libbed. But enough writers are employed by our TV and radio stations today to write out *in one year the entire work of all copyists who created by hand all the books in Europe during the Middle Ages* from 500 to 1500 A.D., when printing was invented.
>
> Jack Wilson, one of the last radio dramatic story editors, says: "good writers can start anywhere in broadcasting; as copywriters or news editors on small stations, or as assistant gag writers. It doesn't matter where or how you start out. If you have talent, it will show. A writer learns by writing, and you don't start in the top drawer in any field, except maybe if you write a smash best-seller novel. You also have to build an immunity to rejection slips and turned-down manuscripts. Very few people get to be TV or radio writers on their first try, or even on the second or third try. You have to have patience." Jack Wilson's advice to young writers is extremely practical. First, *listen* to radio, *watch* TV, and get to know how the professionals do it. Then practice the craft and try to sell materials either to local TV or radio outfits or, by mail, to bigger production organizations. The one thing a young writer should not do is pack up his bags and head for New York or Los Angeles in the mistaken belief that he has a better chance in the big city than in his home town. He doesn't. . . . Jack notes . . . "don't be fooled that you can get a lot of money for 'hack' writing that's easy to knock off. No matter what you are working on, and you may hate the darn program, your finest effort is required. In a way, it's just as hard to be a bad writer as it is to be a good one. There is no easy way to use the twenty-six letters in the English alphabet in their infinite combinations."
>
> In TV or radio, the term "writer" applies to anyone who prepares broadcasts which are not spontaneously produced, although sometimes writers prepare notes from which a performer spontaneously ad-libs. A writer is therefore considered the employee of one or another of agencies which produce broadcasts. Writers are paid according to the type of employer for whom they work and the extent of the service which they perform for him.

Every arm of broadcasting employs writers of one sort another, either on a free-lance basis or on a permanent payroll. Some writers work for individual stations; others work for networks. Some work for both. Network jobs are, of course, better paying and generally considered more important than station jobs, but most network writers start out as employees of stations. Independent producers, syndicated TV program producers, and film producers hire many writers to produce the vast amounts of material they consume. These authors are frequently highly specialized.

The most interesting type of writing for broadcasting, many believe, is dramatic writing. . . . Daytime TV is replete with relatively well-written versions of radio's old soap operas. Independent program producers and film producers keep creating a never-ending stream of filmed westerns, gangster shows, pseudohorror films, domestic comedy films, and animated stories for children and for adults also. And don't forget the TV "specials," productions of superior plays and original musicals. . . . Never attempt to market any dramatic script which does not fit the format of the kind of TV shows presently on the air.

Whenever writers are mentioned in broadcasting circles, you frequently hear talk about literary agents and their role in selling the output of authors. Rarely does a writer for TV or radio need a literary agency unless he operates as a free-lance author, selling his output to the highest bidder. Free-lancers usually write for dramatic programs and their scripts are bought for "one-shot" programs. . . . Literary agents help free-lance dramatic writers to place their manuscripts with production companies or to search out assignments. For their services, agents receive at least ten per cent of the sale price of each script the author writes. Most literary agents will sign contracts only with writers who have established reputations and whose work is known to be marketable. *Remember that ten per cent of nothing is nothing.*

Jane Caper, former producer of the TV interview program "Panorama" on WTTG, Washington, D.C., and a producer of ABC's "A.M. America," has suggested that a person wishing to break into television — as a writer, on interview shows, or in any capacity — should seek an internship at a local station. "There are so few jobs available," Caper has said, "that in most instances this is the only way to get experience and exposure." The intern should not be afraid to take the initiative. "If you have ideas, type them up and give them to the producer. Let the producer know you are willing to work hard and long hours." She has advised that, if at all possible, one should seek experience with live shows, hopefully in some on-the-air as well as in a production capacity.

Commercials

The three areas in which there is the greatest opportunity — that is, in which most writers are employed — are commercials, news, and drama. Kirk Polking, director of *Writer's Digest* School, analyzed careers for copywriters for a *Writer's Digest* article, "The TV Copywriter":

Of all the writing jobs today, the network television commercial copy-writer probably gets paid more, for less actual *writing,* than any other writer. Charlie Moss, whose copy jobs include the American Motors account and others handled by the Wells, Rich, Greene agency, points out, "I may spend no more than 15 minutes a week at the typewriter. Much of the rest of my time is spent sitting around this table with art directors and account executives analyzing a client's product and trying to find the right idea to sell it in one minute." *Idea* is the key word here and many top agency copy chiefs say they're looking for "concept creators," not writers. "*Writers* we can always hire," says one creative supervisor. "What's harder to find is the guy with a new idea, a fresh approach — someone who can create the theme for a brilliant, visual short story, with a sales message, in 60 seconds."

. . . Ron Rosenfeld, a copy chief at Doyle Dane Bernbach, says, "We're not necessarily looking for copywriters as such. We want people who have a great sense of the graphic and are good at thinking in pictures."

. . . The television commercial copywriter has to sell the client first before he can sell his idea to the public. How does he do this? . . . A client says, "Too many young copywriters come in with only one idea and can't do a good job of showing why it will effectively sell the product. They're too jealous of their own idea — maybe they're afraid they'll never get another. A real professional can lay aside an idea you don't like, and come up with five others and show you 11 good reasons why each one would be effective."

. . . "There's a screaming need for good TV commercial copywriters," says Ed Carder, Director of the Radio and TV Department of Ralph Jones, "but the writer has to have a thorough basic understanding of the English language, how TV and radio work and the discipline to work within time and space limitations."

. . . What about freelancing in this field? It usually takes the form of moonlighting. A small agency will go to a copywriter at a leading agency whose style they like and ask him to do a job on the side. Mostly the agencies work with their own staff people and know fairly well what their next year's needs are going to be in the way of personnel based on their client list. Rarely has an agency bought a TV commercial idea submitted by a writer through the mail. Some of the larger clients and agencies have a form letter rejecting all such submissions automatically to protect themselves from claims of plagiarism. A writer who has what he thinks are some new, fresh approaches to the TV commercial might do best to work with local agencies first, contacting them by mail, with a resume of his professional experience and asking for an appointment to present several specific commercial ideas for specific clients of the agency. If he's good, he'll get a chance.

. . . Most agencies agree that a good liberal arts background is essential for any copywriting job. Since TV copywriting also requires a knowledge of the things the motion picture camera and the TV studio can and cannot do, background in these areas is also helpful.

Several Doyle Dane Bernbach copywriters discussed in *DDB News* how they judge copywriters and offered some comments of value to the person seeking to break into the field. In describing what she seeks in going over someone's portfolio, Sue Brock said, "The first thing I look for is whether there is an ad there that I would have okayed. And then, if there are none like that, whether there is the germ of a good idea that perhaps was goofed up in the execution. Then, after you've decided that there is something there that is fresh or exciting, you call the person in, and at that point you are influenced by the person's personality. If she sits there hostile and full of anxieties, you lose interest, because this is very much team work, and all the little belles and stars have a very rough time." Judy Protas stated that "in this business, where criticism is very much the order of the day, a writer whose personality can't stand up to criticism would fall apart at the seams." Brock added that "you have to have a pretty good opinion of yourself or you won't survive. You have to have a pretty strong ego, because everyone here is willing to criticize — traffic, the messengers, everyone. And if it happens to be your boss who's criticizing, you're going to have to change your copy." Protas concluded that "you have to know when to stop discussion. You're expected to fight for your opinion, but not start whining and arguing defensively over something in which only your ego is involved."

George Grey, president and general manager of WBSM-Southern Massachusetts Broadcasting Company, has this principal advice for the person who wishes to obtain a job writing commercial copy: "Learn to write a simple, declarative sentence." He seeks, from experienced and inexperienced applicants both, the ability to write "simple, clear, short sentences, using a lot of nouns and verbs, a limited number of adjectives, and very few adverbs." He wants people who "can express a thought in the simplest terms. Nothing loses a listener more quickly than high-flown imagery. My advice to my own writers is: tell them, tell them what you told them, then tell them again." Although he wants people who have had experience in the real world and who understand the client's business goals and the purposes of the commercials they write, paramount are "the techniques of thinking, habits of study, organization of time and energy, and self-discipline that people who have a college education presumably have learned, and which are all essential for one to be a successful professional broadcast writer."

News

With the increased emphasis on local news, jobs for news reporter-writers at local stations have increased as well. Desired preparation for a career in broadcast journalism varies with station and station managers. In some instances a pure journalistic background is preferred; in others, specialization in television and/or radio techniques is wanted; in still other cases judgment and news sense is subjectively evaluated, with training a secondary consideration. Stanley S. Hubbard, as president and general manager of Hubbard Broadcasting, Inc., described in *Television/Radio Age* what he looks for:

What is a news person? Is a news person qualified because he has a degree from a university which says he graduated in journalism? Or is a news person qualified because he has held a job someplace as a news person? I think not. I think that a news person, in order to really be considered capable, has to prove that he or she has news ability and "news sense." The time restrictions involved in producing television news require that in order to be successful, a television news person has to have genuine news sense. It is not possible, insofar as my experience has indicated, for a person to learn news sense in a journalism school. . . . Journalism schools can prepare you very adequately to go to work in a news room at a TV station and learn how to successfully fit into the mechanism, but just because a person successfully fits into the mechanism, it is a mistake to think that a person necessarily has news sense or the judgment required of a licensee in the discharge of his public responsibilities.

Background, formal or informal, is required, of course. News sense without knowledge is the other half of the loaf that includes knowledge without news sense. In light of the attention being directed to local and regional events on local stations, Barbara Allen recommends that as a potential reporter-writer, "1) you need to be familiar with every aspect of city government, the people who make up the power structure in your community, the business and industries that support your area's economy, your schools, colleges and local personalities, 2) the breadth and depth of your knowledge about people and government and art and politics and educational science and social and economic problems will be the underpinnings of your value as a journalist, and 3) your function and responsibility is to see what seem to be isolated events against the background of the forces which cause those events."

Teresa McAlpine, managing editor of all-news radio station WEEI in Boston, looks for some experiential background when interviewing potential beginning newswriters. She first determines whether the applicants have some experience in writing broadcast news, "which requires different skills than writing for newspapers. At WEEI our beginning writers write news for broadcast from many sources, including personally conducted telephone interviews from which they prepare stories. Previous broadcast newswriting is essential. It can have been with a college station or a non-paying internship somewhere . . . as long as it's broadcast writing."

The second thing McAlpine looks for is the applicant's ability to write simple sentences in conversational style. She expects the writer to have a sense of news judgment, and she tests applicants by giving them print stories, having them rewrite for radio, and judging whether the writer found the proper lead for radio and presented it in a "catchy, conversational style." Finally, she looks for speed. Fast-breaking radio news stories frequently have to be written very quickly. "To the good newswriter," she says, "all of this comes naturally."

As for education, McAlpine believes that a liberal arts background is the best preparation, coupled with a continuing knowledge of what is going on in the world from assiduous reading of newspapers and magazines and listening and watching broadcast news. If the applicants have little or no previous experience in broadcast newswriting, they can balance that off by having a communications major or degree. She also believes that courses in radio and television writing will have taught the applicants the essential forms and techniques and that "this is a definite plus."

Irving Fang, in his book *Television News*, reported on the preferences of news directors in hiring young people from among five categories of preparation. First preference was for a reporter with two years' experience and no college education, and close behind was preference for a college graduate in broadcast journalism with no experience. Very low in preference were college graduates with a different major and no experience, a local resident junior college graduate with no experience, and a broadcasting trade school graduate with no experience. Majors other than broadcast journalism, in order of preference, included political science, English, liberal arts, history, general journalism, and telecommunications. The most important ability looked for was that of writing, with other skills, including reporting and on-air personality, far behind. The personal qualities most desired are eagerness, enthusiasm, self-motivation, and energy. Fang also listed the behavioral attitudes a broadcast journalist should have, according to the American Council on Education for Journalism:

1. Ability to write radio news copy.
2. Judgment and good taste in selecting news items for broadcast.
3. Ability to edit copy of others, including wire copy.
4. Knowledge of the law especially applicable to broadcasting.
5. Knowledge of general station operation.
6. Understanding of the mechanical problems of broadcasting.
7. Appreciation of broadcasting's responsibility to the public, particularly in its handling of news.
8. Ability to work under pressure.
9. Ability to make decisions quickly.
10. Speed in production.
11. Familiarity with the various techniques of news broadcasting (including first-person reporting, tape recordings, interviews, remotes).
12. Knowledge of newscast production (including timing or back-timing of script, opens and closes, placement of commercials, production-newsroom coordination).
13. Ability to gather news for radio/tv.
14. Ability to read news copy with acceptable voice quality, diction, etc.
15. Ability to find local angles in national or other stories.
16. Quickness to see feature angles in routine assignments.
17. Ability to simplify complex matters and make them meaningful to the listener or viewer.

It is estimated that there are about twenty thousand newswriting positions in radio and approximately the same number in television throughout the country. Yet, each year, there are more applicants than there are job openings. In addition, salaries vary widely. In the early 1980s they ranged from about $10,000 per year at small stations to more than $30,000 at networks (translate the relative differences into the inflation figure existing at the time you read this).

Where do you look for a job as a newswriter? Everywhere and anywhere! If you're breaking into the field, try the small stations first, where you can get experience doing everything, in and out of news, in and out of writing. If you want or need to live and work where there are predominantly large stations, be prepared to start as a copyperson or in another beginning position. Be aware, however, that it is extremely difficult to go up the ladder in a network or similar large operation, and the lack of experience and competitive structure may keep you on a rung of the ladder quite removed from newswriting for a long time, if not forever. Most experienced newswriters and managers recommend the small station route as the one with the better chance. If you are studying in a journalism, communications, broadcasting, or similar department, your professors will already have contact with stations in your state or region, and usually recommend capable graduating students for jobs. You can, of course, contact stations anywhere in the country yourself; ask your professors for help in preparing your resume, and don't forget the experience you obtained, it is hoped, with the university's noncommercial station or with a local commercial station while working on your degree. Your professors can also refer you to national organizations and associations that have placement services. One of the principal groups is the Radio-Television News Directors Association in Woodland Hills, California. Journalist-applicants pay a small fee.

There are some free-lance newswriter-producers, but these are few and far between and usually are people who have achieved sufficient recognition that they can name their own spots and terms. For the less experienced and renowned, however, local television and radio stations do provide some outlets. If you are a writer and have a camera that you can use well and/or a tape recorder that you can be creative with, you can frequently provide special features on local events. Local history, geography, civic affairs, local and state holidays, and unusual happenings and personalities offer a plethora of possibilities. This might be something worthwhile trying while you're still in college, on your own-time, part-time basis. You can get experience with a public television and/or radio station, if there is one, and experience and payment with a local commercial station. Some larger stations employ students as news stringers to cover campus news, particularly athletics.

Playwriting

"Breaking into television is more difficult than for any other writing field," according to former television writer and vice president of RKO Radio, Art Mandelbaum. "It requires plotting a game plan at least as intricate as plotting the structure of a story or teleplot." Mandelbaum has suggested several guidelines for those who wish to write for sitcom or continuing television series:

1. Study very carefully the particular series you want to write for and analyze every major character.

2. Simultaneously find out, if possible, the rating of the series to determine if it will still be on the air the following year. All series shows are assigned to writers by the producer before the season starts, so that even if your script is read and bought, it won't be seen, probably, for about a year-and-a-half. For this reason, too, don't write anything too timely that might be out-of-date by the time the program is aired.

3. Find out the demographics of each show; contact the networks and learn who watches, where the heaviest audience is.

4. It is essential that you obtain an agent in Hollywood. It is a waste of time to send material directly to a producer.

5. An agent can provide you with fact sheets provided to writers on every show. The fact sheets brief writers on formats, requirements and taboos. The Writers' Guild sends out information on all shows to its members.

6. After studying a particular show, provide your agent with a great many ideas for that show. Don't lock yourself into one show idea. If you come up with 50 one-paragraph thumbnail sketches, your agent will have enough to present to the producer even if the first few are immediately shot down.

7. If your agent sells a show idea, then you can get a contract for a treatment — and you can break into the Writers' Guild.

8. Make sure you are grounded in the classics. Basic themes and plots are modifiable and, if you study TV shows, you'll note that they are constantly used.

9. Don't let all your friends read your work. By the time their critical appraisals are finished you'll find that your head is spinning and/or you'll be revising your scripts into something you didn't intend to say in the first place.

10. If an agent offers suggestions that conflict with your ideas concerning a particular show, follow the agent's advice. As a beginner, trying to break in, you are totally dependent on an agent.

11. TV writing is a continuing compromise. The first thing you're pushing is the detergent; the second thing is the content.

Mandelbaum's practical approach combines a range of attitudes; some writers and producers are extremely optimistic about the extent of artistic creativity and social impact possible for the writer of television drama; others are extremely pessimistic and cynical. All agree, however, that you must have the talent to write plays, must write drama that fits the needs and format of the program series (including the dramatic specials that are not continuing-character series), and must know the potentials and the limitations of the medium.

The editors of *Writer's Digest* analyzed the television play market in a pamphlet entitled *Jobs and Opportunities for Writers:*

Television has to fill at least 18 hours every day with fresh, appealing material. This necessity makes it one of the best markets for freelancers. It's one of the highest paying, and producers are constantly looking for new ideas and new scripts. Most new show ideas come from freelancers and many of the subsequent scripts are written by other freelancers. Good dialogue writers will find TV a highly rewarding market. . . . TV producers usually accept scripts only through agents, which means that writers cannot submit work directly to them. But writers can keep themselves informed on the current market picture through *Writer's Digest,* whose issues publish information on new TV shows along with practical articles on TV script writing. The annual *Writer's Market* contains a detailed list of agents' names and addresses.

Television and film writer Alfred Brenner has stated in *Writer's Digest* that "the technological revolution in communications — pay TV, cassettes, cable, satellites, etc. — is already upon us. For the writer, it's a world . . . of expanding markets. . . . For a writer, the only way to break into television . . . is by writing a professional script."

The Writers Guild of America, West, provides a list of agents, noting those willing to look at the work of new writers. Before submitting a script to an agency, however, send a summary and the agency will send you a release form if it is interested in seeing the full script or treatment.

More than one playwright has been quoted anonymously about what happens to a writer in Hollywood: "They ruin your stories. They butcher your ideas. They prostitute your art. They trample your pride. And what do you get for it? A fortune!"

Although writing television play scripts does not provide the lucrative income that writing feature films does, the following figures indicate that a successful writer can do very well financially. The basic minimum rates negotiated by the Writer's Guild of America, from July 1, 1983, to June 30, 1984, are, for the teleplay only, $6,406 for the 30-minute script; $8,642 for the 60-minute show; and $15,410 for the 120-minute program. Fees for both the story and teleplay for the same time periods are $8,993, $13,135, and $23,456, respectively. From July 1, 1984, to June 30, 1985, the payments for the teleplay alone are $6,982 for 30 minutes; $9,420 for 60 minutes; and $17,414 for 120 minutes. For the story and teleplay they are $9,737, $14,317, and $26,506, respectively.

As a sobering thought, however, keep in mind that in 1981 the 8,000 members of the Writers Guild, East and West, had an average individual income of less than $20,000 per year. On the average, you might do better in insurance or plumbing.

Cable and Corporate Television

Cable and corporate television are, at the moment, the two fastest-growing new areas with opportunities for writers. As new technology develops, so will jobs for writers. By the time you read this, video discs and interactive television may well be opening entirely new vistas for writers.

What is significant about cable and other new technologies is that they are expected to provide greater possibilities for a larger variety of dramatic writing, at least until such time as they become duplicates of what has become staple television broadcast station drama. Fred Silverman, former network president, stated in a 1982 interview with David Crook in the *Los Angeles Times* that "the networks are vulnerable in entertainment. . . . Cable is just taking it away from free TV." His own entry into cable television production is predicated on his belief that by the early 1990s cable would command about half of the total viewing audience.

Frank R. King, director of video training for the John Hancock Mutual Life Insurance Company, stated that if you are planning to enter the corporate video field, you should "pick an industry you think you might enjoy." Students should prepare themselves by learning the content areas of the specific industries in which they are interested. However, more important for the writer than knowing the industry or video techniques, King says, is the ability to write creatively, to use the language correctly, including the basics, and to work with people. He advocates conscientious study in script writing courses. He advises people applying for jobs in corporate video to bring, if at all possible, a demonstration tape or reel, with a clearly labeled indication of what the applicant did in the production. If the applicant can afford it, a tape or reel should be left for review by additional persons. If that is not possible, the applicant should bring and leave some sample scripts.

College Preparation

What are the attitudes of station managers toward college graduates in general? *Broadcasting* has cited a study by Frederick N. Jacobs that found that most radio managers have unfavorable attitudes toward college students, with almost two-thirds stating that communications graduates don't understand commercial broadcasting. Some three-fourths say that there is no substitute for experience, with almost half of the managers believing that colleges are not preparing students adequately for a broadcasting career. Although most think that college training is of some help, only a small percentage has more positive than negative opinions about the importance of a degree in broadcasting. A principal concern is that communications departments do not prepare people with a combination of philosophical understanding and practical application, but tend to go too much in one direction or the other.

Professional broadcast training on the undergraduate level is available at about 300 colleges and universities, with more than 100 offering master's degrees and about 30 having doctoral programs. About 150 junior and community colleges have radio-television programs or courses.

Copyright

You can't copyright an idea. If you are creative, you will find that some time, some place, one or more of your ideas will be appropriated without compensation or credit to you. It's happened to all of us, and series formats, script outlines, and concepts for various kinds of programs have from time to time been adapted or even wholly used by unscrupulous broadcasters. On the other hand, there are many ideas, script concepts, and formats that can be thought up by more than one person at virtually the same time, and when you see or hear on the air under someone else's name a creation that you had submitted to a network or station or agency, it might not be a rip-off at all. However, inasmuch as all broadcasting offices require you to sign a release for the purpose of protecting themselves in instances where your submission was not original or the first one received, you can never quite be sure!

The answer is copyright. Unfortunately, not everything that the writer creates for television and radio is copyrightable.

Ideas for and titles of radio or television programs cannot be copyrighted. According to the United States Copyright Office, narrative outlines, formats, plot summaries of plays and motion pictures, skeletal librettos, and other synopses and outlines cannot be registered for copyright in unpublished form. Copyright will protect the literary or dramatic expression of an author's ideas, but not the ideas themselves. If you want to copyright a script, it has to be more than an outline or synopsis. It should be ready for performance so that a program could actually be produced from the script.

The Copyright Office states the following about materials not eligible for copyright: "Works that have not been fixed in a tangible form of expression. For example: choreographic works which have not been notated or recorded, or improvisational speeches or performances that have not been written or recorded. Titles, names, short phrases, and slogans; familiar symbols or designs; mere listings of ingredients or contents. Ideas, procedures, methods, systems, processes, concepts, principles, discoveries, or devices, as distinguished from a description, explanation, or illustration. Works consisting entirely of information that is common property and containing no original authorship."

Unpublished scripts in complete form or a group of related scripts for a series may be copyrighted. If a script is a play, musical, comedy, shooting script for a film, or a similar dramatic work, it may be copyrighted under Class PA: Works of Performing Arts. The Copyright Office describes this class as including "published and unpublished works prepared for the purpose of being 'performed' directly before an audience or indirectly 'by means of any device or process.' Examples of works of the performing arts are: music works, including any accompanying words; dramatic works, including any accompanying music; pantomimes and choreographic works; and motion pictures and other audiovisual works." The latter includes television and radio. Registering a particular script protects that script only and does not give protection to future scripts arising out of it or to a series as a whole.

Television and radio writers should note that there is an additional category that might sometimes apply to their works. Whenever the same copyright claimant is seeking to register both a sound recording and also the musical, dramatic, or literary work embodied in the sound recording, Form SR: Sound Recordings should be used.

You may obtain copyright forms and detailed explanations of how to determine what is copyrightable as well as the procedures for obtaining a copyright by writing to the Copyright Office, Library of Congress, Washington, D.C. 20559. The copyright fee of $10 protects your work for the life of the author plus 50 years.

Another form of script protection, if you don't wish to apply for a copyright, is the Script Registration Service of the Writers Guild of America, West, which is available for a fee to both members and nonmembers. The oft-used self-addressed registered mail approach could have some value in some future litigation, but more formal registration is advised for better protection.

Glossary of
Broadcast Terms and Abbreviations

AM Amplitude modulation, relating to transmission of sound.

American Research Bureau (ARB) Market research company that conducts surveys.

Aperture The diameter of a camera lens opening, also called an iris opening, which controls the amount of light permitted to reach the film.

Arbitron Rating service of ARB that conducts television viewing surveys.

A roll, B roll The practice of putting interview material on one projector, non-interview on another, resulting in the designation of one or the other by A roll or B roll when preparing the final script.

Ascertainment primer Former FCC requirement that a station applying for a license or for renewal must survey community problems and show how programming has dealt and would deal with these problems.

Associated Press (AP) One of the wire services used extensively by news programs.

Automation Use of computers to control some radio equipment and to perform some duties otherwise required of personnel.

Bite A recorded quote, used in documentaries and news programs.

Blending Combining and sending out over the air two or more different sounds at the same time.

Boom A crane used in television that holds a microphone or camera at the end, making it possible to follow or move closer to the performers. Also, the movement of the crane with the camera or microphone to and from the subject.

Bridge A sound, usually music, connecting two consecutive segments of a radio program.

Bumped Rapidly changed intensity.

Bumper Material added to the beginning or end of the principal part of a commercial or to the end of a program that is coming up short.

Cable Wired, as differentiated from over-the-air or broadcast, television transmission; see **Coaxial cable.**

Cart Audio cartridge. Radio scripts usually specify a cart number, which designates segment to be inserted at a given place in a program; some scripts use the term *cut* with a number referring to the segment on audiotape.

Chain break Network break for national or local ads.

Character generator Electronic device that cuts letters into background pictures.

Chiron See **Character generator.**

Chroma key Electronic effect that can cut a given color out of a picture and replace it with another visual.

Close-up Filling the TV screen with a close view of the subject. As with other shot designations, it has various gradations (e.g., medium close-up) and abbreviations.

Coaxial cable Metallic conductors that carry a large bandwidth and many channels; wired television.

Control board Instruments that regulate the volume of output of all radio microphones, turntables, and tapes and can blend the sounds from two or more sources.

Co-op announcement Multiple sponsors on a network commercial; individual messages locally spotted.

Crane shot See **Boom.**

Crawl Movement of titles on screen.

Crawling titles Titles that move slowly and across the screen.

Cross-fade Dissolving from one sound or picture to another; see **Dissolve.**

Cross plug An announcement for one of the station's programs or the advertiser's other products.

CS Close shot. Frequently used for **CU.**

CU Close-up.

Cut In film, instantaneous switch from one picture to another, created in film editing room; also used to designate end of a shooting sequence. In television, instantaneous switch from one camera to another. In radio, see **Cart.**

Cutting Moving abruptly from one sound or picture to another.

DBS Direct broadcast satellite: permits an individual with receiving dish to pick up designated satellite signals; sometimes called satellite-to-home transmission.

Deep focus The longest and shortest distances in which the camera can get the sharpest image on any given shot, aiming at a three-dimensional illusion.

Demographics Analysis of audience characteristics.

Detail set A constructed detail of the set to augment close-ups.

DISS Dissolve.

Dissolve Fading from one picture or sound into another; see **Cross-fade.**

Dolly A carriage with three or four wheels on which a microphone or camera is mounted. Also, the movement of the carriage with the camera toward or away from the subject.

Drive time Automobile commuter hours, important in determining radio programming formats and placement of commercials.

ECU Extreme close-up.

EFFX Effects.

EFP Electronic field production, the use of minicam equipment to produce commercials and other non-news materials away from the studio.

EFX Effects.

Electronic synthesizer Computerized device that can mix and prepare for replay varied sounds, including music.

ENG Electronic news gathering, the use of minicam equipment to cover news stories.

Equal Time rule Congressional and FCC rule that bona fide candidates for the same political office be given equal time for radio and television broadcasts.

ET Electrical transcription; when used with a number (e.g., ET #6) refers to a segment on a record to be used in a program. Preceded the use of tapes ("cut #6") and cartridges ("cart #6").

EXCU Extreme close-up.

EXT Exterior; designates setting in a film script.

Fade, fade in, fade out Gradual appearance or disappearance of sound (in radio) or picture (in television).

Fairness Doctrine Congressional and FCC requirement that if only one side of an issue that is controversial for a given community is presented by a radio or television station in that community, comparable time must be provided for the other viewpoints.

FAX Facsimile; the transmission of written material or pictures through wire or radio. Used to designate segments in a television news program.

Federal Communications Commission (FCC) Government agency regulating the use of the air waves.

Federal Trade Commission (FTC) Governmental agency with some regulatory power over advertising.

Feed Transmission from a remote site.

FF Full figure shot.

Fiber optics Extremely fine fiberglass threads that can carry many more channels than coaxial cable wire transmission.

Focal length Relates to the size of a lens in terms of its principal focusing characteristics and determines how large the image will be at different camera distances.

Follow shot Movement of carriage and camera alongside of or with subject.

Freeze-frame Stopping the action and holding on a single frame.

FS Full shot.

Full-service station A radio station providing two or more types of music, news, talks, features, and so on, as differentiated from a specialized station providing predominantly one service (or one form of music or format).

FX See **FAX.**

Gamma correction Adjustment of contrast in a film negative.

Gobo A cutout device enabling the camera to frame a subject or to get a special effect.

Hollywood style Television directing style that leans principally on traditional Hollywood filmmaking techniques.

ID Station identification.

Instant replay Playback of a videotape even as it is recorded, used frequently in live sports events.

INT Interior; designates setting in a film script.

Intro Standard material used to introduce every program or designated segments within a program in a series; also called stock opening.

ITFS Instructional Television Fixed Service, a relatively inexpensive microwave system that permits point-to-point transmission of instructional, professional, and other materials.

ITV Instructional television; in the United Kingdom, Independent Television (private television not associated with the BBC).

Key A special effect combining two or more video sources, cutting a foreground into a background.

Kine, kinescope The early television picture tube and, before videotape, the term for recording a television program by filming it off the kinescope through a monitor.

LA Live action.

Laser Acronym for light amplification through simulated emission of radiation; a developing technique for multichannel and multidimensional television transmission.

LCU Large close-up.

Lead-in, lead-out The material introducing the substance of a program, such as a recap preceding the daily episode of a soap opera, and the material at the end of a program preparing the audience for the next program.

Limbo Performer, through lighting and position of camera, stands out from a seemingly nonexistent background.

Live-type taped Television directorial technique that uses the continous-action procedures of the live show.

Logo Visual identification symbol of a station, company, or product.

LS Long shot.

Magazine format A program format with a number of different segments not necessarily related in content.

Magnetic tape Tape coated with magnetic particles, used in television for recording, storage, and playback of programs or other materials.

Matte A process by which two different visual sources are combined to appear to be one setting, such as placing a performer on one camera into a setting on another; same as **key,** but can add color to the image. Also spelled *mat* or *matt.*

MCU Medium close-up.

Microwave Transmission on a frequency 1000 MHz and over (not receivable by ordinary home receiver), used for special point-to-point materials.

Miniature A setting used to simulate one that can't be economically built or located live.

Minicam Lightweight, easily portable camera and tape system that facilitates highly mobile news gathering and remote coverage; see **EFP, ENG.**

Minidocumentary A short documentary feature most often used in magazine-type television programs.

Mix In film, rerecording of sounds to blend them together; in radio, combining several sound elements onto a single tape or track; in television, the point in a dissolve when the two images pass each other (the term is sometimes used in place of **dissolve**).

Montage Blending of two or more sounds or series of visuals.

MOR Middle-of-the-road, a radio format combining popular and standard music.

Mortise A cutout area of a picture where other material may be inserted.

MS Medium shot.

MTC Magnetic tape composer.

MU Music.

Multiplex In radio, transmitting more than one signal over the same frequency channel, the additional signals referred to as being transmitted on subcarriers; in television, feeding the signals from two or more sources into one camera.

National Association of Broadcasters (NAB) A voluntary association of television and radio stations. Until their abolition in 1983, the NAB's Radio and Television Codes of Good Practice served as self-regulatory guides for much of broadcasting.

New York style Television directing style that relies heavily on the stage and on the continuous live-action early television techniques.

OC, O/C Off-camera.

On mike Microphone position in which the speaker is right at the microphone; this is the position used if none is indicated.

Outro Standard material used at the end of every program or of designated segments in a program in a continuing series; also called *stock close*.

Pan Lateral movement of the camera in a fixed position.

Panto Pantomime.

Participating announcement The commercials of several advertisers who share the cost of a program.

PB Pull back, referring to camera movement or action of zoom lens.

POV Point of view.

Preinterview Establishment of general areas of questions and answers with an interviewee prior to the taping or live interview.

Prime-time Rule PTAR or Prime-Time Access Rule; FCC requirement that television stations allocate at least one hour during prime time (7 P.M.–11 P.M. EST) every evening to nonnetwork programming.

Promo Promotional announcement; see **Cross-plug.**

PSA Public service announcement.

PTV Usually means public television; sometimes used to mean pay television.

Quadruplex The use of four overlapping heads on a videotape recorder in order to produce tapes of almost-live quality.

Remote Program or materials, usually live coverage, produced at a site away from the studio.

Responsive television Frequently called interactive television, functions principally as audio response in cable hookups and in **ITFS**; developing into computer-based multimedia response systems.

Routine sheet A detailed outline of the segments of a program, frequently including designation of the routines or subject matter, performers, site if remote, time, and so on.

Rundown sheet Sometimes used interchangeably with **Routine sheet,** but generally not as detailed.

SC Studio card.

Scenario Film script outline.

SE Sound effects.

Segue Transition from one radio sound source to another.

Service announcement Short informational announcement, not necessarily completely of a public service nature but similar in form to the **PSA.**

SFX Sound effects.

Sitcom Television situation comedy, the staple of television programming in the 1970s and early 1980s.

SL Studio location.

SOF Sound-on-film; frequently describes a news insert, but also refers to other format segments.

SOT Sound-on-(video)tape; same use as **SOF.**

Split screen Two or more separate pictures on the same television screen.

Storyboard Frame-by-frame drawings showing a program's (usually a commercial's) video and audio sequences in chronological order; essential in preparing and selling commercial announcements and sometimes required in showing development of a film story.

STV Subscription or pay television.

Super Superimposition of one picture over another in television.

Switching See **Cutting.**

Synthesizer See **Electronic synthesizer.**

Tease A program segment, announcement, intro, or other device to get the attention and interest of the audience.

Telop An opaque projector with the trade name Balopticon that shows opaque graphics rather than transparencies; also referred to as Balop.

Tilt Vertical movement of the camera from a fixed position.

Titles Credits and other printed information on the television screen.

Track, track up Following a subject with a camera (see **Follow shot**); raising the intensity of the sound.

Travel shot Lateral movement of the dolly and camera.

Treatment See **Scenario.**

2S Two-shot, the inclusion of two performers in the picture.

United Press International (UPI) One of the wire services used extensively by news programs.

VC, VCU Very close-up.

Videotape Magnetic tape used for recording, storage, and playback of segments for or an entire television program.

Vidifont See **Character generator.**

VO, V.O. Voice-over; the narrator or performer is not seen.

VCR Videocassette or videocartridge recorder.

VTR Videotape recorder.

Wide angle lens A lens of short focal length which encompasses more of the subject area in the picture.

Wipe A picture beginning at one end of the screen that moves horizontally, vertically, or diagonally, pushing or wiping the previous picture off the screen.

Wirephoto Photo transmitted through telephone for use in news broadcasts.

WS Wide shot; used as a synonym for long shot or full shot.

Wrap, Wrap-up The closing for a news program.

XCU Extreme close-up.

XLS Extreme long shot.

ZO Zoom.

Zoom Changing the variable focal length of a lens during a shot to make it appear as if the camera were moving to or away from the subject; similar to the **dolly** technique without moving the carriage or camera.

Suggested Readings

Policy and Production

Barnouw, Erik. *A History of Broadcasting in the United States*. In three volumes: *A Tower in Babel* (to 1933), *The Golden Web* (1933–1953), *The Image Empire* (from 1953). New York: Oxford University Press, 1966, 1968, 1970.

Barnouw, Erik. *The Sponsor: Notes on a Modern Potentate*. New York: Oxford University Press, 1978.

Bittner, John R. *Broadcast Law and Regulation*. Englewood Cliffs, N.J.: Prentice-Hall, 1982.

Blum, Eleanor. *Basic Books in the Mass Media*. Urbana: University of Illinois Press, 1980.

Connors, Tracy Daniel. *Dictionary of Mass Media and Communication*. New York: Longman, 1982.

Ginsburg, Douglas H. *Regulation of Broadcasting: Law and Policy towards Radio, Television and Cable Communications*. St. Paul, Minn.: West Publishing Company, 1979.

Head, Sydney W., with Christopher H. Sterling. *Broadcasting in America: A Survey of Television, Radio and New Technologies*. 4th ed. Boston: Houghton-Mifflin, 1982.

Hilliard, Robert L., ed. *Radio Broadcasting*. 3d ed. New York: Longman, 1984.

Hilliard, Robert L., ed. *Television Broadcasting*. 2d ed. New York: Longman, 1984.

Johnson, Joseph, and Kenneth K. Jones. *Modern Radio Station Practices*. 2d ed. Belmont, Calif.: Wadsworth, 1978.

Millerson, Gerald. *The Technique of Television Production*. New York: Focal Press, 1979.

Sterling, Christopher H., and John M. Kittross. *Stay Tuned: A Concise History of American Broadcasting*. Belmont, Calif.: Wadsworth, 1978.

Wurtzel, Alan. *Television Production*. 2d ed. New York: McGraw-Hill, 1983.

Zettl, Herbert. *Television Production Handbook*. 4th ed. Belmont, Calif.: Wadsworth, 1984.

Commercials

Heighton, Elizabeth J., and Don R. Cunningham. 2d ed. *Advertising in the Broadcast Media*. Belmont, Calif.: Wadsworth, 1984.

Orlik, Peter B. *Broadcast Copywriting.* 2d ed. Newton, Mass.: Allyn & Bacon, 1982.

White, Hooper. *How to Produce an Effective TV Commercial.* Chicago: Crain Books, 1981.

Zeigler, Sherilyn K., and Herbert K. Howard. *Broadcast Advertising: A Comprehensive Working Textbook.* Columbus, Ohio: Grid, 1978.

News

Bliss, Edward J., Jr., and John M. Patterson. 2d ed. *Writing News for Broadcast.* New York: Columbia University Press, 1978.

Broussard, E. Joseph, and Jack F. Holgate. *Writing and Reporting Broadcast News.* New York: Macmillan, 1982.

Fang, Irving E. *Television News.* 3d ed. St. Paul, Minn.: Rada Press, 1981.

Garvey, Daniel E., and William L. Rivers. *Newswriting for the Electronic Media.* Belmont, Calif.: Wadsworth, 1982.

White, Ted, et al. *Broadcast News Writing, Reporting and Production.* New York: Macmillan, 1983.

Wimer, Arthur, and Dale Brix. *Workbook for Radio and TV News Editing and Writing.* 5th ed. Dubuque, Iowa: Wm. C. Brown, 1981.

Drama

Baker, George P. *Dramatic Technique.* Reprint of 1919 edition. Westport, Conn.: Greenwood Press.

Cousin, Michel. *Writing a Television Play.* Boston: Writer, Inc. 1975.

Goodman, Ellen. *Writing Television and Motion Picture Scripts That Sell.* Chicago: Contemporary Books, 1982.

Rodger, Ian. *Radio Drama.* London: Macmillan, 1983.

Rowe, Kenneth T. *Write That Play.* 2d ed. New York: Funk & Wagnalls, 1969.

Stedman, Raymond W. *The Serials: Suspense and Drama by Installment.* 2d ed. Norman: University of Oklahoma Press, 1977.

Trapnell, Coles. *Teleplay: An Introduction to Television Writing.* New York: Hawthorn Books, 1974.

Willis, Edgar E., and Camille D'Arienzo. *Writing Scripts for Television, Radio and Film.* New York: Holt, Rinehart & Winston, 1981.

Other

Brenner, Alfred. *TV Scriptwriter's Handbook.* Cincinnati: Writer's Digest Books, 1980.

Clark, Bernadine, ed. *Writer's Market*. Cincinnati: Writer's Digest Books (published annually).

Eastman, Susan Tyler, and Robert Klein. *Strategies for Broadcast and Cable Promotion*. Belmont, Calif.: Wadsworth, 1982.

Edmonds, Robert. *Scripting for the Audio-Visual Media*. New York: Columbia University Teachers College Press, 1978.

Garvey, Daniel E., and William L. Rivers. *Broadcast Writing*. New York: Longman, 1982.

Hilliard, Robert L., and Hyman H. Field. *Television and the Teacher*. New York: Hastings House, 1976.

Johnson, Donald F. *Copyright Handbook*. New York: R. R. Bowker, 1978.

LeBaron, John. *Making Television: A Guide for Teachers*. New York: Columbia University Teachers College Press, 1981.

Maloney, Martin, and Paul M. Rubenstein. *Writing for the Media*. Englewood Cliffs, N.J.: Prentice-Hall, 1980.

Mattrazzo, Donna. *Corporate Scriptwriting*. Philadelphia: The Media Concepts Press, 1980.

Nash, Constance, and Virginia Oakey. *The Television Writer's Handbook*. New York: Barnes and Noble, 1978.

Polking, Kirk, and Leonard S. Meranus. *Law and the Writer*. Cincinnati: Writer's Digest Books, 1978.

Routt, Edd, James B. McGrath, and Frederic A. Weiss. *The Radio Format Conundrum*. New York: Hastings House, 1979.

Rowlands, Avril. *Script Continuity and the Production Secretary in Film and TV*. New York: Focal Press, 1977.

Index

S

Y

Z